Medieval Religious Women in The Low Countries

THE 'MODERN DEVOTION', THE CANONESSES OF WINDESHEIM AND THEIR WRITINGS

In the last decades of the fourteenth century a new religious movement arose in the northern Low Countries, the so-called 'Modern Devotion', which had a major influence upon religious life in Europe in the later middle ages. It was particularly popular with women, thousands of whom were attracted to it; but until now there has been no study of the women who played a part in the movement. This book seeks to fill that gap, through a case study of the Chapter of Windesheim and the mystical and religious texts its sisters produced, which may be regarded as typical of the female spiritual experience of the Modern Devotion. The author analyses texts by such important canonesses as Salome Sticken, Alijt Bake and Jacomijne Costers, placing them in the context of daily life in the convent; of especial importance also is the anonymous sisterbook of the largest convent at Diepenveen, which provides a rich source of historical information on the movement. He shows that although the women were all concerned with improving religious life in their convents, their opinions and attitudes as to how best to do so varied dramatically, leading to conflict with both other members of the convent, and the male leaders of the Chapter; he pays particular attention to Bake's vision of a mystical spirituality, which ultimately led to her ejection from the convent and exile.

WYBREN SCHEEPSMA gained his doctorate from the University of Leiden. He teaches at the Hogeschool Leiden.

This translation has been supported by a grant from the
Netherlands Organisation for Scientific Research

Medieval Religious Women in The Low Countries

THE 'MODERN DEVOTION', THE CANONESSES OF
WINDESHEIM AND THEIR WRITINGS

Wybren Scheepsma

Translated from the Dutch by
David F. Johnson

THE BOYDELL PRESS

Translation © David F. Johnson 2004

All Rights Reserved. Except as permitted under current legislation
no part of this work may be photocopied, stored in a retrieval system,
published, performed in public, adapted, broadcast,
transmitted, recorded or reproduced in any form or by any means,
without the prior permission of the copyright owner

Translation first published 2004
The Boydell Press, Woodbridge

ISBN 1 84383 048 5

Originally published 1997 as
Deemoed en devotie: de koorvrouwen van Windesheim en hun geschriften
by Prometheus, Amsterdam
© Wybren Scheepsma 1997

The Boydell Press is an imprint of Boydell & Brewer Ltd
PO Box 9, Woodbridge, Suffolk IP12 3DF, UK
and of Boydell & Brewer Inc.
PO Box 41026, Rochester, NY 14604–4126, USA
website: www.boydellandbrewer.com

A catalogue record of this publication is available
from the British Library

Library of Congress Cataloging-in-Publication data
Scheepsma, Wybren, 1962–
 [Deemoed en devotie. English]
  Medieval religious women in the Low Countries : the 'modern devotion',
the Canonesses of Windesheim, and their writings / Wybren Scheepsma ;
translated from the Dutch by David F. Johnson.
    p. cm.
Includes bibliographical references (p.   ) and index.
 ISBN 1–84383–048–5 (hardback)
1. Canonesses Regular of Windesheim – Spiritual life. 2. Devotio
moderna. I. Title.
BX4294.S3413 2004
271'.97–dc22   2003021874

This publication is printed on acid-free paper

Typeset by Pru Harrison, Woodbridge, Suffolk
Printed in Great Britain by
St Edmundsbury Press Limited, Bury St Edmunds, Suffolk

CONTENTS

Preface		vii
Abbreviations		ix
1.	**Introduction**	1
	1.1 A Pious Religious Women's Movement	2
	1.2 The Search for Inner Meaning	16
	1.3 The Writings of the Canonesses of Windesheim and Their Reception	24
2.	**Aspects of Life in the Convent**	31
	2.1 The Inhabitants of the Convent	31
	2.2 Postulance, Taking the Veil, Profession	38
	2.3 Education and Training	41
	2.4 Year, Week, Day	47
3.	**Communal Devotion and Piety**	51
	3.1 Liturgical Celebrations	51
	3.2 Chapter of Faults	56
	3.3 Silence	61
	3.4 In the Sweat of Thy Face	62
	3.5 Copying and Illuminating	65
	3.6 Religious Nourishment	70
	3.7 Rest and Recreation	76
	3.8 Words of Inspiration	76
4.	**Living with Texts**	83
	4.1 Reading for a Pure Heart	84
	4.2 Reading with the Pen?	90
	4.3 Devout Exercises	96
5.	**Written Instructions**	111
	5.1 A Rule of Life for Devout Sisters	113
	5.2 Devout Epistles	119
	5.3 Five Letters on the Reformation of Mariënberg in Helmstedt	125
	5.4 The Collations of Johannes Brinckerinck	129

6.	**Devout Biography and Historiography**	135
	6.1 The Diepenveen *Viten*	*136*
	6.2 Learning Virtues	145
	6.3 The Work of Griete Essinchghes	152
	6.4 The *Kroniek Bethanië*	159
	6.5 Chronicle and Sisterbook	165
7.	**Two Spiritual Friends from Facons**	171
	7.1 Jacomijne Costers	172
	7.2 An Account of a Journey through Hell	175
	7.3 Reform through Literary Means	181
	7.4 Mechtild van Rieviren and Her Comforting Conversations with Christ	189
8.	**Alijt Bake, a Woman with a Mission**	197
	8.1 Biography	198
	8.2 Reading, Writing and Erasing	202
	8.3 Three Moments in the Literary Career of Alijt Bake	208
	8.4 Audience and Dissemination	223
9.	**Literature and the Choir Nuns of Windesheim**	227
	9.1 Language and Literature in Daily Life	228
	9.2 The Role of the Pastors	232
	9.3 The Windesheim Choir Nuns as Authors	238
Bibliography		245
Index		271

PREFACE

In recent decades the study of medieval women's history has virtually taken off. Because the available source materials pertain for the most part to women in religious orders, the focus has been on nuns, Beguines, anchoresses and other such religious women. In the meantime it has become well known that there was a remarkable flourishing of female religious in the southern Netherlands of the thirteenth century. This is to some extent due to the fact that most of the source texts from this era were written in Latin, and as such have been accessible to the international scholarly world. It is a much lesser known fact that a powerful new impulse in female religious living manifested itself in the northern Netherlands. The Modern Devotion, the reform movement founded by Geert Grote of Deventer, attracted during the late fourteenth and fifteenth centuries thousands of women in northwestern Europe. That this second religious woman's movement is less well known may be attributed to the fact that in this case the source texts are for the most part in Middle Dutch, a language read by few scholars outside of Belgium and the Netherlands. As a partial remedy to this unfamiliarity, this study of a small yet essential element of the second movement of women religious – the writings of the choir nuns of Windesheim – is offered in the language of international scholarship.

I completed my doctorate at the University of Leiden in 1997 with the dissertation *Deemoed en devotie. De koorvrouwen van Windesheim en hun geschriften* ('Piety and Devotion: The Choir Nuns of Windesheim and Their Writings'), which was published by Uitgeverij Prometheus in Amsterdam as volume XVII in the series Nederlandse literatuur en cultuur in de middeleeuwen (Dutch Literature and Culture in the Middle Ages). The translation of this book was made possible due to generous funding from the Nederlandse Organisatie voor Wetenschappelijk Onderzoek (Netherlands Organisation for Scientific Research). The book has been abridged in a number of significant ways in order to keep both the cost and size of the book within reasonable bounds. The main text of the original, with the exception of a few minor corrections and additions, has been translated in its entirety. The extended appendices which appeared in the dissertation, however, have been excised, and the number and scope of the footnotes greatly reduced. As a result of these measures the bibliography, too, appears here in a more abbreviated form, though on the other hand a number of publications in English have been added. Moreover, an honest effort was made to bring the bibliography up to date, but only with respect to the choir nuns of Windesheim and their spiritual way of life. This book will undoubtedly meet the demands of any reader whose goal is to gain familiarity with the writing women of the Modern Devotion and their works. Anyone wishing to pursue further research in this area, however, will inevitably wish to consult the Dutch original.

I would like to thank David F. Johnson for the expertise and enthusiasm with which he translated a text from a relatively new and unfamiliar field. I owe thanks to Caroline Palmer of Boydell & Brewer for her conscientious editing and production of the book. Finally, Ingrid Biesheuvel deserves thankful acknowledgement for her meticulous editing of the notes, bibliography and index.

Wybren Scheepsma
Spring 2003

ABBREVIATIONS

Below are listed sigla for manuscripts frequently cited in this book, followed by other abbreviations, with full bibliographic information for works cited in abbreviated form. The edition used, where available, is given in parentheses, as is any existing English translation. Where no edition exists, I have provided the manuscript information.

B	MS Brussel, KB, 8849–59; a collection of histiographical texts concerning the Modern Devotion, including among others some Latin excerpts from the Diepenveen sisterbook (for an overview of its contents and some available editions, see Carasso-Kok 1981, no. 204)
D	MS Zwolle, Rijksarchief Overijssel, Coll. van Rhemen, inv. no. 1; the 1534 redaction of the Diepenveen sisterbook from the Meester-Geertshuis (ed. Brinkerink 1904, 1–368)
DV	MS Deventer, SAB, Suppl. 198 (101 E 26); the 1524 redaction of the Diepenveen sisterbook from that monastery
G	MS Deventer, SAB, Suppl. 208 (101 F 25); sisterbook from the Meester-Geertshuis in Deventer (ed. de Man 1919, 1–256)
KB	Koninklijke Bibliotheek; Kongelige Bibliotek (Royal Library).
SAB	Stads- of Athenaeumbibliotheek (Deventer) (City or Athenaeum Library).
UB	Universiteitsbibliotheek (University Library)
Vienna	MS Vienna, Österreichische Nationalbibliothek, s.n. 12.827; contains among other things the complete works of Jacomijne Costers
ABB	Archief- en bibliotheekwezen in België / Archives et bibliothèques de Belgique
AGAU	Archief voor de geschiedenis van het aartsbisdom Utrecht
AGKKN	Archief voor de geschiedenis van de katholieke kerk in Nederland.
Bereijdinghe	Jacomijne Costers, *Bereijdinghe tot het Heijlich Sacrament* (MS Vienna, ff. 63v–66v)

ABBREVIATIONS

BHS	Berliner historische Studien
Brief	Alijt Bake, *Brief uit de ballingschap* (ed. Spaapen 1967b, 353–67)
CM, *Constitutiones monialium*	Liber constitutionum sanctimonialium ordinis Sancti Augustini <Capituli Windeshemensis> (ed. van Dijk 1986, 726–833)
Collatie I	Johannes Brinckerinck, *Van der bekeringhe* (ed. Moll 1866a, 111–21; trans. van Engen 1988a, 223–30)
Collatie II	Johannes Brinckerinck, *Van berespinghe* (ed. Moll 1866a, 121–6)
Collatie III	Johannes Brinckerinck, *Van der ghehoersamheit* (ed. Moll 1866a, 126–34)
Collatie IV	Johannes Brinckerinck, *Van der oetmoedicheit* (ed. Moll 1866a, 134–43)
Collatie V	Johannes Brinckerinck, *Van den heiligen sacrament* (ed. Moll 1866a, 143–7; trans. van Engen 1988a, 231–4)
Collatie VI	Johannes Brinckerinck, *Hoe wi sellen striden teghen die ghebreken ende teghen die sinlicheiden* (ed. Moll 1866a, 148–55)
Collatie VII	Johannes Brinckerinck, *Van den arbeide van buten ende van binnen, ende hoe wi ons oefenen sullen in den ghebeden des daghes ende des nachts* (ed. Moll 1866a, 155–62)
Collatie VIII	Johannes Brinckerinck, *Hoe wi dat leven ende die passie ons liefs heren na sellen volghen* (ed. Moll 1866a, 162–7)
Collatie IX	Johannes Brinckerinck, *Van swighen* (ed. de Vreese 1898, 233–5)
Drij beloften	Jacomijne Costers, *Van de drij beloften der religieusen* (MS Vienna, ff. 86r–88v)
DS	M. Viller, F. Cavallera and J. de Guibert (eds.), *Dictionnaire de spiritualité ascétique et mystique: doctrine et histoire*, 17 vols., Paris, 1932–95
Epistel I	*Hier begynt een devoete epistel, ghescreven tot sommeghen susteren van Jherusalem buten Utrecht die te Diepenven ghesent waren om hem te proeven* (ed. Brinkerink 1907, 324–38)
Epistel II	*Hier beghynt een ander epistel* (ed. Brinkerink 1907, 388–96)
Epistel III	*Hier beghynt een ander devoet epistel, gheschreven totten selven zusteren: woe si hem oefenen solden inden waeldaden ende inder passien ons lieven heren Jhesu Cristi* (ed. Brinkerink 1907, 397–409)
Kroniek Bethanië	MS Mechelen, Stadsarchief, EE XXVI; the first part of the largely unpublished *Kroniek van Bethanië te Mechelen* (fragments published by Cordemans de Bruyne 1896, 60–82 and *passim*)

ABBREVIATIONS

Kroniek Sint-Agnes	MS Ghent, Bibliotheek van de Minderbroeders, Ua50 (fragments published in Lingier 1993, *passim* and Willems 1842, 154–73)
Lanck leven	Jacomijne Costers, *Die op lanck leven stelt al sijn hopen* (ed. Roose 1958)
Lessen van Palmzondag	Alijt Bake, *De lessen van Palmzondag* (ed. Spaapen 1968b, 235–61)
Lichtere weg	Alijt Bake, *Een lichtere weg* (an expansion appended to *Vier kruiswegen*) (ed. Spaapen 1966, 58–61)
Louteringsnacht	Alijt Bake, *De louteringsnacht van de actie* (ed. Spaapen 1968c, 359–421)
MB	L.-E. Halkin, R. Aubert, L. Milis *et al.* (eds.), *Monasticon belge*, 7 vols., Luik, 1890–.
Memorie	Alijt Bake, *Van die memorie der passien ons heren* (ed. Scheepsma 1994, 118–26)
Merkelike leeringhe	Alijt Bake, *Een merkelike leeringhe* (ed. Lieftinck 1936, 21)
Mijn beghin ende voortghanck	Alijt Bake, *Mijn beghin ende voortghanck* (ed. Spaapen 1967a, 218–301 and 321–50)
Mijns herten lief	Jacomijne Costers, *O mijns herten lief eenich een* (MS Vienna, ff. 42v–44r)
Mst	*Middeleeuwse studies*
MStB	*Middeleeuwse studies en bronnen*
MTU	*Münchener Texte und Untersuchungen zur deutschen Literatur des Mittelalters*
Naem- en doodtboeck	Christophorus Caers, *Naem- en doodtboeck der rectooren, priorinnen, canonikerssen, conversinnen, donatinnen en donaten des cloosters genoemt Facons* (MS Antwerp, Rijksarchief, Facons, no. 96)
NAKG	*Nederlands(ch) archief voor kerkgeschiedenis*
NLCM	*Nederlandse literatuur en cultuur in de middeleeuwen*
OGE	*Ons geestelijk erf*
Previlesien	Jacomijne Costers, *Previlesien van Sint Joannes Evangelist* (MSVienna, ff. 89r–102r)
Register	Christophorus Caers, *Register van het beginsel, voortganck ende gedenckweerdichste geschidenissen [. . .] des cloosters van O. L. Vrouwendael in Valckenbroec, genoempt Facons* (MS Antwerpen, Archief van het bisdom Antwerpen, K 92)
Scouwenden leven	Alijt Bake (?), *Van drien punten die tot enen scouwenden leven behoren* (ed. de Man 1937, 567–9)
Trechter en spin	Alijt Bake, *De trechter en de spin* (ed. Scheepsma 1995e, 230–4)
Van de perfectie	Jacomijne Costers, *Van de perfectie* (MS Vienna, ff. 86r–88v)

ABBREVIATIONS

Vier kruiswegen	Alijt Bake, *De vier kruiswegen* (ed. Spaapen 1966, 18–58)
Visioen en exempel	Jacomijne Costers, *Dit is het visioen en exempel vande gelucksalige religieuse suster Jacomijne Costers, met bijnaem Zirix, een religieus van ons clooster* (ed. Scheepsma 1996c, 161–84)
Vivendi formula	Salome Sticken, *Vivendi formula* (ed. Kühler 1914, 362–80; trans. van Engen 1988a, 176–86)
VL	K. Ruh *et al.* (eds.), *Die deutsche Literatur des Mittelalters. Verfasserlexikon*. Berlin, 1978–.
Volmaeckt leven	Alijt Bake (?), *Van drije pointen die toebehooren een volmaeckt leven* (ed. Scheepsma 1992a, 151–3)
Weg van de ezel	Alijt Bake, *De weg van de ezel* (ed. Spaapen 1968a, 11–32)
Weg der victorie	Alijt Bake, *De weg der victorie* (ed. Spaapen 1969, 280–304)
Zusterboek Sint-Agnes	Formerly MS Emmerich, Stadtarchiv, 1206, of which only a handwritten transcription survives (ed. Bollmann and Staubach 1998, 35–307; fragments published in Liesen 1891, 1–14 and Hövelmann 1971, 52–62)

1

Introduction

'WHEN WOMEN apply themselves devoutly they often receive more grace and stand in greater favour with God than men do.'[1] Johannes (or Jan) 'Brinckerinck (†1419), whose words these are, knew what he was talking about. He devoted his entire life to the pastoral care of women. Brinckerinck was one of the pioneers of the Modern Devotion (*Devotio Moderna*), the spiritual reform movement which flourished in the late medieval Low Countries and which profoundly influenced religious life in northwestern Europe. The Modern Devotion provided an opportunity for a large number of women who wished to adopt a spiritual lifestyle. They found in Johannes Brinckerinck one of their most fervent advocates.[2] Brinckerinck did his utmost to teach the numerous female followers of the Modern Devotion how they could give expression to the communal life that his movement advocated. The acquisition of such Christian virtues as obedience and humility was, in his view, their most important task. The sisterbooks kept by the sisters that have survived from a number of institutions under his leadership show, via the lives or *viten* of dozens of pious sisters, how this spirituality of humility – *ootmoed* was the term preferred by the Modern Devout – was to be put into practice.[3] These *viten* lead one to suspect that the spiritual ideal which Johannes Brinckerinck held up to them was very much in keeping with the needs shared by many women.

Brinckerinck urged the nuns to apply themselves in their youthful years to keeping a book of virtues, so that they might read from it later in life.[4] This practice is a characteristic one, not only because followers of the Modern Devotion stressed virtuousness, but also because books and writing played an important role in their spiritual life. Some female members of the movement followed Johannes Brinckerinck's advice literally. They applied them-

---

[1] *Collatie VI*, 150. The collations of Johannes Brinckerinck are discussed in greater detail in §3.8 and §5.4.
[2] There are five known *viten* of Johannes Brinckerinck; cf. Scheepsma 1996a, 334 n. 5.
[3] The terms *vite/viten* are used here throughout to refer to the distinctive biographies of devout brothers and sisters of the Modern Devotion. For more on how this genre is to be distinguished from the Latin *vitae* or saints' lives see Chapter 6.
[4] *Collatie I*, 112 (cf. n. 1).

selves to writing spiritual texts in which the theme of virtuousness was often discussed. Most of these authors followed closely the lead provided by their founder. Only Alijt Bake of Ghent consciously departed from this path. She had personal experience of the divine blessing which according to Johannes Brinckerinck fell more often to women than to men, and she wrote candidly about it. Because she felt that the path that led to the divine experience had more to offer her, she left the path of humility and devotion forged by the Modern Devotion behind her, and with dire consequences.

It is a rather exceptional phenomenon for medieval women themselves to produce texts. Yet the works of the women of the Modern Devotion are relatively unknown. This study seeks in part to fill this gap by focusing on the texts of the most productive group, the Canonesses of the Chapter of Windesheim (§1.3). But first some attention should be paid to the history of the Modern Devotion (§1.1), as well as to the spiritual beliefs of this movement (§1.2), with, of course, particular stress on the female contribution to it.

1.1 A Pious Religious Women's Movement

Johannes Brinckerinck and the followers of the Modern Devotion were preceded by numerous other church reformers. With great regularity, almost from the very inception of Christianity, religious reform movements have arisen which have striven after a life of simplicity for their fellow believers. Time and again they found their inspiration in the gospel of Jesus Christ and took as their model the first Christian communities established by his disciples, the Apostles. The medieval reform movements were often the thorn in the flesh of the Christian church. They criticised the elitism and lust for power of the clergy and the wealth and ostentation of the Church establishment. They were initially suppressed because their ideas were considered heretical. Pope Innocent III (reigned 1198–1216) was the first to realise that for the Church to ignore or brand these religious movements as heretical was wrong, both in principle and from a practical point of view. He integrated the apostolic ideals of poverty and preaching by affording Francis of Assisi (†1226) and Dominic Guzman (†1221) the opportunity to found new (mendicant) orders. It was through such orders that outbursts of religious enthusiasm among the faithful could be channelled. On the other hand, Innocent III resolutely opposed groups who in his eyes advocated truly heretical ideas. The new Franciscan and Dominican orders were of great help to him in this endeavour.

The German historian Grundmann was the first to study the medieval religious movements as a constantly recurring socio-religious phenomenon. In his classic study, *Religiöse Bewegungen im Mittelalter*, he recounts the history of these movements down to the middle of the fourteenth century.[5] Grundmann

---

[5] Grundmann 1977; see also the English translation, Grundmann 1995.

considers these medieval marginal groups with their deviant spiritual ideas to be Christian religious movements, but at the time they were firmly branded as heretics. According to the prevailing view, innovations in religious practice were to come from within the Church. And yet the impetus for change often came from circles more or less removed from its central establishment.[6] Particularly striking is the contribution of women to these medieval reform movements, so that Grundmann posits the existence of a 'Religiöse Frauenbewegung'. This term, which has found general acceptance, can be the cause of some confusion. Its word-order and grammar would suggest that it refers to a kind of emancipation movement *avant la lettre*, which demanded for women a place within the church hierarchy.[7] Rather, it was a movement carried by women religious (*mulieres religiosae*). And this is the meaning which this study gives to the term 'Religious women's movement'.

The thirteenth century is considered its Golden Age, and the Maas–Rhine region the cradle of medieval women's religiosity. Women turned *en masse* to the spiritual life. New convents had to be founded in large numbers to accommodate them. While initially it was the orders of the Premonstratensians and Cistercians who accepted these women into their ranks, from the thirteenth century on this task fell to the Franciscans and the Dominicans.[8] But there were other opportunities open to them besides the traditional monastic life. Some women sought out utter isolation and became anchoresses, others adhered to the ideal of practical brotherly love and became nurses in hospitals. And it was in the diocese of Liège that the Beguines movement was started. There women formed small religious communities without taking the official monastic vows. The Church had continual difficulties with these women, who could not or would not fit into its hierarchical structure. The success of the Beguines – Beguinages were founded in large numbers throughout northwest Europe – led ultimately to their severe persecution at the hands of the Inquisition.[9]

The rise of the Modern Devotion in the last decades of the fourteenth

---

[6] Grundmann 1977, 5–6.
[7] For a discussion of the feminist perspective on the term 'religiöse Frauenbewegung', see Degler-Spengler 1984, 88. As potentially better alternatives she suggests 'women's religious movement', or 'religious movement among women'.
[8] Degler-Spengler 1985 provides a historical overview of the spiritual care of women by the monastic orders (*cura monialium*). For a general treatment of the medieval female Cistercians, see Nichols and Shank 1995; the Dominicans will be dealt with in detail below.
[9] On the Beguines in the Netherlands, see for example Nübel 1970 and Koorn 1981. On the literature of the Beguines see Peters 1988a, 41–100, Ruh 1990–9, vol. 2 and McGinn 1991–8, vol. 3.

century fits the pattern outlined by Grundmann for the previous centuries.[10] Yet again a reform movement was founded out of dissatisfaction with the miserable state of the Church in this century – the Western Schism constituted its low point: from 1378 two popes fought for control over the Church of Christ, one in Rome and the other in Avignon. The Modern Devotion, too, was carried to an important degree by the enthusiasm and idealism of women: women devout outnumbered their male counterparts three to one.[11] There is sufficient reason to speak of a 'second religious women's movement' in the late fourteenth and the fifteenth century, the direct result of the advent of the Modern Devotion. One of the questions which this study seeks to answer is how far this second, pious women's movement may be considered comparable to the first.[12]

Although the Modern Devotion has been the subject of intense study for over a century now – hence the rather cursory treatment of its history here – the female Modern Devout have for the most part received little attention.[13] Post regards the women as the passive, receptive part of the movement, because they do not preach or carry out any pastoral activities. In his view they were only active in the sense that through their personal conversion and devotion to their leaders they were able to reform many other women.[14] And in research devoted to medieval religious women's movements, which during the last two decades has received new impetus, the Modern Devotion and the second religious or 'devout' women's movement have occupied a

---

[10] Cf. van Dijk 1994a. Grundmann ends his study in the middle of the fourteenth century, but mentions in his introduction a significant number of later reform movements to which his observations are relevant; the Modern Devotion is one of these (Grundmann 1977, 1–3). A recent survey of late medieval reform initiatives that have been the subject of study is provided by Elm 1980b, whereas Elm 1989 contains studies of a large number of reforms within religious orders and other institutions.

[11] This ratio is an average one; specific calculations are to be found in Rehm 1985, 16, Post 1954a, 160–7 and Post 1968, 265–72.

[12] On the second religious women's movement of the Modern Devotion, see especially Koorn 1981, 25–35.

[13] Dols 1941 provides a bibliographical overview; the journal *Ons geestelijk erf* provides an annual bibliographical update. Important surveys of the state of research are provided by Alberts 1958 and Weiler 1984b (the 'female question' is not treated by either of them). The most recent monograph on the Modern Devotion is Post 1968. *Moderne Devotie. Figuren en facetten* 1984 gathers in one place a great deal of recent literature and knowledge; Andriessen, Bange and Weiler 1985 covers a great number of articles on this movement. The scholarly discussions of the Modern Devotion are still largely conducted in Dutch and German. Important overviews in English are Hyma 1950, Hyma 1965 and Post 1968; van Engen 1988a is especially useful because it introduces and translates a number of characteristic texts of the Modern Devotion.

[14] Post 1968, 259 and 497; he is, incidentally, the only one to give reasons for devoting relatively little attention to the women.

merely marginal position.¹⁵ It seems therefore desirable to provide here a brief outline of the Modern Devotion as a religious women's movement.

The establishment of a religious women's community was one of the first tangible results of the conversion of Geert Grote (†1384).¹⁶ On 20 September 1374, he opened his parental home to poor, unmarried women who wished to live the spiritual life; in this he was following the example of the Deventer vicar Hendrik Stappe, who had left his home to pious women upon his death.¹⁷ Grote retained two chambers and a few other rooms for his own use, which served as a base of operation for his successful preaching tours through the northern Low Countries. In 1379 a charter was drawn up for the Meester-Geertshuis ('Master Geert's house') – the name by which it was later known – by the magistrates of Deventer, who exercised judicial authority over the sisters. Here we may recognise the influence of Geert Grote himself. Initially each of the occupants of the house in Deventer ran her own household. The sisters had to live from the money they earned by their own efforts; begging was strictly forbidden. Grote repeatedly advocated regular manual labour as a means of achieving inner purity. Particularly striking is the stipulation that the Meester-Geertshuis could not form the basis of a new spiritual order. The Pope had forbidden it, and neither Geert Grote nor the town of Deventer had any intention of opposing his order.¹⁸

After Geert Grote's death in 1384 the spiritual leadership of the sisters devolved to Jan van den Gronde. One of the original devotionals, he was an undeniably brilliant preacher, but a poor leader.¹⁹ Upon his death in 1392,

---

¹⁵ It goes beyond the scope of this work to provide any overview here pretending to exhaustiveness; in the course of my discussion I shall cite numerous publications. Important for the situation in the Netherlands are the collection of articles in Mertens 1992, and Vandenbroeck 1994a, which surveys female religiosity in the southern Netherlands from the thirteenth to the seventeenth centuries.

¹⁶ Studies devoted to Geert Grote and his religious beliefs are to be found in for example Post 1968, 51–175 and Epiney-Burgard 1970.

¹⁷ On Hendrik Stappe's foundation, see Nübel 1970, especially 209–15.

¹⁸ On the history of the Meester-Geertshuis, see de Man 1919, especially X–LXIX; Post 1968, 259–65; Epiney-Burgard 1970, 146–58 and Rehm 1985, 35–7. A definitive investigation into the Netherlandic sisterhouses, such as Rehm 1985 provides for the northwestern region of Germany, is unfortunately lacking. There exist a short and a long version of the statutes of the Meester-Geertshuis, both printed in Post 1952. Post develops there the theory that the second version, dated 13 July 1379 and to which Geert Grote attached his seal, is a forgery created between the years 1395 and 1397 (cf. Post 1968, 260–5). Weiler 1995, on the other hand, does not believe it is necessarily a forgery: he dates the first redaction to 1374, the year in which Grote opened up his house, and regards the second redaction as an improved version which, in conformity with the script, may be dated to 1379. In my view Weiler's argument should be preferred, if for no other reason than that it allows us to abandon the idea of a later forgery.

¹⁹ On Jan or Johan van den Gronde as the rector of the Meester-Geertshuis, see de Man 1919, XXIX–XXXI; cf. Kühler 1932, 64–7.

van den Gronde was succeeded by Johannes Brinckerinck from Zutphen, who had as a youth belonged to the group of followers who accompanied Geert Grote on his preaching excursions. A number of them went on to live as brothers in the house of the Deventer vicar Florens Radewijns, who had assumed leadership of the movement after Geert Grote's death. Johannes Brinckerinck spent his entire life in the Heer-Florenshuis ('Lord Florens's house'). Under his direction the common life of the sisters in the Meester-Geertshuis began to take shape. The possessions and income of all of its inmates were put into a communal coffer and measures were taken to care for the sisters who were elderly or sick. The inhabitants of the Meester-Geertshuis were therefore later referred to as the 'Sisters of the Common Life'. While Johannes Brinckerinck was not the originator of this lifestyle, he was a great supporter of it.[20] The Sisters of the Common Life are counted among the 'semi-religious': they lived in a community, but unlike the 'full religious' they were not bound by the three monastic vows of poverty, obedience and chastity.[21] In this respect the Sisters of the Common Life strongly resemble the Beguines; the most important distinction between the two groups is that the Sisters kept no private possessions.[22]

The passionate Johannes Brinckerinck provided the women's movement of the Modern Devotion with new fervour. As it turned out, there was a great demand for the semi-religious lifestyle that he advocated. The Meester-Geertshuis originally comprised sixteen sisters, but when Brinckerinck died in 1419 their number had grown to one hundred and fifty. In Deventer by around 1400, moreover, four new houses had been established: the Lamme-van-Diezehuis, the Kerstekenshuis, the Brandeshuis and the Buiskenshuis. All four were brought under the spiritual authority of Johannes Brinckerinck.[23] Upon his death the spiritual care of the Sisters was

---

[20] Post 1952 suspects that the 'forged' second redaction of the statutes of the Meester-Geertshuis (see note 18) was composed by Brinckerinck *cum suis* in order to protect the Sisters from accusations of heresy, given the fact that they go to great lengths to demonstrate that the Deventer sisters were not Beguines. But Weiler 1995 demonstrates that Geert Grote himself may have seen the necessity of diverting this suspicion away from the women in his house. His reconstruction led Post to regard Johannes Brinckerinck as the main force behind the 'common life'. If we accept Weiler's dating, then Geert Grote himself must have provided the impetus for this lifestyle. Incidentally, Koorn 1985, 300 had already noted the existence of a number of Beguinages where the 'common life' had been introduced earlier (cf. *Moderne Devotie. Figuren en facetten* 1984, no. 6, Koorn 1992, 106 and Weiler 1995, 130–2).

[21] My guide for the use of ecclesiastical terms (in Dutch) was van Dijk and Mertens 1993; the terms 'semi-religious' and 'full religious' are defined on p. 358.

[22] On the differences and similarities between the Beguines and the Sisters, see Koorn 1985, Rehm 1985, 40–2 and Koorn 1986.

[23] About the Deventer sisterhouses not much is known; see, among others, H. Kronenberg 1917; Schoengen 1941, 49–53; Post 1968, *passim*; Persoons 1984, 60–3; and Koch 1985, 43–7.

assumed by Brinckerinck's brothers in the Heer-Florenshuis; the pastoral care of the Sisters evolved into one of the primary tasks of these and others of the Brothers of the Common Life.[24] Deventer developed into one of the most important centres of the Sisters of the Common Life movement, though sisterhouses in other northern Dutch cities like Amsterdam, den Bosch, Haarlem, Utrecht and Zwolle reached similar proportions.[25]

The background to the Modern Devotion's successful introduction of the 'Common life' is still insufficiently known. The preference for the semi-religious life was certainly a factor in their distrust of ecclesiastical institutions, including the monastic orders.[26] The entire Church was tainted and therefore the Modern Devout were compelled to seek refuge in an alternative religious framework. Seen in this light, the independent status of the Brothers and Sisters of the Common Life constitutes a clear protest against the establishment. But more prosaic factors of a socio-economic nature also emphatically asserted themselves. The foundation and maintenance of convents required significant sums of money, money which the young and not yet firmly established movement did not always have at its disposal. The creation of a lifestyle whereby each sister had to earn her place in the house through spinning and weaving – the brothers relied primarily on the copying of books for their income – made it possible for them to live the spiritual life relatively cheaply.[27]

The Modern Devout were by no means revolutionaries intent upon toppling the established order of the Church. Their orthodox beliefs are apparent, for example, in the history of the founding of the convent in

---

[24] No further attention will be paid here to the Brothers of the Common Life. They have been studied intensely, despite their small numbers. Further information about the Brothers may be found in Leesch, Persoons and Weiler 1977–. Important studies include Hyma 1950, van der Wansem 1958, Post 1968, especially 197–258, 343–468 and 551–631, Elm 1985 and Weiler 1997. On the role of the Brothers in the spiritual care of the Sisters of the Common Life, see Rehm 1985, 113–42 and 190–203.

[25] Post 1968, 269 gives some figures for Dutch houses. Rehm 1985, 212–24 arrives at lower but nevertheless respectable totals for the sisterhouses of northwestern Germany. On developments in Utrecht and Holland comparable to the situation in Deventer, see Koorn 1992, 107–14.

[26] Cf. van Engen 1993 on this anti-monasticism.

[27] Cf. Mol 1992, 61–6, for more on the socio-economic backgrounds of the women's movement of the fifteenth century. The flourishing of the sistershouses of the Common Life exhibits important similarities with the rise of the Beguine movement in the thirteenth century: according to Degler-Spengler 1984 the Beguines, too, chose the semi-religious life in the face of insufficient financial resources (they did not usually come from the highest social circles). Degler-Spengler seeks the roots of the Beguines among the lay establishment developed by the Cistercians in the twelfth century: lay brothers and sisters were poor layfolk who in exchange for labour were allowed to join the monastic community without becoming monks or nuns.

Diepenveen.²⁸ With his enthusiastic preaching Johannes Brinckerinck also moved the hearts of a number of wealthy woman. After the death of her husband, the lord of Ruinen, Zweder van Rechteren (†1407) was expelled from her castle. She became an important patron of the Modern Devotion and wished ultimately to devote her own life to Christ. Jutte van Ahaus (†1408) was abbess of the nunnery (*stift*) of Vreden in Westphalia, but under the influence of Johannes Brinckerinck she, too, was converted to the life of poverty and obedience. Elsebe Hasenbroecks from Oldenzaal was widowed at an early age. She felt a strong attraction to the new spiritual movement in Deventer and went so far as to abandon her three children in order to live the life of the Modern Devout. None of these women, who would later prove to be so important to the Modern Devotion, could initially live in the Meester-Geertshuis, for the statutes restricted its occupancy to poor and unmarried women.²⁹ It was for this reason that Johannes Brinckerinck founded in 1400 a new sisterhouse with more liberal rules of admission. To this end he acquired a plot of land in a marsh bearing the descriptive name of *Diepenveen* ('deep peat-bog'), five kilometres north of Deventer. It functioned originally as a branch establishment of the Meester-Geertshuis.

Slowly but surely the plans which Brinckerinck must have had for his foundation from the very beginning started to take shape.³⁰ It was probably in 1407 that he definitively severed the ties between Diepenveen and the Meester-Geertshuis. In that same year he received permission from the bishop of Utrecht to turn Diepenveen into a convent that would follow the rule of St Augustine. The parish priest of Deventer, under whose authority the sisterhouse of Diepenveen fell, also gave his permission for the conversion. From his actions we may deduce that Johannes Brinckerinck considered the

---

[28] The history of Diepenveen is treated in detail in Kühler 1914. New contributions to the history of this convent appear in Scheepsma 2002; see especially van Dijk 2002 and Koorn 2002.

[29] The life of Zweder van Rechteren is in DV, ff. 112r–129r and D, ff. 21b–31c, and in an abridged translation from the Latin in B, ff. 185r–192r (on this manuscript, a chronicle of a century of the Modern Devotion, see Scheepsma 1996a, 226–8 and 237). On her special significance for the Modern Devotion see especially van der Wansem 1958, in particular 87–90 and 183–90 (edition of charters); see also Kühler 1914, 56–8 and Post 1968, 204 and 274. The life of Jutte van Ahaus is to be found in DV, ff. 129v–150v and D, ff. 31c–45c, and in B, ff. 226v–231r. The life of Elsebe Hasenbroecks is in DV, ff. 87v–108v and D, ff. 107a–117d, and in B, ff. 232r–234v. Zweder van Rechteren and Jutte van Ahaus appear also in the so-called. '*Apocalyps*-visioen' (apocalyptic vision) of Hendrik Mande, in which a number of the pioneers of the Modern Devotion appear. This, the sixteenth vision of Mande, is edited by de Vooys 1903, 81–8; for more on this text see Mertens 1986, 114–17 and Mertens 1996a. The third woman to appear in this vision is Stine Tolners, canoness regular of Diepenveen (cf. §2.3, n. 69).

[30] Cf. the foundation narrative of Diepenveen incorporated in the *vite* of Johannes Brinckerinck as preserved in DV (especially ff. 7r–14v) and B (especially ff. 29v–32r; ed. Brinkerink 1902).

monastic life to be the highest form of spiritual life. Given the degree of care he devoted to the convent, Diepenveen may be considered his crown achievement. On St Agnes's day (21 January) 1408 the *clausura* was established in the new convent and at the same time twelve sisters were given their habits. Zweder van Rechteren did not live to see this great day. Jutte van Ahaus was given her habit on her deathbed on 22 January 1408 and died the next day.

In 1412 Diepenveen was admitted to the Chapter of Windesheim, the monastic union that originated in 1395 from the monastery of that name near Zwolle. Geert Grote and the Brothers of the Common Life were actively involved in the foundation of the monastery at Windesheim. One of the reasons the semi-religious had for their foundation was the improved chance of survival of their spiritual ideal within the established institution only a monastery could provide. But that cannot have been their only reason: Geert Grote and the Modern Devout faced formidable opposition, it is true, but they were never really persecuted.[31] Grote was not fundamentally an opponent of the monastic life, even though he sharply criticised the state of the spiritual life within the established orders. He stayed in the Carthusian monastery of Monnikhuizen near Arnhem – the Carthusians were the only ones who in Grote's view were not in need of internal reform – and recommended the monastic life to a number of people. He wrote, for instance, a letter of recommendation on behalf of Berthold ten Hove to the prior of Eemstein near Sint-Geertruidenberg, which was founded in 1382.[32]

From approximately 1383 plans were made for the foundation of a monastery on the land of Berthold ten Hove, called Windesheim.[33] One of the driving forces behind this endeavour was Johannes Brinckerinck, who at the time still intended to become a monk. In 1387 the new monastery's church was consecrated and Berthold ten Hove and five other brothers were given their habits. The six of them had previously lived in Eemstein for a period in order to learn the customs of the order. Like Eemstein, the Windesheim monastery wished to follow the rule of St Augustine. According to one account Geert Grote had recommended this rule because the lifestyle of the Augustinian canons regular most closely resembled that of the Modern Devout; according to another it was because Grote wanted to honour the famous mystic Jan van Ruusbroec (†1381).[34] Van Ruusbroec was prior of

---

[31] On the persecution of the Devout and the Inquisitions see de Man 1926 and Post 1957, vol. 2, 340–6.

[32] For Grote's position on monasticism, see Post 1968, 51–66. He played an active role in the foundation of Eemstein (Kohl, Persoons and Weiler 1976–84, vol. 3, 196 and Mertens 1995b, 120).

[33] For the position of Geert Grote and the Brothers on Windesheim see van der Wansem 1958, 75–85.

[34] Johannes Busch in his *Liber de origine Devotionis Modernae* (Grube 1886, 263; on Busch see §1.3) and Thomas a Kempis (†1472) in *Dialogus noviciorum* (Pohl 1922, 77–8) and *Chronica Monte Sanctae Agnetis* (Pohl 1922, 487), respectively. See van der

Groenendaal near Brussels, an establishment that also followed the rule of St Augustine.[35] Eemstein was founded by, and upon the model of, this Brabantine monastery; the driving force behind this foundation was Jan van Schoonhoven (†1432).[36]

The monastery at Windesheim became very prosperous, both materially and spiritually. Its success soon rendered it a model for other monasteries. In 1395 the Chapter of Windesheim was established, a monastic union of male and female canons regular, with Windesheim as its headquarters. Eemstein was a member of this new organisation, as was Mariënborn near Arnhem and Nieuwlicht near Hoorn. It was thought that within this organisational structure the monasteries could best stimulate and inspire each other. At the annual gathering in Windesheim the Chapter General gave decisions, following extended discussion, that were binding for the entire Chapter.[37] The union grew quickly, especially when, in 1413, the Chapter of Groenendaal, with its seven monasteries, and, in 1430, the Chapter of Neuss, with fifteen foundations, were absorbed into the Windesheim organisation. The Chapter of Windesheim continued to grow until, at the end of the fifteenth century, it reached its highest point with nearly a hundred member monasteries, most of them situated in present-day Belgium, Germany and the Netherlands.[38] By virtue of this the Chapter of Windesheim was at least numerically a dominant factor in the monastic life of northwest Europe.

Wansem 1958, 78–80 on these and other readings. Van Engen 1992 discusses a Brabantine tradition which regarded van Ruusbroec as the founder of the Modern Devotion.

[35] There is a considerable body of literature on Jan van Ruusbroec and Groenendaal. A popular introduction to his life and work is provided by Verdeyen 1994; see also Ruh 1990–9, vol. 4, 29–82 and Warnar 2003. A great deal of material is compiled in the catalogue *Jan van Ruusbroec* 1981. Bos and Warnar 1993 and Mertens 1995a provide collections of recent discussions of van Ruusbroec's work. Van Ruusbroec's works were published in Jan van Ruusbroec, 1944–8; a new edition (with an enface translation in English) is presently being prepared, of which several volumes have already appeared (Jan van Ruusbroec, 1981–).

[36] Jan van Schoonhoven, canon regular of Groenendaal, had studied in Paris. He is especially famous for his defence of van Ruusbroec's teaching against the Chancellor of the University of Paris, Jean Gerson. He is the author of a couple of spiritual treatises and a number of sermons. For a brief treatment see Gruijs 1974. On the monastery of Eemstein see van Herwaarden, de Boer, van Kan *et al.* 1996, 337–43.

[37] On the Chapter's administration see van Dijk 1986, 49–65. The resolutions of the Chapter were taken the first year (*ordinatae*), in the following year confirmed (*confirmatae*), and yet a year later definitively approved (*approbatae*). Many such resolutions have been preserved in the so-called *Acta Capituli Windeshemensis*, a partial edition of which is provided by van der Woude 1953.

[38] The standard work on the history of the monastery and Chapter of Windesheim remains Acquoy 1875–80; more recent studies include Post 1968, especially 292–313, 502–20 and 632–80, Kohl 1989 and van Dijk 1994b. For individual monasteries, see Kohl, Persoons and Weiler 1976–84; cf. the chronological overview in van Dijk and Hendrikman 1996.

Moreover, in the course of the century it played an active role in reform initiatives in a multitude of other monasteries.[39]

Convents of female religious remained in the clear minority within the Chapter of Windesheim: only thirteen of them were admitted into the union. This imbalance was not due to a lack of interest on the part of the convents – on the contrary: in 1436 Pope Eugenius IV issued a decree forbidding the Chapter of Windesheim to admit any more convents. The Pope did this at the express request of the Windesheimers.[40] The immediate impetus was a proposal by the prior of the monastery of Bethlehem at Herent (near Leuven) that a number of convents, over which Bethlehem had spiritual care, be admitted to the Chapter.[41] The Chapter General decided to apply the key to the door, as it were, and by that means stave off in advance a great influx of convents.[42] The chief motivation behind this decision lay in the fear of the heavy burden of responsibility for the material administration of these houses. After all, the admission of convents meant that the responsibility for their economic and juridical well-being lay with the Chapter. Apparently the weight of responsibility for the *cura monialium*, the spiritual care of nuns, was not the deciding factor in the formulation of the papal decree. For every convent required at least one, and usually more than one, priest to celebrate mass and provide the sacraments, a fact that could put a significant strain on monastic personnel. Although the Chapter General could not be accused of excessive enthusiasm in this regard, there were nevertheless quite a few of the brothers of Windesheim who devoted themselves to the spiritual care of nuns. This usually involved monastic houses that did not belong to the Chapter but which nevertheless felt an affinity to it. For the German monas-

---

[39] Kohl 1989 discusses the Chapter of Windesheim as a reform movement in greater detail (cf. also Axters 1956, 243–79). A few studies in which the importance of Windesheim for reform is touched upon include Becker 1980 (the Benedictines; Congregation of Bursfeld), Elm and Feige 1981 (the Cistercians; Colligation of Sibculo) and Mol 1992 (the Crutched Friars). It is noteworthy that the term *reformatio* was used by the Windesheimers for both the reformation of an existing monastery and the foundation of a new one (van der Woude 1947, 71–2).

[40] On the decree in question see Acquoy 1875–80, vol. 2, 74, Hofmeister 1941, 169, van der Woude 1953, 31, Rehm 1985, 44–5 and van Dijk 1986, 29. As early as 1431 the Chapter General had determined that individual monasteries could not take steps to incorporate new convents of female religious (van der Woude 1953, 24).

[41] Persoons 1984, 81–2.

[42] The dismissive attitude of the Windesheimers is strongly reminiscent of the orders disposed towards reform in the thirteenth century. Even then the administrative leaders of the Cistercians, Franciscans and Dominicans attempted to limit their responsibility for the *cura monialium*, which had been imposed upon them by the Pope. Yet even among these orders there were a fair number of monasteries or brothers who nevertheless felt a strong commitment to the *cura monialium* (Degler-Spengler 1985).

tery of Gaesdonck near Goch, for example, the *cura monialium* was its primary task: it served no fewer than twelve nunneries.[43]

Thus it was that only thirteen nunneries received the privilege of joining the Chapter. One of these lay in present-day Germany (Engelendaal at Bonn), four in Belgium (Barberendaal at Tienen, Bethanië at Mechelen, Facons or Mariëndaal at Antwerp, Galilea at Ghent), and eight in the Netherlands (St Agnes in Dordrecht, Bethanië in Arnhem, Brunnepe near Kampen, St Maria and St Agnes in Diepenveen, Jeruzalem in Utrecht, Mariënburg in Nijmegen, Mariënveld or Oude Nonnen in Amsterdam, Onze Lieve Vrouw in Renkum).[44] Of this select group of convents Diepenveen was the most important and the most influential; it is considered the mother convent of the Windesheim nunneries. Sisters from Diepenveen were sent to Barberendaal, Bethanië in Mechelen, Galilea, Bethanië in Arnhem, Jeruzalem and Mariënveld in order to teach the nuns there the observance of Windesheim.[45] The monastery of Johannes Brinckerinck provided the model for the female monastic life according to the principles of the Modern Devotion. In the course of the fifteenth century the Windesheim manner of life exerted an increasingly significant degree of influence on the women's religious movement. In order to understand this development, we must return to its roots.

In the early years of the Modern Devotion many hundreds of women sought and found a place in the newly founded sisterhouses. Whether or not they chose this lifestyle out of principle, the life of the semi-religious was not, apparently, an end in itself. Even before the turn of the century a number of the spiritual leaders of sisterhouses, such as Wermbold Buscoop, Hugo Goudsmit and Gijsbert Dou, endeavoured to establish firmer control over the Sistermovement. The spread of the independent lifestyle of the Sisters, which strongly resembled that of the suspect Beguines, was followed closely by the Inquisition. A number of brother- and sisterhouses, especially those situated in the western Netherlands, therefore decided to adopt the Third Rule of the Order of St Francis. Innocent III accepted this third rule – alongside the first of the Franciscans and the second of the Poor Clares – in order to provide layfolk, too, with the opportunity to lead the spiritual life. The members of these houses are usually regarded as semi-religious, for they did not take vows. In 1401 the Chapter of Utrecht was founded, an organisation of former brother- and sisterhouses which observed the Third Rule of St Francis. A

---

[43] On the judicial aspects of the *cura monialium* carried out by the Chapter of Windesheim see especially van Dijk 1985.

[44] Kohl, Persoons and Weiler 1976–84 discuss a total of sixteen Windesheim convents, but according to van Dijk 1986, 38 the membership of at least two of them is suspect (the German houses of St Petrus at Heiningen and St Trinitatis at Dorstadt), whereas Onze Lieve Vrouw Presentatie at Oostmalle only entered the Chapter union in 1612, well after the medieval period.

[45] Cf. Kühler 1914, 313–26; Diepenveen reformed at least eleven other monasteries and sisterhouses in Belgium, Germany and the Netherlands.

portion of this devout movement was thus quickly integrated into the structure of the Church. The Chapter of Utrecht achieved dimensions on a par with Windesheim: eighty-two houses, of which only a small number were inhabited by men. Although it followed a Franciscan rule, the Chapter of Utrecht did not belong to the Franciscan Order. It was independent, but strongly influenced by the Modern Devotion.[46]

A number of the foundations of the Chapter of Utrecht, however, aspired to a higher form of monastic life. In 1418 the bishop of Utrecht, Floris van Wevelinckhoven, granted a number of these monasteries permission to adopt the Rule of St Augustine. Thus the foundation was laid for the monastic union known as the Chapter of Sion (or the Chapter of Holland). The driving force behind this movement in the early years was Willem Clinckaert of Schoonhoven, who sometimes gives the impression that he wanted to establish his own personal chapter in Holland, next to that of Windesheim, out of a desire for revenge. But for the most part the members of the Chapter of Sion followed the Windesheim model, though the Chapter retained its own character. A notable distinction between the two is that in the Chapter of Windesheim it was the chief monastery which enjoyed the greatest influence, whereas in the Chapter of Sion greatest power was wielded by the Chapter General. Another difference is the parity in numbers between the male and female house in the Chapter of Sion: there were seven of each.[47]

Ultimately the tendency to adopt the monastic life manifested itself in practically all the ranks of the Modern Devotion. At the organisational level this found expression in the formation of collegiate unions like the Chapters of Utrecht and Sion and the *colloquia* of Zwolle and Münster, in which the Dutch and the German Brother and sisterhouses, respectively, were united.[48] Within these larger contexts the member houses could monitor and inspire each other to adhere to their commonly avowed ideal. Post distinguishes three important phases in this process of monasticisation: the adoption of a

---

[46] On the history of the Chapter of Utrecht, see for example Post 1968, 269–72. Van Heel 1939 includes a brief discussion of the affiliated monasteries. At the time of writing a *monasticon* of the Chapter of Utrecht is being prepared at the Free University of Amsterdam, under the direction of K. Goudriaan. The first results of this project are to be found in Goudriaan and Mertens 2000.

[47] The history of the Chapter of Sion was written by Ypma 1949. On Windesheim's influence on the Chapter of Sion, see van Dijk 1986, 539–91 and van Dijk 1987b. For Willem Clinckaert and the Chapter of Sion see Goudriaan 1995.

[48] On the formation of the Chapter see Stutvoet-Joaknecht 1990, 139*–140* and van Dijk 1992, 120–1. The Chapters of Cologne (1427) and Zepperen (1434) were formed after the model of the Chapter of Utrecht. Cologne united brothers, sisters and tertiaries in northwestern Germany (de Kok 1939), Zepperen houses from the southern Low Countries (van Heel 1953). On the *colloquium* of Münster, which united a number of German brother- and sisterhouses, see Rehm 1985, 123–42 and Hinz 1997; about the *colloquium* of Zwolle, which united houses in the present-day Netherlands, little is known (Rehm 1985, 124 and Weiler 1997, XXII–XXIII).

rule, a stricter observance of it, and ultimately the adoption of the *clausura*.[49] Apparently the severe limitation of freedom of movement was regarded as the crown of the religious life; the so-called monastic enclosure movement was extremely influential within the Modern Devotion. Strict enclosure became a part of observance in virtually every convent, though there were many male monasteries which adopted a limited form of enclosure, such as, for example, Groenendaal, Mariënborn near Arnhem, and Korsendonk near Oud-Turnhout.[50]

This development increased greatly in momentum, especially in the second half of the fifteenth century, and also within the devout women's movement. More and more sisterhouses endeavoured to emulate the monastic life as closely as they could. Sometimes they stopped at the Third Rule of St Francis, sometimes they adopted the Augustinian Rule, but often a house just graduated from the Third Rule to membership of the Augustinian order. An illustration of this is the evolution of Sankt-Michaëls convent at Lübeck: its inmates lived first as poor women, then as penitents, next as Sisters of the Common Life, and finally as Canonesses.[51] In the male branches of the Modern Devotion, too, one sees this same tendency towards monasticisation. Hence in 1461 the Chapter of Windesheim accepted the Leiden house Hiëronymusdaal (or Lopsen), which was founded as a kind of brotherhouse and subsequently functioned as a tertiary monastery of the Chapter of Utrecht.[52] In all of this one must not lose sight of the fact that the monastic life was considerably more expensive than the semi-religious life. Without a firm economic foundation, the monastic life was an impossibility.

The monasticisation of the Modern Devotion is the expression of a more widespread striving for a stricter spiritual life which manifests itself especially in the second half of the fifteenth century. There are many reasons for these stricter attitudes.[53] The call for change came primarily from below, from the brothers and sisters themselves, and their spiritual leaders supported these initiatives wholeheartedly. The latter developed the need to maintain control of the situation. The Sisters of the Common Life stood, after all, under constant suspicion of heresy. It was easier to exercise control over an organisation that

---

[49] Post 1957, vol. 2, 97–175 is inclined to regard the 'common life', in which the Modern Devotion had its origins, as an exceptional intermediate stage in what he sees as a *monastic* reform movement. Post 1968, 493–4 refers in this context to Johannes Busch, who characterises the Modern Devotion as primarily a monastic movement.

[50] On the enclosures see Prims 1944.

[51] On Sankt-Michaël, see Rehm 1985, *passim* and Feismann 1994.

[52] Obbema 1996, 126–7 and Weiler 1997, 187–9.

[53] Stutvoet-Joanknecht 1990, 135*–153* provides an overview of this field of influence; according to her the Middle Dutch translations of Thomas of Cantimpré's *Liber de apibus* were made to facilitate the transition of the sisterhouses to the Augustinian rule after the model of Windesheim.

possessed a clear structure than over a large number of independent houses.[54] And yet the desire to lead the monastic life must have been a strong one among the Sisters themselves. For most of them it would have represented the highest and surest path to salvation. Ave Sonderlants (†1452) lived in the sisterhouse in de Wijngaard in Utrecht, where she 'chose a sure thing above an unsure one'[55] and became a canoness regular in the convent of Diepenveen.

As more and more convents adopted the Augustinian rule, the sphere of influence of the Chapter of Windesheim expanded. The way of life of the sisters of Windesheim continued to serve as the great model and for this reason many former sisterhouses and tertiary houses wished to join them, but the gates remained closed to these new nunneries. In order to come as close as possible to the Windesheim ideal, many monasteries adopted the statutes of the Windesheim convents in a more or less derivative form. This was the case for the Chapter of Venlo, a union of monasteries formed in 1455 in the bishopric of Liège, as well as for a large number of non-affiliated monasteries.[56] Many houses also tried to procure a confessor from a Windesheim male monastery. In both ways, which were naturally very often combined, the Chapter of Windesheim left its mark on the spiritual life in several hundred convents in northwestern Europe.[57]

The Modern Devotion was of tremendous significance for the religious women's movement in the later Middle Ages. The figures compiled by Post concerning the dimensions of the spiritual community in the present-day Netherlands on the eve of the Reformation testify to the veracity of this claim. Of the just under ten thousand female religious he counted at the beginning of the sixteenth century, approximately eight thousand of them belonged to the Modern Devotion: Sisters of the Common Life, tertiaries, and canonesses regular.[58] The total figures for the dimensions of the devout women's movement in the fifteenth century are unknown, but given the fact that, for example, the sisterhouse ten Orthen in den Bosch already counted five hundred members by the middle of the century, then we must be prepared to assume similar numbers for that period.[59] The influence on the pious

---

[54] The actions of the papal legate Nicholas of Kues or Cusanus (on him see also §5.3), who made a tour through the Netherlands in 1451, were of great significance in this regard. He strenuously propagated the Windesheim observance and forbade the foundation of new brother- and sisterhouses. The foundation of the Chapter of Venlo would appear to be the direct result of Cusanus' actions.

[55] ... *vercoes [. . .] dat seker voer dat onseker* (D, f. 159a; cf. DV, f. 361r).

[56] On the Chapter of Venlo see van Dijk 1986, 591–648.

[57] According to the estimation of van Dijk 1986, 30. See Rehm 1985, 44–53 on the relationship between Windesheim and the sisterhouses.

[58] Post 1954a, 160–7.

[59] Post 1968, 269; a sister-establishment was built in nearby Vught, with room for two hundred women.

women's movement of the Chapter of Windesheim must have increased in the course of the fifteenth century. It would not be going too far to posit that fully half of the ten thousand devout sisters who existed around 1500 were within the Windesheim sphere of influence, though a much smaller portion of these would have belonged directly to the Chapter itself. Thus, despite its restrictive policy of admission, the Chapter of Windesheim was a dominant factor in the second religious women's movement.

The tide changed around the year 1515. Once again the Church was confronted by a sense of distrust among the faithful and a loud call for change. The next reform movement rocked the very foundations of the Catholic Church and would ultimately lead to schism. In 1517 the Augustinian hermit Martin Luther inaugurated the Reformation by nailing his ninety-five theses against indulgences to the door of the church of Wittenberg.

1.2 The Search for Inner Meaning

The Modern Devotion is one of the most influential spiritual movements prior to the Reformation. It comes as no surprise therefore that there are some who have wished to view this movement as a precursor to the Reformation. The protestant preacher and church historian Willem Moll may be regarded as one of the founders of the study of the Modern Devotion. His interest was fed by curiosity about the roots of Protestantism.[60] One of his successors, Albert Hyma, went much further: in his view the Modern Devotion constituted a Christian Renaissance and as such should hardly be considered part of the Catholic Middle Ages.[61] This view was refuted by R. R. Post. In his seminal study of the Modern Devotion he emphasises the Catholic character of the movement and the strict orthodox views of its members.[62] In the previous section it was argued that the Modern Devotion falls within the sphere of influence of the decline of the Church and the succession of medieval reform movements. Given that there was but one Christian Church, then the Modern Devotion must indeed be regarded as a Catholic movement. The longing for interiorisation of the spiritual life which this movement reveals is reflected, perhaps, in the Reformation, but it appears with no less force in the Counter-Reformation. The emphasis upon a personal relationship with God is thus not an exclusively Protestant theme.

One may reasonably expect from a reform movement that it seeks to implement significant spiritual innovations, especially if it includes the adjective 'Modern' in its name. But in this compound we should not necessarily attribute the sense of 'innovative' or 'original' to the word. What the Modern

---

[60] The results of this research are recorded in Moll 1854; on the protestant founders of the study of the Modern Devotion, see Mertens 1991, 130–1.
[61] Hyma 1965.
[62] Post 1968.

Devout strove for was a new, 'modern', resurgence of the old strength of mind that had made Christianity great. The pioneer mentality of the Apostles, the unity of the first Christian communities, the simplicity and purity of a young yet internally strong movement, these were the primary inspirations of Geert Grote and his Modern Devotion.[63] This vision was anything but exceptional, for virtually all of the medieval reform movements drew upon the ancient apostolic ideals. And in other respects too the Modern Devout can take relatively little credit for innovations of any substance. They owe their success in particular to their skill at putting existing ideas and methods into practice on a large scale and disseminating them widely, and doing so with rare energy and effectiveness. We turn now to examine more closely a number of characteristic aspects of the Modern Devotion, in order to give some sense of its essence. It is well to note at the outset that most general observations on the Modern Devotion are based on what we know about their male representatives.

The great appreciation for the individual religious life as a distinguishing characteristic of the Modern Devotion has always attracted the most attention. But this may be the case because the movement has also usually been viewed from a Renaissance perspective. That interest in the spiritual life of the individual is not an innovation to be credited to the Modern Devotion need hardly be argued. After all, Francesco Petrarch (†1374) observed that in spiritual matters, too, man is ultimately left to his own devices.[64] Moreover, the Modern Devout respected personal experiences in this regard only up to a certain point, as Alijt Bake was to learn in 1455 (see Chapter 8). None of this detracts from the fact that personalism in matters of religion was for the first time widely disseminated under the Modern Devout. Even in the spirituality of the simple Sisters of the Common Life individual religious experience comes to the fore. Weiler has tried to understand the Modern Devotion's individualising approach with the aid of insights from French history of ideas. The Modern Devout were compelled to begin the necessary spiritual reformation with themselves because the Church had become unreliable. Geert Grote and his followers developed a psychologically oriented method which revealed to the individual believer the sinfulness of his nature. In this way he discovered not just his vices, but also what true virtue entailed. With

---

[63] The name 'Moderne Devotie' for the movement referred to here was as far as is known first used by Henricus Pomerius (†1469) in *De origine monasterii Viridisvallis*; he calls Geert Grote the *fons et origo modernae devotionis* ('source and origin of the modern devotion', [de Leu] 1885, 288; cf. Verdeyen 1981, 142); cf. Johannes Busch (for more on him, see §1.3), who comments on this name in the prologue of his *Liber de origine Devotionis Modernae* (Grube 1886, 245-7). The term had been verified earlier by Heinrich Seuse, whose work was embraced on a massive scale by the Modern Devotion. See further Staubach 1994, 200-1 and Mertens 1996c, 163 n. 2.

[64] It was no accident that Petrarch's *De vita solitaria* was popular among the Modern Devout (Enenkel 1987).

the help of this (self-)knowledge a new religious person could be created. In an ongoing individual process of spiritual construction the Modern Devout learned to reject flawed 'building materials' and use only approved ones to build a new, inwardly reformed person.[65]

Of great importance to this process of construction was the examination of personal conscience, to which the Modern Devout devoted several hours of each day. In order to track their progress, they drew up lists of vices and/or good intentions and resolutions. That the Modern Devout were concerned with the outer as well as the inner life may be clearly seen in a text that was circulated widely in their circles: the *Profectus religiosorum* ('The Development of the Religious Person') by the Fransciscan David of Augsburg (†1272). This guide for novices not only provides the young monk with a firm footing in moral issues, but teaches him as well the proper way to walk or sleep, how much he may eat each day and when he may laugh.[66]

'Consciousness-raising' texts like the *Profectus* were warmly received within the Modern Devotion. It is fair to say that not only the Modern Devout's individual activities but most of the communal ones as well were intended to improve their spiritual life. The Modern Devout supported each other in their endeavours and reprimanded one another when necessary. They conducted open discussions with their fellow brothers and sisters about their progress towards virtue. In this way they constructed not just new persons, but reformed communities as well.

The process of spiritual reform is traditionally based upon the trinity *lectio > meditatio/ruminatio > contemplatio* (for more on this see Chapter 4). The Modern Devotion was responsible for innovation within this framework that had a tremendous impact on religious literature. To the Modern Devout, books and writing were extremely important pillars of this meditative process. In this regard Geert Grote himself was an inspirational model: books were his great passion, and the only thing he spent any significant amount of money on after his conversion. The reading of religious texts was a great help to him in his own inner conversion, and in order to reach the hearts of others he wrote several treatises and a great number of letters. He translated various breviaries, including Heinrich Seuse's *Horologium aeternae sapientiae* ('Clock of Eternal Wisdom'), from Latin into Middle Dutch, and he also translated the works of Jan van Ruusbroec into Latin, in order that a wider audience might read them.[67] In their love of the book Geert Grote and his followers were part

---

[65] Weiler 1984b, 173–6. This perspective is illustrated with the example of Geert Grote in Weiler 1992.

[66] On the dissemination of the *Profectus* among the Modern Devout, see among others Stooker and Verbeij 1993. No manuscript from any of the Windesheim convents has been identified, but Alijt Bake was probably familiar with this text.

[67] On the translations of the divine office see van Dijk 1990 and van Dijk 1993; on the van Ruusbroec translations see de Baere 1993; cf. Staubach 1991, 418–20.

of an important development in late medieval reform movements: the use of literary means for the dissemination of religious ideals.[68] The Modern Devout incorporated this medium into their daily practice on a large scale and with exceptional efficiency. The 'Pragmatische Schriftlichkeit' ('pragmatic literacy'), which according to recent German scholarship manifested itself more and more in the late Middle Ages, reaches a highpoint with the Modern Devotion.[69] This functional approach to literacy resulted in a loss of interest in the original contents of texts, and respect for traditional conventions of genre disappeared for the most part as well. The Modern Devout created in the process a new, utilitarian religious literature, consisting of all manner of reworkings, adaptations, summaries and hybrid forms. Because of this, in addition to its sheer quantity, it is hard to give a brief overview of the literary production of the Modern Devotion.[70]

The women of the Modern Devotion were of overriding significance for the vernacular component of this tradition. Grundmann describes one of his most important conclusions as follows: 'Wo sich Männer mit theologischer Bildung der religiösen Frauenbewegung annahmen, war der Boden für eine volkssprachliche Literatur bereitet.'[71] The vernacular languages had earned a place in the Church as the spoken word, especially in preaching and prayer, but the written ecclesiastical language was Latin. Theological discourse was carried out within a circle of well-trained clergy, for whom Latin constituted not a hindrance, but rather an obvious and appropriate medium. Only after a great number of women adopted the spiritual life in the thirteenth century was there an audience with a desire to read the Bible themselves, but with too little education to be able to read the Latin. We find a very early example of this in the diocese of Liège; it was there that the priest Lambert (†1177) translated the life of St Agnes into French verse for the benefit of a number of women, perhaps Beguines. According to Grundmann the pinnacle of this development was ultimately reached in the 'German mysticism', of which the Dominicans Meister Eckhart (†1328), Johannes Tauler (†1361) and Heinrich Seuse (†1366) are the most important representatives. All three were committed by their order to the care of the Dominican nunneries in the Rhineland, which flourished tremendously in the fourteenth century. The meeting of these theologians and mystics with such literary talents and the

---

[68] Williams-Krapp 1986–7 and Williams-Krapp 1993, 301. Schreiner 1992 discusses a large number of written reform materials.
[69] On 'pragmatische Schriftlichkeit' see Keller, Grubmüller and Staubach 1992; the concept is applied to the Modern Devotion in Staubach 1991.
[70] On the vernacular literature, see Mertens 1989a and Mertens 1993, for the Latin see Staubach 1991 and Staubach 1994.
[71] Grundmann 1977, 457.

Dominican nuns who put themselves in their care formed the breeding-ground for a rich and varied mystic oeuvre in the vernacular.[72]

This mystic literature was not produced exclusively by male pastors who wished to be of service to a female audience. Many religious women did not limit themselves to reading and listening, but took to composing texts themselves and thus created the famous tradition of female mysticism.[73] With their relatively uneducated female audience in mind they wrote for the most part in the vernacular. Moreover, many of these women did not have sufficient knowledge of Latin to be able to write in that language.[74] A number of the first religious women to produce their own corpus in the vernacular lived in the southern Netherlands and wrote in Middle Dutch: the Cistercian nun Beatrijs van Nazareth (†1268) and the Beguine Hadewijch, whose activities are usually dated to about 1250.[75] In the first half of the fourteenth century there was a great deal of literary activity among the Dominican nuns, usually resulting in autobiographical accounts of the mystical life and *Schwesternbücher* or 'sisterbooks', collections of the life stories of sisters in a given convent.[76] Mention should also be made of the fact that a large body of mystic literature was produced in Latin, in particular by such influential authors as the Cistercian Bernard of Clairvaux and the Franciscan Bonaventure. In the mystic tradition Latin and the vernacular went hand in hand, though not always as equal partners. In general we may posit that in matters of mysticism the vernacular enjoyed a certain degree of preference, whereas when theological matters entered the picture, Latin was preferred. It is significant that it is exactly the mystical-theological works of writers like Bernard and Bonaventure that were not translated into Middle Dutch. The cleric reserved for himself the exclusive right to write about and debate such lofty themes. In that regard Latin functioned as an effective barrier.[77]

The meeting of the second religious women's movement and the leaders of the Modern Devotion also had consequences for religious literature in the

---

[72] Grundmann 1977, 452–75. For German mysticism see Ruh 1990–9, vol. 3.

[73] Lewis, Willaert and Govers 1989 provide bibliographical data on German female mysticism, as well as Beatrijs van Nazareth and Hadewijch. Peters 1988 treats the history of the origin of this female mystic tradition in great detail.

[74] Enough exceptions are known. The Cistercian abbess of the German convent Helfta, Gertrud the Great (†1301/2) wrote a body of mystic writings in Latin (Lewis, Willaert and Govers 1989, 196–218; see also Ruh 1990–9, vol. 2, 314–37) and the two oldest known *Schwesternbücher* from Adelhausen and Unterlinden were composed in Latin (Lewis 1996, 10–15 and 35–9).

[75] On Beatrijs and Hadewijch see for instance Ruh 1990–9, vol. 2, 138–57 and 158–232, respectively, and McGinn 1991–8, vol. 3, 166–74 and 200–22, respectively.

[76] On this *Viten- und Offenbarungsliteratur* in general see Ringler 1980 and Peters 1988; for the *Schwesternbücher* in particular, see Lewis 1996 (cf. also Chapter 6, where *Schwesternbücher* and sisterbooks are distinguished).

[77] Surveys of the mystical tradition of the Occident are provided by Ruh 1990–9, McGinn 1991–8 and Dinzelbacher 1994.

vernacular. The fifteenth century constitutes a highpoint in the production of manuscripts in the Low Countries, a phenomenon for which the Modern Devotion may largely be credited.[78] A significant peak in this production manifests itself in the third quarter of the fifteenth century, unmistakably linked to the increase in monasticisation.[79] Not only were many books produced during this period, but new works were made available as well. Both (!) Middle Dutch translations of Thomas of Cantimpré's (†1272) *Bonum universale de apibus* or *Bienboeck* ('The Book of Bees') produced after 1450, were intended to serve as a guide to monastic life for new canonesses regular.[80] This production was not restricted to the Sisters of the Common Life, the tertiaries and the canonesses regular, for whom the many Middle Dutch devotional manuscripts were produced.[81] Latin texts and manuscripts were also produced on a large scale for the male establishments.[82]

The Rhineland mysticism of the fourteenth century is famous not for the volume of its manuscript production, but for the expressiveness of this new literature created, often collaboratively, by Dominican theologians and nuns. Did the priests within the Modern Devotion who were charged with the *cura monialium* also create such an original body of literature? Can the same be said of the female Modern Devout? It is certainly true that the use by women of various forms of religious literature was promoted by the Modern Devotion. But the attitude towards this religious literature was predominantly receptive. The Modern Devout knew the canon well and preferred to draw from that pure and trustworthy source; hence the translations of, for example, David of Augsburg's *Profectus* and Thomas of Cantimpré's *Bienboeck*. Even when they wrote new texts – and they did this on a large scale – the Modern Devout tended to rely heavily on the spiritual tradition, with a preference for that of the ascetics. They were especially reserved towards the mystic literary tradition, which speaks openly and unreservedly about the human relationship with God. This somewhat narrow-minded cultural climate was not conducive to the development of a truly new literature or mode of expression.

---

[78] On manuscript production in the fifteenth-century Low Countries, see Gumbert 1990, 24–79. I know of no such available data for Belgium and northern Germany, where the Modern Devotion was also strongly represented.

[79] Cf. Mertens 1995b, 129 and Mertens 1993, 364 n. 42 for possible explanations for this 'manuscript explosion'.

[80] Stutvoet-Joanknecht 1990, 129*–153*.

[81] On monastic owners of Middle Dutch religious manuscripts, see Stooker and Verbeij 1997.

[82] The 'wall catalogue' (a large piece of parchment attached to the wall, upon which are recorded the library's holdings) from the monastery Lopsen in Leiden (see §1.1) mentions around two hundred Latin works, which is certainly not extravagant for a male institution. In his edition of this catalogue, Obbema rightly maintains that modern research tends to neglect the Latin texts and manuscripts of the Modern Devotion (Obbema 1996, 120–34, in this case 129; cf. Mertens 1991, 138).

INTRODUCTION

The apprehensive attitude of the Modern Devout towards mysticism is clearly seen in the meeting between Geert Grote and Jan van Ruusbroec, which took place in the monastery at Groenendaal around 1378. Grote was impressed by van Ruusbroec, having become familiar with the latter's mystic teachings through his writings. The two engaged in a fundamental discussion of the meaning of the mystical experience. Van Ruusbroec was firmly convinced that the Holy Spirit resided in his heart and allowed himself to be guided by this assurance. He dared to trust in divine grace, which infused his actions and teachings with an aura of wisdom and joy. Grote, on the other hand, who was no stranger to the experience of God, was of the opinion that the mystic from Groenendaal was not possessed in a sufficient degree of the fear of God. By this he meant that van Ruusbroec had too little fear of God's wrath, which would be brought down upon mankind for its sins. This somber view would always be uppermost in Grote's attitude towards life.[83]

The spirit of its founder has always remained recognisably present in the spirituality of the Modern Devotion. Gerard Zerbolt van Zutphen (†1398), the brilliant friar from the Heer-Florenshuis, who died at an early age, developed a penitential attitude to life based on asceticism. In his view man is torn between the heavenly Jerusalem and the earthly Jericho. It behooves him to seek after self-knowledge in order to become aware of this ambiguity. Zerbolt recommends three means that lead to self-knowledge: independent soul-searching, admonishment by others and confrontation of the passions of the soul. Armed with the new self-knowledge the believer sets course once and for all down the path to Jerusalem. By means of all manner of spiritual exercises he tries both externally and internally to emulate Christ. Gerard Zerbolt preferred to dedicate himself to practical asceticism, which he himself could control, rather than to wait for the mystical meeting with God in the spirit.[84]

Although asceticism held the dominant position in the spiritual beliefs of the Modern Devotion, there did exist a mystical undercurrent. It manifested itself particularly in the context of the Chapter of Windesheim. The roots of this mystical tradition extend back to van Ruusbroec and Groenendaal. The unification of the Chapters of Windesheim and Groenendaal sealed the incorporation of this tradition.[85] At the beginning of the fifteenth century there was

---

[83] The encounter between van Ruusbroec and Grote is described exhaustively by Henricus Pomerius in his *vite* of van Ruusbroec, chapters 8–10 (ed. [de Leu] 1885, 288–90 and Verdeyen 1981, 142–5). Much shorter is the account given by Peter Hoorn in the *vite* of Geert Grote (ed. Kühler 1909, 349–51). On the difference in outlook between van Ruusbroec and Grote see Weiler 1984c (where only Hoorn's text is cited).

[84] Zerbolt's main treatises are *De reformatione virium animae* and *De spiritualibus ascensionibus*. Mahieu 1941 prints the Latin text (with translation), van Engen 1988a, 245–315 a slightly abridged English translation. On Zerbolt see further Gerrits 1986.

[85] A few south Netherlandish Windesheimers view van Ruusbroec, not Geert Grote,

a small active circle of mystics, whose members included, among others, the prior Johan Vos van Heusden (†1424), the librarian and Bible translator Jan Scutken (†1423), the visionary Hendrik Mande (†1431) and the mystical author Gerlach Peters (†1411).[86] Gerlach Peters is the only one to have left behind original mystical teachings. For Gerlach, a demeanour of humility before God formed the basis for the devout life. Only when one has managed, starting from this fundamental attitude, to achieve purity of heart (*puritas cordis*) can one also experience the pouring in of divine grace (which takes place constantly within man). This joyous encounter with God was for Gerlach Peters the very essence of the inner life. This contemplative element is much more prominent with him than it is with Gerard Zerbolt, who nurtures fewer expectations of grace and is therefore a greater advocate of strict penitence.[87]

In an excellent study, Mertens demonstrates how the Modern Devotion gradually and increasingly distanced itself from mysticism during the course of the fifteenth century.[88] Hendrik Mande had to overcome resistance from his fellow brothers at Windesheim who had their doubts about his visionary talent. Mande compares his critics with a dog in the haystack who barks at the approaching cows and horses: he may not be able to eat the hay himself, but nor will the animals that can be allowed to do so.[89] According to Mertens, during the fifteenth century the Modern Devotion developed a mystical tradition in which mysticism was in fact banished to the margins.[90] Suspicion of the unverifiability of the mystical experience and fear of the emergence of heretical ideas shape this spirituality. This growing reticence is certainly not unrelated to the great influx of women, in whose judgement there was little confidence. In order to provide these women with a more realistic and achievable life ideal, the contemplative element was gradually banished from the life ideal of the Modern Devout. They were presented with a spirituality based on

---

as the founder of the Modern Devotion. Thus for example Petrus Impens (†1523), canon regular at Bethlehem in Herent, in his chronicle *Compendium decursus temporum monasterii christifere bethleemitice puerpere* (see further van Engen 1992). Warnar 1995, 133–47 notes the important differences between the literature written in the convents in Brabant and that written in the more northerly Windesheim convents.

[86] On the mystical circle in Windesheim see Mertens 1995b, 120–2.
[87] Kors 1996 edits Gerlach Peters's *opera omnia* and provides it with an introduction; cf. van Engen 1999.
[88] Mertens 1995b.
[89] Cited by Mertens 1995b, 121–2. On Mande as visionary, see Mertens 1989b.
[90] By 'mystical culture' Mertens understands a spiritual culture the ideal of which is determined by the experiences of the mystic. Aided by this concept it is possible to position the Modern Devotion – and perhaps the entire fifteenth century – within the long mystical tradition that begins in the early Middle Ages and ends only in the eighteenth century. The Modern Devotion knows and recognises the mystical experience, but nevertheless considers the mystical path to be too extreme. Van Dijk 1984, 103 considers this attitude 'the tragedy of the Modern Devotion': it remained mired in asceticism and never achieved a full mystical flowering.

solace and resignation, whereby at the very most some literature with a mystical tint was consulted.[91] This shift in the spiritual culture of the Modern Devotion reflects its struggle with the theme of mysticism. The Modern Devout were ultimately not able to provide a serious place in their spiritual life for the mystical experience, which by definition is a personal and unverifiable phenomenon. In the end they preferred the regular communal life of the convent, for this seemed to them to provide the surest and safest path to salvation.

1.3 The Writings of the Canonesses of the Chapter of Windesheim and Their Reception

Literature and reform of the religious life go hand in hand in the Modern Devotion, even among the women, despite the fact that women had very little influence. In the second religious women's movement a small number of women emerged as authors, all of whom did their best to disseminate or preserve a religious ideal through spiritual texts. From a literary viewpoint the Windesheim canonesses constitute a special group, for it is this circle that produced the lion's share of writings by women among the Modern Devout. Apparently the literary climate for women was more favourable in the Chapter of Windesheim than anywhere else. And yet within that monastic community itself little if any importance was conceded to these female authors: they are utterly absent from the *Catalogus scriptorum Windeshemensium* produced by Petrus Trudonensis (†1674).[92] The literary activity of Windesheim canonesses regular, which covers approximately the period 1425–1525, is, so far as we know, concentrated in four convents: Diepenveen, Galilea, Bethanië (Mechelen) and Facons. What follows is a brief overview, by way of introduction, of the most important authors and writings of the Windesheim canonesses, in more or less chronological order.

As the first prioress of Diepenveen, Salome Sticken (†1449) was an important support for Johannes Brinckerinck. After his death she was primarily responsible for keeping his ideal alive. She ruled the convent of Diepenveen from 1408 to 1446 with great severity and brought the spiritual life there to great heights. In about 1435 this famous reformer was asked to compose a religious handbook for women who wished to live according to the precepts of the Modern Devotion. This *Vivendi formula*, or 'Rule of Life', deals in some depth with the inner life of the women devout.

The Windesheim canoness with the largest and most widely disseminated oeuvre is Alijt Bake (†1455). Virtually immediately after her arrival in Galilea she had serious disagreements with the prioress, Hille Sonderlants (†1445), who just a few years earlier had come from Diepenveen in order to establish

---

[91] Willeumier-Schalij 1990.
[92] Ed. Lourdaux and Persoons 1968.

Windesheim practices in the new monastery in Ghent. Bake felt that the prioress put too much emphasis on externals, whereas she herself valued the inner spiritual life more highly. Ultimately Alijt Bake was able to win the trust of the community and in 1445 she succeeded Hille Sonderlants as prioress. During her priorship Bake wrote a number of texts, all of which dealt with her mystical teachings. Most intriguing is *Mijn beghin ende voortganck* ('My Beginning and Progress'), a spiritual autobiography, in which she describes her difficult early years at Galilea.

Alijt Bake's stubborn self-willed behaviour had far-reaching consequences. In 1455 she was removed from her office and banished by representatives of the Chapter General of Windesheim. That her literary activities had something to do with her removal is apparent from a striking resolution passed by the Chapter General that very year:

> No nun or sister, no matter what her status, may, either personally or through an intermediary, copy books which contain philosophical teachings or revelations [i.e. mystical texts], whether these originate in her own mind or that of her sisters, on penalty of imprisonment; henceforth should any such be discovered, it is the responsibility of all to ensure that they are immediately burned as soon as they are found or heard tell of; nor should any dare to translate such texts from the Latin into Dutch.[93]

This 'injunction against writing' of 1455 reflects again the official stance of the Chapter of Windesheim towards the mysticism issue. Writing about mystical experiences, in previous centuries the essence of religious women's literature, was now definitively forbidden.[94]

As far as is known no Windesheim canoness wrote any truly mystical texts after 1455, though one still encounters 'revelations' in their works and numerous other reminders of their long mystical tradition. An important work is the Diepenveen sisterbook, in which sixty lives of virtuous sisters from this convent are compiled. These *viten* were written by their fellow nuns, who on behalf of the entire convent recorded these remembrances of the dead. This sisterbook took shape during the course of almost a century,

---

[93] *Nulla monialis aut soror cuiuscunque status fuerit conscribat aliquos libros, doctrinas philosophicas aut revelationes continentes per se interpositamve personam ex sua propria mente vel aliarum sororum compositas sub poena carceris si qui inposterum reperti fuerint praecipitur omnibus quod statim illi ad quorum conspectum vel aures pervenerint eos igni tradere curent, similiter nec aliquem transferre praesumant de latino in theutonicum* (ed. van der Woude 1953, 53). On the three phases of the resolution of the Chapter of Windesheim see §1.1, n. 37; the prohibition against writing returns in the *Acta* of 1456 and 1457 (van der Woude 1953, 54 and 56). In 1466 there followed a resolution in which it was yet again stipulated that women were not allowed to translate books from Latin without permission of the Chapter General (van der Woude 1953, 67 and 68).

[94] Axters 1956, 168 was the first to make the connection between this order and Alijt Bake's actions.

roughly in the period between 1450 and 1525. The lives present examples of sisters who exemplified their ideals in an exceptional way, recorded for the benefit of younger generations of Diepenveen sisters. The Diepenveen sisterbook is thus 'a book full of virtues', just as Johannes Brinckerinck must have intended. It is at the same time also a chronicle, in which the history of Diepenveen is recorded in the form of life histories.

The *Kroniek Bethanië* in Mechelen also describes the history of a convent, but unlike the sisterbook the choice here was the traditional chronicle format. In 1486 one of the nuns from Bethanië was given the task of writing the convent's history. She did this in the form of brief annual synopses. Subsequently an account was given from year to year of the most important events, right up until the dissolution of the convent in the French period. Thus it is that this chronicle contains a wealth of information, especially concerning the exterior aspects of life in the convent; the Diepenveen sisterbook, on the other hand, deals predominantly with spiritual matters.

At the end of the fifteenth century it was Jacomijne Costers (†1503) who in the convent of Facons in Antwerp led a small group of women seeking a more profound spiritual life. Jacomijne repented on her sickbed. In a vision she was taken before Christ by malicious devils, who there demanded her soul. She decided to mend her ways, and those of her fellow sisters. In order to persuade the nuns she committed to writing a detailed account of her terrible journey to hell. In addition she wrote a number of shorter spiritual texts, including a refrain. One of the sisters in whom she found a willing audience was Mechtild van Rieviren (†1497). A number of this sister's internal dialogues with Christ have been preserved.

This overview would not be complete without a mention of Sister Bertken (†1514), without doubt the best known fifteenth-century female author from the Netherlands. Bertha Jacobs, illegitimate daughter of the canon regular Jacob van Lichtenberg, lived for about six years as a canoness in the Windesheim monastery of Jeruzalem, in Utrecht. She left the monastery in 1456 or 1457 in order to live as an anchoress in a cell at the Buurkerk in Utrecht. There it was that she wrote her corpus of mystically tinted spiritual works that were to make her so famous. These include, among others, a treatise on Christmas Eve, perhaps inspired by a vision, as well as a number of songs. Because these spiritual works were composed only after she had been enclosed, they will not be considered in this study. That is of course not to deny that as far as their spirituality and function are concerned, the works of Sister Bertken have a close affinity with the writings of the Windesheim canonesses.[95]

Unlike the works of Bertha Jacobs, the writings of the Windesheim nuns have received hardly any attention from literary critics. In the classic Dutch literary histories one will search in vain for the names of Alijt Bake, Jacomijne

---

[95] On sister Bertken see for instance Vynckier 1988 and van Aelst 1997.

Costers or Salome Sticken. It is true that many of these authors were 'discovered' rather late – Costers is mentioned for the first time in 1926, Bake in 1936 – but even after such discoveries Netherlandicists have paid scant attention to their work. Axters was the only one to conduct a thorough and systematic study of their literature, in his *Geschiedenis van de vroomheid* ('History of Piety'). But he did not study their works as literary artifacts: Axters used the texts composed by the Windesheim canonesses as evidence for their pious convictions.[96]

One of the reasons for the treatment of the Windesheim canonesses as second-rate authors is undoubtedly their gender. The great Dutch literary histories were written predominantly by men. Literary historians were on the whole not interested in the achievements of female writers, which had the effect of further marginalising their already less than prominent role. However, during the second decade of the twentieth century this gap was partly filled by the appearance of Basse's history of Dutch literature written by women. Basse does indeed note that, thanks to the Modern Devotion, the fifteenth century produced a great deal of literature written by women, but he goes on to fill practically the whole of the next section on the Middle Ages with the work of only one woman: Hadewijch.[97] There must be more going on here than meets the eye. The Windesheim nuns wrote virtually exclusively religious prose, and that happens to be precisely the genre anathematised a century and a half ago by Jonckbloet, the founding father of Middle Dutch literary studies. Because religious prose did not, in his view, live up to the highest standards, especially those determined by an aesthetic norm, the genre was of no significance to literary history.[98] Jonckbloet's powerful voice has exerted so much authority that religious prose has barely, if at all, found a place in the canon of Middle Dutch literature. Only the mystical prose of Jan van Ruusbroec and the varied works of Hadewijch have managed to win a place in the canon since then. In recent years a change has taken place that has brought medieval religious prose within the purview of literary history.[99] Moreover, the interest in religious women's literature, stimulated by the flourishing field of the history of women, has never been greater than it is now.

This study is aimed at the role which religious prose played in the lives of the nuns of Windesheim. All the texts in whose composition they had an active role are discussed in detail here. To this end I have chosen a literary theoretical approach marked by a historical cultural-studies perspective. According to this methodology medieval texts are studied in the historical contexts of their composition and function. Generally speaking, a monastic

---

[96] Axters 1956, 152–70 and also Axters 1967, *passim*.
[97] Basse 1920–1; cf. Aercke 1994.
[98] See especially Jonckbloet 1851–5, vol. 2, 259–62 and vol. 3, 484–7.
[99] Mertens 1991; the position of religious prose in the literary canon is discussed on pp. 131–3. See Ruh 1979 and Steer 1987a for religious prose in the German-speaking area.

order constitutes a sharply demarcated cultural entity – more so than a city or court, for instance – within which in a precisely circumscribed way a very pronounced philosophy of life is put into practice.[100] The intersection of texts by the canonesses of Windesheim with their cultural-historical contexts generates new insights which can lead to better interpretations of the texts. On the other hand, literary criticism also contributes to cultural history, for the canonesses of Windesheim reveal themselves nowhere more clearly than in their writings. A careful study of these works from a literary historical perspective increases our knowledge of the lives and thought of these women.

The historical-functional approach is also apparent in the structure of this book. In the following three chapters a number of contextual aspects are addressed: the historical reality of life in the convent, commonly held religious rituals and the organisation of the spiritual life of the individual. Subsequently the texts and their authors are taken up, in an order which globally speaking moves from fixed – not to say orthodox – to more liberal forms and attitudes. Chapter 5 is devoted to a number of strongly didactic texts, among which is Salome Sticken's *Vivendi formula*. In Chapter 6 the focus is on historiography: the Diepenveen sisterbook and the chronicle of Bethanië. Chapter 7 studies the monastery of Facons, where Jacomijne Costers and Mechtild van Rieviren established a new reform movement, while Chapter 8 deals with Alijt Bake who, partly by means of her writings, attempted to legitimate her spiritual authority, a move that would prove fatal. The approach chosen here is accompanied to some extant by the danger of fragmentation. Therefore a concluding chapter has been added which surveys and takes stock of current knowledge of the position which literature held in the lives of the Windesheim nuns. At the same time Chapter 9 seeks to establish their place in the larger context of the medieval religious women's movements.

Several written sources are available for the historical reconstruction.[101] Approximately eighty medieval manuscripts and early printed books survive from Windesheim convents, many of which have been consulted for this study.[102] Of great historical importance are the *Constitutiones sanctimonialium ordinis Sancti Augustini Capituli Windeshemensis*, available in van Dijk's thorough edition. The daily programme followed by the nuns of Windesheim

---

[100] Concerning literary historiography based on cultural circles see van Oostrom 1985, especially 211–12.

[101] The point of departure was in each case the *Monasticon Windeshemense*, which provides for each Windesheim convent an overview of sources, literature, history, and bibliography (Kohl, Persoons and Weiler 1976–84). Moreover the *Monasticon belge* has also proved useful in this regard.

[102] The Middle Dutch manuscripts identified as to provenance from the Windesheim convents are listed in the catalogue published by Stooker and Verbeij 1997. I refer the reader further to the online version of the Bibliotheca Neerlandica Manuscripta (http://www.leidenuniv.nl/ub/bnm/). For the Latin manuscripts see the *Monasticon Windeshemense* and *Monasticon belge* (see previous note).

is described exhaustively and with great care in these constitutions. The only extant redaction of the constitutions dates to just after 1443.[103] Little information of this kind is available for the previous years.[104] This is where the literary sources can help to fill in the gaps. Almost all of the texts written by the Windesheim nuns provide information about life in the convent, sometimes in passing.[105] The most important source of information concerning the nuns' daily lives, but also their attitudes, is the Diepenveen sisterbook. Among other narrative sources the work of Johannes Busch (†c.1480) should receive first mention, as he was one of the most important chroniclers of the Chapter of Windesheim and the Modern Devotion. These include especially the *Liber de origine Devotionis Modernae* and his book on the reform work carried out under the auspices of Windesheim, *De reformatione monasteriorum*.[106] Furthermore there is the work of Christophorus Caers, prior of Facons from 1640 to his death in 1673. He wrote a chronicle of this monastery entitled *Register van het beginsel, voortganck ende gedenckweerdichste geschidenissen* ('Register of the Origins, Progress and Noteworthy Events'), and a *Naem- en doodtboeck* ('Book of Names and the Dead'), in which the names of all the deceased sisters as well as the priors and benefactors of Facons were recorded.[107]

All of these sources must necessarily be treated with a certain degree of caution, because without exception they tend to idealise reality. The constitutions describe an ideal situation which in practice can never have been fully realised, and chroniclers are often inclined to enhance somewhat the words and deeds of their subjects. Even in one of the most important sources, the sisterbook, the primary aim is never an objective representation of the facts. Nevertheless, provided they are approached with some reserve, these sources do provide enough leads – they are also often enough the only means – for the construction of a reasonably trustworthy picture of historical reality. Moreover, it is possible to compare the various sources with one another.

In order to put the picture thus constructed into its context, periodic references are made to the situation among the canons of Windesheim, whose constitutions comprise the main source for the canonical statute.[108] Other

---

[103] Ed. van Dijk 1986, 726–833. There was also an (unedited) translation in Middle Dutch available (cf. van Dijk 1987a).
[104] In the manuscripts of the *Acta Capituli Windeshemensis* used by van der Woude 1953 in his edition (see §1.1, n. 37), numerous Chapter resolutions concerning canonesses have apparently been left out (van Dijk 1986, 203–12).
[105] On daily life in the Windesheim convents, see Persoons 1980.
[106] Busch wrote three great historical works, the full titles of which read *Liber de origine Devotionis Modernae, Liber de viris illustribus* and *Liber de reformatione monasteriorum ordinum diversorum* (ed. Grube 1886). See Debongnie 1937 and Iserloh 1983.
[107] On Christophorus Caers and his works see Persoons 1993d, 564 and 576–7 and Scheepsma 1997, 245–6.
[108] The *Constitutiones Capituli Windeshemensis*, however, have not been edited yet (cf. van Dijk 1986, 13–46).

INTRODUCTION

groups of religious women provide further interesting material for comparison. In this regard it is primarily the other women's movements which sprang from the bosom of the Modern Devotion that receive consideration. The Sisters of the Common Life and the tertiary nuns, with their semi-religious manner of life, are fairly far removed from the nuns of Windesheim. Much closer are the Canonesses of the Chapters of Sion and Venlo, as well as all manner of other convents that adopted the Rule of St Augustine. The frame of reference is broadened even further by the Windesheim practice of opposition to the situation among the Dominican nuns from the order province of Teutonia. It is precisely there that the foundation is laid for German mysticism: Eckhart, Seuse and Tauler were all active there, and the Dominican *Schwesternbücher* were written in that region. The Windesheimers were aware of the trend-setting role of the Dominicans in the realm of the *cura monialium*, and therefore for the composition of the rule for 'their' nuns they drew heavily on the Dominican constitutions, which had already amply proved their worth.[109] During the fifteenth century an internal reform movement arose within this famous order which in its tendencies bears a similarity to the Modern Devotion.[110] The new observance gained a foothold in a small number of Dominican convents in Germany, among the most famous of which were St Katharina in Neurenberg and St Nikolaus in Undis at Strasburg. The developments that transpired in both of these reformed convents constitute a benchmark for the assessment of the position that the religious literature women held in the lives of the canonesses of Windesheim.[111]

---

[109] Van Dijk 1986, especially 256–85.
[110] On the reforms of the Dominican nuns in the Netherlands, see Wolfs 1985a, 1985b and van Dijk 1986, 276–85.
[111] On the reforms in the province of Teutonia in the fifteenth century, see Barthelmé 1930. St Katharina at Neurenberg was founded in 1295 and immediately joined the Dominican order. An attempt at reform in 1397 failed, but in 1428 the observance was finally adopted. St Katharina is famous for its huge library of manuscripts, which must have contained between 500 and 600 codices and is the direct result of the reformation (Ruf 1939, 570–8, Schneider and Zirnbauer 1965, XI–XXXIV; see furthermore Schneider 1983, 70 n. 1). Fortunately fully half have been preserved in the Stadtbibliotheek of Neurenberg (described by Schneider and Zirnbauer 1965, 1–429; see also Schneider 1983). A list of the books in this formerly private collection was drawn up between 1451 and 1457 (ed. Ruf 1939, 578–96), and furthermore a general catalogue has survived in which the general collection was recorded up to approximately 1500 (ed. Ruf 1939, 596–38). Moreover two programmes of reading for the refectory are known for the years 1429–31 (ed. Ruf 1939, 638–50) and 1455–61 (ed. Ruf 1939, 650–70); cf. Hasebrink 1996 and Lewis 1996, 62–3. St Nikolaus in Undis, situated just outside the walls of Strasburg, joined the Dominican order in 1428 and was reformed in 1431. Most of the 86 surviving manuscripts date to a later period (cf. Rüther and Schiewer 1992).

2

Aspects of Life in the Convent

ON 4 SEPTEMBER 1412 an eminent company from the county of Holland arrived at the new convent in Diepenveen. Its most important members were the Lady van Heenvliet, her niece Katharina van Naaldwijk, Joost Claesz – later Johannes Brinckerinck's successor as prior of Diepenveen, but at that time still procurator of the Windesheim monastery of Rugge, near Brielle – and the Heenvliet family chaplain. The eighteen-year-old Katharina had had to travel incognito because of the very real threat of abduction. Her father, Lord Hendrik van Naaldwijk, was marshall to the count of Holland, Albrecht of Bavaria. Katharina was thus an exceptionally attractive marriage prospect. She, however, had chosen the heavenly groom, a choice which her parents, pious as they were, had approved, however much it pained them. Katharina passed up a splendid position in the world for a life of poverty, obedience and loneliness.

The conversion of the noblewoman Katharina van Naaldwijk made quite an impact at the convent of Diepenveen too. It was not just her conversion, but also the way she put her religious ideal into practice that evoked great admiration. It is partially on account of this that the biography of her and her sister Griete is one of the most detailed and thorough in the Diepenveen sisterbook.[1] This combined biography is therefore exceptionally well suited to serve as the guide for an introduction to life in a Windesheim convent. In what follows, I offer an overview of the persons who lived there and the most important functions that had to be carried out (§2.1). Next are described the three stages that a novice nun had to complete (§2.2). Special attention is given to the education and the training of the Windesheim novice (§2.3), and finally we shall consider how life in the convent was structured temporally (§2.4).

2.1 The Inhabitants of the Convent

The thirteen nunneries that were admitted to the Chapter of Windesheim were already unique for that fact alone, but there is more reason to regard

---

[1] The *viten* of Katharina and Griete van Naaldwijk are found in DV, ff. 226r–266v, D, ff. 45c–70a and B, ff. 225r–226v (Carasso-Kok 1981, no. 204; 32).

this group as an elite. The Windesheim convents boasted among their inmates a considerable number of daughters from high noble circles. This was the case, for example, at Onze Lieve Vrouw in Renkum, founded in 1405 by Reinald IV, duke of Guelders, and patronised thereafter by him and his successor, Arnold II. Walburg van Gelre (†1509), Duke Arnold's niece, entered the convent of Onze Lieve Vrouw in 1457. Her mother Walburg van Meurs (†1459), wife to Willem van Egmond and Bar, Duke Arnold's brother, asked to be buried there.[2] Such examples, which could be multiplied many times over by that of Katharina van Naaldwijk and others, demonstrate that the Windesheim convents generally had strong ties with the highest social circles. Most of the canonesses came from the upper strata of society, the nobility and municipal patriarchy. The Sisters of the Common Life and tertiaries were derived on the whole from the lower classes.[3]

In the Windesheim convents of canonesses regular it was the divine office, the daily prayers observed at the canonical hours, which formed the pivot of their existance. The canonesses (also: choir nuns or canonesses regular) were the most important members of this monastic community, for they were the ones who carried out this eternal prayer. For Katharina van Naaldwijk the saying of divine office would become her life fulfilment. And when choir nuns like herself were not in the chancel, they were occupied with other religious duties. They were able to devote themselves almost exclusively to a life of prayer. The position of choir nun or canoness was therefore regarded as the highest monastic state.

That the canonesses of Windesheim were able to devote almost all of their time to the monastic life was thanks in large part to the *conversinnen* (*conversae*). These lay sisters took monastic vows, wore a habit that differed only slightly from that of the choir nuns and lived together with them within the walls of the convent. Within the praying and working community that constituted a convent as a whole, they were the ones who performed the extensive duties of maintaining the household. They were expected to be present at the most important celebrations – albeit in the church, not in the chancel – but their main charge was to perform all kinds of labour: brewing beer, baking bread, washing clothes, polishing shoes, and so forth.[4]

Women who had not made profession, but nevertheless were members of the community, also lived in the Windesheim convents. Three categories of such women can be clearly distinguished: *donatrices, familiares* and lay sisters.

---

[2] Cf. Scheepsma and Tersteeg 1992, 108–9 (dukes Reinald and Arnold), no. 35 (Walburg van Gelre) and p. 126 (Walburg van Meurs). Reinald IV also founded the Windesheim convent of Bethanië at Arnhem.

[3] Weiler 1985, 403–12; cf. Rehm 1985, 212–24 on the German sisterhouses. Already mentioned at §1.1 is the eminent status of Zweder van Rechteren, Jutte van Ahaus and Elsebe Hasenbroecks from Diepenveen.

[4] *CM* 4 is concerned with the lay sisters. For background on the lay sisters see the articles in Elm 1980a and Degler-Spengler 1984.

The constitutions make absolutely no mention of these members of the cloister, yet it seems clear that they comprised a considerable portion of the community. *Donatrices* were women who had given their wordly possessions to the convent in exchange for lodging and care until their death.[5] Moreover, there were often *familiares* present, a category of women that resists definition. In the male monasteries these *familiares* were for the most part craftsmen who found employment within the monastery.[6] We know of a few *familiarissen* by name from the convent of Bethanië in Mechelen, but it is inconceivable that they served as 'craftswomen'. Jacoba van Loon-van Heinsberg served as abbess in the aristocratic cloister in Thorn, and her companion Christine van Rijswijk came from that establishment as well (on these two see §6.5). Finally, there were also female labourous living in the Windesheim convents, also referred to as *lekenzusters* or lay sisters. This is somewhat confusing, given the fact that the *conversinnen* (or *conversae*), who did make profession, were also referred to by this name.[7] The *buitenzusters* ('outside sisters') in Diepenveen, who tended the livestock outside the convent's walls, undoubtedly fall within this category of lay sisters.[8] It is striking that two incunables, from 1480 and 1489, have survived from the Diepenveen library which, according to the *ex libris*, belonged to these *susteren buten dat besloot*.[9] Even the working sisters, it would seem, could possess religious literature of their own.

The status bestowed upon a sister – 'nun', 'lay sister' or *'donatrix'* – was inextricably tied to medieval class awareness. Katharina van Naaldwijk was installed practically as a matter of course as a canoness, for it was a position appropriate to her standing (for more on this see §2.2). When her mother Elisabeth approached Johannes Brinckerinck for a place in Diepenveen for her second daughter, Griete, she was seriously disappointed. Griete van Naaldwijk was deemed unfit for the rigorous life of a canoness by virtue of her weak health. That Lady van Naaldwijk accepted this judgement was regarded by those in Diepenveen as a sign of her great piety.[10] True to his

---

[5] According to the *CM* 1.2.299 *donatinnen* owed obedience to the prioress (cf. van Dijk 1986, 92).

[6] Kohl 1980, 85.

[7] The status of lay sisters may be compared to the lay brothers in the Windesheim male establishments (cf. Kohl 1980, 79–90 and van Dijk 1986, 70–83).

[8] See for example DV, ff. 241r–v and D, ff. 54d–55a: in 1419 the so-called 'outerworks' were brought within the priory walls, but nine sisters remained outside to serve guests and tend the livestock.

[9] Deventer, SAB, Inc. 209: Otto of Passau, *Boeck des gulden throens of der XXIV ouden*, GL, Utrecht, 30 March 1480 (Kronenberg 1917, 209; *Incunabula in Dutch Libraries* 1983, no. 3462) and Deventer, SAB, Inc. 160, Jacobus de Voragine, *Sermoenen op die evangelien doer dat gehele jaer*, Peter van Os, Zwolle, 6 November 1489 (Kronenberg 1917, no. 160; *Incunabula in Dutch Libraries* 1983, no. 2604).

[10] DV, ff. 237r–240r and D, ff. 52b–54c; cf. the case of Armgert van Lisse in DV, ff. 287r–v and D, f. 172c.

status as Geert Grote's student, the inspired Johannes Brinckerinck wanted to make selections purely on the basis of personal qualifications. Nevertheless, in actual practice the social status of the nuns often exerted an influence on relationships within the monastic community.[11]

It was not unusual for a few men to be present in the convents, either *donaten* ('donators') or *lekenbroeders* ('lay brothers'), who performed all manner of crafts or trades. They lived in outbuildings within the convent walls. That these men were members of the monastic community in its broadest sense may be deduced from Johannes Brinckerinck's motto, to the effect that he had founded Diepenveen not just for maidens and widows, but for *manspersone* ('men') as well (DV, f. 101). Brinckerinck felt it was also his responsibility to look after the spiritual welfare of these unprofessed brothers. When he learned that the lay brother Gert Velthuis was having a spiritual crisis, he rushed to the oil-press where Gert worked to give him support and encouragement.[12]

Finally, we often find men in or near the Windesheim convents who were there for reasons of a religious nature, without actually having joined the ranks of the clergy. Such is the case, for instance, with Gerd Nyehof, who went to Diepenveen with his wife. The couple were already legally separated, but decided to follow the monastic life more closely.[13]

A medieval convent was a microcosm of society in which numerous tasks and functions of both an administrative and domestic nature had to be carried out by the members of the community. We shall discuss here only the administrative functions.[14] Each Windesheim priory was led by a prioress, chosen from the group of canonesses over thirty years of age.[15] If the need arose a suitable nun could be drawn from another convent. Katharina van Naaldwijk was approached no fewer than three times to become prioress of another priory, but her superiors refused to let her go.[16] Every year the prioress offered her resignation to the Chapter General. If she was old or ill or for some other reason unfit – Daya Dierkens (†1491), prioress of Diepenveen from 1472–8, for example, was too strict – then the prioress could be replaced

---

[11] One example from Bethanië in Mechelen: in 1503 prioress Liesbeth van Bergen (†1503) was entombed with high funerary honours in a grave beneath the choir (*Kroniek Bethanië*, 1503), in which her legal sister Helena van Bergen had already been buried, at fifteen years of age, in 1480 (*Kroniek Bethanië*, 1480). A grave beneath the choir was generally reserved for especially prominent nuns. It will have been no coincidence that Hendrik van Bergen (†1502), one of the prioress's brothers, was bishop of Kamerijk/Cambrai (Strubbe and Voet 1960, 266; cf. Chapter 7, n. 1).
[12] DV, ff. 26v–27v.
[13] See Rudolf Dier van Muiden (cf. §5.4, n. 82) in his *Scriptum* (ed. Dumbar 1719, 70; cf. Kühler 1914, 102–3).
[14] In *CM* 2, a separate paragraph is devoted to practically all of these offices.
[15] On the appointment of the prioress, see *CM* 1.2; cf. van Dijk 1986, 309–25.
[16] DV, f. 252r and D, f. 62a; mentioned are Jeruzalem in Utrecht and a convent in Brabant.

without too much loss of face.[17] Finally if the situation threatened to get out of hand, there was the option of placing the prioress on non-active status at the annual visitation. This happened to Alijt Bake in 1455.

It was of the utmost importance to have a prioress who had the trust of the community. She was the one who provided leadership in the life within the convent walls.[18] The nuns were duty bound to show her respect and obedience; they addressed her usually as *mater* ('mother'). The leading role of the prioress manifested itself through a variety of tasks. In the divine office she had a special ceremonial role; among other things, she said the blessing. The brief admonition which she delivered each day during the celebration of prime gave her the opportunity to inspire the other nuns spiritually. Finally, the chapter of faults on Fridays was the place where the prioress addressed and punished violations of monastic law.

Should the prioress be absent, due, for example, to illness, then her duties were assumed by her second-in-command, the subprioress.[19] The subprioress was not elected, but appointed by the prioress. At Diepenveen in 1420 Salome Sticken appointed the twenty-six-year-old Katharina van Naaldwijk as her second-in-command.[20] According to the sisterbook a curious competition developed between these two, which is illustrative of the way in which the leading functionaries were viewed by this source. Salome Sticken had her subprioress take her place in the choir on feast days, even if she were not ill. Katharina van Naaldwijk may have had a fine voice, but that is presumably not the reason behind Sticken's behaviour. During her long tenure as prioress (1412–47) she made repeated attempts to be relieved of her office because she much preferred to live in humility and obedience than to have to exercise authority.[21] It would appear that she wished to retreat within herself in the choir. Katharina van Naaldwijk was obliged to obey her prioress and lead the choir, though she, too, preferred not to play such a prominent role. This eminent nun would sometimes lash out at imaginary flies or butterflies with her veil in an attempt to convince her fellow sisters that she was not in her right mind and thus unfit for leadership. Katharina said many a time that if she had known beforehand that she would have to exercise authority at Diepenveen, she never would have entered the convent.[22] 'Not wanting to lead' is practically a topos in the biographies of the Diepenveen nuns to whom a leadership role fell, which is not to say that it was not based on

---

[17] The biography of Daya Dierkens is given in DV, ff. 407v–409v and 410v–413r and D, ff. 186b–188a and 189b–190c; on her tenure as prioress, see DV, f. 412r and D, f. 189c–d.
[18] On the duties of the prioress, see CM 2.1.
[19] On the subprioress, see CM 2.2.
[20] DV, f. 242v and D, f. 55c–d.
[21] DV, ff. 214v–215r and D, f. 15c–d.
[22] DV, ff. 242r–v and D, f. 55c, and DV, f. 242v and D, f. 55d, respectively.

truth.²³ This was a means of emphasising that they were good leaders in that they understood the great responsibility that accompanies leadership.

The supervision of the material affairs of the convent rested with the *procuratrix*.²⁴ She too was appointed by the prioress, and it was to the latter that the *procuratrix* had to report. The Diepenveen sisterbook praises Elsebe Hasenbroecks, because as *procuratrix* she freed Salome Sticken from the burden of concern over material issues, thus allowing her to concentrate all of her energies on spiritual leadership.²⁵ The sisterbook presents the cooperation among the 'trinity of ladies' Salome Sticken, Katharina van Naaldwijk and Elsebe Hasenbroecks as a model for teamwork among convent superiors.²⁶

Of the remaining obedientiaries – sacristan, precentoress, cellaress, chamberess, etc. – we mention here only the *armaria* or librarian.²⁷ She was responsible for maintaining the library and also for managing the convent's writing materials, such as paper, parchment and pens. It goes without saying that nuns with a special love for books and texts were appointed to this position. We know the names of two nuns who were librarians at Diepenveen, Zweder van Rechteren and Katharina van Naaldwijk.²⁸

Furthermore, every convent had a *rector*, who was responsible for the pastoral care of the nuns.²⁹ The relationship between the prioress and the rector was as follows: 'The prioress need not promise obedience to the rector, rather they should promise mutual loyalty and assistance to one another.'³⁰ Although the prioress was the only superior in the convent and thus held a position of independent authority, there were a limited number of situations in which she could take no action without the permission of the rector. In

---

[23] Cf. Breure 1985a, 242–5.
[24] On the *procuratrix*, see CM 2.3.
[25] DV, ff. 213v–214r and D, ff. 14d–15a (cf. DV, f. 103r–v and D, f. 113c–d, where the same formula appears in a different context).
[26] DV, f. 243r and D, ff. 55d–56a; cf. the passages from the previous note. Salome Sticken was prioress from 1412–47, Katharina van Naaldwijk was subprioress from 1420 (Griete van Ahaus succeeded her around 1437; cf. DV, f. 215r), and Elsebe Hasenbroecks was *procuratrix* from 1408 to 1441 (but from around 1437 on, Trude van Compostel also fulfilled that office; cf. DV, f. 215r).
[27] CM 2.11, concerning the librarian, has been frequently published: Meinsma 1902, 111–25 provides a synoptic Latin–Middle Dutch edition; Christ 1942, 10–11 gives an edition of the Middle Dutch ms Gaesdonck, Collegium Augustinianum, 15; Foncke 1916 edits the Middle Dutch ms of statutes Mechelen, Stadsarchief, S II, 1 from Bethanië in Mechelen. On the Windesheim librarian see Lingier 1993, 286–9.
[28] DV, f. 117r and D, f. 24c (Zweder) and DV, ff. 242v–243v and D, ff. 55d–56b (Katharina). Zweder van Rechteren died in 1407; it would appear, then, that Diepenveen possessed a library from the very beginning.
[29] On the rector see CM 5.1.1–63 (no separate section is devoted to his duties).
[30] *Priorisse non tenentur promittere obedienciam rectori, sed possunt sibi invicem promittere fidelitatem et assistenciam* (CM 5.1.94–5).

actual practice the rector functioned 'more as an advising, controlling and sanctioning instrument of the Chapter General than as a pastor of the nuns'.[31]

The rector was not elected by the nuns, but rather appointed by the Chapter General or by the *commissarius* of the convent in question. The pastoral care of the nuns (*cura monialium*) was entrusted to a select group of priors, the so-called commissioners, from the Windesheim Chapter. In 1433 the pastoral care of Diepenveen was entrusted to the prior of Windesheim, that of Groenendaal to the prior of Barberendaal, and that of Bethanië in Mechelen to the prior of Rooklooster. The office of commissioner was granted to the person, not the function of prior; it was therefore not automatically transferred to any given prior's successor. In actual practice this usually did happen. For certain events, such as ceremonies of profession and the annual visitation, the commissioner himself would appear in 'his' convent. The day-to-day business within the convent, however, was the purview of the rector, who often came from the commissioner's monastery.[32]

A rector had to be a consecrated priest, as his most important task was the carrying out of sacramental duties. He conducted the daily mass in the convent and served as confessor to the nuns. In the larger convents there was so much to do that rectors could appoint assistants – *socii* or companions – if the convent could afford the expense, that is.[33] Generally speaking one or more extra priests were usually in demand, to assist the rector in reading mass and with confession. Quite often a non-consecrated brother was stationed in the convents, a lay brother, for example, who made himself useful by taking upon himself tasks the nuns were not capable of performing themselves.[34] Rector and *socii* comprised a small religious community within the convent, and they were usually housed in a separate building on the convent's grounds. The clergymen did their best to observe the major canonical hours, and together with the lay brothers they held the chapter of faults once every fortnight, led by the rector.[35] According to Johannes Busch, who served as rector of Brunnepe from 1431 to 1434, this life of saying mass, hearing confession and reciting the divine office was boring in the extreme – but previously he had held a high function in the bishopric of Magdeburg.[36]

---

[31] Van Dijk 1986, 844.
[32] On the *cura monialium* in Windesheim female houses see Hofmeister 1941, 256–70, van Dijk 1985 and van Dijk 1986, 87–8.
[33] *CM* 5.1.71–2; cf. van Dijk 1986, 29.
[34] Kühler 1914, 102 discusses the example of the lay brother Herman Scoenbeke from Diepenveen, who on behalf of the convent was involved in the settlement of an estate.
[35] On the chapter of faults for the brothers, see *CM* 5.1.60–3.
[36] Grube 1886, 706–7. Luckily for Busch, he was again sent to Germany in 1434 on a reform mission.

2.2 Postulancy, Taking the Veil, Profession

The first step towards becoming a member of a convent was the *postulancy*: a woman proclaimed her desire to join a convent. The *Constitutiones monialium* of Windesheim contain strict rules regarding the acceptance of new nuns. Girls younger than twelve were not admitted; they had to be at least fourteen to take the veil. The postulants were also required to be thoroughly prepared before they were admitted.

> We therefore decree that in all those who would be received it first be ascertained that they be possessed of discrimination and forethought, so that they be admitted not for privilege of any kind, nor riches, nor rewards, nor any other matter pertaining to worldly pomp or avarice of this world.[37]

Women whom no one in the convent knew personally or who did not bear a letter of recommendation had to go through a trial period of at least six months:

> during which time they shall be tested as to whether they are steadfast in their resolve in fully renouncing the vanities of this world through the casting off of secular clothing, through physical labours and humblings, through prompt obedience on each and every harsh thing, through mortification of their own will and senses, through the observation of silence and prayers, through willing acceptance of rebukes and corrections, through ardour in vigils and abstinences, through promptitude and through whatever other similar things they might be tested by, and whether they truly wish to be dead to the world and themselves and to live with God in the one true holy religion.[38]

The admittance of new nuns was clearly not taken lightly: a nun unsuited to the monastic life could naturally become the source of great discord in the long term.[39]

Strong leaders like Johannes Brinckerinck followed these selection procedures to the letter. In the spring of 1412 Joost Claesz arrived at the monastery

---

[37] *Pro suscepcione igitur quarumlibet adveniencium hanc primam discrecionem ac sollicitudinem tenendam esse censemus, ut neque pro dignitate generis neque pro diviciis neque pro muneribus neque pro qualibet alia re ad mundi pompam vel avariciam huius seculi pertinente alique suscipiantur* (CM 3.1 22–6).

[38] *... in quo tempore probande sunt, utrum proposito sint constantes ac pompis seculi perfecte renuncient per abiectionem vestium secularium, per exercicia laboris et humiliaciones, per promptam obedienciam ad queque et aspera, per mortificacionem voluntatis et sensus proprii, per observanciam silencii et quietis, per sedulitatem in lectionibus sacris et oracionibus, per gratam suscepcionem increpacionum et correctionum, per alacritem in vigiliis et abstinenciis, per promptitudinem et per quelibet similia, in quibus probari possit, an veraciter mundo et sibi ipsis mori et Deo in profectu sancte religionis vivere velint* (CM 3.1. 36–47).

[39] The demands placed on postulants are described in CM 3.1.22–63.

of Windesheim with the message that Katharina van Naaldwijk had converted and now sought a suitable convent.[40] The prior superior, Johan Vos van Heusden, recommended the recently founded Diepenveen. Together with Joost Claesz and a number of other Windesheim priors he travelled to Diepenveen to procure a place for Katharina – a clear indication of the importance the prior superior of Windesheim attached to the investiture of this lady of standing. Johannes Brinckerinck, however, rejected the wealthy Katharina, because he feared that she would not be able to endure the poverty and hard labour which in his view formed the very basis of life at Diepenveen. Neither the prior of Windesheim nor the other priors could convince him otherwise. In the end it was the prior superior's order that compelled Brinckerinck to admit Katharina. The good name of the Naaldwijk family was the deciding factor for Johan Vos van Heusden.[41]

If a postulant was found to be suitable, then she could be veiled. The postulancy was brought to an end by a gathering in the chapter house, attended by the entire convent. There the postulant asked to be admitted to the community. The following phrases from the rite provide a good impression of the atmosphere. The new nun knelt before the prioress, who asked her: *'Quo est peticio tua?'* ('What is your request for?'). She answered: *'Peto Dei misericordiam et vestram confraternitatem'* ('I request the mercy of God and your confraternity'). If the postulant replied to a number of questions to her satisfaction, the prioress said, *'Dominus det tibi hec omnia adimplere, ut ad vitam eternam possis pervenire'* ('May the Lord grant you to fulfil all these things, so that you may be able to attain eternal life'). The convent voiced its approval with 'Amen'. The novice-to-be placed her hands in those of the prioress, who on behalf of the entire community said *'Ex parte Dei et nostra recipimus te et concedimus tibi societatem nostram'* ('On behalf of God and of us we receive you and grant you our fellowship'). The investiture of the new nun was a separate ceremony which took place in the priory chapel, on the steps of the altar. There the new nun was veiled by the commissioner or another Windesheim prior (who might under certain circumstances be replaced by the rector). The novice received the habit from this ecclesiastic. A white veil and a sleeveless scapular, the long choir tunic, distinguished her from the professed nuns and lay sisters.[42]

---

[40] According to the sisterbook it was more frequently the case that women came to the postulancy through the intervention of a relative or acquaintance among the clergy. The first contacts for Salome van den Wiel the older were made by her brother Thonis from the brotherhouse in Zwolle (DV, ff. 308r–309v and D, ff. 165d–166c); the entrance into the convent of Jutte van Culemborg was arranged by the unnamed procurator of Mariënborn near Arnhem and the rector of the Heer Florenshuis, Egbert van der Beeck (DV, ff. 378r–380v).

[41] DV, ff. 230r–231r and D, f. 48a–d.

[42] On the veiling see CM 3.1. An illustration of the habit of the novice nun is given in van Dijk 1986, 353; the clothing of the novice lay sister is not explicitly specified (cf. CM 4.3.1–5).

The Diepenveen sisterbook provides an impressive description of the investiture of Katharina van Naaldwijk by Johannes Brinckerinck (6 September 1412). Many of those present were moved to tears, including the clergy, which made for rather disorderly choral singing. To impress upon Katharina the significance of her new status, the rector had her tread upon her splendid fur-trimmed cloak, which lay spread over the steps of the altar.[43]

When the novitiate of at least a year had drawn to a close, there was another plenary gathering in the chapter house. The novice was afforded the opportunity to leave the community. If she chose to remain and make her profession, she was given the task of composing her letter of profession. If she was not able to do this on her own, she was to have someone else write the letter, which she then signed with a cross. By copying the monastic vow herself, she would become better aware of its meaning.[44] The zealous Katharina van Naaldwijk went further than the constitutions demanded. She wrote not just the letter of profession, but copied the Augustinian Rule as well, in order to better fix it in her mind.[45]

The profession proper took place in the priory chapel. This ceremony was embedded in the liturgy of a festive celebration of the mass. The mass was in principle led by the *commissarius*, and otherwise by another Windesheim prior. The novice lay kneeling before the altar, her habit lying beside her. This garment was consecrated with holy water, whereupon the novice removed her old habit and put on the new one. Subsequently the prior placed upon her head the black veil, the distinctive mark of the professed nun.[46] The newly consecrated nun, standing upright near the altar, then read her profession letter for all to hear, kissed it and prostrated herself upon the altar steps. The prior confirmed her profession, following which mass was said and the new nun could go to confession.[47]

The canonesses or nuns of Windesheim made profession in Latin, but the lay sisters were allowed to use the vernacular. So far as is known, of the several hundred profession formulas written in the Middle Ages by Windesheim nuns, only one, in Latin, survives, with a Diepenveen provenance. The text is as follows:

> I, sister N, twelve years of age, came to Diepenveen in the year 1475. I, sister N, promise steadfastness and conversion of morals, perpetual continence, renunciation of property and obedience according to the Rule of St Augustine and the constitutions of our Chapter General, in the presence of God and all the saints and Lady Salome, prioress of this monastery, which was built in honour of the Holy Virgin Mary and St Agnes and the canonesses

---

[43] DV, ff. 234r–236r and D, ff. 50b–51b.
[44] CM 3.3.7–10; cf. van Dijk 1986, 386–90.
[45] D, f. 60d; cf. DV, f. 250r–v (both cited in §4.2).
[46] For an illustration of the habit of a Windesheim nun, see van Dijk 1986, 353.
[47] On the profession, see CM 3.3.

who came after her. In the presence of Lord Theodoricus, prior of Windesheim. In the year of our Lord 1483.[48]

Identifying the persons mentioned in this formula is an easy matter. 'Lady Salome' is Salome van den Wiel the younger, prioress of Diepenveen from 1478 to 1490. 'Theodoricus prior of Windesheim' refers to Dirk Grave, who held this office from 1459 to 1486.[49]

2.3 Education and Training

The Windesheim novice underwent a rigorous programme of education and training.[50] The new nuns were assigned a mistress of novices who during their novitiate would serve as their mentor and advisor. Griete van Naaldwijk was placed in the care of her sister Katharina, together with three other novices. The lessons Katharina taught her sister represent the essence of the Windesheim educational programme.

> And she [= Katharina] taught her [= Griete] assiduously how she should humble herself before the sisters if she were admonished, and how she should go to them in silence and subjugation and be attentive to them, and that she should burden her heart with daily contemplation of the suffering of our Lord and many other things. She taught her sister those things she did herself, in order that the enemy should not find her heart to be empty and fill her with idle fantasies and illusions of the world, and more particular things which she after the fact would have great difficulty in expiating if she did not now assiduously guard herself against them and give herself over to internal exercise.[51]

---

[48] *Ego soror N, veni Diepenveen MCCCCLXXV etatis anno 12. Ego soror N, promitto stabilitatem et conuersionem morum, perpetuam continentiam, carentiam proprij et obedientiam secundam regula sancti Augustini et constituciones capituli nostri generalis, coram deo et omnibus sanctis dompne Salome, priorisse huius monasterij, quod constructum est in honore Beatissime Virginis Marie et Sancte Agnetis et illi canonice succedentibus. In presentia domini Theoderici, prioris in Windesem. Anno domini MCCCC LXXXIIJ* (MS The Hague, Meermanno-Westreenianum, 10 F 14, f. 13v (a parchment leaf bound into the MS); cf. *CM* 3.3.16–22 for the official text.

[49] Kohl, Persoons and Weiler 1976–84, dl. 3, 613 and 511, respectively.

[50] Cf. Lingier 1993, 282–6.

[51] *Ende sie lerde sie vlitelick hoe sie hoer solde veroetmodighen voer die sustern alsmen hoer vermande, ende dat sie swighende ende bughende bij hem hene solde gaen ende hem bedienstachtich solde wesen, ende dat sie hoer harte stedelick solde becummeren mit dechlickscher offeninghe des lidens ons lieven heren ende voert ander punten. Soe als sie selven dede, soe leerde sie hoer, op dat hoer harte niet ledich ghevonden and worde vanden vianden ende hoer dan inbrachte ydele fantasien ende verbeldinghe vander warlt ende voergaender dijnghe die sie namaels quelke quit solde conen worden, weert dat sie hoer daer nu niet vlitelick teghen and satte ende hoer tot inwendighen offeninghen gheve.* (DV, ff. 240r–v; cf. D, ff. 54b–c). These formulas correspond closely to chapter 3.2 of the *CM*, devoted to the training of novices.

Thus the in-house training of Windesheim novices had two primary focuses. The first was the teaching of skills and customs pertaining to daily life in the priory: they taught the young nuns not just how to sing loudly and softly – necessary skills for the choir – but also, for example, how they should approach superiors with humility. A second focus was on the teaching of the requisite disposition and the construction of the inner spiritual life (for more on this, see Chapter 4). Vigorous intellectual training was clearly not a part of this educational programme.

The statutes do stipulate as a prerequisite that postulants must be able to read and sing well.[52] This meant that they had to be able to decipher the Latin choirbooks used in the liturgy, and thus to sing the liturgical texts in the appropriate fashion. The Windesheimers admitted into the order only women who already possessed these skills. Usually they had already completed their schooling, otherwise they would first attend school at the priory. To get some sense of the average intellectual level of the canonesses of Windesheim, we must attempt to ascertain which educational programmes women had access to in the Middle Ages. But we may at the outset note that their opportunities were limited: education was at this time by and large the province of men.[53]

Katharina van Naaldwijk fulfilled in all respects the requirements stipulated by the constitutions, 'For she could read Latin and had a splendid voice for singing'.[54] Katharina received an education commensurate with her status from her grandmother, Sophia van Teilingen. For a girl from high noble circles in the county of Holland, a stay in the Benedictine abbey at Rijnsburg (near Leiden) was a matter of course.[55] 'And when Lady Katherina had reached the proper age for schooling, Lady Sophia sent Katherina to the priory of Rijnsburg so that she might there learn her psalter.'[56] Learning to read with the aid of the Book of Psalms – in Latin – had for ages been an important component in the education of medieval ladies.[57] Most of the

---

[52] CM 3.1.58–63; cf. the *Acta* of 1441: *Quod in domibus monialium nulla ad investitionem admittatur nisi prius docta fuerit legere et cantare, ut valeat horas suas persolvere* (van der Woude 1953, 36).

[53] On education in the medieval Netherlands see Post 1954b, Nauwelaerts 1980 and van Buuren 1995.

[54] *Want sie conde wal Latijn lesen ende hadde ene bequame guede stemme toe sijnghen* (DV, ff. 234r–235v; cf. D, f. 50d).

[55] On the school in Rijnsburg, which also had a schoolmaster, see Hüffer 1922, 108–10, Post 1957, vol. 2, 183 and Bot 1990, 178.

[56] *Ende als jonfer Katherina quam tot bequamer oeltheit toe leren, soe sande jonfer Sophia Katherinen toe Rensbarghen int cloester om daer toe leren horen psalter* (DV, f. 226v; D, f. 46a).

[57] 'Learning her psalter' is the expression used in the Diepenveen sisterbook to indicate that a nun could read Latin and to a certain degree understand it (cf. DV, f. 198r and D, f. 5a, on Salome Sticken); cf. Grundmann 1978 on the relatively high level of literacy among noble women: in his view they are therefore in one sense the founders of medieval vernacular literature.

Windesheim convents had a considerable number of noble women living in them. We may assume that many of these enjoyed an education comparable to that received by Katharina van Naaldwijk.[58] They were familiar to some degree with the psalter, but their level of competence in Latin would of course have been determined by individual talent.

It is not entirely clear where the numerous girls who came from the municipal patriarchy and higher bourgeoisie were supposed to have learned their Latin. In many cities girls could attend school, though these were 'elementary schools', where the curriculum stopped at the *Donaet* (= Donatus). The *Donaet* is a brief Latin grammar that stood at the beginning of the Latin curriculum, to which only boys were admitted. If girls wished to learn Latin, they had recourse only to private tutors or schools. Perhaps it was such a school that Berte van der List, later a canoness at Diepenveen, attended.[59] We have data concerning one nun who received private instruction, namely the intelligent (*subtijl van sinne*) Lubbe Snavels, daughter of an alderman of Zwolle.[60] Lubbe received lessons in Latin from the cleric Gerlacus, who was supervised by Jan Cele, the famous rector of the town school of Zwolle and a friend of Geert Grote.[61]

Given the absence of a clearly structured programme of education for girls, it is understandable that the convents should themselves have provided some degree of training for their future nuns.[62] Diepenveen is the only Windesheim convent that we know for sure housed a *scole* for future sisters.[63]

---

[58] Some data follows concerning the education of some other noble nuns from Diepenveen. DV, f. 177v; cf. D, f. 118a: Dymme van Rijssen was schooled in the nunnery of Hoog-Elten near Emmerich (on this establishment see for example Koch 1994, 29–31; Dymme does not appear in Koch's index of the inmates of Hoog-Elten); DV, f. 374v: Jutte van Culemborg was trained at Vreden. We have little data on Griete van Ahaus and Fye van Galen, nuns of Freckenhorst near Münster (on this establishment see Kohl 1975); concerning them see DV, ff. 319v–322r and D, f. 146a–d (Griete) and DV, ff. 322r–323r and D, ff. 146a and 146–7a (Fye).

[59] Rembert van der List, Berte's uncle and educator, *hielt sie ter scolen ende liet sie leren synghen ende lesen* ('sent her to school and had her learn to sing and read'; DV, f. 109v). The phrasing is not very explicit and leaves open the possibility that Berte first attended the 'elementary' school and only later learned Latin.

[60] DV, ff. 303r–v (cf. Lingier 1993, 458 n. 54) and D, ff. 86d–87a and 89d.

[61] On Johan Cele see Rayez 1974.

[62] In the case of the fourteenth-century Dominican nuns, the internal schooling was provided both by the older nuns and by the friars (especially by means of sermons) (Lewis 1996, 266–72).

[63] It has frequently been assumed that the school at Diepenveen fulfilled a regional function (cf. Moll 1864–71, II-2, 246 and 278, Acquoy 1875–80, vol. 2, 191, Brinkerink 1904, 164 n. a and Kühler 1914, 310–11). It would appear, however, that when Diepenveen was enclosed, only girls intended to be entered into the convent were schooled there. This was at any rate the case for the 'children' whom Daya Dierkens (see also §2.1, n. 17) taught as reformer of the German convent Hilwartshausen (DV, ff. 408r–410r and D, ff. 187a–188a).

In the early years the programme was rather ad hoc, but it was to become gradually more structured in nature.[64] A schoolmaster was appointed, the *socius* Otto Poten, who led the school until his death in 1420.[65] From 1413 on Otto was assisted by the aforementioned Lubbe Snavels; she may even have succeeded him.[66] Later on the office of headmistress was filled by well-educated nuns. Two of these we know by name, Fenne Bickes (†1458) and Daya Dierkens (†1491). Of the former it is said that she taught the *sustren*, of the latter that she was charged with 'children'.[67] The specification of different pupils probably reflects the development of the convent school at Diepenveen. Initially, professed nuns who did not yet possess the required skills were educated there. Later on the convent school was most likely attended only by postulants and novices.

In the early years in Diepenveen there were, after all, quite a few adult nuns who were sufficiently enthusiastic, but not yet proficient enough, to participate in the office in choir. For example, Stine Tolners was admitted to the ranks of the canonesses in 1416, but from then on had to attend school under Otto Poten.[68] There she received instruction primarily in Latin grammar, an experience that must have proved somewhat daunting to a nun who was no longer young. When asked if Stine had any time left over for her spiritual exercises, she replied: 'I appeal to my friends in eternal life for prayer and assistance with all my cases and tenses, for I can do little else.'[69] When the convent at Diepenveen was finally established, it was probably offered very young candidate postulants who had already been prepared for monastic life in its own school. Conversions of adult women will have become a relatively rarer phenomenon by this time.

The young pupils were subjected to a regimen comparable to that of the secular schools. The sisterbook records a moving anecdote concerning Liesbeth van Heenvliet, who as a ten-year-old girl had chosen to enter Diepenveen and received her training there.

> Sister Elsebe Hasenbroecks had commanded her that she should not speak Dutch without permission. And then it happened that during the night she became ill and had no basin or other container in which to vomit. She dared not speak in Dutch, but she could not yet speak in Latin. Then that obedient

---

[64] Jutte van Ahaus (†1408) taught a young girl to read her psalter (see below).

[65] DV, f. 108r and D, f. 117b, DV, f. 235v and D, f. 51a, DV, f. 251v and D, f. 61c, and DV, f. 303v and D, f. 87c; B, f. 234v (edition in Brinkerink 1904, 96 n. c and Lingier 1993, 455 n. 28); and van Slee 1908, 337 (necrologium). For Otto Poten, see Kühler 1914, 243 and Lingier 1993, 283.

[66] DV, f. 303v and D, f. 87c.

[67] DV, f. 52r and D, f. 129b (Fenne Bickes) and DV, ff. 411v–412r and D, f. 189c (Daya Dierkens; on her see also n. 64 and §2.1, n. 17).

[68] The *vite* of Stine Tolners appears in DV, ff. 295v–301r and D, ff. 85a–89b.

[69] *Al myne casus ende tempere pleghe ic toe senden mynen vrenden int ewighe leven voer ghebet ende lof, want ickes niet anders maken en kan* (DV, f. 298v; D, f. 86c–d).

child, maiden Liesbeth, cried out: 'Soror, lackus basinus', and produced the best Latin she was capable of in order to avoid being disobedient.[70]

Sister Elsebe's measures may strike us as severe, but the students in the Latin schools were likewise forbidden to converse in any tongue but Latin both in class and on the streets.[71] The 'school' at Diepenveen simply maintained a similar standard.

It would appear, then, that there was a great need for instruction in Latin among the nuns in the new foundation of Diepenveen. The curriculum of Otto Poten, who must have been a formidable teacher, concentrated on this very aim. Moreover, he surrounded himself with a group of already well-educated nuns; Katharina van Naaldwijk and Lubbe Snavels were among this circle of 'disciples'.[72] The nuns of this talented group also occupied themselves predominantly with the study of Latin. Otto Poten's lessons will have been concerned primarily with the comprehension of theological issues. This hunger for knowledge of the language of the Church may be seen as a sign of the fervour that was current in Diepenveen at the time.[73]

To put it another way: whenever a strong reform movement manifested itself in a community of women, there was a concurrent desire for knowledge of Latin. When three nuns from Brunnepe became involved in the reformation of the Saxon priory of Mariënberg near Helmstedt, the creation of a conventual school was therefore an important goal. Johannes Busch, the leader of this reformation, selected these candidates partially because of their proficiency in Latin. Sister Tecla was even charged with teaching the Saxon nuns Latin grammar (for more, see §5.3).

Perhaps a reference to Latin lessons from the chronicle of Facons should also be seen in this light (Chapter 7 deals with this convent). Sister Margarita van Achterhout (†1521) had a testament drawn up in which she granted to her convent an annuity of one pound, 'whereby she desires that the young nuns be allowed to learn Latin until they are proficient in it'.[74] Perhaps this testament is related to the restoration of the religious life that was initiated at

---

[70] *Suster Elsebe Hasenbrocks had hoer verbaden dat sie ghien Dues and solde spreken sonder oerlof. Ende doe waert hoer eens quelke inder nacht dat sie moste overgheven ende sie and hadde ghien becken of ander riesscap in toe breken. Ende sie and dorste ghien Duusch spreken ende dat Latijn and conde sie doe noch niet. Doe riep dat ghehoersame kint jonfer Liesken: 'Soror, spielus beckelus', ende macte Latijns als sie beest conde, op dat sie niet onghehoersam and weer* (DV, f. 279r; cf. D, f. 77c–d).
[71] See for example Nauwelaerts 1980, 368 and van Buuren 1995, 228.
[72] DV, ff. 250r and 251r–251v, and D, ff. 60d and 61c (Katharina van Naaldwijk), and DV, f. 302r and D, f. 87c (Lubbe Snavels); on Lubbe's knowledge of Latin see also DV, ff. 300r and 304r, and D, ff. 86d–87c.
[73] Cf. Williams Krapp 1995, 1–2 on the relationship between reform and education in Germany in the fifteenth century.
[74] . . . *waer dat sy begeert datmen de jonge susteren souden soe lanck laten Latyn leeren tot datzet costen* (*Naem- and doodtboeck*, p. 90).

Facons towards the end of the fifteenth century. It tells us at any rate that there was a Latin curriculum at Facons. But Margarita van Achterhout appears to be the first to put the reformation into perspective. In virtually the same breath she established a *pitantie*: the sum of six guilders, to be spent by the nuns on herbs for their sausage and stew.[75]

In the medieval world 'being educated' was virtually the same thing as 'knowing Latin'. Taking this as our point of departure when we attempt to assess the intellectual level within the convents of Windesheim, we may infer that for women it was high indeed, even though the statutes place no emphasis on it whatsoever. The nuns had at any rate enough Latin to be able to give voice adequately to the liturgical texts. But in every convent there must have been a number of nuns whose knowledge was considerably deeper, like the aforementioned Sister Tecla of Brunnepe, or Truke van der Beek from Diepenveen, who translated Latin texts into Middle Dutch at sight during readings in refectory.[76] When compared to their male counterparts (or the Brothers of the Common Life), they were at a disadvantage, of course. There would have been few among them who could achieve the level of the average canon regular of Windesheim.[77]

Such a comparison does not tell us much about the level of practical knowledge among the Windesheim nuns. Perhaps Jutte van Ahaus from Diepenveen is a good representative of the average level of literacy in this circle. Jutte was abbess of the convent at Vreden, but sought a purer form of religious life. She corresponded with Johannes Brinckerinck about her conversion, but had her letters copied by a scribe. Brinckerinck, however, wanted to meet the doubting abbess face to face and finally asked her to answer a letter in person, for 'he could read a difficult hand'.[78] Jutte, then, could write, even though her skills with a pen left something to be desired. The former abbess knew Latin, as well, for having finally arrived at Diepenveen, she there taught a young girl to read her psalter. But the child complained of her teacher that she could not immediately provide Dutch translations for all the Latin words.[79] We may observe, then, that Jutte van Ahaus could read and write – skills which did not always go together as a matter of course in the Middle Ages. She had enough Latin to be able to read the psalter, but her knowledge of the psalms – without doubt the best known texts from Scripture – had its limits.[80]

---

[75] By means of such *pitanties* nuns could ensure that they would be commemorated on the anniversary of their death: on that day wine or some special dish would be served.

[76] DV, ff. 329r–v (cited at §3.6); cf. DV, ff. 336r–337r: both Truke and her sister Beatrix knew Latin well and therefore were allowed to take the veil.

[77] On the use of Latin and Middle Dutch among the Modern Devout in general, see Scheepsma 1996a, especially 212–14.

[78] *Hie konde wal quaet scrift lesen* (DV, f. 131r; cf. D, f. 32d).

[79] DV, f. 136v and D, f. 37a.

[80] The situation of the nuns of Windesheim is comparable to that of the Dominican nuns in Germany in the fourteenth and fifteenth centuries (Ochsenbein 1992).

Jutte van Ahaus's example illustrates why beyond the liturgy the vernacular was so dominant in the convents of Windesheim (and in practically every other female establishment in the Middle Ages). Reading Middle Dutch or Middle Low German would have posed no great obstacle for the canonesses regular of Windesheim, though writing them would have proved difficult for some. It goes without saying that the situation with Latin was significantly more problematic. This explains why the vernacular played such an important role in the female houses. Not just the educated nuns, but the entire convent had to be able to understand what was said or read.

2.4 Year, Week, Day

The rhythms of life in the monasteries of Windesheim were wholly determined by the liturgical calendar and the recitation of the divine office. The calendar comprises an annual cycle in which the most significant events in salvation history are observed. The core of the ecclesiastical calendar consists, of course, of the most important events in the life of Christ: expectation (Advent), birth (Christmas), passion and death (Lent), resurrection (Easter), ascension, and the descent of the Holy Spirit (Whitsuntide). Furthermore, this liturgical calendar celebrates, in addition to a number of other sacred moments from the life of Jesus, the saints produced by the Church. They were the ones, after all, who followed Christ's example and where necessary gave up their lives for their belief in him. By following the liturgical calendar from day to day, week to week and year to year, each individual was constantly spurred on to imitate Christ.

In the later Middle Ages the number of saints and feast days increased dramatically, thus overcrowding the calendar. A movement arose which advocated a return to the old rite of the Church of Rome, with its limited number of saints' days and less elaborate celebrations. The Chapter of Windesheim felt the influence of this movement when it drew up its own calendar.[81] Even so, the Windesheim calendar printed in 1488 numbers nearly eighty feast days.[82] These were divided into several grades or ranks. The *Constitutiones monialium* of Windesheim distinguish five, in ascending order: *feria, festa IX lectionum, duplex, duplex maius* and *supra* or *solempnitas*.[83] This hierarchy of feasts was given clear expression in the liturgical celebrations. An important distinction was that between an office read and an office

---

[81] On the Windesheimse calendar, see van der Woude 1949, Franke 1981, 35–43 and van Dijk 1986, 212–20.

[82] Ed. van der Woude 1949. This calendar is contained in the *Breviarium Windeshemense*, printed by Gerard Leeu in Antwerp on 15 October 1488 (on this Windesheim breviary see Kruitwagen 1914).

[83] Van Dijk 1986, 393 n. 3, and also 219, 357 and 399. The calendar of 1488 also distinguished feasts of three recitations (van der Woude 1949).

sung; the latter lasted much longer and for that reason alone was held on certain feast days. Also, for example, four candles were lit on the altar on high feast days during vespers, matins, and high mass, whereas during feasts of only nine recitations just one was lit, and on work days none.[84]

The Chapter of Windesheim sought to implement a uniform execution of the liturgy in all of its member monasteries, though small modifications were possible. Every monastery celebrated the feast of its patron saint as a high feast (thus with four candles, among other things), regardless of his rank on the calendar.[85] It would seem that over the years much more variation became possible. The chronicle of Bethanië in Mechelen describes the following adaptations to the liturgical celebration, for which the visitor Gerardus vanden Clooster (†1546), prior of St Agnietenberg from 1504 to 1530, had given dispensation.

> Likewise he has also granted that for St Margaret a *duplicibus fest<um>* be held, at the behest of our venerable mother Magrita Oddyns [prioress 1512–41].
>
> Likewise that a *duplex festum* be held for the holy virgin St Berbele as requested by many sisters and her spiritual daughter Sister Barbare Speelberch.[86]

The correspondence of names indicates that personal preferences could play a significant role in these modified celebrations.

Within the framework of the liturgical year, the week was the most important temporal unit.[87] The weekly liturgical cycle was based on the psalms, all one hundred and fifty of which were read or sung in the choir office. For the nuns of Windesheim the week began on Sunday, the day of Christ's resurrection. Sunday was celebrated as a feast day. The rest of the days were in the main considered *feria* ('workdays'), unless the calendar called for them to be celebrated as a feast day. The canonesses took turns as *hebdomadaria* or week-sister. It was their task for that week to lead devotions and prayers. First in line was the prioress, followed by the subprioress and thereafter the oldest nun, and so on. The principle of seniority played a role in the weekly rotation of choir sides: one week the *hebdomadaria* was drawn from the right side of the choir, the prioress's side, the next week she was drawn from the left side, where the subprioress sat.[88]

---

[84] On the use of candles, see *CM* 2.8.41–54 and van Dijk 1986, 357.
[85] *CM* 2.8.54–5.
[86] *Item hy heeft oock ghegunt datmen hout van sincte Margrieta duplicibus fest<um>, duer die begeerte onser eerwaarde mater Magrita Oddyns . . . . Item datmen hout vander heyliger maget sincte Berbele duplex festum door beede van veel susteren ende synder geestelycker dochter suster Barbare Speelberch* (*Kroniek Bethanië*, from one of the unnumbered final leaves of the codex).
[87] On the liturgical week, see Harper 1991, 46–8.
[88] The *CM* deals with the *hebdomadaria* at 2.10.

The celebration of the liturgy also determined the daily routine of the nuns of Windesheim. Each day the eight liturgical hours of the divine office were recited or sung: matins, lauds, prime, terce, sext, nones, vespers and compline. In addition a conventual mass was sung each day, accompanied by the choir.[89] In practice the greatest differences existed between Sundays and feast days on the one hand, and work days (*feria*), on the other. The lay sisters attended only a few of the celebrations on work days. On Sundays and feast days – some hundred and fifty in all; a feast day could also fall on a Sunday – the canonical hours were sung by the entire convent, with both the lay sisters and other nuns present in the church. On these days, too, various individual or group religious observances took place, and there would also have been time for recreation.

Following is a global schedule for a Sunday or feast day in a Windesheim convent, with special attention to the moments at which religious literature, in whatever form, was used.[90]

00:00	matins and lauds; return to bed
05:00	prime
07:00	terce
09:00	sext and nones
10:00	celebration of mass
11:00	dinner (with reading)
12:00	meditation and religious reading
13:00	recreation, singing lessons, conversation, study, etc. (possible collation by the rector)
15:00	vespers
16:30	supper or evening drink with reading (also known as 'collation')
18:00	compline
18:30	religious reading or meditation
19:00	retire to bed

The times given are approximations only. A feast's higher ranking could cause a celebration to be drawn out considerably. Moreover, the schedule had to make allowances for the changing length of the day in the course of the year.

Two hours are of particular importance with regard to the use of non-liturgical religious literature. During the midnight celebration of matins, regardless of the feast hierarchy, one of three nocturns was included. Nocturns contained two important parts. The first consisted of three psalms, always preceded and followed by an antiphon. The second part consisted of

---

[89] On the celebration of the conventual mass, see *CM* 3.5.
[90] The most important source here is the sacristan's tolling schedule (*CM* 2.8), presented in van Dijk 1986, 358. Compared to the schedule in Persoons 1980, 91 (more frequently published) the most significant deviation is the beginning of matins, in that scheme at 4:00 a.m.

the recitations or readings from Scripture, preceded by prayer and blessing and followed by antiphonal singing (versicles and responses). In principle the first reading was taken from the Bible, the second from the lives of the saints and the last from patristic literature. Each reading was preceded by the singing of a psalm, prayer and blessing, and ended with a sung reply, the responsory. It was in this office of readings that the tone for the day in a spiritual sense was established.[91]

The office of prime consisted of a hymn, three psalms and a reading from the Augustinian Rule, all of which were conducted in the chapel. Thereafter the convent removed itself to the chapter house, where the celebration of prime was continued.[92] Here, among other things, the *martyrologium* was recited: the nuns learned which saint's day was to be celebrated the next day and which other saints were to be commemorated. Furthermore there was room towards the end of prime for a word from the prioress. This might take the form of an announcement, consultation on particular business or the assignment of daily tasks, but the prioress could also issue an admonition, if occasion demanded it. The sources reveal precious little about the nature and contents of these admonitions.[93] No doubt abuses in the convent would have been the subject of discussion among the nuns. In any concrete sense we know anything only about the admonitions of Salome Sticken from Diepenveen, who found grist for her mill in everyday situations. She once pointed out to the convent the exemplary obedience of the priory's cat, who contritely left the hall when she was admonished for her loud mewing.[94]

---

[91] On the celebration of matins *CM* 3.4.69–120; cf. Harper 1991, 86–97. See also Martimort 1992, 66–105.

[92] On the celebration of prime see *CM* 3.4.140–59; cf. Harper 1991, 98–100. On the reading from the Rule see the introduction to Chapter 5, n. 5.

[93] Cf. *Kroniek Bethanië*, 1557, where prioress Maria de Latere is praised because 'she has given the convent many a good admonition to the chapter'; on their contents, alas, not a word. In practice it is not easy to distinguish the admonition at prime from the speech with which the prioress opened chapter of faults on Fridays (see also §3.2). The Diepenveen sisterbook also mentions addresses to the chapter by Johannes Brinckerinck and cites them profusely (DV, f. 32r and *passim*). Is it possible that Diepenveen and/or Brinckerinck were unique in this regard (see further §3.8)?

[94] DV, ff. 200v–201r and D, ff. 6d–7b.

3

Communal Devotion in Piety

THE CHOICE OF life in the convent is a choice for the communal life. Many of the religious devotions required of the sisters of Windesheim were performed communally. The Diepenveen sisterbook speaks in awe of Elsebe Hasenbroecks, who continued to take an active part in the life of the convent at an advanced age.

> For when she was eighty-six years old and nearly blind and deaf she nevertheless steadfastly continued to go both day and night to choir and refectory and chapel, and she would remain there until the end.[1]

Elsebe's dedication to the life of the convent was apparent to her fellow canonesses by her participation in a number of important communal exercises. Generally speaking these may be divided into two groups, the religious and the material. First among the religious exercises to be discussed here are the choir services (§3.1). Strictly speaking these should not be considered simply one of the many devotions, because the performance of the office in choir constituted by far the canonesses' most important duty. They devoted many hours each day to the choir office. The other religious exercises were the weekly chapter of faults or correction (§3.2) and adherence to silence (§3.3). Next came a number of physical exercises: manual labour (§3.4 and 3.5), congregating in refectory (§3.6) and the hours of rest and recreation (§3.7). Finally, I will consider the collation, a collective spiritual exercise characteristic of the Modern Devotion, the meaning of which within the Chapter is not entirely clear (§3.8).

3.1 Liturgical Celebrations

With their detailed rules for the celebration of the choir office and conventual mass, the *Constitutiones monialium* provide ample indication 'Of the care bestowed upon the heart of the canonical communal life, the divine office,

---

[1] *Want doe sie was van sesentachtentich jaren ende bijna blint ende doef, doe ghenck sie noch nachtes ende dages stedelicken toe choer ende toe reventer ende toe chapittel, ende daer toe bliven totten eijnde toe* (DV, ff. 104v–105r; cf. D, f. 114d).

especially in the Windesheim convents'.[2] In the Catholic service the life of Christ is repeatedly commemorated; its rituals render the events in his life visible once again. For this reason a solemn and high-minded celebration of the liturgy was the best thing the nuns could offer the Church of Christ. The recitation of the divine office was the very pulse of life in the convents of Windesheim. The oft-repeated psalms, antiphons, hymns, sequences, responsories, etc. from the divine office belonged among the texts most frequently read, sung and heard in this milieu.[3]

From the very beginnning the Windesheimers placed a great deal of emphasis upon uniformity of liturgical practice throughout the entire Chapter. At its foundation in 1395 an editorial committee was established and charged not only with the drawing up of constitutions, but also with designing their own liturgical order.[4] The Windesheim order is codified in three liturgical manuals: the ordinary, the manual and the calendar.[5] Johannes Busch remarks further that standard redactions of other liturgical books were also established, such as the missal, gradual, antiphonary, lectionary, capitulary and martyrology. It is not without pride that he writes that such liturgical unity was achieved in this way that it could have been implemented throughout the world.[6] In principle the canonesses of Windesheim celebrated the liturgy in the same way as the male canons regular. The usually minor differences in actual practice have mostly to do with the fact that the canonesses were not priests, as most canons were, and thus were not able to perform certain rituals.[7]

The choir in which the canonesses of Windesheim celebrated the office differed considerably from that of the canons. A special gallery was usually built on the west side of churches in the convents for the canonesses regular, who after all were not to have any contact with the world. In the church below, beneath the nuns' gallery, there was room for the lay sisters, separate from the layfolk with their families and any other persons, such as guests, who sat all

---

[2] Van Dijk 1986, 402. *CM* 3.4 and 3.5, respectively, deal with the choir service and the conventual mass.
[3] On the Catholic liturgy, see Harper 1991.
[4] On this committee, see for example van Dijk 1986, 214–15.
[5] These books were used particularly by the sisters involved in the organisation of the choir service, such as the cantrix, the sacristan and the sister of the week (*hebdomadaria*). On the Windesheim calendar, see §2.4. An *ordinarius* is a liturgical guide in which directions were given as to the rank of any one day, which rituals it was to be celebrated with and what was to be read and/or sung. For the medieval *ordinarius* see Martimort 1991, 48–85; on the Windesheim *Liber ordinarius*, see Franke 1981 and van Dijk 1986, 212–20. On p. XV Franke names as one of his sources MS Brussel, KB, 5156 (531), a missal from Barberendaal in Tienen (Persoons 1972, 1354–5). The *Manuale Windeshemense* contained certain texts for fixed celebrations, such as rites of profession, extreme unction, etc. (van Dijk 1986, 221–7).
[6] Ed. Grube 1886, 95 and 310–11, respectively.
[7] Van Dijk 1986, 395–402.

the way in the back. The canonesses regular could observe, from their high vantage point and from behind a screen, the sacramental rituals performed around and upon the altar (on the east side), without being seen by anyone else. It was in this isolated choir that the nuns performed their liturgical duties.[8]

In the nuns' gallery pews were built on the north and south sides. Each canoness had her own designated place in the pew, depending on when she had made profession. Thus two choirs were formed, each responding to the other in song. The choir was led by the cantrix (lead singer). She divided the tasks and 'rolls' among the sisters, provided the tempo and pitch for each song, and intervened when things threatened to go amiss.[9] Naturally a musically talented nun with a fine voice was sought for this task. The first cantrix of Diepenveen, Gertrud Monnickes (†1426), had such a beautiful voice that, according to the sources, her fame as a singer extended as far away as Rome.[10] Her later successor Liesbeth van Arden (†1485), however, appears to have been appointed on account of the volume rather than the quality of her voice: when Liesbeth let loose the rector left the church in haste, because she *ludde als een vaer* ('lowed like a heifer') (DV, f. 369v).

The liturgical celebrations in the convents of Windesheim were above all simple and sober. Normally only monody was provided for in the service; part-song was regarded as an expression of vanity, though it was resorted to on feast days. In the course of the fifteenth century we may detect a development towards a somewhat richer liturgy. Musical instruments, especially the organ, were sometimes used during the office.[11] We find indications of this in the convents as well. Master Jan Gielis (†1560), second *socius* in Bethanië at Mechelen, is praised in the chronicle for the skill with which he accompanied the choir with his stringed instrument.[12]

Celebrating the divine office was the most important duty of the canonesses of Windesheim. This appears both from the scope of their office and the manner in which it was observed. Not only did the canonesses observe all the liturgical hours of the office on a daily basis, but they also observed the Hours of the Virgin Mary.[13] The liturgical *horarium* (Book of

---

[8] On the nun's gallery, see Eman 2002.
[9] On the cantrix see CM 2.9.
[10] DV, f. 48v and D, f. 127b.
[11] For more on music and liturgy in the Windesheim convents see Ewerhart 1955, 133–57 and Hascher-Burger 1998; cf. Hascher-Burger 2002.
[12] *Kroniek Bethanië*, 1560. Jan Gielis also had a splendid singing voice; did the canonesses know this only from his celebrations of mass, or did he add luster to the choir song with his voice?
[13] CM 3.4; the Hours of Mary on lines 130–9. On the divine office see Harper 1991, 73–108, on the office for Mary Harper 1991, 133–4. Christine van Rijswijk left the convent of Bethanië in Mechelen in 1467 because the recitation of the major services was too much for her; she moved to a house where only the Hours of Mary were recited (on her see §6.5).

Hours) was augmented by the recitation of a conventual mass.[14] It bears repeating that all such offices were recited in Latin.[15] Illustrative of the significance this bore is the lamentation uttered by Hubert van Lochem, priest of Jeruzalem in Venray, when he learned that the nuns had received dispensation from the bishop of Liège to recite the liturgy in the vernacular during the transition to the rule of St Augustine, until such time as they had sufficient command of Latin: *Hie mach sien woe hie dat verantwoerdet* ('He would have to see how he justified this').[16] The liturgy was supposed to be sung in Latin, and that was all there was to it. If we compare the liturgical practice of the Windesheim canonesses with that of the related Chapter of Sion, it becomes apparent just how high their standards were. The canonesses of Sion recited only the Office of the Virgin Mary – albeit in Latin – and this took the place of the Divine Office.[17] Even further down the scale were the sisterhouses and tertiary houses, where it was usual for a paraliturgical office to be recited from the Book of Hours that was derived from the divine office. These sisters recited while they worked, for example, the *Hours of Eternal Wisdom* of Heinrich Seuse (in Geert Grote's translation).[18]

The observation of the liturgy entailed a significant physical exertion, as well. The Diepenveen *viten* frequently praise the sisters for attending choir day and night, as Elsebe Hasenbroecks seems to have done. Having to rise at midnight for matins must have been particularly taxing for the nuns' constitutions. Some of the canonesses never got used to it. In one of her dialogues with Christ, Mechtild van Rieviren from Facons describes a moving event in her convent (see also §7.4), Sister Janneke looking on in envy as her fellow nuns went to matins relatively refreshed, while she could barely keep her eyes open.

> It happened once that one of our fellow sisters asked me [= Mechtild] to pray on her behalf to God that he should aid her and fortify her so that she might the more easily rise for matins during the night, for it was very difficult for her. But when I had addressed my beloved [= Christ] and had forgotten my fellow sister, he said to me: 'Tell your fellow sister Janneke to bear this hardship at matins out of love for me, for it pleases me greatly. And the more difficult it is for her, the more it pleases me that she should

---

[14] On the conventual mass see *CM* 3.5.

[15] But in the early years of Bethanië in Mechelen sister Katharina Holanders lived there, and she *las haer ghetyden int Duetsche* ('read her hours in Dutch'; *Kroniek Bethanië*, 1431). It would appear that this was tolerated in the beginning.

[16] Verschueren 1949, 701. On Jeruzalem in Venray see further §5.2.

[17] Ypma 1949, 31–2 and 106–7.

[18] When Diepenveen was still a sisterhouse, the *Hours of Eternal Wisdom* were also recited there (DV, ff. 196r–v and 103r–104r, and D, ff. 4b–c); for these hours see Weiler 1984a, 11–47 (introduction) and 50–92 (edition with translation).

see the reward that I hold for her on account of it. She would be displeased with me were I to deprive her of it.'[19]

Christ's 'answer' is typical for the later period of spirituality of the Windesheim canonesses: they willingly underwent this daily physical suffering out of love for him.

Another problem, for most of the nuns, was the difficulty of Latin. Trude van Beveren (†1428), canoness at Diepenveen, often carried a book containing the texts for the day with her, in order to ask, when time allowed, a fellow sister who knew more Latin to explain it to her.[20] And yet even this not-so-learned sister was totally immersed in the texts of the office. Her *vite* describes how appropriate passages sometimes came to Trude unexpectedly.

> It happened once that she was drawing water from the well when a verse came to her that she had recited at nocturns, namely: *Haurietis aquas in gaudio de fontibus salvatoris* etc. ['You shall draw waters with joy out of the saviour's fountains' (Isaiah 12:3)]. This inspired her to such a degree that she paid no heed to the work she had done and drew the water so passionately that she hardly realised what she was doing, such was the strength of her ardour.[21]

This anecdote shows how the daily life of the Windesheim canonesses had become intertwined with the texts of the liturgy. Trude van Beveren drew not only water, but also strength from the well, thanks to the passage from Scripture that she had read during matins (and perhaps also thanks to the fact that she had understood at least this verse).

Passages from the liturgy crop up surprisingly often in accounts describing the deaths of the sisters contained in the sisterbook. A nun like Katharina van Naaldwijk tried even while on her deathbed to participate in the divine office by reciting appropriate psalms, sequences and hymns in her mind.[22] Jutte van Culemborg (†1503) went even further while she lay dying.

---

[19] *Het is eens gebeurt datter een van onse medesusteren mij [= Mechtild] badt dat ick voor haer soude willen bidden dat Godt haer toch wilden helpen and verstercken dat sy wat beter snachts ter mettenen mocht comen opstaen, want het haer seer crachtich viel. Maer als ick mijnen beminden had gesproken en mijn medesuster hadde vergeten, soo seijde hij mij: 'Segt uwe medesuster suster Janneken datse die moeijelijckheit vande mettenen ter liefden van mij verdraecht, want ick daer groote genucht in heb. and hoet haer swaerder valt, hoet mij meer behaecht dat sij den loon sach die ick haer daer voor bewaer. Sy soudet mij ondanck weten dat ick haer daer af beroofden'* (MS Vienna, f. 51r).

[20] Cf. D, f. 102b and DV, f. 164r.

[21] *Sunderlinghe op een tijt doe stont sie ende puttede, doe quam hoer een vars in dat sie des nachtes inder noctornen ghelesen had ende dat was dit: Haurietis aquas in gaudio de fontibus salvatoris etcetera. Daer was sie soe vuoerrich mede dat sie bij na alden arbeit vergat ende puttede soe vuoerrichlick dat sie nauwe and woste wat sie dede van groter vuoerricheit* (DV, f. 164r–v; cf. D, f. 102c–d).

[22] DV, f. 253v and D, ff. 62d–63a.

She sought texts that fitted her precarious situation and hit upon the responsories for Good Friday.

> In the days before her death she was constantly singing and very cheerful. Then it happened that one of her disciples was sitting with her and said to her that it was time to go to sleep. 'What difference does it make,' she said, 'I have remained awake with them so many hours, they can surely do so for one. It is, after all, my last hour.' Thus she lay there, singing, and with her at that time were sister Fenne Godschalkes and Truken Essinchghes, her disciples, and she made them sing with her the two responsories that are sung on Good Friday eve, the *Velum templi sissum est* ('And behold the veil of the temple was rent in two from the top even to the bottom, and the earth quaked'; the murderer on the cross cried 'Lord, remember me when thou comest into thy kingdom' (Matt. 27:51; Luke 23:42)). And they sang so loudly that they could be heard throughout the house.[23]

These choices made by Sister Jutte, from the wealth of liturgical texts available to her, were not arbitrary. In the final hour of her own life she wanted to experience in song the death of Christ one last time. Naturally she could sympathise entirely with the good murderer, who asked for mercy at the threshold of death.[24]

3.2 Chapter of Faults

The concept of correption (Dutch *kapittelen*, French *chapitrer*) has its roots in a monastic religious exercise to which the Windesheimers attached great significance: the chapter of faults. Paul's appeal to the Thessalonians to support and urge each other on (1 Thes. 5:11) was heeded by the earliest monastic communities. The monks gave testimony of their inward life to the monastic community and did public penance for their sins. Since the time of Benedict of Nursia (†547) only the external sins were exposed, i.e. transgressions of the rule, the constitutions and the customs of the order. Inner sins

---

[23] *Des daghes voer hore doet doe wolde sie ommer synghen ende see was zeer vrolick. Doe was ene van horen discipelen bij hoer, die sede hoer dat dat onder slaepueren weer. 'Wanne', sede sie, 'ic heb soe mannich ure mit hem ghewaket, sie moeten wal ene ure mit mi waken. Het is doch myn leste ure.' Dus lach sie al in enen synghen ende bij hoer wa<ren> op dat pas suster F<enne> Godschalkes ende Truken Essinchghes, hoer discipula, ende sie moste<n> mit hoer synghen die twie responsen diemen and goeden vridaghe nacht synget, als Velum templi sissum est (Dat clet des tempels is ghescoert ende al die eerde heeft ghebevet. Die mordener <an>den cruce riep: 'Ghedenct mynre, here, als ghi comet in dijn ricke').* Ende dat sanck sie soe lude dat men sie over alt huus horde (DV, ff. 383r–v). The second responsory, in spelling of the sisterbook, is: *Tenebre facte sunt dum cruxifissent Jhesum.* Both verses are derived from the story of the Passion (cf. Matt. 27: 45–56, Mark 15: 33–41, Luke 23: 44–9 and John 19: 28–37).

[24] See Grijp 1997 on facing death with song; cf. Lewis 1996, 168–70.

had to be accounted for during confession, the personal admission of guilt to a priest.[25]

The chapter of faults found a place in the spiritual life of all the monastic orders. It was an institution that fulfilled a range of functions in these religious communities. First and foremost it carried a spiritual significance: by pointing out each other's sins and shortcomings and exhorting one another, the members of the community became better monks and nuns. If this exercise in guilt and penance proceded harmoniously, moreover, the sense of community was strengthened. Its second function lay principally in the realm of maintaining order. In a monastic community the inmates live in very close proximity to one another and they are very much thrown into each other's company, a situation that could easily lead to tensions running high. In the enclosed female houses such as the Windesheim ones this danger was even greater than in the male establishments, which were considerably more open. In this area of tension the chapter of faults could channel internal differences and conflicts in the right direction. Finally, the chapter of faults functioned as a kind of internal court, where cases concerning transgressions against the laws of the monastery could be heard.

In the Windesheim convents the chapter of faults was normally held on Fridays, the day of the crucifixion, but it could be rescheduled if it conflicted with the celebration of a high feast day. Only the canonesses were present at this weekly gathering. The chapter of faults followed directly after prime, the second half of which was celebrated in the chapter house (see §2.4). The *Constitutiones monialium* regulate correption closely, as it was regarded as an essential instrument for maintaining the observance.[26] Congregations for the chapter of faults were usually led by the prioress, though she could also delegate that task to another capable sister.[27] But even if she did not actually direct it, she was required to be present. None of the canonesses were allowed to be excused from participating in the chapter of faults. Even the sisters in the infirmary could be accused and punished, at least if their condition was not too grave.[28]

The chapter of faults began with a general exhortation by the prioress or the sister in charge. It is only the correptory exhortations of Salome Sticken of Diepenveen that we are in any position to assess, for the sisterbook describes them in quite some detail.[29] They are summarised there as follows:

---

[25] For a historical overview of the chapter of faults, see Schmitz 1953.
[26] On the chapter of faults, see *CM* 3.6.
[27] Salome Sticken regularly had subprioress Liesbeth van Delft stand in for her (DV, ff. 57v–58r and D, ff. 132b–c).
[28] On the sick or infirm and the chapter of faults, see *CM* 2.6.46–54.
[29] Hardly any distinction is made in the sources between the exhortations sometimes given by the prioress during prime (see §2.4) and the introductory remarks to the chapter of faults.

Her exhortations were as ardent as a burning flame, so that the sisters sorely regretted it if circumstances prevented them from attending the chapter of faults or any other place where the sisters gathered; they felt then that they had missed something very worthwhile. Her exhortations were to become more steadfast in all virtues, to fast and deny ourselves and to take pains to humble ourselves towards one another; and everyone should exert herself to be the most humble and to steal virtue for herself and everyone should strive to outdo the others in virtue – this we must all do – and to love the virtue we find in another, and to humble ourselves such that we are not guilty of sluggishness and indolence, and always to strive where we are able and may to devote our hearts to our Lord, yea, and to cleave to him, to confess to him our weaknesses and shortcomings, and to pray and beseech him passionately for assistance in travelling the path to the kingdom, and to love him warmly and to follow him with ardent fervour and with great thankfulness, and to do those things that we are obliged to do and to persist in doing so with ardent assiduousness, for God loves a cheerful giver (2 Cor. 9:7).[30]

Salome Sticken's *vite* describes here somewhat nostalgically a spiritual programme in which the principles of piety of the female Windesheimers are clearly expressed. The exhortations of its first prioress were thus to remain an enduring source of inspiration in Diepenveen.

Directly after the exhortations of the prioress there followed a collective castigation of the novices. Inexperienced as they were, they were not yet subjected to individual admonitions concerning their behaviour. Only after the novices had left the chapter house did the chapter of faults begin for the professed nuns. The constitution regulates the procedure to be followed very precisely, partly, no doubt, because of the painful situations that might arise. By turns, and beginning with the youngest, each of the canonesses came forward to the centre of the chapter house. After they had sought pardon (*venie nemen*), i.e. bowed down and touched the ground with their hands –

---

[30] *Hoer leringhe weren zeer vuoerrich als ene barnende vlamme, dat hem die susteren zeer toe liden hadden als die saken eyschede dat sie nit wesen en konde daermen capittel hielt of anders daer die susteren vergadert weren, dat hem plach toe duncken dat sie wat grotes verlaren hadden. Die leringhe weren toe toehardinghe alre dogheden, toe starven ende uutghaen ons selves ende pynen ons toe veroetmoedighen onder malkanderen; ende een yghelick pyne hem die mynneste toe wesen, ende die dogheden toe stelen, ende een yghelick den anderen in dogheden baven toe gaen-dat mosten wy wal doen-ende mynnen die dogheden in enen anderen, ende veroetmodighen ons dat wi soe niet en sijnt, dat onser tracheit ende versumelheit scolt is, ende ommer vlitich toe wesen onse harte altoes waer wy conden ende mochten bij onsen lieven heren toe hebben, jae, in hem toe cleven, hem toe belien onse crancheit ende onse ontbliven, ende bidden ende begheren hartelicke van hem om hulpe den coninclicken weech toe wanderen, ende hem hartlicke toe mynnen ende mit vuoerrigher begherten hem an toe hanghen mit groter dancberheit, ende die dijnghe die wi sculdich weren toe doen ende toe holden dat wi dat mit vuoerrigher vlitichheit solden doen, want den bliden ghever mynt God* (DV, ff. 198v–199r; cf. D, f. 5c–d).

the ultimate gesture of humility – they confessed whatever transgressions they might have committed against the rules of the convent.

> And when she says that she can think of nothing else or she ceases to speak, the prioress says: 'Does anyone wish to accuse this sister?' and if anyone should wish to accuse her, she shall not use many words, but will do so simply in the following manner: 'Our sister has done or failed to do this, or said this or that', naming the sin. And having been accused, she shall then humbly seek pardon, saying: 'I am guilty.' Thereafter, having been commanded to do so, she shall rise. But if she does not accept her guilt, she shall, while standing, say: 'Mother, I do not recollect having done or said what my sister accuses me of.'[31]

In order to prevent accusations motivated by revenge, a sister thus accused was not allowed to lay something at the feet of her accusers in the same session.

It fell to the prioress to pronounce the verdict. She was aided in this task by an elaborate penal code, in which appropriate penalties for transgressions of various degrees of seriousness, from the lightest to the most serious, were prescribed.[32] The most serious transgression, for example, was incorrigibility or disdain for punishment, the sentence for which might even be incarceration. The disciplinarian Salome Sticken seems to have added her own sanctions, apparently for sisters who according to the penal code did not deserve punishment.

> She castigated those sisters with humble clothing, torn and patched surplices and veils. She would also have them wear an apron upon their heads or some such, and the buttons cut from old nightshirts would serve the more fastidious sisters as their paternoster. And all the while she would castigate them by assigning them humbling tasks, such as begging for bread before the other tables at refectory with a dish, or kissing the feet of the sisters at the other tables or seeking pardon or submitting to a beating.[33]

---

[31] *Et cum se dixerit non recolere plura vel loqui cessaverit, dicat priorissa: 'Vult aliqua sororem istam proclamare?' Quod si que eam proclamare voluerit, non exaggeret verba, sed simpliciter proponat in hunc modum: 'Soror nostra fecit vel omisit aut dixit hoc vel illud' nominando culpam eius. Proclamata vero veniam humiliter accipiens dicat: 'Mea culpa'. Deinde iussa iterum surgat. Si autem culpabilem se non recognoverit, dicat breviter stans: 'Mater, non recordor me hoc fecisse vel dixisse, quod soror mea dicit'* (CM 3.6.18–26).

[32] See the code of punishments in CM 3.7–11; cf. the schematic overview in van Dijk 1986, 414–16.

[33] *Sie ofende die susteren mit oetmodighen clederen, subtijlen ende wilen, ghescoert ende ghelappet. Sie plach hem oeck wal enen scorteldoeck op dat hovet toe setten ende dier ghelick, ende die cnope die vanden olden slaprocken weren ghesneden, dat weren sommigher curioser susteren hoer paternosteren.<Ende onderwijlen worden sie van hoer geoefent myt oetmoedigen werken> als broet toe bidden int reventer voer die tafelen in een scottel of die voete toe cussen ander tafelen ofte te venien, of een rode op den rugghe toe draghen* (DV, f. 200r–v; cf. D, f. 6c). The phrase between brackets is from manuscript D. DV

This was a prioress who, entirely in the spirit of the Bible, punished lovingly. According to the sisterbook her authority was accepted by the sisters: they regarded those who were treated most severely as Salome's most beloved children.[34]

Going by the sisterbook, which certainly does not provide a representative reflection of reality, the transgressions correpted in Diepenveen were not very serious ones. Some, for example, were accused of offences which in our eyes would seem rather altruistic. Sister Trude van Beveren was accused and punished for using too much material in her undoubtedly benign striving to clothe the sisters adequately. Jutte van Ahaus was accused because she offered warm water to the sisters too frequently, and because she wished to warm herself by the fire too often. And Sister Jutte van der Beeck often put wool she had spun into the baskets of the other sisters, so that she herself frequently came up short at the weighing of each day's production. Finally, Katharina van Naaldwijk was frequently correpted because she appeared for work late; the reason for this, however, was that she was always helping the other sisters with advice and assistance.[35] The idealising agenda of the sisterbook has the concomitant effect that everyday shortcomings such as spitefulness, envy and jealousy are hardly so much as mentioned. The *viten* present almost exclusively flaws that are in fact virtues taken to excess. The sources reveal precious little about serious crimes against monastic law. A rather poignant case is that of Sister Fenne Stuermans of Diepenveen, who was repeatedly chastised during the chapter of faults, and later also during a visitation. Katharina van Naaldwijk was the only one to recognise that the sister *groet ghebreck in hoer hovet had* ('was not in her right mind'), but otherwise had a good heart. When the visitators returned the next year, Fenne Stuermans had alas already become insane (*al gheck*, DV, ff. 248v–249r; cf. D, ff. 59d–60a).

Although in principle correption was a tool for enforcing the monastic rule, it could also easily take on a spiritual dimension. Katharina van Naaldwijk, for example, regularly accused herself of offences she had not committed, in order thus to undergo public humiliation (and to add another virtue to her arsenal).[36] In its idealistic early days it would appear that the entire convent of Diepenveen maintained the same attitude. Salome Sticken had to work hard to find material for her exhortations, so exemplary was the life lived by the inhabitants of Diepenveen.

is corrupt: in the margin of f. 200r *Onderwile mit oetmodighen wa[rck]en* has been added.
[34] DV, f. 200v and D, f. 6c–d.
[35] DV, f. 170r and D, f. 99b (Trude van Beveren), DV, f. 142r–v and D, ff. 40c–41a (Jutte van Ahaus), DV, f. 324r (Jutte van der Beeck) and DV, f. 248v and D, f. 59c–d (Katharina van Naaldwijk).
[36] DV, f. 242v and D, f. 55c.

And if she had nothing, she would find something, for she understood the hungry desire of the sisters. She often turned a thing into a fault that was in the sisters something praiseworthy rather than a fault, because she did not otherwise know where to find the spiritual sustenance they longed for.[37]

Prioress and convent worked as one to ensure that the chapter of faults was a serious exercise in humility. The sisters asked for admonitions that they in fact did not deserve; the mother superior did her level best equally to find causes for which to reprimand her flock.

Salome Sticken's *vite* reflects in her a model sister who understood the deeper sense of correption like no other.[38] In her long tenure as prioress she humiliated the sisters as much as she could because she knew that the spiritual freedom of mankind lay in self-disengagement. Towards the end of her life she was allowed to step down as prioress and was treated like any other canoness during the chapter of faults. It was then that Sister Salome demonstrated to others how one should bear the accusations.

> It happened once at the time when the sisters are informed of their shortcomings that she was so gloriously chastised by the others that she surpassed them all. She became then so calm and inwardly drawn to our Lord that she lost control of her limbs, so that she had to be carried there.[39]

Salome Sticken exulted in that moment because for a brief time she was one with the mocked and taunted Christ. In her deep realisation of this she lost control over body and spirit.

3.3 Silence

One of the pillars of the Christian monastic tradition is the practice of *silentium* or silence. In communities of monks and nuns there were often mutually agreed upon hours of the day during which no conversation was allowed. This exercise carries both ascetic and mystical aspects. Silence is something that people must impose upon themselves, for not speaking goes against the grain of human nature, which compels people to seek contact

---

[37] *Ende als sie ghiene sake and hadde, soe vant sie ioe wat, want sie bekende die hongherighe begherte der susteren. Sie macte vake een ghebreck van een dijnck dat meer toe prisen was inde susteren dant ghebreck was, omdat sie niet and woste waer siet onder tijden nemen solde hen broet toe gheven daer hem inden gheeste na verlanghede* (DV, ff. 199v–200r; cf. D, f. 6b).

[38] In *Vivendi formula*, f. 376r–v, Sticken herself lays out her position on the chapter of faults succinctly (for a translation, see van Engen 1988a, 185–6). For a daring appraisal of Sticken's opinions on the spiritual life, see Weiler 2002.

[39] *Op een tijt alsmen den susteren hoer ghebreke plach toe segghen, soe waert sie soe glorioes ghemaket vanden anderen dat sie alden anderen boven ghenck. Soe waert sie dan soe suetlicke ende inwendelicke ghetaghen tot onsen lieven heren dat sie hore leden niet mechtich and was, dat men sie daer hen draghen moste* (DV, f. 212v; cf. D, f. 14a).

with their fellows. When members of the monastic community opt for silence, they do this to teach themselves and others the difference between what is unimportant and what is worthwhile. For the mystically inclined authors the value of silence lies especially in this latter aspect. By maintaining silence at appropriate moments they create the opportunity to let God enter into themselves.[40]

In the *Constitutiones monialium* a striking stress is placed on the silence which the sisters of Windesheim are strictly to observe. The composers of these statutes go much further in this regard than their sources, the constitutions for the Windesheim canons regular and the constitutions for the Dominincan nuns.[41] On the face of it there is little reason to seek a contemplative reason behind this increase in severity. In composing the *Constitutiones monialium* the Windesheim canons were undoubtedly of the opinion that it was a good idea, even more so than for themselves, to teach the canonesses to control their tongues. The chapter dealing with silence in the *Constitutiones monialium* is the only one to undergo intermediate revision, in the years 1456–8. On that occasion it was given a more logical structure and furthermore a few relaxations were added. This would indicate that the original chapter was so strict that in practice the sisters were unable to follow their statutes faithfully on this particular point.[42]

In the Windesheim convents there were a few rooms in which absolute silence reigned. This was the case in particular in the consecrated space of the priory church, but also in refectory, in the dormitory and in the lavatory speaking was strictly forbidden. Moreover, the constitutions impose significant temporal restrictions. On workdays and during the hours of mandatory labour silence is in principle to be maintained at all times. On such days the sisters would have had little more than three quarters of an hour to speak to one another. On Sundays and feast days there was somewhat more room for conversation, especially at midday, but there were restrictions then, as well. These will in practice have resulted in keeping mutual contact between the sisters to only the barest of essentials. Often they would have restricted their conversation to topics that really mattered to them.

3.4 *In the Sweat of Thy Face*

The time-honored Benedictine adage *ora et labora* expresses succinctly how in the existence of the monk the life of work and the life of prayer are to be combined. In the convents of the Chapter of Windesheim, where incidentally

---

[40] On monastic silence, see for example Salmon 1947, Gehl 1987 and Miquel and Dupuy 1990; cf. Ruberg 1978.
[41] Cf. van Dijk 1986, 531–2 and van Dijk 1988. In addition strict enclosure is recommended (cf. §1.1).
[42] On silence see *CM* 3.13 (first redaction) and 5.2 (second redaction).

the Rule of St Augustine was followed, great significance was attached to this combination: one ought to live by the labour of one's hands. The most important source of income for the Windesheim convents was the land they possessed, but the work of farming and animal husbandry was for the most part carried out by the lay sisters and servants. The choir nuns could not take to the fields, as they were enclosed within the walls of the priory. They did have access to the gardens, which were usually laid out within the walls. But the canonesses of Windesheim earned most of the money for their convents through the production and processing of textiles and hand-made articles, for example liturgical paraments. Given the wealth of many of the Windesheim convents, the sisters' income was not really necessary. They were, however, required to engage in manual labour, for that formed an integral part of the ascetic way of life of the Windesheimers.

In the constitutions of the Windesheim female houses it is rare for any of the many strict rules to be legitimised by biblical passages. Yet in the opening section of the chapter on manual labour we encounter no fewer than three in succession.[43]

> For idleness is the enemy of the soul and the nourisher of vices, therefore in the convent no woman shall be idle, but diligently see to it that on workdays from prime to compline, with the exception of the hours and times during which they are to observe the divine office, or when those who are appointed to do so are engaged in instruction, all and sundry who are able shall perform manual labour for the common good, according as it has been ordained or established, for she who is engaged in labour is not easily overcome by temptation. For by God it was told to man that 'In the sweat of thy face shalt thou eat bread' [Gen. 3:19]. And the Apostle said: 'If any man will not work, neither let him eat' [2 Thess. 3:10]. And the prophet: 'For thou shalt eat the labours of thy hands' etc. [Ps. 128:2].[44]

Apparently it was necessary to bring to bear considerable powers of persuasion to convince the sisters that idleness constituted a threat to salvation and that manual labour provided the most efficacious remedy against it.

Most of the canonesses of Windesheim originated from the upper echelons of society. In these circles, for example the court of Holland-Beyeren where

---

[43] On manual labour see *CM* 3.14; cf. van Dijk 1986, 438–9.
[44] *Quia ociositat inimica est anime et nutrix viciorum, nulla in clausto maneat ociosa, sed diligenter observetur, ut ferialibus diebus a prima usque ad completorium, exceptis horis et temporibus, quibus divino officio debent interesse, seu quando doctrine vacant que ad hoc sunt deputate, operibus manuum pro utilitate communi omnes et singule que possunt insistant, prout ordinatum ver commissum fuerit, quia non de facili a temptacione capitur que exercicio bono vacat. A Domino enim dictum est homini, quod in sudore vultus vesci debeat pane suo* [Gen. 3:19]. *Et apostolus dicit: Qui non laborat non manducet* [2 Thess. 3:10]. *Et propheta: Labores manuum tuarum quia manducabis etcetera* [Ps. 128:2] (*CM* 3.14.1–13).

Katharina van Naaldwijk came from, a strong shame culture was prevalent: human behaviour was judged in terms of honour and shame.[45] Against this background the conversion of someone like Jutte van Ahaus, abbess of Vreden, takes on greater relief. She learned from Johannes Brinckerinck to humble herself rather than be honoured. This eminent abbess thereupon decided to take up spinning – to her disappointment she was unable to learn how to weave – to the great horror of the damsel nuns at Vreden.[46] Only fine needlework was thought appropriate for ladies of nobility: both Katharina van Naaldwijk and her niece Liesbeth van Heenvliet were accomplished embroiderers.[47] The fact that Jutte van Ahaus humbled herself by taking up the dirty and unpretentious work of spinning confirmed for the Modern Devout the sincerity of her conversion.

One may deduce from the constitutions that spinning was the most important form of manual labour for the canonesses of Windesheim.[48] Other sources show unequivocally that spinning and weaving were done at St Agnes at Dordrecht, Facons, Galilea and Diepenveen. An entry in the chronicle of Facons reveals that textile production was not among the most popular activities there. At her profession in 1477 sister Catharina Steeyncx stipulated that her donation would be spent as follows: 'That it be applied to the working of wool, so that the sisters may be relieved of this task.'[49] Catharina Steeyncx succeeded in convincing convent authorities, who were after all the shepherds of the observance, to accept this breach of Windesheim spirituality. But the prior superior became enraged when he heard the news and wrote an extremely angry letter to Facons. Yet the damage was done: from 1477 on spinning and weaving were no longer carried out in Facons.[50] How the sisters in other convents felt about spinning and weaving is not known, but it would seem that not everyone accepted this work with the same degree of enthusiasm.

Manual labour could assume other forms besides spinning and weaving. The *vite* of Katharina van Naaldwijk and her sister Griete describes how they helped the lay sisters with baking, brewing, churning, shoe-polishing,

---

[45] On honour and shame, to name but one example, see Peristiany 1966.
[46] DV, f. 139r–v and D, ff. 38d–39a; on Jutte van Ahaus, see §1.1, n. 29.
[47] DV, f. 229r and D, f. 47c (Katharina van Naaldwijk); DV, ff. 284v–285r and D, f. 81a–b describe a number of works produced by Liesbeth van Heenvliet.
[48] CM 5.2.34–47; in the old redaction, CM 3.13 the range of possible forms of manual labour are not specified. The chapters on silence (CM 3.13 and 5.2) and manual labour (3.14) have much in common, because the imposition of silence posed problems especially during labour (cf. bijv. van Dijk 1986, 439). On spinning see also Persoons 1980, 95.
[49] *Datmen die doen soude totten arbeyde vanden wollenwerck, opdatmen de susteren dat afnemen soude* (Naem- and doodtboeck, p. 83; cf. Register, f. 21v).
[50] *Naem- and doodtboeck*, p. 83; cf. Register, f. 21v. Apparently his protests stopped at the letter; there is no mention of the incident in the Acta Capituli Windeshemensis.

wool-combing, dish-washing, the cleaning of chamber-pots and all kinds of chores in the kitchen.[51] The fact that sisters of Katharina's and Griete's social standing worked with their hands is presented in the sisterbook as an expression of humility (despite the fact that Griete was a lay sister). This raises the suspicion that they might have been virtually exempt from manual labour. Social rank did play a significant role in the division of labour at Diepenveen, as revealed by the biography of Souke van Dorsten (†1480) from Sneek in Friesland.[52] She brought an endowment of no less than one thousand guilders with her to Diepenveen, yet participated diligently in the household chores. One of the sisters once asked her why she worked so hard: hadn't she contributed enough to the convent? Souke's exemplary reply deserved to be immortalised in the sisterbook. 'In all my days it never occurred to me to do less. The strongest are obliged to do the hardest work. I do not want to hear you say that again.'[53] It is to be wondered whether other wealthy and prominent sisters were possessed of the same strength of character as Souke van Dorsten.

3.5 Copying and Illuminating

Besides the production of textiles, the Constitutions mention another form of manual labour which merits separate discussion in the context of this study: the copying of manuscript books.[54] A limited number of sisters passed (a portion of) their hours of required labour in writing, for example Armgert van Lisse from Diepenveen:

> She remained passionate in her later years and performed common labour industriously. She continued to copy handsome and extremely edifying books for the convent, thanks to a testament, when she was seventy years of age.[55]

In the view of the Modern Devout, copying religious literature was an especially appropriate form of labour. On the one hand it provided the opportunity for building a well-stocked library, and on the other hand, during the hours he was engaged in copying, the scribe was continuously exposed to

---

[51] DV, f. 241v and D, ff. 54d–55a.
[52] The *vite* of Souke van Dorsten is found in DV, ff. 371r–374r.
[53] 'Daer en hebbe ic nij myn levedaghe opghedacht dat ic daer die myn om doen solde. Ende wie die starchste is, die is sculdich dat zwaerste warck toe done. Ic en mach niet horen dat ghi dat segt' (DV, f. 373v).
[54] CM 5.2.36–9.
[55] *Sie blef noch zeer vuoerrich in horen oelden daghen ende vlitich voerden ghemienen arbeit. Sie scref noch suverlicke ende zeer lerlicke boeke den cloester voer een testament doe sie was van soventich jaren* (DV, ff. 289v–290r; cf. D, f. 174c).

religious literature.[56] We shall now examine the place this characteristically monastic form of manual labour held in the female religious houses.[57]

To begin with there was a great and perpetual need for new liturgical books in the convents of Windesheim. Because of their intensive use, these books were subject to heavy wear and tear. A passage from the sisterbook of Diepenveen demands our special attention in this regard. Sister Liesbeth van Arden, professed in 1416, is praised in her *vite* precisely for her paltry collection of books.

> She was poor in books and all other possessions. She had a nocturn book and a shabby vesperal and a little diurnal in two parts; these were all her books. And her gradual and other choir books were not well made.[58]

All in all Liesbeth possesses a respectable number of books, all of which serve a function in the performance of the divine office. This rich collection must surely have resulted from the position of cantrix that Liesbeth van Arden held (see §2.2). It is at any rate very unlikely that every sister at Diepenveen possessed as many liturgical books as this cantrix.

And yet there are indications that the canonesses of Diepenveen possessed at least one little manuscript containing certain liturgical texts. Due to a shortage of resources in the early years great frugality would have been the rule, and therefore mediocre singers like Trude van Beveren would not have been given their own choirbook. She would have been compelled for each service to write the (constantly changing) text on a slate.[59] And Beatrix van der Beeck had her fellow sisters copy a *capittelaer* ('capitulary') and a *salter* ('psalter') for her own use.[60] If we assume that every canoness in Diepenveen eventually came to possess one or two manuscripts of liturgical texts, then there must have been hundreds of them. There were, after all, over one hundred canonesses in Diepenveen around the year 1450.[61] Added to this were the large and undoubtedly much more expensive liturgical books,

---

[56] On book production more generally see Kock 1999; on the spiritual aspect of the copying of religious books see Mertens 1989a, 191–3 and Staubach 1991, 434–5.

[57] Lingier 1993, especially 289–93, discusses book production in the convents of the Modern Devotion, the most important cases being Diepenveen and Sint-Agnes at Ghent (on this convent see Goossens, Trio and van Mingroot 1989). See also her forthcoming dissertation on this subject. I use the situation in St Agnes as a reference for the general state of affairs in the Windesheim convents.

[58] *Sie was zeer arm van boecken ende van allen dynghen. Sie hadde een noctorna ende een onnosel versperstucke ende een diornaelken van twien stucken; dat weren al hoer boecken. Ende hoer graduale ende ander sanckboeke die en weren niet vromme* (DV, f. 370v).

[59] DV, f. 163v and 168r, and D, f. 101d and 102b.

[60] DV, f. 341v. Because sister Beatrix had herself asked her family for the necessary money and materials, Salome Sticken forced her to wear the new books about her neck for several days as punishment.

[61] Cf. Johannes Busch, *Liber de origine Devotionis modernae*, cap. XXXVI; ed. Grube 1886, 339.

which had a permanent place in the choir, and from which the sisters would presumably have performed their collective singing. The collection and maintenance of this body of books would have required considerable financial outlay on the part of the Windesheim priories.[62] Unfortunately, we are forced to acknowledge that next to nothing remains of this treasure trove of liturgical books.[63]

In the scriptoria of the Windesheim convents – when they existed – it was primarily liturgical books that were copied. The Diepenveen sisterbook reports of various sisters who were involved in the production of books. Most phases of the process were carried out on the premises.[64] Katharina Lippen (†1452) cut the necessary parchment (or paper?) to size.[65] The copying could then begin. The scribes mentioned copied indeed for the most part liturgical books. This was the case, for example, with Ave Sonderlants (†1452): 'She wrote a fair hand, and thus it was that she faithfully aided the choir by copying books, both with and without notes.'[66] The production of choir books with notes was the most highly qualified form of copying. Also mentioned as scribes of liturgical works in Diepenveen are Zwene ter Poorten (†1439), Griete van Algeerden (†1440) and Gertrud ter Poorten (†1452).[67] The sisterbook makes no mention of manuscript illumination, although an illuminated Bible made in Diepenveen survives.[68] It was Lubbe Snavels's (†1450) task to correct the books which had been copied, a job she was very well qualified for thanks to her knowledge of Latin.[69] Finally,

---

[62] In 1551 prioress Maria de Latere of Bethanië in Mechelen ordered all the choir books to be inspected and bound, which cost her more than seven Rhine Guilders. At the same time she had a new martyrology made and bound (*Kroniek Bethanië*, 1551).

[63] Practically the only one to survive is the splendid MS Tilburg, Stichting Theologische Faculteit, Haaren 31, an antiphonary written at Windesheim in 1409 and eventually ending up at Mariënveld in Amsterdam (or Oude Nonnen, i.e. Old Nuns) (van de Ven 1990, no. 24 and Korteweg 1992, no. 111).

[64] Cf. Kühler 1914, 298–9 and Lingier 1993, 289–91.

[65] DV, f. 344r.

[66] *Sie conde wal scriven, alsoe dat sie den choer doe trouwelicke bijstont in bocken toe scriven, beyde ghenoetiert ende onghenotiert* (DV, f. 361v; cf. D, f. 159b).

[67] DV, f. 68r and D, f. 136c (Zwene ter Poorten), D, f. 89c (Griete van Algeerden) and DV, f. 69r and D, f. 137a–b (Gertrud ter Poorten).

[68] MS London, Victoria and Albert Museum, George Reid MS 23, consisting of two codices ending on 28 September, 1450 and 9 July, 1453, respectively (the detailed colophons are cited partially in Byvanck and Hoogewerff 1922–5, vol. 3, 34).

[69] The constitutions provide rules for correcting the Old and New Testaments, but are silent concerning liturgical and other kinds of works: *Libros veteris ac novi testamenti vel eos, cum quibus divina celebrantur officia, sine generalis capituli consilio nullus emendare presumat, nisi cum exemplaribus domorum nostrarum emendatis, nisi iudicio rectorum vel fratrum discretorum error aliquis manifestus appareret* ('No one shall presume to correct the Old and the New Testament or those books with which the divine office is celebrated without the advice of the Chapter General, unless they be

Lubbe was skilled in the art of bookbinding, in which craft she was assisted by a certain Sister Wyse.[70]

It was not only liturgical books that were copied in the context of *ghemienen arbeit* ('common work') but also books for the refectory and the library. Maria Weels (†1472), for example, third prioress of Facons, performed 'much labour in the copying of liturgical books and books for refectory'.[71] As far as is known none of the fruits of her labour has survived. It is certain that a number of the extant Diepenveen manuscripts were written by the sisters themselves, as appears from their colophons.[72] During the period from 1451 to 1454 Adriaen Mant (†1460) copied the biggest part of a cycle of seventy-seven sermons by Beernt Arborstier, divided among three codices (see §3.6). In 1466 Sister Griete des Vrien wrote her name in a manuscript containing among other things the second and third letters written by Jan van Schoonhoven to Eemstein. Her hand is also to be found in another manuscript containing primarily works by Modern Devout such as Gerard Zerbolt and Gerlach Peters; it was probably written around 1440.[73] The third Diepenveen scribe known by name is Griete van Houdaen, a lay sister, who around 1425 produced a manuscript containing the works of Jan van Leeuwen.[74] The books produced by these three sisters would have found a place in the priory library or the refectory.

In some of the Windesheim convents books would have been copied *pro pretio*, i.e. for payment. Most priories would have had a scriptorium of some kind, staffed by a few competent sisters, thereby meeting the minimum requirements for commercial copying.[75] Some care had to be taken, for only manuscripts copied on workdays could be sold. Writing on Sundays or feast days counted as Sunday labour for ecclesiastics, and such labour could not earn money. In the *vite* of Salome van den Wiel the younger it is reported that

---

corrected from books in our house, lest any manifest error in the judgement of the rectors or brothers be perpetuated') (*CM* 2.11.21–5).

[70] On Lubbe Snavels see DV, f. 303v and D, f. 89d (where sister Wyse is not mentioned).

[71] ... *menigen arbeyt gedaen met schryven van choorboecken ende refterboecken* (*Naem-* and *doodtboeck*, p. 33; cf. *Register*, f. 13r).

[72] For a number of Diepenveen manuscripts, see the exhibition catalogue Wierda 2000.

[73] MS Deventer, SAB, I, 50 (10 T 3) mentions the name Griete (see Gumbert 1988, no. 348 and pl. 746a and Wierda 2000, no. 11). The other MS is Deventer, SAB, I, 49 (101 E 7); see *Jan van Ruusbroec* 1981, no. 124, Kors 1991, 64 and 109–22 and Wierda 2000, no. 6.

[74] MS Deventer, SAB, I, 55 (101 F 5); see *Jan van Ruusbroec* 1981, 283 and Wierda 2000, no. 4.

[75] The *Kroniek Bethanië*, 1455 mentions the construction of a scriptorium (ed. Cordemans de Bruyne 1896, 74). See also the entry for the year 1463: the scriptorium was situated in the same (east?) wing as the work house and the chapter house; above it was a dormitory.

she copied books on workdays, which might suggest, among other things, that she wrote for the outside market.[76] Books copied on Sundays and feast days could be added to the priory's library.[77] Griete des Vrien's manuscript mentioned above, for example, was completed on the octave of St Agnes; it was given a place in the library of Diepenveen itself.

The sisterbook tells us that Griete van Algeerden (†1440) also sometimes copied for money.[78] Little is known about the exact nature or volume of scribal work commissioned at Diepenveen.[79] According to a number of surviving invoices from St Agnes in Dordrecht, manuscript copying was a significant source of income for that convent. In 1475 the production of linen earned the priory one hundred and ninety-seven guilders and five cents, whereas copying brought in thirty-five guilders and twenty cents.[80] Just what kind of books the sisters at St Agnes copied can no longer be determined. No manuscripts from this priory have so far been identified.

The convent Bethanië in Arnhem had a scriptorium that must have been comparable in size and production to that of the priory in Dordrecht. Two splendid exemplars from the scriptorium of Bethanië, dating to the second half of the fifteenth century, have been preserved. Both were produced by the canoness Margriet Block. A Latin breviary from 1451 ultimately found its way into the collection of the dukes of Parma.[81] Sister Margriet completed a Middle Dutch Book of Hours in 1469, which now among other things contains the *ex libris* of the fifteenth-century family Hop.[82] The provenance of these manuscripts suggests that they were commissioned by lay persons. Proof that the scriptorium of Bethanië continued to produce manuscripts on commission is provided by a letter, dated 1472, from a certain Brother Bernard to Griete Vromoeds, a sister from Bethanië. In this letter he touches among other things on the design and cost of a Book of Hours which is to be written and illuminated at the priory in Arnhem for one Gertken Kocx.[83]

We can only conclude that in the convents of Windesheim the copying of books held special significance in the context of required manual labour. It may be said with certainty of five of the seven Windesheim convents that

---

[76] DV, f. 318v.
[77] Kruitwagen 1907, 97–120.
[78] D, f. 89c (not in DV).
[79] The only documented instance is the commission of a capitulary and a psalter by Beatrix van der Beeck (see text and also n. 60).
[80] Overvoorde 1896, 73. In 1482 *scriven* ('writing') brought in only nine guilders and twenty cents, minus one farthing (p. 79).
[81] MS Milan, Biblioteca Nazionale di Brera Gerli, MS 60. See Bénédictins du Bouveret 1976, no. 13012 for the Latin colophon, and further *Moderne Devotie. Figuren en facetten* 1984, 275.
[82] MS Arnhem, Openbare bibliotheek, 287; cf. Gumbert 1988, no. 327 and pl. 576b and van Bemmel 1999, 191–5.
[83] Arnhem, Rijksarchief in Gelderland, Archief Klooster Bethanië bij Arnhem, 52.

they either possessed scriptoria or produced manuscripts: St Agnes in Dordrecht, Bethanië in Arnhem, Bethanië in Mechelen, Diepenveen and Facons. Of the remaining houses one may reasonably assume that there were sisters engaged in writing during the obligatory hours of labour. Within the movement of female devout it was the canonesses of Windesheim who led the way in book production.[84] And yet only a relatively limited number of sisters were involved in the actual copying.[85] For the canons regular, on the other hand, the copying of religious texts constituted the single most important form of manual labour, one in which theoretically everyone participated.[86] For most of the canonesses regular this obligatory manual labour consisted of spinning, weaving and needle-work.

3.6 Religious Nourishment

The entire monastic community gathered together for daily meals in the refectory. These gatherings were also intended to reinforce the sense of community, not through busy conversation, but rather by enjoying the meal in silence and listening to the refectory reading. Thus the community received both physical and spiritual nourishment. The refectory reading was a significant institution in the monastic life in the late Middle Ages, the importance of which is often underestimated.

Normally speaking two meals a day were served in the Windesheim priories. To modern sensibilities this would appear to be a form of fasting, but in the Middle Ages hardly anyone ate more than two meals a day. Observance of the great or monastic fasts may certainly be accounted the stricter forms of asceticism: in wintertime, which lasted from Holy Cross day (14 September) to Easter Eve, the sisters of Windesheim fasted on Monday, Wednesday and Friday. Added to this were certain further restrictions associated with ecclesiastical fasts, among others during Advent and Lent, preceding Easter. In principle 'fasting' amounted to the sisters having just one meal a day; moreover some sisters abstained on certain fast days from meat and dairy products.[87] During fasts it was the evening meal that was cancelled; the communal gathering in refectory nevertheless took place, and the sisters received something to drink while they listened to the reading. The

---

[84] Cf. van Eeghen 1941, 25–7, who points to significant discrepancies in the involvement in book production between canonesses regular and tertiaries in fifteenth-century Amsterdam.

[85] Lingier 1993, 291 counts thirteen nuns involved in copying at St Agnes in Ghent, of a total of one hundred and thirty nuns mentioned by name in the convent's chronicle. There is no reason to assume that more than ten per cent of the Windesheim canonesses performed their manual labour in the form of copying.

[86] Cf. Kock 1999, 16–54 (with numerous references to the literature).

[87] On the significance of food and fasting for medieval female religious, see for example Bell 1985 and Bynum 1987.

evening gathering in refectory was also sometimes called the 'collation'.[88] The afternoon meal took place following the celebration of nones; on fast days this service had to end at or around 11:00. The evening meal or drink preceded compline, so at about 17:30.[89]

Once the sounding of the bells had announced that the meal or collation had begun, the convent gathered at the entrance of the refectory. The sisters entered in the same strictly established order of preference maintained in the choir itself. The *hebdomadaria* or sister of the week entered first in prayer and blessed the high table. Only then were the sisters allowed to take their seats. Once all were seated, the reader began that day's reading. The sisters took turns as reader for a week. The constitutions prescribe that they were to prepare ahead of time and have sufficient material to read.

> The reader shall have been provided with books before the blessing, and with the place at which to begin the reading, and reading material sufficient for the entire refectory. She shall not begin the reading until the din of those present has ceased, nor shall the sisters touch their food until, a small portion of the reading having been read, the prioress has given the sign or they see she has begun to eat.[90]

It was one of the tasks of the prioress to assure that the reader read well. If necessary, she was obliged to correct her.[91]

The constitutions make no explicit mention of it, but we may assume that the reading was conducted primarily in the vernacular. After all, the canonesses were not the only ones present during refectory: the less well-educated lay sisters were there, too. The written sources provide two important pieces of evidence in this regard. Concerning Truke van der Beeck the Diepenveen sisterbook remarks: 'She studied eagerly and delved into the Latin books and was wont to translate from Latin into Dutch during refectory.'[92] And the chronicle of Bethanië praises the *socius* Nicolaas de Dinter (†1518; see §9.2) among other reasons because 'he has frequently translated a number of homilies for us from Latin into Dutch, which the sisters eagerly

---

[88] Van Dijk 1986, 465–6 provides an outline of the days of abstinence and fasting.

[89] The data underlying this section have been drawn from CM 2.5 (mistress of refectory), 3.19 (refectory), 3.20 (fasting) and 3.21 (collation). The starting times are derived from the saxton's tolling schedule in van Dijk 1986, 358; see also the outline in §2.4.

[90] *Debet autem lectrix ante benedictionem provisa esse de libris et loco incipiendi lectionem et ut legenda per totam refectionem sufficiant. Lectionem non incipiat, antequam strepitus residencium cesset, nec sorores cibum attingant, priusquam, lecta clausula, priorissa signum dederit vel eam attingere viderint* (CM 3.19.16–20).

[91] See CM 2.1.37–9; cf. CM 3.7.11 and 13–14 on possible punishments for the reader.

[92] *Gherne studdierde sie ende zeer studioes was sie inden Latinschen bocken ende sie plach vake uten Latien in Duus toe reventer toe lesen* (DV, f. 329r–v).

read during refectory'.⁹³ Whether Latin was never used in refectory is still an open question. It is possible that texts which everyone was expected to know, like the rule and the statutes, may have been read at table in Latin. It may have been the case that half way through the meal there was a shift to the vernacular. The texts that Truke van der Beeck translated were apparently only available in a Latin version at Diepenveen, and Nicolaas de Dinter, too, seems to have translated material in Latin he had to hand. The question remains whether these texts were originally read in Latin, but later on translated because as the fifteenth century progressed, fewer and fewer of the sisters entered the convent with a good command of Latin. Be that as it may, the vernacular was the predominant medium in refectory.

The constitutions have much to say about how to ensure an orderly conduct of refectory, but concerning its contents they are much less specific. The cantrix appointed the reader and provided her with an appropriate text. The summary description of the reading plan shows that the material was in many cases a given:

> It falls to her to indicate to the readers at table what and when they shall read. On feasts and days with propers the homilies of the holy fathers are read first of all. On Saturday, however, the rule shall always be read, unless some feast or other matter should prevent this.⁹⁴

It was from the Rule of St Augustine that a chapter would be read on Saturdays, unless an important feast was to be celebrated on that day.⁹⁵ A number of Sundays and feast days on the liturgical calendar had fixed homilies, which were keyed directly to the lesson or special significance of that particular day. During the Middle Ages the term 'homily' was used mainly for sermons by Church Fathers such as Origen, John Chrysostom, Jerome, Gregory the Great, the Venerable Bede and sometimes Augustine. On those days with fixed homilies the reading at refectory was determined by the liturgy.

For a significant number of days the refectory reading programme was thus predetermined. Only if there was time to spare after the refectory reading or homily might the cantrix choose other texts. It will be obvious, partly because the cantrix was also in charge of directing the choir services, that in choosing her texts she would have given consideration to the time of

---

⁹³ *Hy heeft ons dic overgheset sommighe omelien uutten Latyn int Dietsche, die de susteren geeren ten refter ghelesen hadden* (*Kroniek Bethanië*, 1518).

⁹⁴ *Ad ipsam pertinet legentibus ad mensam, quid et quando legere debeant, ostendere. Omelie sanctorum patrum in festis et hiis diebus, qui proprias habent, primo omnium leguntur. Sabbato tamen regula semper legitur, nisi propter festum aliquod seu aliam convenientem causam preveniatur* (CM 2.9.20–4).

⁹⁵ There was also a brief reading from the Rule during prime (see §2.4); on the reading from the Rule see the introduction to Chapter 5, n. 5.

year. Undoubtedly one of the most significant restrictions in all of this would have been the quality of the library, which in the less wealthy convents would hardly have been very high. The *Constitutiones monialium* provide no further direction on the contents, though the constitutions for the Windesheim canons do include such a provision: 'The *lector* is to read the histories competently and the sermons and homilies attentively.'[96] The reading at refectory consisted, then, of two components: lectures, sermons and homilies on the one hand, *historiae* on the other. This narrative literature, which would of course have been religious prose, would have included, for example, chronicles and saints' lives. It is striking that this passage has been left out of the *Constitutiones monialium*; there is, however, little reason to suppose that the canonesses' programme of refectory reading differed in any substantial way from that of the canons.

Because the programme of refectory followed by the canonesses of Windesheim remains rather schematic, we shall turn our attention briefly to the convents of the reformed Dominicans in the province of Teutonia, where the sources are fuller in this regard. A striking degree of emphasis was placed there on communal refectory reading as an instrument of reform.[97] At St Katharina in Neurenberg, reformed in 1428, a new programme of refectory reading was introduced.[98] On Sundays and feast days the sisters of St Katharina read the prescribed Gospel pericopes and/or a sermon or homily for that day. On normal workdays the selection was the legend of the saint whose day it was to be celebrated according to the church calendar, or another text relating to him or her.[99] Thus the Dominican nuns of St Katharina read predominantly sermons and saints legends in refectory: the same division of material prescribed by the Windesheim constitutions.[100]

In the German-speaking areas during the fifteenth century there appears to be a link between initiatives of reform in a given monastery and the presence of manuscripts containing saints lives, such as the *Legenda aurea*, for example.[101] During that same century large numbers of manuscripts were produced containing Middle Dutch and Low German translations of the *Legenda aurea*. The women in the reform movements of the Modern Devotion

---

[96] *Historias legit expedicius, sermones et omelias attencius* (van Dijk 1986, 462).
[97] Williams Krapp 1986, 357.
[98] Ed. Ruf 1939, 638–50 (programme 1429–31) and 650–70 (adjusted programme 1455–61); cf. Hasebrink 1996.
[99] V. Mertens 1979, 279. Both Williams Krapp 1976, 291–5 and V. Mertens 1979 maintain that the widely disseminated German legendary *Der Heiligen leben* originated round about 1380 in the context of the Dominican reformation movement, the centre of which lay in Neurenberg and the most important convent of which was St Katharina. This legendary contains around 250 *vitae*: one text for every day that was not a Sunday or feast day.
[100] Hasebrink 1996, 213–14.
[101] Williams Krapp 1981 and Williams Krapp 1986, 356–64.

constitute their chief audience. It seems logical that all of these manuscripts of saints' lives served a single purpose in refectory or private reading.[102] In this context we may assume that on workdays in the convents of Windesheim the *vite* of the saint of the day was read in refectory.

The extant corpus of manuscripts from Windesheim circles can go only so far towards confirming the picture outlined here. Against all expectations, for example, hagiographical texts are not well represented in the libraries of the Windesheim canonesses. Not a single manuscript of the *Legenda aurea* or any other legendary has been preserved from any of the thirteen houses. There are a few manuscripts extant containing a smaller number of saints' lives.[103] These could well have been used for reading in refectory, though this might be said of most of the manuscripts surviving from the Windesheim convents.

In practice it is difficult to identify manuscripts intended specifically for refectory. None of the existing manuscripts, as far as I am aware, indicate explicitly that they were intended for refectory. Manuscripts do sometimes show signs that their texts were to be presented orally, as indicated by notes in the margins. But the question remains as to whether such a distinction existed for the larger specimens. Given the high cost, it would have been better to produce manuscripts that were multifunctional.[104] Nevertheless it is

---

[102] Martimort 1992, 100: 'Ils [= medieval legendaries] ont été compilés plutôt en vue de la lecture au réfectoire ou de la *collatio* du soir des monastères ou même, plus largement, pour l'édification personelle.' Cf. the typology of hagiographic manuscripts in Phillipart 1977, m.n. 115–17.

[103] Possibly originating in Diepenveen are: MS Deventer, SAB, I, 43 (101 F 9), containing a calendar and one hundred and ten *passiones, vitae* and *exempla* (cf. Alberts 1961 and Williams-Krapp 1986, 68 (MS Dv2)); MS Deventer, SAB, I, 33 (10 W 6), containing diverse *vitae*, among which a number from the south Netherlandish translation of the *Legenda aurea* (Williams-Krapp 1986, 69 (Dv6)); MS Deventer, SAB, I, 46 (191 D 5) (Williams-Krapp 1986, 68 (Dv1)). Hagiographic in nature but not a legendary is MS Brussel, KB, 12.166 (3875) from Bethanië in Mechelen, containing Konrad von Eberbach's *Exordium magnum cisterciense*, with biographies of St Bernard and his first fellow brothers (Deschamps 1972, no. 62; cf. §6.2, n. 54). The convent of canonesses regular St Agnes in Maaseik, which applied for membership in Windesheim but eventually joined the Chapter of Venlo, owned an ample collection of hagiographical manuscripts. On the convent see Persoons 1976; for more on hagiography see Mulder-Bakker 1987. M. van Dijk 2000 illustrates the functions of reading saints' lives in female religious circles using the Life of St Barbara.

[104] Persoons 1980, 94 assumes the existence of a separate (modest) library of manuscripts for the refectory in the Windesheim convents; cf. Costard 1992, on the (relatively large) collection of manuscripts with sermons from the sisterhouse, later Augustinian convent Nazareth in Geldern. Costard is of the opinion that most of these sermon manuscripts functioned in the context of private reading, though she does not exclude the possibility of their being used in refectory (p. 208). The numerous sermon manuscripts from the reformed Dominican convent St Nikolaus in Undis in Strasburg appear to have been used primarily for private reading (Rüther and Schiewer 1992).

safe to assume that the primary function of manuscripts containing homilies in their entirety was for reading in refectory.[105] The same holds true for books containing sermons by such well-known preachers as, for example, Johannes Tauler.[106] Surviving from Diepenveen is a cycle of seventy-seven sermons by Beernt Arborstier, prior of the Windesheim foundation Thabor in Friesland from 1449 to 1454. The prior of Thabor had originally preached the sermons to the lay members in his monastery, but they were also considered suitable for the sisters of Diepenveen. The sermons are arranged according to the liturgical year and deal mainly with lessons from Scripture for high festivals. This makes them ideally suited for use in refectory.[107] It is worth noting that the collection bearing Arborstier's name contains seven sermons written by Tauler.[108]

Taking all of this into account, we may posit that reading in refectory was certainly important for the canonesses of Windesheim – consider the detailed rules governing every gathering in refectory – but that this reading had a less essential role than among the German reformed Dominican nuns, for example. The fact that the passage concerning the contents of the reading, which does appear in the *Constitutiones Capituli Windeshemense*, was left out, may be an indication of this: if the Windesheimers had truly regarded the reading at refectory as a means of the reformation of female religious, they would more likely have inserted a more elaborate programme of reading here. The absence of detailed instructions for reading such as those for the Dominican nuns of St Katharina is also evidence of this. Naturally these reformed Dominicans turned to the tradition that had made their order great and that had produced preachers of Johannes Tauler's calibre. Ultimately the Modern Devout valued individual reformation exercises more highly.

---

[105] MS Deventer, SAB, I, 35 (10 W 5) was given by the priest Johannes van Warendorf of Cologne to Diepenveen in 1414. It contained among other things seven homilies by John Chrysostom in praise of Paul and other patristic works. Another gift to the convent included three books of homilies, none of which has survived (DV, f. 110v; cf. D, f. 162d). MS Brussel, KB, 12.050–12.052 (1216) from Facons contains various homilies and sermons from Church Fathers in the vernacular.

[106] MS Brussel, KB, 2283–4 (1167) from Galilea in Ghent contain several dozen sermons by Tauler. Another example is MS Brussel, KB, II 6644, also from Galilea, that contains the sixty-five articles of the passion of Jordan of Quedlinburg; a number of his sermons are also included there (Deschamps 1972, no. 82). On both authors see further §8.3.

[107] The sermons of Beernt Arborstier are preserved only in the Diepenveen manuscripts Deventer, SAB, I, 71 (101 D 13), I, 72 (101 D 14) and I, 73 (101 D 14); I, 72 and I, 73 were written in their entirety by Adriaen Mant (see §3.5) and her hand can be seen in I, 70 from f. 138v onwards. For more on these manuscripts, see Steensma 1970, 202–3, Gumbert 1988, no. 356 and pl. 711 and Wierda 2000, nos. 8–10; Steensma 1970, 204–21 discusses the contents of the sermons.

[108] Steensma 1970, 206–8.

3.7 Rest and Recreation

Just as the sisters of the Windesheim convents attended church and worked together, so too they retired to the dormitory as a group. This occurred after compline and the half hour of spiritual reading and meditation, at approximately seven o'clock in the evening. Unlike their male counterparts the nuns did not have individual cells; rather they slept in dormitories where each nun had her own private sleeping cubicle and a bed. The dormitory was one of the places in the priory where absolute silence was maintained (see §3.3). Whoever could not or would not sleep had to remain in bed until the sign was given to rise, and occupy herself with spiritual exercises.[109]

On holy days, when no work was done, the sisters had some spare time for recreation. Of course this part of life in the convent was hardly, if at all, described in the constitutions, thus leaving us pretty much in the dark. In convents in which the spiritual life was held to the highest standards, these hours, too, were devoted to religious exercises. Thus in the afternoons on Sundays and feast days at Diepenveen a communal *toe samensprekinghe* ('address') was held for the entire convent in the chapter house or some other building, at which point some section of the constitutions would be read aloud. On these occasions Armgert van Lisse would often give some of the younger nuns private singing lessons.[110] On Sundays and feast days Truke van der Beek would frequently teach the younger sisters 'something good' about the special meaning of that particular day.[111] Presumably the nuns would have been allowed to devote some time on Sundays and feast days to conversation, or to strolling in the convent gardens. Rare indeed would have been the sister who did not use these precious few hours of leisure time for social exchange, but devoted them to study instead.

3.8 Words of Inspiration

The re-establishment of the 'collations' is one of the most important 'innovations' brought about by the Modern Devout. The Desert Fathers were the founders of this brotherly exercise in exhortation; thanks to John Cassian's (†c.435) *Collationes patrum* there was sufficient knowledge about its structure and contents. Naturally the Modern Devout adapted this observance to meet the demands of their own day. And their use of the term 'collation' was not univocal: the word was also used to designate a variety of other gatherings. With regard to the collation as correptory exercise Mertens distinguishes two main types. The *admonitio* was an observance organised by the Brothers of the

---

[109] For more on the dormitories, see *CM* 3.17.
[110] DV, f. 290r and D, f. 174c. On the reading of the statutes, see the introduction to Chapter 5.
[111] DV, f. 329r.

Common Life for schoolboys, as well as for interested layfolk, on Sunday afternoons. Passages were read from the Bible and the faithful were exhorted to lead a Christian life within the bounds of their own estate. In addition to this the Modern Devout also observed the *collatio mutua*. The members of the community would point out their weaknesses and shortcomings to one another and try to help each other in their quest for purity. As their spiritual leader the rector would be present in the nunneries during these correptory discussions. In actual practice his authority as consecrated priest and learned theologian proved to be so great that the dialogic dimension disappeared entirely and the collation evolved into an address by the rector.[112]

It is possible to trace the development of the *collatio mutua* in the sisterbook of Diepenveen. It contains a number of references to the collations of Johannes Brinckerinck. Brinckerinck would first determine the spiritual concerns of the sisters and then improvise his address to them accordingly. The following passage illustrates how this rector proceeded:

> Once during collation he asked one of the elder devout sisters, Sister Jutte van der Beeck by name, what good things she had thought, as was his wont from time to time to do, for he would question someone and then base his collation on the response. Then she humbly revealed what thoughts she had had.[113]

This collation was no monologue in the purest sense, for it was Jutte van der Beeck who provided the theme. Moreover the sisterbook describes how Salome Sticken – as prioress someone with real authority – also participated in the discussion.[114] The collation as practised by Johannes Brinckerinck did, then, preserve some of its original dialogic nature, but there can be no doubt as to who was in charge. There is clearly no trace here of a correptory exercise in which all sisters took an active part in responding to one another.

Little is known about the frequency of and times at which collation was held at Diepenveen.[115] Based on remarks in passing in the description of Liesbeth van Heenvliet's (†1452) deathbed, it may be inferred that collation was usually held in the afternoon. 'And at approximately one o'clock in the

---

[112] On the practice of the collation generally, see Mertens 1996c, especially 164–9.

[113] *Op een tijt inder colacien vraghede hie eenre alte devoter suster, ghehieten suster Jutte vander Beck, wat sie goedes ghedacht hadde, als sijne maniren ondertijden weren, dat hie ymant wat vraghede ende daer dede hie dan sijne clacie op. Doe sede sie oetmodelicken wat sie ghedacht hadde* (DV, f. 34r–v).

[114] DV, f. 34v.

[115] Based on DV, f. 32r (cited in §5.4) we may conclude that Johannes Brinckerinck also held collations or similar addresses 'in chapter'. It is unlikely that the chapter of faults is being referred to here, as that was a gathering to which only the canonesses had access (§3.2). Is this perhaps a reference to the period when Diepenveen was still a sisterhouse, to certain communal gatherings in the chapter house held then?

afternoon, during collation, sister Liesbeth said to the nurse, sister Griete Harbers, "I'm fading".[116] Sister Liesbeth died on St Martin's day (11 November), a Saturday, as the sisterbook emphatically points out, for Liesbeth had prayed to be allowed to die on this day which had been devoted to Maria.[117] St Martin's was a compulsory feast throughout the Christian world and a feast *duplex maius* for the Windesheimers. Thus it is certain that collations were held on feast days at Diepenveen, and quite possibly this was the case for Sundays as well.

The rector probably made eager use of his collation to take up where the liturgy left off, for example by referring to the lesson.[118] An interesting passage from the sisterbook shows how Johannes Brinckerinck took passages from Scripture as a point of departure for his collations, and at the same time how the nuns received his message. It happened once that Jutte van Ahaus (†1408) was struck by a falling door while carrying a number of chamberpots. She was not bothered by the pain, but regretted very much the loss of the pots, which of course were shattered. Someone asked her what went through her mind as she lay there beneath the door.

> Thereupon she humbly replied: 'At that moment it came into my mind what our father Johan had said during collation concerning Gideon, when he went into battle with the children of Israel, that each of them had a little lamp in his hand and when the enemy approached they shattered their lamps, at which the enemy fled in fear because they saw the flames spring up there, and they were frightened [Judges 7:15–18].[119]

This is followed in the sisterbook by a gloss in which the meaning of the text is explained, presumably by Johannes Brinckerinck.[120] If a person succeeds in resisting his natural attachments, in this case by ignoring physical pain, then the sparks of God's love will spring forth from him. These sparks instill man with meekness, humility and resignation. And so this collation, too, arrives at the pious virtues which constituted the central theme of this spiritual exercise. For Johannes Brinckerinck scriptural exegesis was never the end, but exclusively the means to inspiring the sisters to ever greater devotion.

---

[116] *Ende des middaghes omtrint een uure, alst onder clacien was, soe sprack suster Lizebet totter sieckwaerster, suster Griete Harbers: 'Ick beswege alte male'* (DV, f. 286v; cf. D, f. 82a).

[117] See DV, f. 286v, D, f. 82a and van Slee 1908, 327.

[118] Cf. DV, ff. 69v–70r and D, f. 137c–d, where Brinckerinck asks Gertrud ter Poorten what the reading from the nocturnal is for matins.

[119] *Doe sede sie oetmodelick: 'Ick dachte op dat punte dat onse eerwerdighe vader heer Johan sede inder clacien van Gedeon, doe hie mitten kinderen van Israhel toe stride toech, dat sie ellick lempkens hadden inder hant, ende doe die viande quemen, sloghen sie hoer lampkens ontwie ende doe vloen die viande van anxte om dat sie dat vuoer daer uut seghen springhen, soe worden sie ververt'* (DV, f. 141r; cf. D, ff. 39d–40a).

[120] DV, f. 141r–v; cf. D, f. 40a–b.

The sisters cooperated in this endeavour with enthusiasm, sometimes by taking active part in the collation, but especially by taking notes of what the rector said. An anecdote concerning Alijt Bruuns (†1452) shows that the role of the sisters during collation was mainly a receptive one. 'She was very eager to hear the word of God during collation, and she wrote the most important points down on her tablet, and afterwards she committed them to paper.'[121] Alijt Bruuns went to collation to hear what the rector had to say; in her perception it was he, as the convent's priest and confessor, who spoke the word of God. In order to better remember them, she wrote a number of key words down in her wax tablet. Afterwards these were expanded and committed to paper; it is likely that she would have called upon the memories of her fellow sisters as well. Alijt (and her fellow sisters) would have used these notes to enrich their own spiritual lives. It was along such multiple paths that the rector's words influenced the sisters' way of life.[122]

Even after Brinckerinck's death in 1419 collation was held in Diepenveen – which is evident, among other things, from the passage concerning Alijt Bruuns, who took the veil in 1432 – but the sisterbook never again mentions the name of any other rector in that regard. Nor are any further details concerning the contents of the collations provided. Apparently no one subsequently made as great an impression as Johannes Brinckerinck had with his inspiring speeches. Nevertheless, rectors continued to hold collations and the sisters continued to take notes. The sisterbook tells of Cecilia van Marick (†1503) that she 'was wont to attend collation very faithfully and to write them out'.[123] Consequently Diepenveen boasts a collation tradition that spans the entire fifteenth century, even though its highpoint lay at its inception.

It is usually assumed that collation was practised in all the convents of the Chapter of Windesheim, but there is reason to exercise caution.[124] The *Constitutiones monialium* themselves can be misleading in that they contain a chapter entitled *De collacione et potu*. This deals, however, with the evening meal, which during Lent was reduced to an evening drink (*potus*). There is no mention of exhortations during these gatherings: the sisters ate or drank in silence and listened to the reading.[125] Moreover the rector was not present

---

121 *Seer begherlick was sie dat waert Godes toe horen inder clacien, ende die ma<r>clicste punten scrief sie in hoer tafele om die toe ontholden ende na op pappier toe scriven* (DV, f. 81v).
122 For this method of note-taking, see Mertens 1996b, 87–8. On the collation texts of Brinckerinck and how they came into being, see §5.4.
123 *. . . plach zeer vlitick toe wesen die clacien toe vergaderen ende uut toe scriven* (DV, f. 386v).
124 Persoons 1980, 90 goes so far as to claim that the rector held daily collations in Windesheim convents; as evidence for this he adduces the sisterhouse, later convent of canonesses regular, Sion in Kortrijk (see Nuyttens 1978), but it was not a member of the Chapter of Windesheim.
125 On the collation see *CM* 3.21. In the programme of refectory reading of St

during these meetings, for he and his associates ate separately from the sisters. It seems clear that this cannot be a reference to the *collatio mutua* as we know it from Diepenveen.[126]

Given the fact that nowhere in the *Constitutiones monialium* is there mention of the collation as communal correptory exercise, one may be justified in doubting its general dissemination. These statutes regulate conventual life with a high degree of precision and it is unlikely that the interpretation of the procedures for communal collation gatherings would simply have been left open. It is much more likely that this exercise did not belong to the standard programme shared by all houses of canonesses regular. Diepenveen is the only one of the thirteen Windesheim convents in which collations conducted by the rector were an irrefutably regular occurrence. Beyond this the chronicle of Bethanië does mention a *colatie* once or twice: for example, the prior of the convent of ten Troon in Grobbendonk held in 1530 a celebratory conference on the occasion of rector Tielman Schuerman's jubilee.[127] But this concerned an incidental address – which was, admittedly, exhortatory in nature – and not an exercise that matches the pattern outlined above. Moreover, these instances from the chronicle start to appear for the first time in the sixteenth century. The term 'collation' was used more frequently in this sense within the Chapter, as the chronicle of Johannes Busch illustrates. The collation held at Diepenveen by the papal legate Nicholas of Kues on his tour of the Netherlands was clearly occasional in nature.[128] In his chronicle of the Chapter of Windesheim Busch frequently mentions collations in convents – he held several in convents slated for reform – but even these seem to have been incidental addresses.[129] Only Gerard van Delft from Windesheim held regular inspirational conferences for women: he addressed them to 'Beguines', i.e. Sisters of the Common Life.[130]

Perhaps the explanation for the unusual situation at Diepenveen lies in the unique history of this priory, which after all was founded as an auxiliary of the Meester-Geertshuis, a sisterhouse, in other words. The sisters' way of life was initially the subject of great controversy. The author of the treatise *Super modo vivendi* defends the Brothers and Sisters of the Common Life energetically. He maintains stridently that women too have the right and obligation

Katharina in Neurenberg there is usually a separate mention of what would be read during collation (i.e. the evening meal) (cf. §3.6).

[126] Van Dijk 1986, 470–4 does note an evolution in the term 'collation' whereby the emphasis came to be placed on the spiritual aspect (i.e. the reading from Scripture) rather than on the meal itself. Even so, the constitutions still make no mention of the *collatio mutua*.

[127] *Kroniek Bethanië*, 1530. The same prior held a collation at the jubileum of cantrix Jacoba van Doenereyn (*Kroniek Bethanië*, 1537).

[128] Grube 1886, 339. On Nicholas of Kues see §5.3.

[129] See Grube 1886, index, lemma *Collatio, Ansprache an die Laien und Klosterfrauen*.

[130] Ed. Grube 1886, 78.

to admonish and inspire one another to virtue, as long as they do not in the process stray into the realm of theological subtleties.[131] Conducting sessions of mutual admonition was apparently an important aspect of the piety of the Sisters of the Common life, as it was for the first inmates of Diepenveen.

The *vite* of Jutte van Ahaus (†1408), who experienced only the sisterhouse period of Diepenveen, indicates the existence of a thriving collation practice in her day. Her application of the collation on Gideon has already been mentioned. Elsewhere it is recorded how on holy days sister Jutte took note of 'good points' on little pieces of paper, bits of text which she later put to use in her meditations. She derived a number of these good points from the collations of Johannes Brinckerinck.[132] Finally, it was Jutte van Ahaus's custom on holy days to address the young girls in an edifying manner and to teach them the Lord's Prayer and the Ave Maria.[133] In this instruction of layfolk we may discern something of the *admonitio* held on Sundays by the friars for school children.[134]

When Diepenveen underwent enclosure, this form of evangelisation was no longer possible. Such was not the case with the *collatio mutua*, even though it was a form of pious observance better suited to the semi-religious than to the canonical way of life. The collation seems to have been especially popular among those who had not taken monastic vows. The canons of Windesheim did not practise the collation as a form of brotherly correction.[135] Collations were held in the male houses, but they were intended for lay brothers and *donates*, who on Sundays and feast days were addressed by one of the canons.[136] The surviving manuscript tradition confirms this impression, as most of the manuscripts pertaining to the practice of collation come from

---

[131] Ed. Hyma 1926, 48; cf. van Rooij 1936, 181–2. *Super modo vivendi devotorum hominum simul commorantium* is attributed to Gerard Zerbolt van Zutphen (see §1.2) (van Rooij 1936, 74–90 and Hyma 1921). Hyma 1926 provides the edition, van Rooij 1936, 165–98 an exhaustive summary. *Super modo vivendi* is part of a body of texts which justify and defend the unfettered lifestyle of the first Brothers and Sisters of the Common Life, along with *De libris teutonicalibus et de precibus vernaculis*, *Tractatus de vestibus pretiosis* and *In quendam inordinate gradus ecclesiasticos et praedicationis officium affectantem* (van Rooij 1936, 47–90).

[132] DV, ff. 143v–144r (cited in §4.2); cf. D, ff. 41b–c. See as well the parallel passage in Latin in B, ff. 229v–230r (cited by Mertens 1996c, 177 n. 78). Brinckerinck is praised in the 'Frensweger manuscript' (MS Utrecht, UB, 8 L 16) for the collations he held for the sisters of the Meester-Geertshuis and Diepenveen, in which no distinction whatsoever is made between the two modes of living (Alberts and Hulshoff 1958, 65–6).

[133] DV, ff. 138v–139r and D, f. 38c; Trude van Beveren did the same (DV, f. 171r–v and D, f. 100a).

[134] Cf. Mertens 1996c, 169 n. 31.

[135] See Acquoy 1875–80, vol. 1, 154–8 on the collation: here, too, it refers to the evening meal; cf. Grube 1886, XXIII.

[136] On the collation for lay brothers and *donates* see especially Mertens 1996c, 169 n. 30. Relevant passages are to be found in Grube 1886, 87, 91 and 201.

circles associated with the Brothers and Sisters of the Common Life.[137] I may therefore conclude that the community of Diepenveen had grown attached to the collation; this may be attributed especially to the authority of Johannes Brinckerinck. His successors seem to have perpetuated the collation tradition at Diepenveen, whereby it apparently assumed a different character.[138] The question remains, however, whether collations were indeed conducted by the rector on Sundays and feast days at any of the other Windesheim convents.[139]

---

[137] Mertens 1996c, 170–4 discusses various *collationalia* (manuscripts containing material for the collation): MS Anholt, Museum Wasserburg, Fürstlich Salm-Salm'sche Bibliothek, MS 45 (*Hic aliqua sequuntur ex vitisfratrum nostrorum*) is a product of the St-Gregory's house in Emmerich (ed. van Engen 1988b, 195–217); MS Deventer, SAB, I, 61 (11 L 1) contains Florens Radewijns's *rapiarium* from the Heer-Florenshuis (see van Woerkum 1951, 115–17 and Mertens 1996c; this manuscript quickly found its way to the library at Diepenveen (see further §5.1, n. 32); on the 'collatieboek' (collation book) of Dirc van Herxen (†1457), of which both a Latin and a Middle Dutch version were in circulation, see van Buuren 1993. Mertens 1996c, 174–81 provides an overview of manuscripts containing collation texts: these are without doubt texts of addresses held in the sisterhouses and recorded by Sisters of the Common Life. The collations of Johannes Brinckerinck alone constitute an exception to the rule because they are for the most part based on written material from Diepenveen (for more on this see §5.4).

[138] The collations of the latter part of the fifteenth century sometimes seem more like exhortatory sermons; cf. Costard 1995 on the sermons/collations of Johannes Veghe.

[139] In the convents of the canonesses regular of the Chapter of Sion the rector held a collation for the prioress and sisters once a month, directly following the chapter of faults, also held on a monthly basis (Ypma 1949, 75).

4

Living with Texts

IN HIS BIOGRAPHY of the Windesheim librarian Jan Scutken, Johannes Busch tells an interesting story about a young monk. The uncertain youngster complained to his more experienced fellow monk that he did not know what he was supposed to do with himself all day in his cell on feast days. Brother Jan advised him to write the words 'Lord, have mercy upon me' on his wax tablet; in this way he tried to convince the young monk that even the smallest of virtues is pleasing to God. Thanks to this wise advice the doubting monk understood that it was enough if he recited the seven penitential psalms in his cell, read something edifying or wrote something worthwhile in his *rapiarium* ('notebook').[1] This anecdote sums up in a nutshell how each individual Windesheimer sought to put to rights his or her inner spiritual life. The young sisters in the convents received instruction in this important aspect of their lives, too, primarily from the mistress of novices, but also from the rector, the prioress or the subprioress. Through years of training, many of the sisters succeeded in gaining a high degree of control over their inner lives. In this they had but one goal in mind: the imitation of Christ

The necessary internal transformation was brought about by means of an on-going process which, in the traditional view, consisted of the stages *lectio*, *meditatio* and *oratio* ('reading, meditation and prayer'). The way in which these stages were organically connected to one another for the Modern Devout is so characteristic of their form of spirituality that it deserves a separate study.[2] This volume restricts itself to questions relating to the meaning the spiritual texts had for the personal spiritual lives of the choir nuns of Windesheim; they were continually reading devout texts, copying them, reflecting on them and meditating on their meaning, and out of this process

---

[1] The anecdote appears in Grube 1886, 196–7; cf. Staubach 1991, 439.
[2] See Goossens 1952 and Goossens 1980 on the early days of the Modern Devotion and Debongnie 1927 on the more advanced meditation technique as developed by Jan Mombaer. See also van Woerkum 1955 and the survey in *DS* (Rousse, Sieben and Boland 1976). The Modern Devotion embodied the transition from *lectio divina* to *lecture spirituelle* (the systematic method of meditation based on selected texts, applied especially by the Jesuits).

of meditation they produced new spiritual texts, which in turn were used by others for their private meditation.³

For convenience, three constituent elements of the Windesheim choir nuns' meditational practice will be dealt with separately here. First to be discussed is the sisters' individual spiritual reading: when and what did they read and what influence did this reading have on their lives (§4.1)? Next we look at the role which writing played – or could play – in the process of intensifying meditation (§4.2). Finally the variety of ways in which the nuns ordered their inner lives is surveyed (§4.3).

4.1 Reading for a Pure Heart

In several places the *Constitutiones monialium* mention the *lectio divina*, the sisters' private spiritual reading, but these references raise more questions than they answer. This is where the nature of the statutes works to our disadvantage, for after all it was the *communal* life in the convent that they were designed to regulate. Issues of a more individual nature, such as spiritual reading or meditation, are not treated in any systematic fashion in the constitutions. There is therefore no chapter dealing with either the duration of the sisters' individual reading hours or what they actually read.

The chapter in the constitutions dealing with the office of *armaria* ('librarian') contains fewer details than one might expect.⁴ There is one important reference regarding the sisters' private reading: 'After prime, when the nuns have left the chapter house, books are requested from the *armaria*, each sister saying, with head slightly bowed, "codicem!" ["a book!"].'⁵ Little is known about the usual location of the library; presumably it was upstairs, next to the church. A nun was specially appointed to receive books on behalf of sick or absent sisters.⁶ Although the procedure for taking out a book is clear enough, some practical questions remain. Did all the nuns go to the library after prime every day, as the citation suggests? It is unlikely that the sisters needed a new book every day, for they did not, after all, have that much time at their disposal for reading. Perhaps a particular day was set for the library to be open, so that nuns who had finished their current book could choose another. Exactly when the nuns were to return the books they had finished is not

---

³ For the process whereby text and meditation interacts and produces new texts among the Modern Devout see esp. Mertens 1989a and Staubach 1994.
⁴ On the librarian see *CM* 2.11; see also §2.1.
⁵ *Finitis primis, codices ab armaria petuntur, cum sorores egrediuntur de domo capituli, singulis cum modica inclinacione dicentibus: 'Codicem'* (*CM* 2.11.13–15).
⁶ *CM* 2.6.17–19: the infirmarian saw to it that, when they could, the sick also took part in choir prayer and spiritual reading. Prioress Liesbeth van Bergen of Bethanië in Mechelen is praised because she provided books so that the sick and the dying could be read to. She herself took great pleasure in reading aloud in the infirmary (*Kroniek Bethanië*, 1503).

mentioned in this chapter; it would seem that this did not happen when the new books were distributed.

In the normal daily schedule of the canonesses there was hardly any room for spiritual reading. Half an hour of preparation time was allotted before the hours of terce, sext and vespers.[7] The *Constitutiones monialium* do not prescribe how this time was to be spent, though the constitutions for the canons regular do. The canons were obliged to spend this half hour reading, which amounts to one and a half hours of required reading time per (work)day.[8] Some canonesses would have read books in preparation for these hours, but prayer and meditation were considered an equally appropriate preparation for the office.

For the Windesheim choir nuns there were indeed more or less required hours set aside for reading. On Sundays and feast days there was time (following the conventual mass?) until noon and for half an hour after the evening meal, to be spent on – silent – spiritual reading or other spiritual exercises.[9] Those for whom these required hours were not enough could conceivably have spent a portion of their free time on Sundays and feast days reading (from noon to vespers); they needed permission from the prioress for this, however.[10] Permission could also be obtained to spend time normally designated for labour on studying (*studio doctrine*).[11] Women like Fenne Bickes, Katharina van Naaldwijk, Lubbe Snavels and Beatrix van der Beeck have already been mentioned, all of them nuns of Diepenveen who had good Latin and enjoyed studying Holy Scripture (§2.3). Presumably the privilege of study was reserved for a few talented women. The constitutions suggest that these nuns had to study mainly in their 'free time'.

In summary we may observe that, compared to the canons of the same chapter, the canonesses of Windesheim were prescribed very little time for reading. On workdays there were no such requirements, and on Sundays and feast days time for reading could be replaced by other spiritual exercises. The programme for the individual as reflected in the *Constitutiones monialium* places little emphasis on spiritual reading. Compared also to the constitutions for the Dominican canonesses, an important source for the *Constitutiones monialium*, the Windesheim sisters enjoyed fewer opportunities for spiritual reading.[12]

---

[7] *CM* 2.8.92–4: this half hour falls between the first and second bell preceding each liturgical hour.
[8] Cf. van Dijk 1986, 360–1.
[9] *CM* 3.13.6–10; this stipulation is left out of *CM* 5.2, the newer redaction of this chapter on silence (see §3.3), but there is little reason to assume that the reading and/or other exercises were dropped from the programme.
[10] *CM* 2.5.104–16; cf. *CM* 3.13.20–2 (cf. n. 9). Probably before this new redaction took effect, the opportunity existed for reading or study with permission.
[11] *CM* 3.14.5–6, cited in §3.4.
[12] Van Dijk 1986, 531; on the female Dominicans, see Lewis 1996, 262–83.

Why is it that the Modern Devotion, exaggeratedly portrayed by some as the movement of the book, placed so little emphasis on reading for the choir nuns, when after all it was they who constituted the highest female echelon of this movement? In van Dijk's view it is precisely in this decreased stress on spiritual reading that the spirituality of Modern Devotion transcends the female canonical tradition.[13] In order to understand this we must gain some insight into that tradition. As a religion of the Word, Christianity demands of its adherents a personal relationship with the Word. The *lectio divina* ('spiritual reading') has therefore been a long-standing element of the monastic life. The reading of Scripture was considered the first stage of prayer, followed by meditation and contemplative prayer. The Modern Devout still respected the classic triad *lectio–meditatio–oratio*, but they added an important shift in emphasis. *Lectio* and *meditatio* became more closely intertwined and eventually hardly distinguishable from one another as separate stages. Reading was for them the handmaiden of meditation, in that it provided a constant source of food for thought. In this way the Modern Devotion also places more stress on the internalisation of faith, which must take place in the heart of the believer. The *Constitutiones monialium* also reflect this shift in attitude.[14]

The Modern Devout put a great deal of thought into the function of spiritual reading. Its founders, including Geert Grote, Florens Radewijns and Gerard Zerbolt van Zutphen, stress the great importance of spiritual reading for the reformation of the inner life. Their vision of this reading may be summarised in six points.[15]

1. The goal of reading is to achieve purity of heart.
2. The texts should be read in their entirety.
3. Reading should take place at established times.
4. Certain points from the reading should be retained, so that one may return to them afterwards.
5. Reading should alternate periodically with prayer.
6. Preference should be given to books on piety and virtue.

The first point links spiritual reading to the essence of the spirituality of the Modern Devotion, inner purity. The Devout do not read with the vain goal of acquiring knowledge, but rather to learn lessons which may be applied to their own situations. This explains, for example, why the well-read Alijt Bake can claim so assertively that she studied no book except the loving heart of our Lord. Spiritual reading had as its ultimate goal the object of bringing the reader closer to Christ.

---

[13] Van Dijk 1986, 531.
[14] Cf. the literature mentioned in n. 2.
[15] This outline is taken from Goossens 1952, 102–3, who bases it on works by Florens Radewijns and Gerard Zerbolt.

The choir nuns of Windesheim were sometimes voracious readers, even though meditative exercises were considered equally appropriate for them. The sisterbook of Diepenveen speaks frequently about sisters who eagerly and assiduously read Holy Scripture. While spiritual reading was highly regarded in this convent, not everyone was able to practise this exercise at the same level. Katharina van Naaldwijk was one of the best-read sisters at Diepenveen. She loved reading so much that she had two or three books with her at all times. When carrying these books became too much for her, her fellow nuns persuaded the prioress to allow Katharina the use of a special book-basket.[16] It would be very useful to know which books appeared in it, but unfortunately the *vite* does not say. Katharina would at any rate have had her *rapiarium*, discussed in detail in the next section, with her at all times.

Given her love of books it is hardly surprising that Katharina van Naaldwijk held the office of librarian at Diepenveen. In that capacity she not only distributed books from the convent's library, but she also made available to the sisters manuscripts owned by herself and her sister Griete. The sisterbook praises Katharina because she tailored her assignment of books to the individual: 'There she served each individual in a friendly and kind fashion according to her estimation of the individual's needs.'[17] With her expertise this keeper of books helped other, less well-read sisters in choosing the most appropriate reading material.

The libraries of the Windesheim convents must have contained a considerable number of books. After all, each nun had to have one book for use at the designated reading times. Ideally there would have been at least as many books in a given convent as there were choir nuns. Round about the year 1450 Diepenveen held more than one hundred canonesses, while Bethanië in Mechelen boasted seventy. The rare instances in which a catalogue or large manuscript collection has survived from a fifteenth-century convent belonging to the Modern Devotion reveal collections numbering dozens and sometimes hundreds of manuscripts. The 'catalogue' of *studierboeken* ('study books') in the tertiary convent St Barbara in Delft lists one hundred and nine books, including two or three copies of the most popular works.[18] Some seventy manuscripts survive from the St Agnes convent in Maaseik, out of a total of nearly one hundred still existing in 1785, according to a list drawn up at the time.[19] There is little reason to assume that the libraries of the average Windesheim convent contained fewer than this, when we consider that it was

---

[16] DV, f. 251v and D, f. 61c.
[17] *[D]aer diende sie enen yghelicken van vrentlick ende mynlick na dat sie miende dat enen yghelicken noetdruftich was* (DV, f. 243v; cf. D, f. 56b).
[18] Moll 1866b.
[19] On the books of St Agnes, see Deschamps 1967, Hermans 1987 and Stooker and Verbeij 1997, part 2, nos. 789–865; on the convent of St Agnes, see Persoons 1976. See also §3.6, n. 103.

in these convents that the level of literacy was relatively high. We must therefore conclude that huge numbers of manuscripts intended (primarily) for private reading have been lost.[20]

In the absence of other data, the contents of the programme of reading for the canonesses of Windesheim must be deduced from the surviving corpus of manuscripts, however incomplete and fragmentary it may be. General instructions for reading or book-lists have not come down to us, and individual preferences can be determined only to a very limited degree. We do know that Augustine was Katharina van Naaldwijk's favourite author, but precisely which works she was familiar with remains unknown.[21] Only Alijt Bake has left us the names of her favourite authors, sometimes even accompanied by a justification. Liturgical works are not included in this survey of the contents of the choir nuns' spiritual reading; among these are also the psalters and books of hours, containing as they do texts pertaining to the divine office. For convenience' sake, texts intended primarily for refectory, such as sermons and saints' lives, are also not considered, though we should certainly acknowledge that they were probably read privately as well.

The extant corpus of books which the canonesses of Windesheim could read privately may be divided into three categories. The first comprises a small number of manuscripts containing patristic works – fewer, incidentally, than one might expect from a movement so emphatically founded upon early Christian principles. The homilies of the Church Fathers would have been read during mealtimes, but texts of other kinds, such as letters or treatises, were presumably read privately. Katharina van Naaldwijk is an example of a nun with a marked preference for the works of the Church Fathers.[22]

The second category consists of now classic authors from the flourishing of mysticism in the twelfth, thirteenth and fourteenth centuries. Richard of St Victor and Francis of Assisi appear once or twice here. Mentioned much more frequently is Bernard of Clairvaux, the author of the medieval concept of the mystical love between God and the human soul. Also well represented here are the Dominican mystics of the fourteenth century. Heinrich Seuse and Johannes Tauler appear most frequently in the manuscript collections of the Windesheim convents.[23] One seldom encounters in these circles their contro-

---

[20] On the fragmentary preservation of spiritual literature from the convents, see Obbema 1996, 91–102.

[21] DV, ff. 250r–v and D, f. 60d.

[22] MS Deventer, SAB, I, 35 (10 W 5), contains, among other things the *Epistola Augustini ad Cyrillum episcopum Hierosolymitanum de laude Jheronijmi* (Lieftinck 1964, no. 21 and pl. 305–7), which she may have read (cf. §3.6, n. 105).

[23] On the dissemination of Tauler in the Netherlands see for example Lieftinck 1936, Axters 1961 and Axters 1970, 243–51: Galilea in Ghent is one of the most important centres for the reception of Tauler (see §8.3). On Seuse see van de Wijnpersse 1926, 20–44, Axters 1970, 180–243 and Deschamps 1989.

versial predecessor and colleague Meister Eckhart, who was accused of heresy.[24]

In the third and last category we find the authors who were members of the Modern Devotion movement itself. Among these I would include also the authors from Groenendaal, Jan van Ruusbroec and Jan van Leeuwen, who may be considered trailblazers for the Modern Devotion; they are fairly well represented in the libraries of the Windesheim convents, though not by their most mystical works.[25] Among the 'true' Modern Devout it is the ascetic writers in particular who stand out: Gerard Zerbolt van Zutphen, Jan van Schoonhoven and Thomas a Kempis.[26] It may be that a conscious literary policy of the Chapter of Windesheim lies behind this, one which preferred to expose the nuns to safe ascetic literature, rather than dangerous mystical fare.[27]

Most striking in their absence from the literature available to the canonesses of Windesheim are the mystics of the first religious women's movement. Van Ruusbroec and van Leeuwen acknowledged the importance of the great Brabantine mystic Hadewijch up to a point, at any rate, and they therefore borrowed from her writings. Most manuscripts containing her works were kept at the Rooklooster, which, like Groenendaal, was situated at the Zoniënwoud and belonged to the Chapter of Windesheim. But the works of Hadewijch are not to be found in the libraries of the convents of the Chapter of Windesheim.[28] The corpus of Hadewijch's works is not large, to be sure, but nor are other, more widely disseminated female mystic authors to be found among the libraries of the Windesheim sisters. In the convent of St Barbara in Delft there were a few manuscripts containing the revelations of Mechthild of Hackeborn and the life of the mystic Mary of Oignies.[29] Of the Dominican authors we encounter most regularly among the Windesheim sisters there are confessors like Tauler and Seuse, who in their orthodox works endeavoured to do justice to the experience-oriented religiosity of their sisters-in-faith. Biographies of Dominicans such as Elsbeth Stagel or Margaretha Ebner, or the *Schwesternbücher* (sisterbooks) with their lives of the

---

[24] On the dissemination of Eckhart see Ubbink 1978 and Ubbink 1985: among the Windesheim convents, only Diepenveen possessed an Eckhart manuscript, i.e. Deventer, SAB, I, 57 (10 W 7), containing the *Reden der Unterweisung*.

[25] On the dissemination of van Ruusbroec see Willeumier-Schalij 1981; on Jan van Leeuwen see Geirnaert and Reynaert 1993.

[26] See the summaries of the monastic libraries in Kohl, Persoons and Weiler 1976–84 and Stooker and Verbeij 1997, respectively; the latter is organised by monastery.

[27] On this cf. Mertens 1995b, especially 128–30: from 1450 on the Modern Devout did read mystical texts, but numerous restrictions were imposed. Williams-Krapp 1993, 302 points to a comparable development in the German-speaking regions.

[28] On the manuscripts of Hadewijch, see Deschamps 1972, no. 24 and Kwakkel 1999.

[29] Moll 1866b, nos. 12, 71 and 103. On the dissemination of Mechtild of Hackeborn in Middle Dutch, see Bromberg [n.d.], especially 118–27.

Dominican female mystics, did not find their way to the Windesheim canonesses. Thus the composition of the convent libraries reflects an atmosphere of somewhat curtailed freedom, especially learning about the mystic experiences of other women. We leave aside the question of whether this was a restriction chosen by the canonesses themselves or imposed by the Chapter, but not without noting again that Alijt Bake probably did know the works of female mystic authors.

4.2 Reading with the Pen?

In his *Speculum imperfectionis* ('Mirror of Imperfection'), finished before 1451, the famous Franciscan Johannes Brugman attacks a number of widespread evil practices among his fellow brothers. The eloquent preacher scornfully condemns, for example, the exaggerated way in which his newly professed brothers cherish their *rapiariola* and *libellulli* ('little books').[30] A *rapiarium* is a collection of excerpts, quotations or sentences with special appeal to the individual collector. Florens Radewijns was regarded by the Modern Devout as the founder of this unique genre.[31] Whether this is true or not, the *rapiarium* is characteristic of the reading and writing practices of the Modern Devotion. By recording important passages from spiritual literature in their personal *rapiaria*, the Devout were better able to internalise them and commit them to memory. Reading the excerpts would in turn prompt a recall of the entire text. Hence the Devout lived as it were in a textual universe, a universe constantly being augmented and expanded. They used texts and writing to stock their memories with good points or sentences and in so doing purify their inner being. Mertens has aptly termed this intensive manner of working with texts 'reading with the pen'.[32]

The marked utilitarian and personal nature of the *rapiaria* is reflected in their rather amorphous physical manifestation. *Rapiaria* consisted in the main of individual collections of loose texts and fragments, written down on scraps of writing material of all kinds: bits of paper or parchment, slates and wax tablets. Such loosely organised collections did not, of course, stand a good chance of surviving the ravages of time. Few indeed have survived. The individual *rapiaria* known to us have in most cases been copied and edited, and thus made accessible to a wider audience, but much of the specifically material character of any given *rapiarium* has been lost in the copying.

Based on both the surviving textual and physical materials, two types of

---

[30] Ed. van den Hombergh 1967, 118–38 (p. 122.8–123.2); cf. van den Hombergh 1985, especially 363 and 370.
[31] Diepenveen possessed a manuscript of Florens Radewijns's *rapiarium* (see §3.8, n. 137; cf. §5.1, n. 32).
[32] On 'reading with the pen' see especially Mertens 1989a, Mertens 1989d and Mertens 1994b.

rapiarium may be distinguished, the chronological and the systematic. In the first type the texts, citations or excerpts follow the order in which the collector encountered them in his reading. The second type arranges the collected material according to some organising principle, for example by author, theme or virtue.[33]

Father Brugman's passionate reaction proves that by the middle of the fifteenth century the *rapiarium* had spread to circles beyond the Modern Devotion. Of particular interest is Brugman's fundamental criticism of this method of reading and writing. He was disturbed by the freedom enjoyed by the individual, in particular by the very real danger that texts or passages would be taken out of context. But Brugman was especially angered by the fact that the value of the communal was being undermined in favour of the individual. Johannes Brugman's criticisms were aimed at newly professed Franciscans who did not possess the gift of discernment when it came to theological matters. What was the status of this sensitive issue among the canonesses of Windesheim and their spiritual mentors?

The *rapiarium* and its accompanying method of reading and writing did indeed become widespread among the ranks of the Chapter of Windesheim. Johannes Busch writes in his chronicle of Windesheim that every monk in that monastery maintained his own *rapiarium*.[34] The most famous example from Windesheim is that of Gerlach Peters, which consisted of scraps of paper and other fragments. After his death his fellow brother Jan Scutken reworked this amorphous material into a coherent treatise, the *Soliloquium*. It was in this guise that Gerlach Peters's *rapiarium* was widely disseminated.[35] And the *rapiarium* method was practised in other monasteries too. The most famous work produced by the Modern Devotion, *De imitatione Christi* by Thomas a Kempis, from the monastery of St Agnietenberg, shows influences of the *rapiarium*.[36] Later in the fifteenth century Jan Mombaer (†1501), canon regular of the monastery at Windesheim, collected a vast amount of material for meditation using the by now tried-and-trusted *rapiarium* method, which he systematically organised in the *Rosetum exercitiorum spiritualium* ('Rose Garden of Spiritual Exercises'). Despite the many examples of the genre, however, there are no rules regulating how one should maintain a *rapiarium* in the *Constitutiones Capituli Windeshemensis*.[37] The Windesheim constitutions regulate the individual's life of prayer, after all, in only the most limited way.

Moreover, the term *rapiarium* itself does not appear in the *Constitutiones*

---

[33] On the *rapiarium* among the Modern Devout see especially Mertens 1988.
[34] Grube 1886, 573.
[35] See Grube 1886, 156–9 and Kors 1996, 162–77; cf. van Engen 1999. On Gerlach Peters see §1.2.
[36] On the *Imitatio* as a *rapiarium* cf. Staubach 1994, 208–9. An English translation of the text is found in Sherley-Price 1952.
[37] Cf. Acquoy 1875–80, vol. 1, 163, who makes use of both historical and literary sources.

monialium, nor is the practice of collecting excerpts from religious texts alluded to in any way. And yet the Diepenveen sisterbook in particular leaves little room for doubt that 'reading with the pen' was a familiar phenomenon among the choir nuns. A passage from the *vite* of Jutte van Ahaus, from before the enclosure of Diepenveen, illustrates succinctly the function of the *rapiarium* in these circles – and that without mentioning the term at all.

> As the sisters on holy days sat committing their good points to paper, this humble woman would sit behind them and ask them modestly and humbly whether she might also dip her pen in the inkpot. She had collected bits and scraps of paper, no doubt cast off by others. She would fill these with good points pertaining to obedience, mortification of the flesh, and self-denial and all things that lead to humility and a feeling of insignificance, and away from placing too much trust in herself, or seeking the esteem of others and anything else that would help her achieve humble submissiveness among all the sisters, both in her heart and in her deeds. Such things and others like them, as well as what she heard during collation or what she read in books or what she overheard others say that would stand her in good stead in her efforts to be dead to the flesh, to resist the temptations of all that was by nature pleasing to her, these things she took great pains to record on her scraps of paper; she filled them so full of writing that one could not pick them up without touching the writing.[38]

Jutte van Ahaus collected 'good points' from various kinds of sources: spiritual treatises, collations by the rector and the words of her fellow sisters. She used the sentences thus gleaned in her efforts to combat her natural urges and in the process achieve a state of higher virtue, the ultimate goal every devout strove for. It goes virtually without saying that Jutte's *rapiarium*, written as it was on loose scraps of paper, has not come down to us.

Zweder van Rechteren, too, kept a *rapiarium* consisting of good points written on pieces of paper:

> She loved the sacred Scriptures with such a passion that she kept on her person little scrolls, some no longer than a finger, some shorter, some

---

[38] *Als die susteren des hillighen daghes een goet punte screven, soe plach dese oetmodighe vrouwe achter hem toe sitten ende bat hem scemelick ende alte oetmodelick of sie wal mede int yncket moste stippen. Soe hadde sie wat lepperkens van pappier vergadert lichte dat een ander verworpen hadde. Dat bescref sie dan soe vol van goden punten die droghen tot ghehoersamheit, toe starven ende uutghaen hoers selves ende al dat tot oetmodicheiden draghet ende tot cleinen ghevolen, ende niet toe betrouwen in hoer selven ende niet gheacht toe wesen, ende wat hoer tot oetmodige nederheit helpen mochte onder al die susteren, van bijnnen inder harten ende van buten inden warcken. Desen ende deser ghelicken ende wat sie hoerde inder clacien of wat sie las inden bocken of wat sie hoerde segghen dat hoer dienen mochte tot aldusdanighen dogheden om toe starven al datter nathuren ghenocklick was, dat pynde sie hoer toe vergaderen op sulke lepkens; die bescref sie soe vol datmen sie nauwe anen conde tasten, men en moste op die scrift tasten* (DV, ff. 143v–144r; cf. D, ff. 41b–c).

longer; these she was wont to carry in her purse and she called them her shields (against evil).³⁹

The texts from two of these 'shields against evil' have been preserved in Zweder's *vite*: 'Poverty without want is like an unsealed letter sent to a great lord' and 'Whatever our superiors say is entirely good and true, and whoever contradicts them is evil and wicked'.⁴⁰ We may perhaps infer from these two texts that 'good points' tended to take the form of spiritual proverbs. But it could also be the case that the other sisters remembered these points precisely because of their pithiness, and that ultimately they were recorded again, in a more definitive form, in the sisterbook. Zweder van Rechteren generously shared her rolls of texts with her fellow sisters, thus disseminating them throughout the convent community.⁴¹ On the whole these 'good points' constituted an important aspect of communication among the sisters at Diepenveen.⁴²

Thus far we have seen that there were two sisters from Diepenveen who, according to modern standards, maintained rather primitive *rapiaria*. The term *rapiarium* occurs in the sisterbook itself just once, and that in connection with Katharina van Naaldwijk. Katharina possessed a blank manuscript, referred to in her *vite* as a *rapiarius*, into which she copied texts and excerpts on a regular basis. She took inspiration from the Augustinian Rule: 'She copied his rule into her *rapiarium* at the proper time, after she had done profession, in order that she might internalise it and follow it the more assiduously.'⁴³ The sisterbook has the following to say about the external appearance of Katharina's *rapiarium*:

> And just how full of goodness her heart was may be seen by her *rapiarius* and her book of the hours of Mary, in which one could hardly find a bit of unwritten space to lay a thumb or finger on, as I myself [i.e. the scribe who wrote MS DV] have often witnessed with amazement.⁴⁴

---

³⁹ *Soe grote mynne ende vuoerricheit had sie totter hilligher scrift dat sie hadde cleine rullekens, som soe lanck als een vingher, sommich corter ende langher; die plach sie in hoer budel toe draghen, die hiete sie horen scilde te wesen* (DV, f. 123v; cf. D, f. 28c).

⁴⁰ *Armode sonder gebreck weer recht als een onbeseghelden bref diemen enen groten heren sende* (DV, f. 122r; cf. D, f. 27c), and *Soe wat dat ons oversten seggen dat is al goet ende waerachtich, ende wie daer teghen secht dat is quaet ende vals* (DV, f. 124r; cf. f. 28c).

⁴¹ DV, ff. 123v–124r and D, f. 28c.

⁴² In the infirmary, the nuns regularly made a point of saying 'something good' to their sick sisters; see for example DV, ff. 253r–v and D, f. 62d (Katharina van Naaldwijk). Sisters on their deathbeds were asked for a 'good point' or sentence by way of a spiritual testament. Dymme van Rijssen offered several sentences, including: *Ghevet u tot ghehoersamheit, soe mochdi blidelick sterven* ('Surrender yourself to obedience and you will die happy'; DV, ff. 180v–181r; cf. D, ff. 120b–c); see also the citation at §6.1. On these spiritual testaments, see Mertens 1989c, 84.

⁴³ *Sie scref goettijt sijne reghele naden dat sie professie had ghedaen in hoer rapiarius, op dat sie sie te beet solde westen ende navolghen* (DV, f. 250r–v).

⁴⁴ *Ende hoe vol godes hoer dat harte was mochmen sien an horen rapiarius ende hoer*

Katharina van Naaldwijk's exact methodology is not entirely clear from this. Presumably once the manuscript she used as a *rapiarium* was full, she began to fill the empty margins and other spaces in her Book of Hours with citations and excerpts. It is just as plausible, however, that she worked on both manuscripts at the same time. At any event, it is certain that Katharina van Naaldwijk's *rapiarium* consisted of two codices, and it is quite possible that there was also a good deal of loose material present. Both manuscripts were preserved after her death, presumably in the convent's library. Although Katharina van Naaldwijk's *rapiarium* was made of much more durable material than the rolls and slips of Jutte van Ahaus and Zweder van Rechteren, nevertheless it was no better structured than theirs. Compiling a *rapiarium* was a life-long project for the Modern Devout. Like her fellow sisters, Katharina van Naaldwijk was constantly looking for new material to add to her collection of texts.

What is striking is how the sisterbook, in the cases of both Jutte van Ahaus and Katharina van Naaldwijk, explicitly draws an immediate connection between a *rapiarium* and the inner life. The fullness of heart of both of these sisters is there to be read in the crowded pages of their *rapiaria*. It was of the utmost importance to keep many good points close to the heart, in order to deny the devil any opportunity of settling there. A full *rapiarium* meant that the writer had taken great pains to commit to memory many valuable and edifying words. From this example, too, the function of the *rapiarium* and that of reading in general clearly emerges: they are there to improve the spiritual life of the individual. Unfortunately, the *rapiaria* of Jutte and Katharina have not come down to us. They would have given us insight into what the choir nuns of Diepenveen read, what they heard at collation and what they talked about in their spiritual discussions.

Judging by the situation at Diepenveen, the activity of recording important sayings and sentences as a means of internalising spiritual values was fairly widely practised. We know, for instance, that Liesbeth van Delft, Alijt Bruuns and Cecilia van Marick took notes during collation on wax tablets, which were later transferred to paper. These excerpts were used during personal reflection. We may assume that most of the sisters at Diepenveen copied texts and fragments in a similar fashion, in order to better commit them to memory or to use them as points of departure for meditation. We can only guess at the manner in and frequency with which that occurred. Perhaps Zweder van Rechteren, Jutte van Ahaus and Katharina van Naaldwijk, the only sisters who are explicitly referred to as compiling spiritual sayings, excerpts or texts, were exceptions to the rule, and most of the others had to make do with a wax tablet from which their temporary texts could be erased.

vrouwen-tijdeboeck, daermen nauwe soe volle spacien an winden en conde daermen enen duem of vingher op legghen en mochte, als ic selven mit verwonderen vake ghesien hebben (DV, f. 251v; cf. D, f. 61c–d).

Maybe the compilation of excerpts in the form of a *rapiarium* was beyond their means. We must take into account the fact that the three aforementioned sisters were all high-born and wealthy and held a status of privilege at Diepenveen.

Little data is available on the state of affairs at other Windesheim convents, but they are so diverse and widely distributed that one may assume that 'reading with the pen' was a generally familiar method for internalising spiritual texts in this milieu. In Bethanië at Mechelen Jacoba van Loon assiduously read and copied holy writings, among others those by van Ruusbroec.[45] And Alijt Bake of Ghent also used a means of writing closely related to 'reading with the pen,' in that she tended to formulate and record her own thoughts and ideas, whereas her fellow sisters restricted themselves to a more passive approach. In other convents associated with Windesheim, too, the nuns copied important texts in order to internalise their contents. The canoness regular Katherine Cauwericx of St Agnes in Ghent, for example, preferred to meditate on the Pauline epistles: 'And her greatest consolation lay in the epistles of Paul, for she would constantly and diligently meditate upon them and would frequently copy many passages from them.'[46]

That so few 'true' *rapiaria* were compiled by the choir nuns, that of Katharina van Naaldwijk forming the exceptional high point in this regard, is due both to their living conditions and to individual opportunity. The canons regular of Windesheim, all of whom compiled *rapiaria*, were much better equipped to do so. To begin with they had more time for reading than the choir nuns, as the previous section makes clear. The compilation of a *rapiarium* among the Modern Devout is organically connected to the process of individual spiritual reading: the excerpts taken always function against the background of the larger text from which they have been drawn.[47] Given the fact that the choir nuns of Windesheim read far fewer texts, the foundation for their *rapiaria* may be seen to be much narrower (and it was more often than not restricted to proverbs and brief quotations). Moreover, the canons of Windesheim had their own cells into which they could retreat to do their copying, reading and note-taking. The choir nuns did not have private rooms, which from a practical point of view made it much more difficult for them to do any writing for their personal use. That Katharina van Naaldwijk was nevertheless able to compile a *rapiarium* is due mostly to her great intellectual abilities, which enabled her to read and excerpt a great deal despite such restrictions. Moreover, her status as a noble-born sister would have given her some advantages.

---

[45] On Jacoba van Loon see §6.5; cf. §4.3.
[46] *Ende haer meeste consolacie was in Paulus Epistelen gheleghen, daer sij haer stedelic in oufende met groeter vliet ende plach daer vele oec uut te scrivene* (Kroniek Sint-Agnes, f. 60r). Cited after Lingier 1993, 459 n. 67; cf. p. 289.
[47] Cf. for example Mertens 1994b and Staubach 1994.

There is one final detail concerning the dating of the witnesses to the production of *rapiaria* and 'reading with the pen': they date mostly to the first half of the fifteenth century. This may be coincidence, but it is also quite possible that in the course of the century the freedom of the female devout was restricted in this regard. Characteristic of the change in the spiritual climate is a passage from the statutes of the convent of Jeruzalem at Venray, which were drawn up when the Augustinian Rule was adopted there in 1467.[48] The newly professed canonesses were forbidden to compile '*rapiaria* or excerpts, that is points gathered here and there from books without any order, for in this way they are often taken out of context'.[49] In light of the prohibition against writing of 1455, we cannot discount the possibility that the canonesses of Windesheim were subject to restrictions on taking excerpts from religious texts. We should be mindful here again of Jan Brugman's outspoken criticisms of the Franciscans' *rapiariola*. Realising how he wished to deny his younger brothers free access to religious literature, we can hardly suppose that the strict Windesheimers will have granted 'their' canonesses much freedom in this regard either.

4.3 Devout Exercises

The *Constitutiones monialium* devotes a separate chapter to rules concerning the sisters' behaviour in the dormitory.[50] The dormitory was one of the spaces in the convent where absolute silence was to be maintained. Sisters who for whatever reason could not sleep were advised to engage in 'devout exercises'.

> From compline to prime no one shall leave the dormitory without permission, unless it be to answer the call of nature or to perform the divine office in the church or to warm herself; for then they are to remain quietly in their beds and devote themselves to God or to lections and prayers, in order that, by means of such respite from daily labour and duties of whatever sort they may be able to amend their past distractions.[51]

Several activities are recommended here, each of which found a place in its own right in the process of internal transformation upon which the devout

---

[48] On Jeruzalem in Venray see §5.2.
[49] *Rabelarien of excerpten, dat syn hier en daer vergaderde punten uut boecken sonder ordinancie, want in desen is duckwile heelheit des sins ghebraken.* MS Grubbenvorst, Ursulinen, archive Jerusalem MS 11, cited after Verschueren 1949, 697; cf. pp. 700–1.
[50] *CM* 3.17.
[51] *A completorio usque ad primas nusquam sine licencia extra dormitorium divertant, nisi pro necessitate nature et ad ecclesiam pro divino officio peragendo sive ad calefaciendum; tunc enim quiete circa lectos suos manentes sibi ipsis et Deo vel lectioni et oracioni vacare studeant, quatenus tali vacacione laboris diurni et quarumcumque occupacionum distractiones preteritas reformare valeant* (*CM* 3.17.10–16).

placed such great emphasis, a process whose basis was formed by the trinity *lectio–meditatio–contemplatio*. Devoting oneself to *Deo vel lectioni* (i.e. holy reading) must surely refer to the recitation of texts from memory, as actual reading would, of course, have been impossible in the darkened dormitory.

The constitutions recommend diverse methods to the sisters for distancing themselves from the concerns of daily life, thus enabling them to come closer to God. Meditative activities, usually referred to collectively as 'spiritual exercises', constituted an extremely important part of the spiritual life of the Windesheim sisters. This section attempts to shed some light on how these choir nuns ordered their internal lives. To this end it seems useful first to establish what the Modern Devout meant by 'meditation'. In modern usage, the term usually refers to a set period of internal reflection on a spiritual subject. To the Modern Devout, however, every moment of spiritual reflection was in fact *meditatio*, wherever and whenever it occurred. They were capable of meditating at all times and in all places, even while working, for instance, or while lying in bed in a darkened dormitory.

Just as the *Constitutiones monialium* are rather vague regarding the specific means whereby one might combat idleness, so too the sisters themselves did not discriminate between the diverse spiritual exercises. That this is so appears, for example, from a passage in the Diepenveen sisterbook concerning Katharina and Griete van Naaldwijk:

> They devoted themselves so utterly to our Lord that they were seldom idle, occupied as they were with good exercises or reading or praying or manual labour.[52]

Manual labour, reading, praying or the performance of exercises were all ways giving oneself over to Christ. The 'good exercises' are thus on a par with spiritual reading, for example, but in practice there was much less time available for the latter activity. The purpose of all such efforts is the struggle against idleness.[53] The fear of falling short in the eyes of God appears also to have dominated the individual spiritual lives of the choir nuns of Windesheim.

In the title of one of the collations of Johannes Brinckerinck a connection is made between manual labour and the performance of internal exercises: 'Concerning external and internal labour, and how we should exercise ourselves in prayer day and night'.[54] By 'external labour' is meant the obliga-

---

[52] *Sie gheven hem soe voerrichlick tot onsen lieven heren dat sie selden ledich weren sie en weren becummert mit goeder offeninghe of sie lesen of sie bededen of deden hantwarck* (DV, f. 242r; cf. D, f. 55b).

[53] Cf. also *CM* 3.2, on the training of novices, and DV, f. 240r–v and D, ff. 54b–c (cited at §2.3), on the lessons Katharina van Naaldwijk gave her sister Griete and other novices.

[54] *Van den arbeide van buten ende van binnen, ende hoe wi ons oefenen sullen in den ghebeden*

tory manual labour to be performed on weekdays; by 'internal labour' is meant constant prayer and meditation. The long hours of monotonous labour in the spinning hall and other work-rooms were perfectly suited for the performance of individual internal exercises, as is demonstrated by Alijt Bake, who, while spinning, contemplated Rulman Merswin's *Neun Felsen Buch* ('Book of Nine Rocks'). Brinckerinck's collation mentioned above is to a great extent devoted to meditation. For the most part the narrative follows the course of a day in a religious community. The message is in essence that one should be occupied in meditation and prayer at all times and in all places, from when one wakes up until one goes to sleep. Certain moments and activities of the day call for special devotions. Brinckerinck took pains to teach the sisters *how* they should give form to their internal lives. In order to be focused on the spiritual from the moment they arose, he recommended the following method:

> In the morning, when you get up, you shall say: 'God, be mindful of my plight. Dear Lord, come to my assistance, for alone I am helpless. Saint Mary, pray for me. My holy angel, pray for me. My holy apostle, pray for me.' Then read this collation: 'Dear Lord, clothe me in your garment of love, of humility and of peace, and protect me against the Enemy, who prepares ambushes against me, in order that I may praise your glorious name forever with a chaste heart and a pure body, you, o God, who lives and reigns forever and ever, Amen.'[55]

We find comparable readings regarding rising in the morning in Salome Sticken's *Vivendi formula*, a rule for devout sisters.[56] She advises the sisters to prostrate themselves humbly before Christ as soon as the clock strikes the hour of matins. The prioress of Diepenveen prescribes a somewhat different kind of meditation material to Brinckerinck, namely a passage from the Passion. But in essence both Brinckerinck and Sticken convey the same didactic message: the mind of each devout sister must be with the divine

---

des daghes ende des nachts (Collatie VII). On the collations of Brinckerinck see §3.8 and §5.4.

[55] *Des morghens, als gi opstaet, so suldi segghen: 'God, wil denken in mijn hulpe. Lieve heer, comet my te hulpe, want ic van mi selven niet en vermach. Sinte Maria, biddet voer mi. Mijn heilighe enghel, biddet voer mi. Mijn heilighe apostel, biddet voer mi.' Ende leest deze collecte: 'Lieve heer, clede mi mit dynen clede der minnen, der oetmoedicheit ende des vredes, ende bescermt mi voer den viant, die my laghen leit, opdat ic mit enen kuuschen hert ende mit enen reynen lichaem mach loven dinen gloriosen name ewelike, die lefste ende reghierste, God, ewelike sonder eynde. Amen (Collatie VII*, 159). The first recommended prayer is a clear allusion to the versicle *Deus, in adiutorium meum intende* (Ps. 69) and the responsory to it, *Domine ad adiuvandum me festina*, with which most hours begin (Harper 1991, 75).

[56] Kühler 1914, 362–9; cf. van Engen 1988a, 176: the first three sections discuss how to achieve a pure spiritual attitude at rising, during mass and the midday meal, and when retiring.

from the moment of waking. The Windesheim constitutions for the canons regular also contain such precepts for the preparations of each new day. Both the canons regular and the canonesses prepared themselves through contemplation for prayer during the first, midnight hour of the divine office.[57]

A prominent moment in the inner life of the sisters was the celebration of the daily mass. The eucharist commemorates Christ's sacrifice for mankind, and it was therefore a most appropriate moment for the sisters to give themselves utterly and inwardly over to him. Brinkerinck's fifth collation is devoted to this sacrament, and the seventh also touches on contemplation of holy mass.[58] Salome Sticken, too, provides extensive instructions for the way in which the sisters are to experience mass. The *Vivendi formula* prescribes a pre-mass confession to Jesus of all unabsolved sins. During the celebration, the sisters should contemplate Christ's suffering and do their best to open themselves up to him.

> Moreover, beloved sisters, if we are fervent and diligent, we can by the grace of our Lord so unfold before us his dear Passion, impress it on our minds, and affectionately unite ourselves to it that we are made ready to do and suffer all that he permits to come over us, be it chastisement, humiliation, temptation, or even the condemnation and rejection of all men.[59]

Next, Sticken recommends calling to mind phrases and images from the Passion as the best method of meditation.

Salome Sticken's long years of experience had taught her that it was no easy task to keep the spirit focused constantly on the divine, especially when one was not engaged in any of the communal religious exercises. The daily activities and responsibilities formed constant distractions. In order to stay focused inwardly, she therefore offered up frequent ejaculatory prayers.[60]

> At all times and places, moreover, lift your hearts up frequently to our most loving Lord Jesus Christ in brief prayers poured out with groans and sighs; for instance, in the psalm 'Create in me a clean heart, O God' [Ps. 51:12], or the hymn 'Come Holy Spirit' or something similar.[61]

---

[57] See CM 3.4.18–22 for the women, and Acquoy 1875–80, vol. 1, 164–5 and van Dijk 1986, 396–7; for the situation among the men, cf. Goossens 1952, 166.

[58] *Collatie V* and *Collatie VII*, pp. 160–1.

[59] Van Engen 1988a, 177. *Quineciam dilectissime sorores, si fervide et diligentes essemus, possemus per gratiam domini nostri amabilem passionem domini Iesu ita revolvere et mentibus nostris inprimere et nos illi affectuose unire, ut parate efficeremur omnia agere et pati, que ipse superevenire permitteret, sive correptio fuerit, sive humiliacio, sive temptacio, sive quod contemnamur et despiciamur ab omnibus hominibus* (Kühler 1914, 366).

[60] On ejaculatory prayers among the Modern Devout, see Mertens 1986, 249–70. Florens Radewijns and Gerard Zerbolt recommend breaking up the reading regularly with short prayers (cf. §4.1).

[61] Van Engen 1988a, 178. *Preterea in omni loco et tempore studebitis corda vestra frequenter erigere ad amatissimum dominum nostrum Iesum Cristum per breves oraciones cum*

As an advocate of such prayers, it is no coincidence that two examples from her own repertoire are included in her *vite*.[62] The first prayer she recited silently before she went to communion to receive the eucharist.

> O, my dearest beloved,
> I pray that Thy holy flesh
> And Thy holy blood
> May be my last sustenance.[63]

The second prayer functioned as a spiritual prostration before Christ.

> O, sincerest beloved, I bow down before you
> And desire you with all my heart.
> May the Holy Trinity preserve me.
> May the Holy Spirit inspire me
> And inflame me and enlighten me
> And unite me with you.
> O, sincerest beloved, this I pray of you.[64]

The rhyme in these brief texts served primarily as a mnemonic function, rather than an aesthetic one, helping the supplicant to remember and recall the prayers more easily. Presumably each sister had her own repertoire of such brief prayers and lamentations.

The same holds true for the individual spiritual exercises, developed for the most part by the sisters themselves. It is likely that no universal meditation method existed for the Windesheim canonesses, though there are bound to have been broad local similarities. Johannes Busch does describe how both canons regular and lay brothers at the monastery at Windesheim meditated on one and the same text, the *Epistola de vita et passione domini nostri Christi et aliis devotis exercitiis* ('Letter on the Life and Passion of Our Lord Jesus Christ and Other Devout Exercises').[65] For every day of the week the *Epistola*

---

gemitu aut suspirio fusas, videlicet 'Cor mundum crea in me, Deus', aut 'Veni Sancte Spiritus', aut simile quid (Kühler 1914, 368).

[62] Ed. Kühler 1914, 220 (in normalised spelling).

[63] *O myn alre lieveste lief, / Ic bidde di dat dijn hillighe vleis / Ende dijn hillighe bloet, / Myn leste spise wesen moet* (DV, f. 209v; not in D).

[64] *O hartelicke lief, ic nighe di / Van al mynen harten begher ic di. / Die hillighe drivoldicheit beware mi. / Die hillighe geest ontsteke mi / Ende make mi vuoerrich ende verlichte mi / Ende verenighe mi mit di. / O hartelicke lief, des bidde ic dy* (DV, f. 209v; cf. D, f. 12b).

[65] Based on Busch (Grube 1886, 32) it has long been assumed that Johan Vos van Heusden (†1424), the first prior superior of the Chapter of Windesheim, was the author of the *Epistola*, but later scholars were not convinced; see for example van der Woude 1947, 149–50 and Hedlund 1975, 6–7. Busch's edition of the *Epistola* is found in Grube 1886, 226–43; Hedlund 1975, 89–110 provides a critical edition of the Latin text. Editions of the vernacular versions are de Bruin 1944–5, 8–23 (Middle Dutch) and Hedberg 1954, 115–63 (Middle Low German); a translation in English is available in van Engen 1988a, 187–204.

provides three points for consideration: one dealing with the beginning of Jesus's life, the second concerning his Passion and death, and the third concerning the saints who followed him.[66] Several manuscripts containing the Middle Dutch or Middle Low German text survive, but none of them comes from a Windesheim convent.[67] It is therefore extremely unlikely that this typically Windesheim meditation text will have found widespread use among the women religious.

Busch published the *Epistola* in Latin, but it is not inconceivable that he first had to translate the text, for it is generally held that this meditation exercise was originally composed in Middle Dutch.[68] This brings us to the question of which language the Windesheimers used for personal prayer. It seems unlikely that the learned canons regular of Windesheim would have preferred the vernacular, for the texts they read for inspiration were written in Latin. Nor was it by any means unusual for the choir sisters of Windesheim to perform their spiritual exercises in Latin. In a bull issued by Pope Alexander VI in 1499 it is even assumed that this is the norm, though implying that the sisters might not know Latin.[69] Probably some Windesheim canonesses regularly used Latin texts as sources of inspiration for their private meditations.[70] Fixed prayers, like the Pater noster and Ave Maria, as well as more well-known passages from the Bible and liturgy, were undoubtedly recited silently by the sisters in Latin. The only silent exercise from a Windesheim canoness whose actual contents are known is that of Katharina van Rijssen from Diepenveen. The sisterbook gives the text in Latin without any further commentary, so apparently this was not all that unusual. It would appear to be an exercise that Katharina contemplated time and again. The limited number of lines that Katharina was required to memorise would

---

[66] On the sources of the *Epistola* see Hedlund 1975, 7–23: among the most important are the *Meditationes vitae Christi* by Bonaventure and the *Vita Jesu Christi* by Ludolf of Saxony.

[67] On the vernacular text and the manuscripts, see Hedberg 1954, 58–71 and Hedlund 1975, 23–5. Unfortunately no information about their provenance is provided, though it appears that most of the vernacular manuscripts originated in the German-speaking regions. The Latin manuscripts do, for the most part, come from Windesheim monasteries (Hedlund 1975, 62–9).

[68] De Bruin 1944–5; de Bruin 1984, 121 speaks more cautiously of a German ur-text. Perhaps this hypothetical vernacular *Epistola* was used in the early years at Windesheim so that the lay brothers might understand it as well. Very early on there was a special library in the monastery, managed by Johan Scutken, containing vernacular books for those with no Latin (cf. Scheepsma 1996a, 225).

[69] This bull, *Circa statum regularium*, has been published by Rehm 1985, 310–17; cf. pp. 49–51.

[70] Two Latin books of hours survive which may have originated at Diepenveen: MS Deventer, SAB, I, 13 (101 E 4) and Deventer, SAB, I, 12 (101 E 1). From Jeruzalem in Utrecht comes the MS Paris, Bibliothèque de l'Arsenal, 858 (Martin 1885–99, vol. 2, no. 858).

have made meditating in Latin considerably easier. Below is the exercise in its entirety:

> Flee, be still, keep quiet for the Lord, on account of whom all things are done, in order that you may please him, consider it enough that your revivification and solace be only in him. For he is the hope of the sighing spirit. Seek him through pious tears and the crying out of a humble heart. Love silence. Seek after solitude. Avoid ostentation. Choose simplicity and concord. Choose to take delight in humble utterances. None appears safely except the one who willingly remains hidden. None speaks safely except the one who gladly keeps quiet.[71]

Significantly, manuscript D, intended for the less well-educated sisters in the Meester-Geertshuis, provides a translation in Middle Dutch.[72]

We have only outside report of the spiritual exercises of the Windesheim sisters. In order to give an idea of the great wealth of form and the many personal variants, a number of these exercises will be introduced in more detail here. The emphasis will fall on the literal contents of the exercises rather than on the technical and methodological aspects of meditation. As usual, the Diepenveen sisterbook provides the most data. Like most of the Diepenveen sisters, Trude van Beveren (†1428) derived her inspiration wholly from the Passion of Christ. She frustrated potential demonic temptations by filling her day completely with exercises.

> She had augmented her hours throughout the day with exercises pertaining to the life and Passion of our Lord, so that the devil had no opportunity to tempt her. But at night he would try to fill her with fear while she slept. It was to no avail. He could not prevail against her, for she was filled with so much good that no evil could get in. She was a holy temple of her bridegroom; only that which belonged to him could enter there.[73]

This Diepenveen sister had a fixed daily programme which she executed with such precision and regularity that one could tell time by it.

---

[71] *Fuge, tace et quiesce soli domino propter quem omnia fiant, ut placeas satage refocillacio tua ac solamen in ipsum tantum sit. Ipse enim spes anime suspirantis. Ipsum pie querunt lacrime clamor quoque cordis supplicis. Silencium ame. Solitudinem inquire. Ostentacionem devita. Simplicitatem et unitatem elige. Ia<c>titacionem humilem optinente te iocundare. Nemo secure apparet nisi qui libenter latet. Nemo secure loquitur nisi qui libenter tacet* (DV, f. 189r–v).

[72] D, ff. 125c–d.

[73] *Sie hadde horen tijt alden dach doer alsoe gheordeniert mit offeninghen vanden leven ende lieden ons lieven heren, dat die duvel ghien tijt en conde crighen hoer toe becaren. Meer des nachtes plach hie sie wal wat toe ververen inden slaep. Het was om niet! Hie en conde niet an hoer wynnen, want sy was vol godes, daer en conde ghien q<u>aet in. Het was een hillich tempel hoers brudegoms; daer en conde niet anders in dan dat hem toehoerde* (DV, f. 171v; cf.. D, f. 100b).

When the sisters did not know what time of the day it was, they would ask Sister Trude. She knew the time so precisely on account of her exercises that it was as if she had heard the bell tolling. Once in a while Sister Griete Deghens, who supervised the workhouse, would ask her what she was thinking. She would then tell her humbly which devout exercise she was engaged in at the time. Sometimes they concerned the Last Supper, and at other times the Passion or something similar.[74]

Trude van Beveren was perhaps unusually precise in the execution of her exercises, but we may assume that most of the canonesses at Diepenveen maintained a programme of meditation of similar scope and intensity.[75]

As a rule the sisterbook offers little by way of explicit detail concerning the manner in which the sisters remembered or structured these exercises. Alijt Bruuns (†1457), Griete ten Kolke (†1453) and Griete Tasten (†1452) used the nine orders of angels – in ascending order of rank: Angels, Archangels, Virtues, Powers, Principalities, Dominations, Thrones, Cherubim, Seraphim – to organise their silent exercises.[76] Certain reflections were associated with each one of these orders, normally dealing with a motif from the Passion. The sisterbook does not reveal whether the meditations of these three sisters corresponded with the theological and cosmological significance of the hierarchy of angels.[77] Alijt Bruuns used another, separate scheme for her nocturnal exercises: 'It was her habit to seek solace each night in the wounds of our Lord.'[78] She would contemplate each of the wounds of the Cross in her mind, considering its meaning and trying to feel its pain. At the same time Alijt felt safe and secure in the wounds of Christ. As the fifteenth century progressed, such expressive representations of the Passion came to be used more and more as a means of intensifying meditation.[79]

Christ's Passion was of course a dominant theme, but not the only one employed by the sisters of Diepenveen in their devout exercises. Many of them chose for themselves 'friends in heaven': saints whom they singled out

---

[74] *Wanner die susteren niet en wosten wat tijde dattet was vanden daghe, soe vraghedent siet suster Truden. Die wostet soe puntelicke bij hore offeninghen of sie die clocke ghehoert hadde. Ende onder tijden plach hoer suster Griete Deghens toe vraghen, die dat werchuus doe verwaerde, wat sie dachte. Soe plach siet hoer oetmodelick toe segghen na dat hoer tijt was dat sie offende. Ondertijden wast vanden aventmael ende in anderen tijden wat anders vander passien ende dierghelicken* (DV, ff. 171v–172r; cf. D, ff. 100b–c).

[75] Cf. for example Souke van Dorsten, who had a separate exercise for every daily activity (DV, f. 373v).

[76] DV, f. 82r (Alijt Bruuns), and DV, f. 345r and D, f. 147d (Griete ten Kolke (cf. §6.1) and Griete Tasten), respectively.

[77] A contemporary view of the choirs of angels is to be found in Dirc van Delft's *Tafel van den kersten ghelove* ('The Table of Christian Faith'), chapter 4 (ed. Daniëls 1937–9, vol. 2, 19–22); van Oostrom 1987 points as well to the convents as a secondary (fifteenth-century) circle of reception for the *Table* (especially pp. 58–63 and 68–9).

[78] *Sie plach alle nachte inden wonden ons lieven heren toe rosten* (DV, f. 82r).

[79] See for example van Herwaarden 1982, especially 184 and Rudy 2000a.

for special worship.⁸⁰ For example, Katharina van Naaldwijk constructed a recurring annual cycle of meditation around St Augustine (28 August) and St Egidius (1 September). She had noticed that dates from the period in which she had undergone her conversion coincided with certain important dates in the lives of these two saints. Moreover, Katharina possessed an image of St Egidius, which she had taken for St Augustine and worshipped as such. Because of these meaningful coincidences Katharina celebrated the feasts of Egidius and Augustine with exceptionally devout exercises; she likewise celebrated lavishly the translation of Augustine's bones (11 October) and the octave of his feast (4 September). Katharina van Naaldwijk felt a responsibility to pay special devotion to a large number of other saints. The divine office having been completed, she would often remain behind in the choir for some time, honouring them with her prayers.⁸¹

Although in principle the nuns would have performed their exercises individually, they sometimes worked together. According to the sisterbook, for example, Griete ten Kolke and Griete Tasten worked their way through the nine orders of angels together on a daily basis.⁸² The sisterbook describes an intriguing mutual exercise in somewhat fuller detail, presumably because it was rather exceptional even by Diepenveen standards. St Agnes was the patron saint of Diepenveen and Trude Schutten had a special affection for her. Therefore she asked Gertrud Huginghes to go with her on an imaginary pilgrimage to the church of St Agnes in Rome. One wonders whether the nuns used a written guide for pilgrims, like, for instance, *Vanden gestant des heiligen landes* ('On the Status of the Holy Land'), for this exercise. Duke Arnold of Gelre's pilgrimage to Rome and the Holy Land in 1450–2 is described in this text, though not in the form of a travel narrative. The holy places are described in such a way that in one's imagination one can wander around them and thus contemplate the most important moments in the life of Jesus. *Vanden gestant des heiligen landes* was written by one Agatha van Aken, and the only extant manuscript containing the text was written in a convent.⁸³

In concrete terms the exercises of the sisters Trude and Griete consisted of an intense cycle of prayers. Their spiritual pilgrimage took shape through special exercises and through the recitation of fifty Ave Marias a day. Sister Trude wanted to depart the day after Epiphany (7 January), and arrive in

---

⁸⁰ A few examples not elaborated on here: Lubbe Snavels had many friends in heaven (DV, f. 304r and D, f. 90a) and Stine Tolners dedicated her Latin *casus ende tempera* (cases and tenses) to the saints (DV, f. 298v and D, f. 86c–d; on the latter see §2.3).

⁸¹ DV, ff. 250r–251r and D, ff. 60d–61b.

⁸² Griete Koetgens and Griete des Vrien also performed spiritual exercises together; they were not, however, to die and embark on the last voyage together as they had so fervently wished to do (see DV, f. 345v and D, f. 117d, and DV, ff. 349v–350r and D, ff. 150c–d, respectively).

⁸³ For information on *Vanden gestant* see Carasso-Kok 1981, no. 271; see further Nijsten 1989 and Nijsten 1992, 148–9.

Rome on the feast of St Agnes (21 January). On an earlier pilgrimage *in mente* she had spent three days in Rome, but how long she wished to remain this time, she could not say. Gertrud Huginghes decided in the end not to accompany her, fearful as she was that she would slow her fellow sister down along the way. Ultimately Trude's imaginary pilgrimage did not last long. She suddenly took ill and died soon thereafter, of all days on 7 January 1417. Thus, according to her *vite*, she did in the end undertake her pilgrimage to St Agnes after all.[84]

Trude Schutten's spiritual pilgrimage to Rome is an exceptional expression of a devotional practice also known as 'piety of sums'.[85] The sisterbook offers further examples of the phenomenon. Every day for thirty years Beatrix van der Beeck (†1500) recited the Lord's Prayer one hundred times along with three *vrouwekrenskens* (chaplets; DV, f. 339v). In all likelihood the latter refers to the reciting of the rosary, for three chaplets constitutes a rosary. By telling her beads three times she would silently commemorate the Passion, the Last Supper and the Resurrection.[86] Much more complex and involved was the devotional exercise devised by Griete van Naaldwijk in honour of St Ursula and the Eleven Thousand Virgins (21 October), an exercise in which the entire convent took part. At her request, whenever one of their sisters lay on her deathbed, the nuns of Diepenveen all recited the Lord's Prayer one hundred times in honour of the Eleven Thousand Virgins, imploring heavenly intercession on behalf of their dying sister. According to the sisterbook, the Lord's Prayer was recited a total of eleven thousand times: thus one hundred and ten sisters would have taken part in this collective exercise (though it is by no means unlikely that the figures have been adjusted to arrive at an appropriate number).[87]

To the nuns of Diepenveen it was no coincidence that Griete died, of all days, on 21 October 1424. When in turn the convent had recited the Lord's Prayer eleven thousand times for her, the dying Griete saw a crowd of white

---

[84] For this specific pilgrimage see DV, f. 66r–v and D, f. 135c–d; on spiritual pilgrimages in general in the Low Countries see Koldeweij 2000 (cf. p. 248), whilst Rudy 2000b refers to a unique practice in this regard in the St Agnesconvent in Maaseik.

[85] In German the term *gezählte Frömmigkeit* is currently in vogue; cf. Angenendt, Braucks, Busch *et al.* 1995. The 'piety of sums' flourished in Dominican circles in southern Germany; cf. Lentes 1993 on St Nikolaus in Undis at Strasburg.

[86] I wonder whether a change in the way meditation was practised at Diepenveen is not reflected here, whereby silent reflection gives way to fixed prayers like the Pater Noster and Ave Maria. Given the date of her death, Beatrix's *vite* cannot have been written before 1500 and thus is one of the later additions to manuscript DV (see §6.3). It is quite possible that these later *viten* represent a changed perspective on the inner spiritual life.

[87] Lentes 1993, 139–41 describes a similar practice among the reformed Dominican nuns of the fifteenth century: according to one 'Sterbeordo', the convent had to say ninety thousand Hail Marys for every sister on her deathbed, a practice which as it were wove a protecting 'cloak of Mary'.

faces all about her. It was usual for the entire convent to gather around their dying sister as she lay on her deathbed, in order to accompany her passing with prayer. Thus it was that Griete asked whether the faces she saw were those of her fellow sisters. Elsebe Hasenbroecks, her nurse, replied in the negative, for only a few were present at the time. It is Elsebe who provides the explanation for what Griete van Naaldwijk must have seen: standing at the threshold of eternal life she saw St Ursula and her eleven thousand virgins gathered around her. Griete van Naaldwijk's story is illustrative of the trust which the Windesheim nuns placed in the intercessory power of the saints and the efficacy of prayers directed to them.[88]

In the devout exercises contained in the Diepenveen sisterbook, the significance of religious literature is actually quite small. We may reasonably assume that in their prayers to the saints the sisters made use of material derived from their legends, and they must at some point have turned to the literature for the numerous articles of the Passion which they always had to hand. But the sisterbook provides precious few examples of the kind of spiritual exercise in which the reading of religious literature and silent contemplation went hand in hand (a form of exercise so typical of the Modern Devotion as a whole). Perhaps this is due to the nature of this particular source, which focuses more on the diligence with which the nuns prayed and meditated than the precise manner in which they did so. After all, the literary climate of this convent may without a doubt be classified as 'good'.

The chronicle of the convent of Bethanië in Mechelen contains a passage concerning the practice of meditation in which reading and contemplation interact directly. Jacoba van Loon–van Heinsberg spent the last years of her life in Bethanïe, from 1455 to 1466. The chronicle praises the pious sister Jacoba,

> who devoted herself with great fervour to the holy scriptures, copying them and reading them, especially those concerning the life and Passion of our Lord, to whom she was greatly devoted, so that she was the first in our house of God to have any knowledge of the hours of the Passion of our Lord divided into twenty-four hours, which she discovered in a book by Lord Jan van Ruusbroec, which hours she frequently copied and had copied up until the time she took ill.[89]

---

[88] Griete van Naaldwijk's exercise is found in DV, ff. 244v–245r and D, ff. 56d–57a. The convent of Diepenveen preserved its treasury of relics in the so-called 'Shrine of Eleven Thousand Virgins' (*Elfduizend Maagden-schrijn*); skulls of one or two of the virgins were among these relics (DV, f. 285r).

[89] *Haer met groote neersticheyt ghevende totter heyliger schriftueren, die te schryven en te lesen, ende dat aldermeest van den leven ende lyden ons liefs heeren, daer sy groote devotie toe hadde, soo dat sy die eerste was die in onsen godtshuyse yet kennes hadde van den uren der passien ons liefs heeren ghedelt in XXIIII uren, die sy vont in een van heer Jans van Ruysbroecx boeke, welcke uren sy dicke schreef ende dede schryven tot in haerer lester sieckten* (*Kroniek Bethanië*, 1455; Cordemans de Bruyne 1896, 78).

As indicated by the inventory drawn up after her death, this prominent woman possessed a personal manuscript containing some of the works of van Ruusbroec, in addition to fifteen other manuscripts.[90] This may well have been the manuscript that provided Jacoba van Loon with the inspiration for her meditation exercises. If that is the case, it would have contained the *Vanden XII beghinen* ('The Twelve Beguines'), for part 4 of this, van Ruusbroec's final work, constitutes a sort of breviary of the Passion. The great events in the life of Christ are described and commented upon, and arranged in order of the eight liturgical hours.[91] Could it be that the further refinement to the twenty-four hours of the day was Jacoba van Loon's own innovation?

This passage containing the meditation of Jacoba van Loon deserves closer scrutiny, in as much as I consider it to be representative of the spiritual exercises of the sisters of Windesheim. The life and Passion of Christ are at the centre here, as they are, incidentally, in almost all the exercises of the Modern Devotion.[92] The exercises are given a structure by the practice of tying parts of the reflection to the hours of the day. Reading, writing and meditation appear to be organically combined in the meditative process. Jacoba van Loon copied her beloved reflections on the Passion according to van Ruusbroec over and over, and when she could no longer do it herself, she had others do it for her. According to the passage cited, the meditation based on van Ruusbroec's commentary on the life and Passion of Christ, introduced by Jacoba van Loon, was taken up by other nuns of Bethanië. This example illustrates well how, despite the personal nature of meditation, the nuns were eager to share their experiences. In such closed monastic communities, the method of prayer or meditation of any given inspired or prominent nun could easily be copied.[93]

From the mid-fifteenth century on, there is a development in the Modern Devotion towards a more systematic and controlled form of meditation. The most important Windesheim representative of this development was Jan Mombaer (†1501) or, in Latin, Johannes Mauburnus. Mombaer, originally from Brussels, entered the Windesheim monastery of St Agnietenberg around 1477. Due to his failing health, he served for a brief period as *socius* at Brunnepe near Kampen.[94] Jan Mombaer was a devourer of books in the best tradition of the Modern Devotion and he collected huge numbers of citations

---

[90] Cordemans de Bruyne 1896, 42 and Persoons 1980, 105 (see further §6.5); cf. Foncke 1932 and Jan van Ruusbroec 1981, 122. For more on Jacoba van Loon, see §6.5.

[91] An edition of the relevant section of *Vanden XII beghinen* appears in Jan van Ruusbroec 1981–, vol. 7a, 402–537; cf. vol. 7, pp. 37–43.

[92] Cf. Mak 1935 and Caron 1985, on the Modern Devout's image of Christ.

[93] It is no coincidence that Jacomijne Costers left instructions for prayer and meditation for her sisters at Facons (see Chapter 7); the example of Alijt Bake, who implemented reforms of the inner life at Galilea, is discussed in detail in Chapter 8.

[94] On the life and works of Mombaer see Debongnie 1927; more recent and concise are Deblaere 1980 and *Moderne Devotie. Figuren en facetten* 1984, nos. 77 and 128.

and fragments in his *collectarium*. His fellow brothers recognised the significance this collection could have, especially for the younger brothers, so they produced copies of it. Mombaer's anthology of citations was disseminated under the title *Rosetum exercitiorum spiritualium* ('Rose Garden of Spiritual Exercises'). In 1496 the *Rosetum* appeared for the first time in print. Because this edition was corrupt, its *auctor intellectualis* – Mombaer collected only citations from others – felt compelled to produce a corrected edition. This made it to the press in Paris in 1510, years after the death of the compiler.[95]

The manner in which Mombaer collected his materials for reflection has its roots in the methods of reading and writing upon which the *rapiaria* are based. The gleanings of this haphazard and unorganised reading process were pulled together in an organised fashion and given a logical structure. The reading material was divided according to a segmented system, providing appropriate material for meditation for every moment of the day. Two important structuring devices were employed to this end: the so-called *rosaria* and groups of seven. The *rosaria* – there are white, red and flaming roses – consist of ten verses, each comprising five sentences, while the sevens consist of seven verses or *disticha* each, which in turn comprise seven or eight sentences. The level of the verses is tied to the seven days of the week, that of the sentences to the eight daily liturgical hours. The *chiropsalterium*, or 'hand psalter', was recommended as an extra mnemonic device, whereby the human hand functioned as a meditative 'map'. By pointing to certain parts of the hand during prayer, the themes associated with each one were automatically evoked for reflection. Using such fixed structures and mnemonic devices (rhyming verses, the *chiropsalterium*), the *Rosetum* constitutes a system whereby all the appropriate themes were touched upon during personal reflection.[96]

The advent and dissemination of the *Rosetum* is clear evidence for the changing attitude towards meditation within the Chapter of Windesheim. Jan Mombaer's new method also spread within the convents of the Chapter: both Diepenveen and Facons possessed copies of the 1510 Paris edition of the *Rosetum*.[97] Hardly anything is known about how extensive its dissemination was, or the manner in which the new method of meditation was introduced. It would appear that the Latin – there was no Middle Dutch translation – formed a considerable barrier for some of the sisters. And yet the presence of

---

[95] No edition of the *Rosetum* is available; Debongnie 1927 touches on its origin and use, spread over several chapters, and Donndorf 1929 provides an intrinsic and theological discussion.

[96] On Jan Mombaer's method of meditation, see among others Debongnie 1927 and Goossens 1980, 917–18.

[97] The Diepenveen manuscript is listed as Deventer, SAB, 113 B 8 KL; see Ledeboer 1867, 99. The Antwerp manuscript appears in the inventory at the time of dissolution of Facons: Brussel, Rijksarchief, Comité van de Religiekas 72/78, f. 160v (cf. §3.5, n. 63).

the *Rosetum* in two of the thirteen Windesheim convents is an indication that it was still quite usual for the canonesses to use Latin material in their meditations. Perhaps those without Latin received instructions concerning the *Rosetum* from the rector or a more learned sister, for example on how to use the *chiropsalterium*. It would appear, then, that the new attitudes towards meditation had a marked influence on the inner lives of the nuns of Windesheim as well.

Confirmation of this supposition is to be found in the work of Jacomijne Costers (†1503) from Facons, who, in the last decade of the fifteenth century, made a case for the reformation of the spiritual life in her convent. It is striking that she attaches great importance to standard prayers like the Our Father and Ave Maria, and hardly mentions any of the freer, individualised spiritual exercises. Jacomijne Costers bequeathed a devotional exercise dedicated to her patron saint, John the Evangelist, in which, compared to her fellow sisters from an earlier period, she pays a great deal of attention to order and systematisation. In her *Previlesien van Sint Joannes Evangelist* ('The Privileges of St John the Evangelist') she employed a numerical structure. Having first worked out the five chief privileges that God granted St John (the fourth is further divided into four parts), a further twenty-one privileges of the evangelist and visionary are discussed. The last one reports that John, like his master, Jesus, was taken up into heaven. Finally, seven items of proof are offered for this miracle, about which the author conceded there were grounds for doubt. This exercise does not achieve the extremely systematic detail and erudition of Jan Mombaer's *Rosetum*, but it is telling that Jacomijne Costers constructed her meditational exercise in a similar way. In the course of her reading, studying and meditating she collected all manner of material pertaining to John, drawn especially from the Gospel, the Epistles and Revelation of John, as well as a *vite* of the biblical visionary.[98] This material was ordered, arranged point by point and written down. The resulting text, the *Previlesien*, was used by Costers – and perhaps other sisters at Facons – as a guide and mnemonic device for her continual devotions to John the Evangelist.

Jacomijne Costers's preference for the visionary John seems an obvious one given her special gift – she herself had visions (see Chapter 7) – yet she treats her subject with a degree of restraint typical of the Windesheim canonesses. So, too, Jesus's beloved disciple John was an important source of inspiration for the German female Dominicans. This interest led among other

---

[98] Costers regularly refers in this text to her sources, for the most part books of the Bible. In *Previlesien*, f. 96r, she names the Gospel of John, his Epistles and Revelation. On f. 101r there is mention of a legend of John, from which she has derived her story of his ascension into heaven. The possible source for this may have been Jacobus de Voragine's *Legenda aurea* in the Middle Dutch translation of the so-called Bible Translator of 1360 (Scheepsma 2003).

things to the new iconography of the Christ–John statue. This representation is derived from the Gospel description of the Last Supper: while the other disciples engage in heated debate concerning which of them will betray Jesus, John rests with his head on Jesus's breast. To the female Dominicans John's pose embodied the epitome of loving submission to the Lord, which, as the brides of Christ, they regarded as their ideal. They therefore installed representations of the Christ–John statue in their convents as constant reminders of this contemplative ideal.[99] As Jacomijne Costers's example illustrates, the choir nuns of Windesheim achieved fewer, if any, such intrinsic and iconographical innovations. Her *Previlesien* reworks familiar themes relevant to John the Evangelist; Costers's innovation lies especially in her systematisation of the material, which optimises its use.[100] The practice of evoking mental images was an inextricable part of the meditational methods of the Modern Devout, but in their use of actual images and representations as an aid to this end, they chose the path of sobriety.[101]

---

[99] On the (interpretation of the) 'Christ–John statue' see Wehrli-Johns 1995 and Lewis 1996, 116–18; see the same for further (art historical) bibliography. In the Dominican reform movement John the Baptist and John the Evangelist each embodied certain aspects of the ideal of contemplation through study. In the Dominican convent of St Katharinental near Diessenhofen there even arose a dispute between the 'baptists' and the 'evangelists' (see further Schiewer 1993). According to Ziegler 1992, the thirteenth-century Beguines in the southern Netherlands introduced the worship and dissemniation of the Pietà, the image of the Suffering Mother with the dead Christ in her lap (but see Tummers 1995 for a critical response). The so-called 'Liège Psalters' also originate from beguine circles; for more on those, see Oliver 1988.

[100] A kind of cult of John does seem to have existed at Facons, given Costers's rejection of the practice of giving one another *sint Jans leskens* ('St John's lessons'; *Drij beloften*, f. 86v, cited in §7.3).

[101] The use of images and statues was certainly not forbidden. In his *Tractatus de quatuor generibus meditationum sive contemplationum* Geert Grote recommended the use of images (woodcuts) as an aid to meditation (ed. Hyma 1924, 302, an English translation in van Engen 1988a, 98–118; cf. Goossens 1952, 202 n. 81 and Waaijman 2000); of course Christ was the most important example. The Diepenveen sisterbook tells of sisters on their deathbed whose last sight was the crucifix hanging in the infirmary: for example DV, ff. 285v–286r and D, f. 81c (Liesbeth van Heenvliet) and DV, ff. 350r–v and D, ff. 150d–151a (Griete Koetkgens). Veelenturf 2000 contains a number of important articles concerning the role played by the arts in the spiritual life of the Modern Devout.

5

Written Instructions

FOR THE Windesheimers, books and writing constituted exceptional and effective instruments of reform. This is perhaps most clearly illustrated by the Chapter's decree of 1434, in which the affiliated monasteries are instructed to burn all paper copies of the *Constitutiones Capituli Windeshemensis* and, where possible, to erase and correct copies on parchment. Every monastery was to procure its own copy of the newly completed revision of the constitutions, to be made from one of the three authorised exemplars circulating through the Chapter.[1] The accurate recording of the Windesheim monastic ideal functioned as a weapon in the fight against spiritual decay, a process that had taken hold time and again in the older orders.[2] By means of an allusion to the Rule of St Augustine, the prologue to the *Constitutiones monialium* explains why writing of this kind is necessary. Unity of form promotes unity of the heart, and that unity can be better preserved if the forms are fixed, so that they may be constantly consulted.[3] The constitutions were to be read in their entirety by the entire convent each year.[4] And the Rule of St Augustine, the spiritual foundation of the Windesheim conventual life, was repeatedly and continually read within the female houses.[5]

---

[1] Van der Woude 1953, 28; cf. Lourdaux and Persoons 1964, 181 and van Dijk 1986, 26–7.
[2] Cf. Schreiner 1992, especially 43–8.
[3] *CM* 0.1–15; cf. the prologue of the Rule of St Augustine (also known as *Praeceptum*); ed. Verheijen 1967, vol. 1, 417–37, here p. 417, 3–4.
[4] See the programme of reading in *CM* 0.48–69; cf. the programme in van Dijk 1986, 293. Section 1.1 was read during the annual visitation, section 1.2 during the election of a new prioress, when appropriate. Sections 2 and 3 were read on Sundays and holy days in the chapter house, until all the material had been gone through. The procuratrix translated and explained section 4, concerning the *conversae*, during Lent for the benefit of the lay sisters, if the convent did not possess a version in the vernacular.
[5] On Saturdays in refectory the reading was drawn from the Rule (*CM* 2.9.20–4; cited in §3.6), likewise a brief passage from the Rule was read at prime (*CM* 3.4.140–59; see §2.4). The Rule of St Augustine itself prescribes a weekly reading (Verheijen 1967, vol. 1, 240–2, 437). Although every Windesheim convent would have possessed at least one manuscript containing the Rule, none survive.

Thus in the Windesheim convents, written instructions for living fulfilled a clear role in maintaining the observance. When the nuns themselves had the opportunity to take up the pen, it was more often than not to lend their fellow sisters spiritual support. This chapter analyses a number of texts in which the primary purpose is instruction. Often not only are their contents but also their transmission associated with a reform movement.

Salome Sticken's *Vivendi formula* is a rule for living for a group of sisters who had only just established a religious community. The famous prioress of Diepenveen had been asked to give them advice in their endeavour (§5.1). And the letters which the nuns of Windesheim frequently sent and received also dealt often with spiritual instruction. Correspondence was one of the few means whereby a nun (bound by enclosure) could make contact with the outside world. But here, too, severe restrictions were imposed; no letters could be written or received without the permission of the rector or prioress.[6] Perhaps it is because of this censure that the few letters that have come down to us from Windesheim nuns are as a rule religious in nature. For the most part these are copies or excerpts; only one letter is an original. In this chapter two groups of letters will be discussed, both of which are the product of a Windesheim reform initiative. The so-called *Devote epistelen* were intended for a number of recently trained nuns from the convent Jeruzalem, in Utrecht (§5.2). The reformation of the convent of Mariënberg at Helmstedt in Saxony by three nuns from Brunnepe produced an exchange of letters between the reformers and the reformed that provides intriguing insights into the practice of such reforms and the mutual relationships between the parties involved (§5.3).[7]

Finally, we return once again to the collations of Johannes Brinckerinck. Brinckerinck spoke before the nuns of Diepenveen and the sisters in Deventer, on which occasions he strove to exhort them to true virtue. These collations were strongly directive in tone: the rector provided rules for behaviour which the sisters were to put into practice. At Diepenveen fairly detailed records were made of these lessons in the spiritual life. These written records form the basis of the 'Collations of Johannes Brinckerinck,' a corpus of texts created and disseminated in a manner so characteristic of the Modern Devotion (§5.4).

---

[6] On letter writing see *CM* 2.1.60–4; see also the code of law, *CM* 3.10.7–10. A salient example is found in DV, f. 309v and D, f. 166d: Johannes Brinckerinck denies Salome van den Wiel the elder, who had only just entered the convent, access to a letter from her mother, reading to her only select passages. Her mother attempts in the letter to convince her to leave the convent, an act which Brinckerinck regarded as the work of the devil.

[7] Constable 1976 provides a typology of the medieval letter; on spiritual letters in Middle Dutch see Mertens 1990 (van Ruusbroec) and Kors 1993. An overview of all letters written by Windesheim nuns is found in Scheepsma 1997, 235–9.

5.1 A Rule of Life for Devout Sisters

The preaching of Geert Grote drastically changed the lives of many people. Hermen Sticken for example, a prominent man from Groenlo, decided to do penance for his sins. He wore a *cilicium* or penitential shirt against his naked skin, over which he put on a hair shirt, and he cut the soles from his shoes. Hermen Sticken also involved his youngest daughter, Salome, born in 1359, in his penitential exercises: she watched as he flagellated himself, and sometimes he even chastised her. At first the penance-minded father had little success, for young Salome sought out the pleasures of the world. In 1390, however, she was converted by Johan de Waal, prior of the convent of Bethlehem in Zwolle and one of Geert Grote's followers. He managed to find her a place in the Meester-Geertshuis. Sticken's qualities as a leader soon surfaced, and she was appointed rectrix. She herself was so little pleased with her position of authority that she fled the sisterhouse in 1407. After having wandered about for a while, Sticken finally arrived at Diepenveen, where Johannes Brinckerinck sought to take advantage of her unmistakable talents. She took the veil as a canoness regular in 1408. And whether Sticken wanted it or not, she was elected prioress of Diepenveen by the convent in 1412. She would hold that office until 1447.[8]

'Being silent, yielding and inclining and being mindful only of the Lord, that was her highest ambition.'[9] A more concise expression of Sticken's view of life is hardly possible. Diepenveen's first prioress appears in the Diepenveen sisterbook as a model of humility, obedience and meekness. With admiration and not a little nostalgia, the sisterbook looks back on the golden age of Diepenveen.

> They loved silence, and they stole humble works in service of one another in secret, so that no one knew who had done these for them. Or, if there was some humble deed to be performed in which they had no part, they would feel greatly wronged and could hardly endure it or get over it for some time. They loved humble works and the shabbiest of clothes and tools and places. That is, they wished to walk the royal road without any pretensions, either internal or external.[10]

---

[8] The life of Salome Sticken is described in DV, ff. 190r–225v, D, ff. 1a–21b, G, ff. 119a–120d and B, ff. 149r–164v. On her life and work, see Kühler 1914, 202–28.

[9] *Zwighen, wicken ende ducken ende den heren allene andachtich toe wesen, dat was hoer hogheste begherte* (DV, f. 194r; cf. D, f. 2d). For more on the phrase *swighen, wiken ende duken* and its variants see §5.2, n. 58.

[10] *Dat silencium waert ghemint, die oetmodighe werken stelen sie malkanderen die ene den anderen diens<t>achtich toe wesen heymelick, dat sie niet and wosten wiet ghedaen hadde. Of alster enich oetmodich warck toe done was, die daer dan niet mede and was, den dochte dat hem groet onrecht ghesciet was ende and conde hem nauwe liden ende in eenre wiellen verwinnen. Sie mynden die oetmodighe warcke ende die snodeste cleder ende die snodeste resscap inden arbeit ende die snodeste stede. Dat is: toe wanderen den*

The actions of Salome Sticken, first prioress of Diepenveen, are associated in the sisterbook with the spiritual ideal of the early days of that convent.

The unusual course of Sticken's career shows how much confidence the leaders of the Modern Devotion had in her abilities. It was probably Johan de Waal who asked her to take the veil at the convent of Our Lady at Renkum, founded in 1405.[11] The politics of Johannes Brinckerinck are also revealing: despite his knowledge of her flight from the Meester-Geertshuis, an inexcusable deed, he accepted Sticken at Diepenveen. He may even have exercised his authority in her election as prioress. The second rector of Diepenveen, Joost Claesz (1419–23), was to remark that a more devout woman than Salome Sticken was not to be found between Diepenveen and Rome.[12] And despite its weak economic basis, she was able to convince the prior of Windesheim, Johan Vos van Heusden, that Diepenveen should admit more than the current limit of fifty nuns.[13] All in all, Salome Sticken was one of the most influential female members of the Modern Devout in her day.

It therefore comes as no surprise that Hendrik van Loder (†1439), one of the founders of the Modern Devotion in Germany, sought her out for advice.[14] Hendrik received his monastic training at Windesheim, where he became a canon regular. He ultimately rose to the rank of prior of the Windesheim monastery of Frenswegen near Nordhorn, an office he held from 1414 to 1436.[15] It was not just this monastery that he helped to flourish, but from there he led the expansion of the Modern Devotion in Westphalia, as well. Loder was involved in the foundation and reform of a number of sisterhouses in this region: Mariënbrink in Borken, Mariënwolde in Frenswegen, Mariëngarde in Schüttorf, Mariënbrink in Coesfeld, and the sisterhouse of Lippstadt in the bishopric of Cologne.[16] We may assume that Hendrik Loder was responsible, together with other experts, for drawing up the statutes for these new establishments.[17] He was less sure about how the internal spiritual life was to be ordered within these convents. For this he sought the help of Salome Sticken.

---

coninclicken wech sonder alle soecklicheit van bijnnen ende van buten (DV, f. 200v; cf. D, f. 6d).

[11] G, f. 120a–b.
[12] DV, f. 202v and D, f. 8a.
[13] DV, ff. 201v–202r and D, ff. 7b–c.
[14] On Hendrik van Loder see for example Bemolt van Loghum Slaterus 1938, especially 58–62, and Kohl 1971, 86–8.
[15] On Frenswegen see Bemolt van Loghum Slaterus 1938 and Kohl 1971, 1–190.
[16] See Kohl 1968, 35–60 (Borken), 61–6 (Frenswegen), 67–83 (Schüttorf) and 84–129 (Coesfeld) and Rehm 1985, 74–8 and 83 (Lippstadt).
[17] According to Rehm 1985, 180–9 no statutes from the mid-fifteenth century in northwestern Germany have survived (some few statutes are printed in appendices 2–4). Kohl 1968 refers on occasion to lost statutes (for example pp. 92–5).

The inscription accompanying the *Vivendi formula* in the only surviving manuscript, Brussels, KB, 8849–59, sheds further light on its origins.[18]

> At the instance and repeated request of the venerable prior at Nordhorn, Hendrik van Loder, Mother Salome Sticken, once prioress at Diepenveen, provided this formulation to serve as the foundation for a spiritual edifice in some new congregation.[19]

From such formulas as *dilecte sorores* ('beloved sisters') it is abundantly clear that Sticken was addressing a female audience. Within the medieval hierarchies of authority it is also unthinkable that a woman should draw up a rule for living for men. Unfortunately, we are not told for which new establishment the *Vivendi formula* was intended. That it must have been in Westphalia seems almost certain, given that Sticken explicitly mentions the prior of Frenswegen as the spiritual leader of her readers.[20] Presumably it was one of the houses mentioned above. The text unmistakably addresses a community of Sisters of the Common Life, for it contains rules for behaviour incompatible with life in an enclosed convent, such as for a visit to town.[21] The leader of the community is referred to as the rectrix, not the prioress. With a newly established sisterhouse as its intended audience, it is extremely unlikely that the *Vivendi formula* was originally composed in Latin. We must assume that Sticken wrote her rule for living in the vernacular, but this original version has not come down to us. That we possess even the Latin version is thanks to an initiative of the Heer-Florenshuis, where around 1500 historical materials pertaining to the Modern Devotion were being collected and compiled. On this occasion a number of Middle Dutch texts were translated into Latin.[22]

The *Vivendi formula* must date to between 1435 and 1439.[23] The *terminus ante quem* is 1439, for that is the year of Hendrik van Loder's death. In the course of her narrative Sticken refers to the physical weakness that prevents her from participating in manual labour.[24] From her *vite* we know that she suffered a mild stroke some ten or eleven years before stepping down as prioress, i.e. in either 1436 or 1437.[25] She must have written the *Vivendi formula* after this event. The only known manuscript was produced on St Margaret's day (13 July) of the year 1501.

---

[18] Ed. Kühler 1914, 362–80; van Engen 1988a, 176–86 provides an English translation.
[19] Van Engen 1988a, 176. *Hanc viuendi formulam edidit mater Salome Sticken, priorissa quondam in Diepenven, ad instanciam et multiplicatas preces venerabilis prioris in Noorthorn, fratris Henrici Loeder, ut esset fundamentum structure in quadam nova congregacione* (Kühler 1914, 362).
[20] Ed. Kühler 1914, 378; van Engen 1988a, 185.
[21] Ed. Kühler 1914, 369; van Engen 1988a, 179.
[22] Scheepsma 1996a, 226–7 and 237.
[23] Cf. Kühler 1914, 360–1.
[24] Ed. Kühler 1914, 374; van Engen 1988a, 182–3.
[25] DV, f. 214v and D, f. 15c.

Sticken's rule for living consists of two parts. The first part is addressed to the sisters and deals with daily life, whereas the second part is intended for the rectrix. This division between material for the *prelaten* ('superiors') and the *ondersaten* ('subordinates') is not unusual in Middle Dutch religious literature.[26] Sticken tells from her own experience how best to provide leadership to a community that wishes to live according to the spirit of the Modern Devotion. She impresses upon the sisters the importance of obeying the orders of their superiors. Central to both sections is the attitude with which the sisters and their rectrix are to perform their tasks. In this respect the *Vivendi formula* differs markedly from statutes and constitutions, which regulate in particular external behaviour and tasks. Instructing, advising, but at times also asking for understanding, Sticken shows her spiritual sisters how they may devote their lives entirely to God.

The first part of the *Vivendi formula* deals with various aspects of life in the sisterhouse. The first three paragraphs – *lombards*, or paragraph markers, appear in the Brussels manuscript – are devoted to the sisters' meditation and personal prayer. Following this, all kinds of subjects are touched on. For example, Sticken explains to her readers or listeners how they are to conduct the chapter of faults in a dignified manner, where and when they are to maintain silence, and why they are to perform manual labour. Here is a passage on obedience, by way of illustration. Sticken refers to her own position at Diepenveen where, thanks to the devoted and obedient efforts of her helpers, she is able to perform her duties in the proper spirit.

> Just as I can with my helpers and sisters, though I am much too unworthy and useless for the office imposed on me. Indeed I bear the burden of office almost without burden when I consider the humble submission of the sisters, how they humbly yield and incline their wills, how they interject about nothing and speak only on that which pertains to their care, how they are intent only upon preserving pure and unsullied consciences and pleasing the Lord alone.[27]

---

[26] See for example the *Bienboeck* by Thomas of Cantimpré (ed. Stutvoet-Joanknecht 1990) and the excerpts from the first sermon of Jan van Schoonhoven to the Chapter General of Windesheim, bearing the titles *Vanden prelaten* and *Vanden ondersaten* ('Concerning the prelates' and 'Concerning the subordinates', respectively; Obbema 1985, 284).

[27] Van Engen 1988a, 179. *Quemadmodum ego facere possum cum adiutricibus meis et omnibus sororibus meis, quamuis indigna sum et nimium vilis et inutilis ad officium mihi impositum. Verumtamen onus officij pene sine onere suffero, quando considero sororum humilem subiectionem, quomodo scilicet humiliter cedant et se inclinent, de nullo se intromittentes aut loquentes preterquam de eo, quod ad curam earum pertinet, ad hoc solum intente, ut consciencias suas puras et mundas conseruare possint et soli Domino complacere* (Kühler 1914, 370).

Sticken even states that the sisters of Diepenveen would without hesitation set fire to the convent if she ordered them to.[28]

The instructions for the rectrix are divided into four parts in this manuscript. In the first section, Sticken relates how the mother superior must be willing to be equal to the sisters as far as she can, in order to avoid jealousy. It is her task to admonish and punish when necessary, but with love and benevolence. Sticken stresses that the sisters who are experiencing difficulties must be treated with tenderness and understanding. From the sisterbook we know that this exemplary prioress acted according to this very spirit. As rectrix of the Meester-Geertshuis she secretly took food from the kitchen for a sister who due to illness tended to eat more than the others.[29] The sections that follow deal with issues of an organisational and routine nature. Under the heading of 'hospitality', Sticken advises the rectrix to choose carefully those sisters who are to serve the guests, for they had to be able to resist worldly temptation. At the same time she argues emphatically for holding a chapter of faults on feast days.[30] She ends her rule for living with a comment on the great importance of maintaining strict silence; here, too, it is thanks to the sisterbook that we know how important this was to Sticken.[31]

Salome Sticken compiled her rule for living with the help of various sources, among them presumably Florens Radewijns's *rapiarium*.[32] Her own experiences as leader of the Meester-Geertshuis and Diepenveen formed the foundation, however, as is evident from repeated references to concrete situations. The way in which Sticken mentions Diepenveen in passing would also suggest that her audience knew the name of this famous convent well. The living examples from experience which she chooses serve to show the new sisters that the heavy demands of the ideals of the Modern Devotion are in fact not as difficult as they may seem.

Another means of convincing the audience of the *Vivendi formula* is the citation of anecdotes and words of wisdom from the Christian tradition. Among other things, Sticken refers to the industrious manual labour of the Holy Desert Fathers in Egypt.[33] Because consultation of patristic sources was

---

[28] Ed. Kühler 1914, 370; van Engen 1988a, 180.
[29] DV, ff. 211r–212r and D, ff. 12d–13d. Could this be an example of *sacra boulimia* (cf. Bell 1985, on *sacra anorexia*)?
[30] In this Sticken was treading on thin ice: the conduct of chapter of faults by semi-religious – the intended audience of the *Vivendi formula* – was a controversial issue in her day (Post 1957, vol. 2, 344); cf. also *Super modo vivendi*, where it is stipulated that the brothers and sisters are obliged to correct one another (see §3.8).
[31] DV, ff. 217r–v and D, ff. 16d–17b; cf. DV, f. 200v (cited in this section) and D, f. 6d.
[32] Van Woerkum 1951, 24 maintains that the *Vivendi formula* shows strong similarities to the *rapiarium* of Radewijns, the *Libellus 'Omnes, inquit, artes'*. An exemplar of this was on hand in the library of Diepenveen, now MS Deventer, SAB, I, 61 (11 L 1) (cf. §3.8, n. 137).
[33] Ed. Kühler 1914, 376; van Engen 1988a, 183.

such standard practice among the Modern Devout in the early years, it is not possible to determine whether Sticken is citing the Lives of the Fathers directly here, or taking this example from the lessons offered by the rector. The situation is different in the case of two citations from Bernard of Clairvaux. Sticken tells how the great Cistercian abbot and his fellow brothers kept silent during manual labour, so that the only thing to be heard was the sound of hoes and other tools.[34] The term Sticken uses here, *legitur* ('one reads'), indicates that she is quoting directly from a written source, probably Konrad von Eberbach's *Exordium magnum*.[35] The formulation of a second citation of St Bernard points as well to a possible direct knowledge of his writings: 'As Bernard says, work of the hands frequently expresses remorse of the heart and makes devotion purer.'[36] Sticken also makes use of a few quotations and statements from well-known Modern Devout. To Geert Grote is attributed the idea that subordinates should always obey their superiors, even if they were ordered to set fire to the house.[37] Immediately following this is a statement by Johannes Brinckerinck, probably drawn from one of his collations. The rector explains that consistent obedience to one's superiors is the most fruitful approach, even if they are possessed by the devil and the orders they give are unworthy. Finally, Sticken refers to a statement by Geert Grote: 'I am abandoned inwardly by the Lord, outwardly I am of no consequence and looked down upon by all men, and to bear this patiently exceeds in merit all contemplation.'[38] With this statement she takes a fairly firm stand against potential attempts on the part of her intended audience to achieve mystical experience.

It is no coincidence that Salome Sticken invokes both founders of the movement of devout female religious, Geert Grote and Johannes Brinckerinck, as venerable authorities. In so doing, she aligns her *Vivendi formula* with an ideal that had proven exceptionally successful. In her rule for female devout, there are two recurrent themes that are characteristic of the Modern Devotion. Sticken demands absolute obedience from the sisters. She discusses both the necessary humility of the rank and file (the *ondersaten*) and the behaviour of those who are called to an office of authority involving tasks of responsibility. The possibilities for shaping the spiritual life according to one's own lights are thus limited, indeed. The second theme addresses the

---

[34] Ed. Kühler 1914, 374–5; van Engen 1988a, 182.
[35] On the *Exordium* see §6.2, n. 54.
[36] Van Engen 1988a, 183. *Teste namque Bernardo, opus manuum sepius exprimit compunctionem cordis et deuocionem puriorem efficit* (ed. Kühler 1914, 376).
[37] Ed. Kühler 1914, 371; van Engen 1988a, 180.
[38] Van Engen 1988a, 184. *Magister Gerardus Magnus, venerabilis pater noster, in quodam loco scribit, quod intus derelinqui a Domino et foris nichilipendi et despici ab omnibus hominibus et hec pacienter posse portare, excedit in merito omnem contemplacionem* (ed. Kühler 1914, 377). This statement does not appear in the works of Geert Grote; cf. Goossens 1952, 145 n. 12.

proper attitude more directly: the sisters must achieve a state of inner detachment and internal submission. The quotation from Bernard of Clairvaux illustrates the central importance of the concept of *compunctio cordis*: the awareness of sin which compels man to humility.[39] Sticken demonstrates that she herself fulfils these requirements, at the end of her section concerning the convent:

> Dearest sisters, I write these simple and crude things to you as if you did not know them. I hope however, that you know many more and greater things than I am able to write.[40]

5.2 Devout Epistles

Into the *vite* of sister Ave Sonderlants a brief biography of Aechte Eernstes (†1444) from Utrecht has been inserted.[41] This pious widow led a devout life, which also had an impact on her children. Her daughter Dyliane took the veil at Diepenveen, another daughter secured a place in the convent of St Cecilia in Utrecht and two of her sons were ordained as priests. And Aechte plays a modest role in the *vite* of Katharina van Naaldwijk as well. In 1413 Katharina's mother, the lady of Naaldwijk, and Katharina's aunt, Heylewich van Heenvliet, travelled to Diepenveen to attend Katharina's profession. When the young Liesbeth van Heenvliet fell ill along the way, it was decided she should be left with the 'spiritual woman' Aechte.[42] Aechte was apparently known to be a trustworthy supporter of the Modern Devotion. In the event, Liesbeth did not wish to be left behind; she continued on, ill, to Diepenveen, never to leave that convent again.

Aechte Eernstes was one of those energetic – and wealthy – figures who provided the new Modern Devotion movement with the opportunity to spread its wings. At the beginning of the fifteenth century she founded, together with a number of other women, a religious community near the chapel of Jeruzalem, just outside the city walls of Utrecht.[43] In due course the plan of converting this community into a regular convent according to the Windesheim observance arose. To this end an appeal was made to the now famous Diepenveen. According to Johannes Busch, first three and later another two sisters from Jeruzalem travelled to Diepenveen to be trained there in the practice of the monastic life. The sisterbook mentions the latter

---

[39] On *compunctio cordis* in this context, see Goossens 1952, 132–41; this attitude forms the basis of spirituality in the Modern Devotion.
[40] Van Engen 1988a, 184. *Sorores carissime, hec rudia et simplicia scripsi vobis, tamquam nescientibus ea. Spero tamen, quod plura sapiatis et maiora, quam scribere valeam* (ed. Kühler 1914, 378).
[41] DV, ff. 360r–v and D, ff. 158c–159a.
[42] DV, f. 272r and D, f. 72d; on Liesbeth van Heenvliet see §6.1, n. 24.
[43] On this establishment, see DV, f. 360v and D, f. 158c–d.

two by name: Clemens van Sconenouwen and Griete van Groenevelt.⁴⁴ When these two sisters returned to Utrecht, probably in 1418, the choir nun Liesbeth van Delft (†1423) and the *conversa* Belie van Düsseldorf (†1444) went with them, in order to lay the spiritual foundation at the new convent. Liesbeth van Delft became rectrix of Jeruzalem in 1418. Two years later she was elected its first prioress, an office she held until her death in 1423.⁴⁵

Aechte Eernstes's young convent sought and found support from the trend-setting convent of Diepenveen. They were allowed to train five nuns there and moreover succeeded in bringing two experienced nuns from Diepenveen to Utrecht. The establishment of the convent of Jeruzalem was also fortified in writing by means of three spiritual letters, known as the *Devote epistelen* ('Devout Epistles').⁴⁶ These letters bear inscriptions and postscripts of the following tenor: 'Here begins a devout letter, addressed to certain sisters at Jeruzalem outside Utrecht, who have been sent to Diepenveen to gain experience in the ways of the order.'⁴⁷ From this it is quite clear that the letters were associated with the reformation of Jeruzalem. The addressees of the *Devote epistelen* must logically have been the five sisters from Jeruzalem – or at least some of them – sent to Diepenveen to learn the Windesheim custom. But who is the author of these spiritual letters?

D. A. Brinkerink, the editor of the *Devote epistelen*, suspects that the letters were written by a sister from Jeruzalem. She would have been writing to her fellow sisters from Utrecht who were then staying at Diepenveen.⁴⁸ It seems rather unlikely, however, that a sister from the recently founded convent of Jeruzalem would have written these letters, for the author of the *Devote epistelen* speaks with great authority and with a deep knowledge of monastic matters. In my view, we should instead look to someone with extensive experience as a leader of female religious. Given their historical context, it is likely that the *Devote epistelen* were sent from Diepenveen to Jeruzalem. It was after all Diepenveen that provided the spiritual foundation of the new convent.⁴⁹ According to this theory, the *Devote epistelen* constitute a written extension of the reform of Jeruzalem. The *Devote epistelen* may have been formally addressed to the sisters staying at Diepenveen, but they provided in fact a spiritual boost for the new convent as a whole. The two convents apparently

---

⁴⁴ Grube 1886, 363–4, and DV, f. 60r and D, ff. 132d–133a.
⁴⁵ The life of Liesbeth van Delft is recounted in DV, ff. 54r–62r and D, ff. 130b–133c. Johannes Busch also writes about her reform efforts (Grube 1886, 364).
⁴⁶ Ed. Brinkerink 1907.
⁴⁷ *Hier begynt een devoete epistel, ghescreven tot sommeghen susteren van Jherusalem buten Utrecht, die toe Diepenven ghesent waren om hem te proeven inder orden.* This is a reconstruction based on the inscriptions in *Epistel I*, f. 33r and *Epistel II*, f. 53r; cf. *Epistel III*, f. 53r. See also Brinkerink 1907, 318–19.
⁴⁸ Brinkerink 1907, 320.
⁴⁹ The text of *Epistel I*, ff. 33r–v, even refers to their stay at Diepenveen.

remained in close contact even after the departure of the five sisters from Utrecht in 1418.

If my hypothesis concerning the origin of the *Devote epistelen* at Diepenveen is correct, then the author of these letters must have held an office of authority there. Inevitably, the name of Johannes Brinckerinck, the man who enjoyed such authority within the movement of female devout, suggests itself. Brinckerinck died in 1419, which places his authorship just within the realm of chronological possibility. Militating against this is the fact that the rector of Diepenveen was not otherwise known to be an author. Moreover, there are other indications that point perhaps to a female author of the *Devote epistelen*; these will be dealt with in the discussion of the texts that follows. Salome Sticken is in that regard the most likely candidate, but we may certainly not rule out the possibility that another wise and experienced nun, for example Katharina van Naaldwijk, might have written these spiritual letters.

The first *Devote epistel* is explicitly addressed to the sisters of Jeruzalem. Frequent references to the *doechteren van Jherusalem* ('Daughters of Jerusalem') of Canticles 3:10–11, and further comparisons of the convent Jeruzalem to the holy city, leave no room for doubt. The author is clearly pleased by the new sisters' choice of the monastic life, but emphasises that that life will only truly begin when they put their choice into practice. They may have left the world physically, but now they must in their hearts take leave of all that they have felt connected to. From the moment when they take the veil only one thing counts: following Christ in his love for mankind. This *Epistel* is devoted entirely to achieving the attitude appropriate for a Bride of Christ.

The author of the *Epistelen* uses not only his or her own knowledge and experience, but draws deeply, as well, from devotional literature. The first *Devote epistel* is based in part on Hendrik Mande's *Een boecskijn van drien staten eens bekierden mensche* ('A Little Book on the Three States of the Convert').[50] Mande distinguishes the following three states: the working life, the spiritual or inner life and the contemplative life. Rather long passages concerning the latter two of these states are included in this epistle, though they have not been copied verbatim.[51] One of the most striking changes is the shift from the first to the second person: Mande uses *wi* ('we'), the *Devote epistel* opts instead for *ghi* ('you'). Like many other devout, Hendrik Mande attempted to internalise a given devotional text entirely by copying it. By 'converting' the pronouns to the first person he was able to personalise the

---

[50] Cf. Mertens 1986, 57–8 and 93–7, respectively. *Een boecskijn van drien staten eens bekierden mensche* has been edited by Moll 1854, vol. 1, 263–92. On Hendrik Mande see also §1.2. He in turn borrowed much from van Ruusbroec, among other things from *Die geestelike brulocht*, *Van VII trappen* and *Vanden XII beghinen* (cf. Willeumier-Schalij 1981, 313–16).

[51] Moll 1854, vol. 1, 278–81 and 291–2.

message more fully.⁵² The author of this *Devote epistel* read Mande's work, took from it what was useful, but adapted the text to the epistolary form.⁵³

The second *Devote epistel* offers a lesson on purity. The letter opens with the words of Christ, 'Blessed are the clean of heart, for they shall see God' (Matt. 5:8). Next the author addresses the intended audience, who have cut all ties with the outside world. In so doing they have taken the first decisive step towards inner purity, but they do not yet know what is necessary for further purification. The spiritual person must strive after three kinds of purity: purity of the body, purity of the heart and purity of the spirit.⁵⁴ These three points are developed one by one in this brief letter, with the greatest attention being paid to the second. Purity of the heart is like a lamp that burns the oil (provided by God) of good will.

In composing these two letters the author has made use of an examplar of van Ruusbroec's *Vanden XII beghinen*.⁵⁵ The chapter concerning the 'tripartite purity' has been fairly faithfully copied.⁵⁶ *Vanden XII beghinen* has in this case been 'read with the pen', as it were, just as Mande's *Boecskijn van drien staten* had been for the first epistle. The author of the epistle follows van Ruusbroec's argument for the most part, but he or she often chooses different phrases and expressions, and either abandons the rhyming passages altogether or converts them into prose. This pattern is broken towards the end of the discussion of the second theme, where the epistle deviates from the source. There is also a brief shift in narrative point of view: the epistle follows van Ruusbroec's imperative forms faithfully, but here shifts to the first person plural. For a moment, then, author and audience are one. It seems unlikely that a priest like Johannes Brinckerinck would identify so closely with his flock.

In this interlude it is argued that purity of heart can only be achieved through *duken, swigen ende liden* ('inclining, being silent and suffering'), a variant of the well-known devout adage *swighen, wiken ende duken* ('being silent, yielding and inclining') – in Latin *tacere, cedere et inclinari* – an expression of submission and humility.⁵⁷ It is striking that the spiritual teachings of

---

⁵² Hendrik Mande follows the same procedure in for example *Een spieghel der waerheit*; cf. Mertens 1994b, 63–6.

⁵³ Cf. Staubach 1994, on the developmental process of reform literature in the late Middle Ages.

⁵⁴ *Epistel II*, f. 47v; cf. the tripartite doctrine of purity of Gerard Zerbolt van Zutphen, which he associates with the communion (Gerrits 1986, 212–19).

⁵⁵ Brinkerink 1907, 321 (using an older edition of van Ruusbroec). On the *Beghinen* see §4.3, n. 91; cf. n. 45: Mande also borrowed from this work for the *Boecskijn*.

⁵⁶ Jan van Ruusbroec 1981–, vol. 7. This chapter is part of volume three of *Vanden XII beghinen*, dealing with the planets. Geert Grote was particularly critical of this astrological section in his letter to van Ruusbroec and the monks of Groenendaal (ed. Mulder 1933, 107–9; see further Ampe 1945, 57–8).

⁵⁷ Brinkerink 1907, 395 n. 41 notes various instances and variations; see also Brinkerink 1904, 7 n. 9.

Salome Sticken are also summed up in the triad *swighen, wiken ende duken* (see §5.1).⁵⁸ And in her *Vivendi formula* Sticken provides a further variant of this expression, when she asks of the Diepenveen sisters that they humbly yield and prostrate: *humiliter cedant et se inclinent*.⁵⁹ Such parallels could be an indication that it was Sticken who wrote the second *Devote epistel*.

Other evidence for her authorship is to be found in the opening of the third *Devote epistel*. The author refers there to a special request from the nuns of Utrecht.⁶⁰ Whether this request was made orally or in writing is not clear, but the phrase does prove that Diepenveen and Jeruzalem remained in contact for quite some time. The author of the epistle writes:

> Dear and beloved ones! You have requested, as I understand, that I should explain to you briefly in writing how you might best observe the good deeds and Passion of our Lord inwardly, in order that you might be inspired and enflamed with love for him.⁶¹

In fact the author considers him or herself too poor (in spirit), too blind and too incompetent to broach the thorny topic of the inner spiritual life. But instead of remaining silent, as the philosopher would do, he or she prefers to reveal his or her deficiencies. After all, Christ will fill one's mouth (Ps. 80:11) with the correct words, and moreover the corn is not to be hidden from the people (Prov. 11:26). She is convinced of the power of her method, however imperfect her own execution of it may be.

> But if I am not able to arrange or write the words in a very appealing and attractive manner, on account of my clumsiness and rudeness, you may yourself rearrange and cast those words in a more pleasing fashion, just as the spirit of God and inspired thought shall guide and teach you.⁶²

The sentiment expressed here is somewhat reminiscent of what we know of Salome Sticken from other sources, though one should keep in mind that too much personal significance cannot be attached to such expressions of humility. Sticken also ends her *Vivendi formula* with a reference to her 'rude'

---

⁵⁸ DV, f. 194r (cited at §5.1) and D, f. 2d; cf. also DV, f. 139r: *toe wicken ende toe ducken*, and D, f. 38d: *te wijken ende duken* (Jutte van Ahaus), and DV, f. 179v: *toe zwighen ende toe ducken*, and D, f. 119c: *tot swijgen ende duyken* (Dymme van Rijssen).
⁵⁹ Ed. Kühler 1914, 370.
⁶⁰ Cf. Kors 1993, 62–3.
⁶¹ *Lieve ende ghemynde! ghi hebt begheert, als my dunct, dat ic u een coerte maniere woelde schrieven, hoe ghi u alre beest oefenen moecht van binnen inden waeldaden ende inder passien ons lieven heren, op dat ghi verwecket mocht werden ende ontsteken tot synre mynnen* (Epistel III, f. 53v).
⁶² *Mer al ist dat ic die worde alsoe suetelick ende alsoe treckelick nit setten of schrieven en kan overmyds mynre plompheit ende rudicheit, ghi moeget selve die woerde in merre mynliecheit veranderen ende formieren, als u die geest Gades ende verlichte reden wael wisen ende leren sal* (Epistel III, f. 54r).

(*rudia*) style of writing.⁶³ A comparable apology for a deficient and unpolished style, as well as the admonition to recast the message in one's own words, occurs too in the sisterbook, in the closing section of a wedding allegory composed by Salome Sticken and Katharina van Naaldwijk.⁶⁴

The third *Devote epistel* advises the sisters of Jeruzalem to conduct their meditational exercises at various times during the day: in the morning after rising, during mass and at night. This tripartite division is a common one for the female Modern Devout; it is also found, for example, in Salome Sticken's rule for living and in the collations of Johannes Brinckerinck. Next follow a number of items of practical advice. The value of the exercises lies in the repetition and in the intensity with which they are performed. The desired blessing may sometimes be long in coming, yet one should nevertheless 'strive to wring honey from the stone' (*pinen honich te sueken uut den steen*).⁶⁵ In this way, and like any serious mystic, the author dismisses the notion of a feverish quest for the divine experience.

The remainder of the third epistle consists mainly of prayers to be used as points of departure by the new nuns. For example, an entire series of prayers is provided for the mass. The first is addressed to Christ and emphasises the great importance of his sacrifice. Next follows a prayer in which Christ's suffering is intensely experienced, at the end of which his wounds are worshipped. The next prayer asks Maria, God's mother, for mercy and intercession through her son. Finally, prayers on behalf of deceased relatives and to the Saints are provided.

The aspiring nuns of Utrecht acquired the necessary practical experience at Diepenveen, but upon their return to Jeruzalem they still needed some spiritual support. In this respect the three *Devote epistelen* provide the finishing touches. The contents of the letters are well suited to meet the needs of a convent in development, which is what Jeruzalem was in 1418. The *Devote epistelen* are reform texts which give expression to the vision of the Chapter of Windesheim concerning certain spiritual matters. This becomes even more evident from the new application they later received. Between 1422 and 1427 a sisterhouse was established in Venray (Limburg), dedicated to St Ursula and her Eleven Thousand Virgins and St Anthony. In 1467 this sisterhouse adopted the Rule of St Augustine. Though its patronage was not changed, the convent was often referred to thereafter as 'Jeruzalem'. It is no coincidence that the only manuscript containing all three *Devote epistelen* comes from this convent. After all, the epistles address the 'Daughters of Jeruzalem', and moreover the newly minted canonesses from Venray found

---

⁶³ Cited at §5.1, n. 40.
⁶⁴ DV, f. 266v; for this wedding allegory, see §6.1.
⁶⁵ *Epistel* III, f. 54v. The quotation and its surrounding text are reminiscent of the exemplum given by van Ruusbroec in *Die geestelike brulocht* (Jan van Ruusbroec 1981–, vol. 3, 335 and 337).

themselves in exactly the same position as their sisters from Utrecht some fifty years earlier, for they, too, were unfamiliar with the intricacies of the monastic life. From the second half of the fifteenth century on, the convent at Venray was spiritually administered from the Heer-Florenshuis. Perhaps one of the brothers from Deventer knew the *Devote epistelen* and saw the opportunity for their renewed use in a new Jeruzalem.[66]

5.3 Five Letters on the Reformation of Mariënberg in Helmstedt

Johannes Busch (†c.1480) is not only the best known chronicler of both the monastery and the Chapter of Windesheim, he was also one of the most important reformers from this circle. The monastery of Sulta near Hildesheim, of which Busch was provost, was the headquarters to a large-scale reform campaign in the German-speaking regions. Johannes Busch's efforts were closely tied to the politics of Nicholas of Kues (1401–64), the papal legate to the German lands, for whom the reformation of the monasteries constituted a prime objective. The activities carried out there by Johannes Busch were vigorously supported by the legate.[67]

In his *Liber de reformatione monasteriorum*, Johannes Busch recounts numerous reforms carried out under the auspices of the Chapter of Windesheim.[68] He does not hesitate to draw attention to his own merits. His account may be regarded as the memoirs of a monastic reformer. One of the endeavours Busch describes in great detail is the reformation of the convent of Mariënberg at Helmstedt, in Saxony, between 1462 and 1465, in which three nuns from the Windesheim convent of Brunnepe were also involved. Six chapters in his *Liber de reformatione* are devoted to this reformation. In the first chapter Busch describes the circumstances and progress of the reforma-

---

[66] The history of Jeruzalem in Venray is described in a fifteenth-century chronicle preserved in MS Grubbenvorst, Ursulinen, archiefdepot Jeruzalem (no shelfmark) (Verschueren 1949, 699–700), and edited by Everts 1866 and L. Peters 1900 (cf. Scheepsma 1996a, 338 n. 70). Verschueren 1949, 693–8 provides a brief synopsis of the history of Jeruzalem, augmented by van Dijk 1986, 684–5. The new convent in Venray had a constitution that bears some resemblance to the *CM*, but it also differs from it in many important ways (van Dijk 1986, 684–95). According to Verschueren 1949, 695 the fifteenth-century manuscript containing the statutes of Venray was written in the same hand as the manuscript containing the *Devote epistelen*. Van Dijk 1986, 687 identifies Albert van den Beesten as the scribe of a manuscript with statutes (MS Grubbenvorst, Ursulinen, archiefdepot Jeruzalem MS 11). Albert van den Beesten, from the Heer-Florenshuis, would thus also have been responsible for copying the *Devote epistelen*.

[67] On Johannes Busch see also §1.3; on his reform activities see van der Woude 1947, 57–141. Meuthen 1982 provides a biographical sketch of Nicholas of Kues; for more on him §1.1, n. 54.

[68] The second book is devoted to the reformation of 25 convents in Saxony (Bange 1996).

tion of Mariënberg. The remaining five chapters consist of copies of letters pertaining to this endeavour. All of them are either written by or addressed to the three nuns from Brunnepe. Not only are these letters unique examples of correspondence by Windesheim nuns, but they provide information about the rationale behind the Chapter's reform efforts, as well.[69]

Busch first describes how in the early 1460s dissatisfaction with the observance had arisen in the convent of Helmstedt. A number of local authorities decided that reformation was needed. Without the concrete help of Windesheim, however, success was not guaranteed, so they called in the aid of the renowned Johannes Busch. His proposal was to send a few qualified nuns from the convent of Brunnepe to Germany. Busch had done pastoral work in Brunnepe between 1431–4 and thus knew the convent well.[70] His choice of the convent in the province of Kampen is an indication that the status of Diepenveen as a centre for reform had slipped somewhat after the middle of the fifteenth century.[71] On 2 May 1462, Johannes Busch presented his plan to the prior superior, Dirk Grave. He received permission to take with him three suitable nuns from Brunnepe, whom he selected with the aid of the prioress. One of the chief requirements for their selection was that they be *in scientiis scholasticalibus eruditas* (freely translated, 'well educated').[72] In the end the choir nuns Tecla and Ida and the *conversa* Aleid were chosen. Concerning the work of the first of these, Busch writes:

> Sister Tecla, who was more than sufficiently well versed in grammar, gave the young girls and the nuns singing lessons and, together with the subprioress, lessons in other subjects, too. Their students made such good progress that they could understand and explain Holy Scripture well, and expertly compose letters or missives in proper Latin, as I have witnessed and verified with my own eyes.[73]

The letters of the sisters of Brunnepe and Mariënberg subsequently published by Busch constitute in his view the best proof of this, as he remarks: *ut in*

---

[69] These five letters constitute chapters XXVI–XXX of *De reformatione monasteriorum*, of which Busch produced two redactions, a first one in 1471 followed by a second in 1473. In the edition by Grube 1886 (of the 1473 redaction), they appear on pp. 622–4, 624–5, 625, 626–7 and 627, respectively. On the reformation of Helmstedt cf. van der Woude 1947, 132–3, Axters 1956, 169, Lingier 1993, 283 and Bange 1996, 147–8.

[70] Van der Woude 1947, 66–7; Busch's precise role is not clear.

[71] According to Van der Woude 1947, 129–30 Busch worked for a brief time in Diepenveen, so he knew the status of the convent first-hand.

[72] Cf. Lingier 1993, 283 and Bange 1996, 148 n. 22.

[73] *Soror Tecla in grammatica competenter docta iuvenes instruxit puellas et moniales in cantu, in scientiis scholasticalibus una cum suppriorissa, que in tantum in eis profecerunt, ut scripturas divinas clare intelligerent, exponere scirent et literas sive missivas in bono latino magistraliter dictarent, sicut ad oculum ipse vidi et examinavi* (Grube 1886, 620–1).

epistolis subsequentibus aperte ostenditur ('as is clearly demonstrated by the letters that follow').

But first there follows a letter from the great reformer himself, which he wrote from the convent of Stederborch, shortly after he had delivered the nuns from Brunnepe in a wagon. He calls the aspirant reformers' attention to their momentous task: the preparation of good souls for eternal life. Busch is convinced that their work will be closely observed and assessed from heaven. He has sympathy for the fact that the change in living conditions and conventions will not be easy for the nuns from Kampen. But they must not recall with longing the flesh pots of Egypt (Ex. 16:3) – in their case the big fish to be had from the river Ijssel in Kampen. Ida, Tecla and Aleid could consider their selection as reformers a great privilege; their work would speed them on their way to heaven.

In the course of the year 1465 the three nuns returned to Brunnepe. On the day after their departure, two letters from Mariënberg were sent after them. The first was written by the prioress Helena and the procuratrix Geseke. Apparently they wrote the letter in the middle of the night, for they write that they must hurry because matins was about to begin. In an informal style they describe the great sadness caused by the departure of the nuns from Brunnepe. Sister Mettike Guestyn, for example, is so sad that she is unable to eat or drink. The sisters Ida, Tecla and Aleid appear to have been much loved in Mariënberg: the prioress and the procuratrix send them 'as many greetings as there are stars in the heaven'.

The second letter from Helmstedt was written by Sister Johanna Penninczac. She writes a brief missive on behalf of the pupils in the conventual school, addressed to sister Tecla, who had taught them at Mariënberg. Sister Johanna also describes the great feeling of emptiness left by the departure of their teacher. Fortunately they will all meet again in heaven. The most important function of the letter, says Johanna, is to demonstrate that the pupils had indeed learned something: they can now compose letters in Latin.

The nuns from Brunnepe found time to answer both these heart-felt missives. And they wrote in Latin, too, which makes their letters the only known texts originally composed in Latin by Windesheim choir nuns. Together Ida, Tecla and Aleid thank the sisters of Helmstedt for their letters full of love, a love which they can hardly repay. The reformers stress that their disciples have been very receptive to their lessons and advice, allowing the love of God to grow within them. This letter shows that the teachings of the sisters from Brunnepe had a dual purpose: they promoted the learning of virtue as well as the comprehension of good texts.

The last letter was written by Sister Tecla, who addresses in particular Johanna Penninczac and her fellow sisters. The former teacher compliments her pupils on their Latin letter. Her lessons have clearly borne fruit. Tecla expresses the hope that the educated nuns will now in turn expose their uneducated fellow sisters to spiritual literature. Perhaps they, too, will participate in the reformation of convents, where they will teach other nuns how to read and write. This wish was in all likelihood fulfilled, for according to Busch Mariënberg was instrumental in the reformation of two other convents.[74]

In 1465 Johannes Busch escorted the three sisters from Brunnepe back to their mother convent by wagon. The immediate occasion for the return was the illness of Sister Tecla, but by then the reformation of Mariënberg could be considered a success. Busch sprinkles his narrative with numerous interesting details concerning the journey, which illustrates once again how the reformation of a convent in the Middle Ages was no trifling task. The story borders on the comical when Busch tells of the fall from the stairs of the rather plump (*spitta satis et pinguis*) sister Ida. She damaged her hip in the fall, with the result that she could not walk and could hardly sit. It fell to Busch, who did not wish to delay the trip until she recovered, to help her into the wagon. After a long trip, with stops along the way at many convents, Ida, Tecla and Aleid eventually arrived home safe and sound.

The correspondence between the nuns of Helmstedt and Brunnepe shows all the signs of topical writing. The tone of the letters is particularly friendly and their messages are personal in nature. Only the letter of consolation written by Johannes Busch is rather formal, though even he manages to strike a cordial tone. But then again, Busch held a church office of authority and led the reformation of Helmstedt. It was from that position of authority that he wrote to the three nuns from Brunnepe concerning the execution of his plans. That their letters have been preserved is thanks only to the historical interest of Johannes Busch. Unlike the *Devote epistelen* to the convent of Jeruzalem, these letters possessed no broader application which would allow them to be used elsewhere as inspiration for the spiritual life.[75] Their relatively wide dissemination is largely thanks to the pride Johannes Busch took in the successful reformation of a convent. It seems that, apart from these letters, the reformation of Helmstedt produced no real reformation literature, though it is to be assumed that the nuns from Brunnepe provided the sisters of Helmstedt with at least one manuscript containing spiritual songs in the vernacular. This is somewhat surprising, given the stress in the letters upon Latin and spiritual literature.[76]

---

[74] Grube 1886, 622.
[75] Cf. Kors 1993, 68: because spiritual letters often speak in general terms about the human condition, there was a greater chance that they would be copied and/or more widely disseminated than letters of a more personal nature.
[76] Wilbrink 1930, 192–215; de Bruin and Oosterman 2001, vol. 2, 760 (H256).

5.4 The Collations of Johannes Brinckerinck

The 'Collations of Johannes Brinckerinck' are the only texts known to us that describe a little of the vision of the spiritual father of the movement of female devout. If it had been left to Brinckerinck himself, we would never have known about the texts of the inspirational speeches on virtue which he addressed to the sisters from Deventer and Diepenveen. The nuns of Diepenveen played an important role in the compilation of the texts now known as the 'Collations of Johannes Brinckerinck'. It is in particular this aspect of the complicated genesis of this corpus of texts that I should like to discuss in more detail here.[77]

The delivery of spiritual addresses or collations in convents and sisterhouses of the Modern Devotion constituted an important task for the rector. Thousands of such addresses must have been delivered, and yet only a few collation texts have come down to us. The most important reason for this is the topical nature of these devout exhortations. The rectors would base their comments on topical issues. They would work from a short outline or sketch, or they would improvise, for example on the deeds of the saint of the day or on a contribution by one of the nuns. Four other collation collections from the Modern Devotion are known from the Netherlands. Two of them are attributed to Claus van Euskirchen (†1520), one to Jasper van Marburg (†1502), and one to Bernt van Dinslaken.[78] The standard pattern is for there to be one manuscript in existence, originating from the convent in which the rector in question had worked. We have two from Claus van Euskirchen, one from the Meester-Geertshuis and the other from Buiskenshuis, but the sisterhouses in Deventer both fell under his supervision; thus they each possessed a collection of collations from their own rector.[79] The dissemination of collation anthologies such as these would seem, then, to be restricted to the circles of the Sisters of the Common Life.

Against this background, the exceptional transmission history of the 'Collations of Johannes Brinckerinck' is put into sharper contrast. Bernt van Dinslaken, Claus van Euskirchen and Jasper van Marburg were active around 1500. It was in about the same period that their collations were written down – perhaps at their instigation or under their direction – and compiled. Johannes Brinckerinck was dead by 1419, but his collations were not brought into circulation until the middle of the fifteenth century. Incorporated into these collections were disparate notes on Brinckerinck's collations

---

[77] The genesis and the transmission of the collations of Johannes Brinckerinck are discussed in Mertens 1996b and Mertens 1996c. Nine collations have been attributed to him (ed. Moll 1866a; some details concerning the editions are to be found in the list of abbreviations).
[78] Cf. Mertens 1996c, 174–81.
[79] See Mertens (in press) on this particular case.

made by the sisters of Deventer and Diepenveen some decades earlier. This material was reworked and reorganised by editors. Thus Johannes Brinckerinck may be regarded as the author of the extant collation texts only in the loosest sense. He might best be termed their *auctor intellectualis*. For the sake of clarity in what follows, the addresses delivered by Brinckerinck will be referred to as 'collations', and their written manifestations as 'collation treatises'.[80]

Thanks to the sisterbook of Diepenveen, we have a fairly precise picture of how the collation material attributed to Johannes Brinckerinck came into existence. The following shows how crucial a role was played by Liesbeth van Delft, later prioress of Jeruzalem of Utrecht.

> When our reverend father Lord Johan Brinckerinck conducted his collations, Sister Elizabeth would sit and write down his words on her wax tablet. And most of what we possess of those [collations], she compiled.[81]

That Liesbeth van Delft took notes during collation is in itself hardly exceptional. The sisters at Diepenveen probably wrote down their good points after every collation as a means of collecting material for private meditation. Sister Liesbeth, however, took notes *during* Brinckerinck's address, thus preserving considerably more of the contents of each collation. Apparently her fellow sisters at Diepenveen, Alijt Bruuns and Cecilia van Marick, who both appear in the sisterbook, did the same thing (see §3.8).

What the exact function of Liesbeth van Delft's collection might have been for the community of Diepenveen is unclear. Did she initially take these notes solely for her own use, as a source of inspiration for her personal reflections? It is more likely that she took them on behalf of the community, for example because the membership of Diepenveen thought it important to have a written testimony to their founder. At any rate these notes – or a copy of the originals – remained behind in Diepenveen when Liesbeth van Delft left for Utrecht. Her work was considered the communal property of the convent. It is no coincidence that the sisterbook speaks of *dat wy daer van hebben* ('what we possess of those'), and as far as is known Diepenveen never possessed a manuscript containing Brinckerinck's collation treatises. Together with the undoubtedly voluminous oral tradition, this spiritual inheritance would have been the source of countless citations of the founder of Diepenveen in the sisterbook. It is as if citing the great Johannes Brinckerinck was a part of literary etiquette at Diepenveen.

Around 1450, probably at the Heer-Florenshuis, the plan was conceived of using the collations of Johannes Brinckerinck as the basis for a guide for religious life. The materials available at Diepenveen and the Meester-Geertshuis

---

[80] Cf. Zieleman 1984, 13.

[81] *Als onse eerwerdighe pater heer Johan Brinckerinck clacie plach toe done, soe sat suster Elizabet ende scref dat uut synen monde in hoer tafele. Ende dat selve dat wy daer van hebben, heeft sie meestlick vergadert* (DV, ff. 58v–59r; cf. D, f. 132c–d).

were collected to that end. The detailed notes taken by sister Liesbeth van Delft were of course of great use in this endeavour. But they must have been rather fragmentary. The coordinator of this project was probably Brother Rudolf Dier van Muiden (†1459) from the Heer-Florenshuis in Deventer. He was at any rate the one who compiled eight thematically organised collation treatises from the collected materials.[82] Rudolf Dier van Muiden had been rector of the five Deventer sisterhouses since 1432, and in that capacity he was a successor to Johannes Brinckerinck. He wrote the *Scriptum*, containing the Latin *viten* of Geert Grote and brothers of the Heer-Florenshuis, as well as a Middle Dutch *vite* of Lutgard van Buderick, contained in the sisterbook of the Meester-Geertshuis.[83]

The identification of Rudolf Dier as the editor of the collation treatises of Johannes Brinckerinck does not entirely clarify their genesis. Mertens distinguishes between two redactions of this coherent corpus of texts. The (short) P-redaction is preceded by a prologue and numbers eight collations; the (long) Maria Magdalene redaction (M) has no prologue, but does include a ninth collation. The question remains as to whether one of the two redactions is the one produced by Rudolf Dier. If not, then two additional editors had a hand in the production of Brinckerinck's collation treatises, or one editor has produced two redactions, perhaps intended for two different audiences. It is worth mentioning in passing that the manuscripts containing these redactions show considerable differences. The case of Brinckerinck's collations is a good example of the complex manner in which new redactions of spiritual texts were constantly produced within the Modern Devotion.

The prologue of the P-group contains an important piece of evidence for a Diepenveen origin for the collations of Johannes Brinckerinck.

> There he [= Johannes Brinckerinck] would often tell and admonish us in his collations that we should strive to be dead to the world and worldly things, and that we should not take the wealthy as our companions, but prefer the poor. 'But should you nevertheless prefer the wealthy to the poor, then I would rather you were all dead and that Diepenveen were a bottomless pit.'[84]

---

[82] In his own *Scriptum* Rudolf Dier humbly mentions *unus* (Dumbar 1719, 19), but in Johannes Brinckerinck's *vite* in B, f. 38v (ed. Brinkerink 1902, 346) he is identified as the compiler of the collations. For a more detailed discussion of this, see Moll 1866a, 106–7 and Mertens 1996b, where the passages in question are cited.

[83] On Rudolf Dier, born at Muiden in 1384, see de Man 1919, XXXV–XXXVI and *Moderne Devotie. Figuren and facetten* 1984, 79. On his works, see Carasso-Kok 1981, nos. 360 (*vite* Lutgard) and 361 (*Scriptum*); cf. Scheepsma 1996a, 220 and 223–4.

[84] *Daer he uns vaken in synen collacien van te seggen plach unde te vermanen dat wy uns solden pynen te sterven der werlt unde der wertlicheyt, dat wy niet en staen na rijcheyden mer arme lude tot unser gheselschap te begheren. 'Mer solde ghy noch na den rijken staen unde nyet na den armen, so weer my lyever dat ghy alle doet weren unde dat Dyepenvene weer een grundeloes kolck'*. This wording appears in all four manuscripts of the

This reference to the name of the convent appears in the sisterbook as well.

> He [= Brinckerinck] was also wont to say that if it came to pass that everyone at Diepenveen should aspire to the best of cells, books, and other materials, he would rather that it reverted to a bottomless bog.[85]

This almost verbatim parallel between the collations and the sisterbook would appear to indicate that the redactor of the P-group used the same source as the authors of the sisterbook. But it is just as likely in this case that Brinckerinck's allusion to Diepenveen had become a commonplace within the Modern Devotion.[86] According to the chronicle of the convent of Jeruzalem, formerly the sisterhouse at Venray (see §5.2), the first rector, Hendrik van Assel, had said to the sisters: 'If I were to learn that no one here performed virtuous works, I would wish that it became a bottomless pit.' The reference to Diepenveen has dropped out entirely from this image.[87]

Manuscript DV of the sisterbook contains an extensive *vite* of Johannes Brinckerinck (ff. 1r–46v). The first section – the chapter divisions are difficult to determine – is a more or less chronological biography, with the emphasis on Brinckerinck's involvement in the foundation of Diepenveen (ff. 1r–15r). The second section consists of a large number of the first rector's noteworthy sayings and deeds. Within this context a separate collection of *dicta* from Brinckerinck's collations and chapter addresses is included (ff. 32r–38r):

> These are some of the points which he taught the sisters and said to them when he addressed them during collation or in chapter. And never did any of the sisters hear them during mass or collation or even in other places, without being moved to greater progress in virtue.[88]

In addition to the collation treatises there exists a fairly extensive collection of *dicta* uttered by Brinckerinck in his collations. These usually crop up in biographies, but they appear as well in Salome Sticken's *Vivendi formula*.

P-group. The one cited here is from MS Düsseldorf, Heinrich Heine Archiv und UB, B 119, f. 61r (cf. Borchling 1914, 89–92).

[85] *Hie plach oeck toe segghen, solde Dyepenven daer toe komen dat een yghelick stonde naden besten cellen, boecken ende anderen riesscap, hie hadde liever dattet weer een grondeloes veen* (DV, f. 46v).

[86] The meaning of the name *Diepenveen* ('deep peat bog') may indeed have contributed to this phenomenon.

[87] Peters 1900, 268: *woeste ic dat men hier gheen doechden in werken en solde, soe wolde ik dattet een grondeloes colck weer*; cf. Mertens 1996c, 180 n. 94. Master Hendrik had contacts in Deventer and knew Geert Grote and Florens Radewijns personally. Did he get Brinckerinck's reference from them? Theodericus Wiel, founder of the brother-house at Emmerich, called his cell in that house 'Diepenveen' (Kock 1999, 48).

[88] *Dit sijn sommighe punten die hie den susteren lerde ende sede als hie hem toesprack onderwilen inder clacien of int capittel. Ende nummermeer en hoerden hem die susteren inder missen of colacien of ock op anderen steden, sie en worden bewecht tot mere voertganck in dogheden* (DV, f. 32r).

Manuscript DV brings many of these scattered sayings together in one place. Nevertheless we are not dealing here with a systematically compiled collection of Johannes Brinckerinck's *dicta*, for elsewhere in the sisterbook there are phrases which do not appear in his biography.[89] The manuscript from Brussels, KB, 8849–59, contains a Latin translation of the Diepenveen *vite* of Brinckerinck (ff. 27r–42r). Here the collection of *dicta* (ff. 44r–55r) is separated from Brinckerinck's biography by a couple of blank pages.[90] Moreover, this section is provided with a prologue and a thematically organised table of contents (ff. 44r–45v).[91]

When the decision was made at Diepenveen to commit Brinckerinck's biography to parchment – which probably took place after 1450 – those who undertook the task could rely on oral tradition, but they also had the material collected by Liesbeth van Delft and her fellow sisters. We know this from the historical sources just cited, but it is also clear from a comparison of the *vite* and sisterbook with the collation treatises. For the most part the similarities are in spirit, rather than the letter.[92] But a few verbally parallel phrases confirm that both texts were dependent on the same source:

> Ghehoersamheit is een alte lichten wech ten ewighen leven mede te comen. Want mochten wi met enen teldenen peerde veer weghes riden, waerom wouden wi te voeten gaen?

> Ghehorsamheit is een alten lichten wech mede ten ewighen leven toe komen. Moghe wy mit enen telderen perde ten ewighen leven comen, waer om wille wij dan toe voete ghaen?[93]

The citation from *Collatie III* comes from the M-redaction. The fairly exact parallels demonstrate here, as they do in the P-group, that material from Diepenveen has been used. We may therefore conclude that sisters from this Windesheim convent, and especially Liesbeth van Delft, were by far the most

---

[89] For example, one might mention two cases from Brinckerinck's *vite*. DV, ff. 25r–v contain a fairly extensive quotation from a collation concerning the significance of manual labour. The phrase on ff. 43r–v, concerning a collation on Gideon, is cited at §3.8.

[90] On the Latin *vite* of Brinckerinck see Carasso-Kok 1981, no. 389; ed. Brinkerink 1902. The *dicta*-collection is cited as *Libellus de dictis Johannis Brinckerinck ad moniales suas* (cf. Carasso-Kok 1981, no. 204), but this title does not appear in the manuscript.

[91] Cf. the Emmerich manuscript *Hic aliqua sequuntur ex vitisfratrum nostrorum*, in which the deeds of the brothers from Deventer are arranged according to their virtues (see §3.8, n. 137).

[92] By way of example I would note the similarities between *Collatie IV*, 138 and DV, f. 42r (concerning the fear of God) and those between *Collatie IX*, 233–5 and DV, ff. 37r–v (concerning silence).

[93] *Collatie III*, 129 (M-redaction) ('Obedience is a very easy path to the eternal life. For if we may travel a great distance on a swift horse, why should we walk?'), DV, f. 40v ('Obedience is a very easy path to the eternal life. If we may arrive at the eternal life upon a swift horse, why should we wish to walk?').

important providers of material for the collation treatises of Johannes Brinckerinck. And while this may never have been their intention, the work of these choir nuns was disseminated on a large scale.

Manuscripts containing Brinckerinck's collation treatises were in great demand in the late fifteenth century. Some fifteen have been identified to date, a surprising number of them in Germany, and the total is likely to increase. The production of these collation treatises is probably closely related to the process of monasticisation that took place within the Modern Devotion from about 1450 on. The transition to life in the monasteries was supported by written instructions for novices. The manuscripts containing the collation treatise often contain other introductions to the monastic life, such as the letter addressed to novices by the Carthusian Heinrich of Coesfeld (†1410). It would seem that in the middle of the fifteenth century there was a shortage of appropriate texts for beginners in which the ideals of the Modern Devotion were adequately expressed. This is the reason why the collations of Johannes Brinckerinck were edited to form eight or nine didactic treatises. The brothers in the Heer-Florenshuis made skilful use of the prestige enjoyed by Brinckerinck as the founder of the movement of devout women. His name was associated with the newly created group of texts in which the devout striving for virtue and communal living was given expression.[94]

---

[94] Cf. Mertens 1995b, 129 and Mertens 1996b, 95.

6

Devout Biography and Historiography

HUNDREDS OF biographies of men and women from various circles of the Modern Devotion exist, all of them written by devoted brothers and sisters. They are usually referred to by the medieval Dutch title *viten*, a term that clearly reflects their relation to the classical saint's life or *vita*. The corpus of biographical literature produced by the Modern Devotion is a remarkable phenomenon, not only because of its size, but also because this genre, created by the Modern Devotion itself, gives such a clear expression of the pragmatic attitude towards literature held by the movement. Moreover, the *viten* provide a kaleidoscopic view of the spirituality of the Modern Devotion, for in them are described individuals who, under constantly changing circumstances, take up the fight for the devout ideal – and win.[1]

All branches of the Modern Devotion produced *viten*. The brothers and canons of Windesheim did this in Latin, the sisters and canonesses opted for the vernacular. Usually devout biographies were included in the larger context of a brotherbook or sisterbook: a collection of *viten* from a given monastery or brotherhouse or sisterhouse, compiled by one or more members of that community. Diepenveen produced a sisterbook as well, the only one of the thirteen female establishments of Windesheim to do so. The *viten* produced by this model convent represent the spiritual ideal of the Windesheim nuns in its purest form. This chapter will deal closely with a few important literary aspects of this work. Thorough consideration will be given first to form (§6.1), followed by contents and function (§6.2), and then authorship (§6.3).[2]

The Windesheim canonesses regular of Bethanië in Mechelen decided in 1486 to write the history of the convent. From that point on they updated their chronicle on a yearly basis. Section 6.4 is devoted to this extremely

---

[1] On the *viten* of the Ijssel region, see Scheepsma 1996a.
[2] A typology of the devout sisterbook is to be found in Scheepsma 1995a; cf. Ruh 1997 and Ruh 1990–9, vol. 4, 313–22. In addition to Diepenveen's sisterbook, known specimens exist from the Meester-Geertshuis in Deventer (ed. de Man 1919), the Lamme-van-Diezehuis in Deventer (partial edition ed. Spitzen 1875), the convent of St Agnes in Emmerich (ed. Bollmann and Staubach 1998) and possibly the Buiskenshuis in Deventer.

thorough monastic chronicle. By way of conclusion we shall compare the chronicle of Bethanië, a specimen of traditional monastic historiography, with the Diepenveen sisterbook, which in a certain sense represents a new direction for monastic historiography (§6.5). By happy coincidence, the chronicle from this convent in Mechelen and the Diepenveen sisterbook may even be compared according to their contents. Both works describe in their own way how the reformation of the new convent of Bethanië was accomplished by two sisters from Diepenveen.

6.1 The Diepenveen Viten

In social communities narrative traditions about the members of the community spring up readily. Such stories deal not only with the living, but often with the dead as well, memories of whom live on in the form of anecdotes and memorable sayings. Sometimes the need for commemorating certain persons and events in writing arises. This was the case among the Modern Devout on a surprisingly large scale. Some forty years after Geert Grote's death, work was begun on his biography. Around the year 1421, two short *viten* in rhyming verse were composed in Latin (one of which is a hymn). Several Latin prose *viten* followed, among them texts by Rudolf Dier van Muiden (†1456), Thomas a Kempis (†1471) and Peter Hoorn (†1479). Numerous adaptations in Middle Dutch were to follow. In this way, then, the biography of the founder of the Modern Devotion was continually recomposed.[3]

At the level of individual monasteries and brother- and sisterhouses, too, written traditions about local history arose. In a model monastery like Diepenveen there was more than enough material available to the membership about its illustrious past. The convent had been founded by the famous Johannes Brinckerinck, and subsequently sisters had lived there who had distinguished themselves by impressive religious accomplishments. Moreover, many of their sisters had been involved in the reformation of other convents. When the decision to record the rich history of Diepenveen was made, they could well have chosen to adopt the classic chronicle form. However, the historiographers of this exemplary Windesheim convent did not do so, apparently because that form was less well suited to their purpose. They realised that it was the more important personalities who had, each in his or her own way, given expression to the ideals of the entire community. The literary genre of the *vite* – and at the macro-level, the sisterbook – emphasises this aspect in particular.

---

[3] On the medieval *viten* of Geert Grote see Carasso-Kok 1981, nos. 215, 216, 293, 301, 324, 347, 361 and 371 and 372; cf. Scheepsma 1996a, 231–8. There is a extensive tradition of the sayings of Geert Grote (see Tiecke 1941, 196–203 and van Engen 1988a, 76–7); cf. §5.4, for the *dicta* of Johannes Brinckerinck.

Precisely when this decision to record the biographies of the Diepenveen sisters was taken is unknown, but it was probably not before 1450. A factor in the timing was certainly that first-hand knowledge of Johannes Brinckerinck and the first sisters was in danger of being lost for ever, because hardly anyone was left who had known them personally. It would also have been apparent that the now wealthy and established Diepenveen was no longer the inspired foundation, struggling for its very existence, that it had been in the early days. In its glory years under Salome Sticken (†1449), the first sisters of Diepenveen had built the convent from the ground up, under the harshest of circumstances, with their own hands. It is no coincidence that the sisterbook describes the first sisters and the early period, when the spirit of Diepenveen and its inhabitants was still strong.

It is in the nature of the sisterbook that it was constantly expanded, each time a memorable person passed away. Sisterbooks are in principle never completed, at least not until the convent they are associated with is dissolved (and in which case they lose their primary function). These expansions were not restricted to regular additions in chronological order, a fact we are able to confirm easily due to the preservation of two complete manuscripts of the Diepenveen sisterbook. Both redactions appear upon closer scrutiny to possess their own distinct character.[4] Manuscript DV was written in 1524; a shelfmark proves that it belonged to the convent of Diepenveen itself. Manuscript D was written in 1534 and belonged to the library of the sisters of the Meester-Geertshuis.[5] The two surviving redactions exhibit too many differences to postulate the existence of a single common exemplar. It must therefore be the case that DV and D go back to separate, now lost, sources. These are referred to as redactions *X and *Y, respectively. In addition, a limited number of *viten* from the Diepenveen sisterbook were translated into Latin. These were included in the anthology of historiographical texts composed by Modern Devout from the Heer-Florenshuis, compiled around 1500 (B).[6]

---

[4] I use the term 'redaction', instead of, for example, 'version', following Steer 1985. Henceforth the phrases 'redaction D' and 'redaction DV' will be used to indicate the different variants in the text of the sisterbook. The phrases 'manuscript D' and 'manuscript DV' will be used to refer to the codicological unity of the manuscripts.

[5] The presence of the Diepenveen sisterbook in the Meester-Geertshuis may be accounted for by the historically close ties between the two houses. A parallel is to be found in Windesheim, where a manuscript containing *viten* of brothers from the Heer-Florenshuis was kept (Scheepsma 1996a, 221).

[6] More detailed information concerning manuscripts D and DV and their place in the stemma of the Diepenveen sisterbook is found in Scheepsma 1997, 240-4. The complex history of transmission of the Diepenveen sisterbook is certainly not unusual for the sisterbook genre. See for example the Unterlinden *Schwesternbuch*: around 1320 Katharina van Unterlinden wrote a Latin redaction, of which two manuscripts have been preserved. At the end of the fifteenth century Elisabeth Kempfin produced a redaction in the vernacular. Both nuns made use in their own

Perhaps the impulse for compiling the sisterbook was provided by the disastrous illness which struck Diepenveen in 1452, and which took the lives of eighteen sisters.[7] This tragedy was preceded by a portentous dream of Sister Alijt Comhaer, in which she was shown that a great wedding would soon be celebrated at Diepenveen, when Christ would come for many of his brides. The use of this wedding imagery would have been a little consoling for the sisters who were left behind, but the loss of more than ten per cent of the convent's population brought primarily despair and desperation. The structure of redaction D clearly reflects the desire to commemorate the victims of 1452 in writing. All eighteen of them receive their own, sometimes very brief, *vite*. The group of texts as a whole is introduced in D with the heading 'The blessed dream dreamt by Sister Alijt Comhaer before her death, of a great wedding that would be celebrated at Diepenveen'.[8] In 1503 and 1504 Diepenveen was again struck by an epidemic; this illness – according to the sisterbook it was not the plague – claimed thirty-one victims (DV, f. 387r–v). In manuscript DV, compiled in 1524, only the *vite* of the first to perish, Cecilia van Marick, has been included in the corpus. It is possible that this new disaster erased for the most part all memory of the first, for in DV the victims of 1452 are no longer listed as a group.

The cycle of *viten* concerning the victims of 1452 could well be the original core of the Diepenveen sisterbook. The collection of *viten* from the Lamme-van-Diezehuis also originated as the result of an epidemic. In 1483 Rector Egbert van der Beeck and seven sisters fell victim to a contagious disease; their *viten* constitute the beginnings of the sisterbook of this house.[9] But in Diepenveen there may well have been *viten* available in 1452 of important persons who had died earlier, for example of Johannes Brinckerinck (†1419), Salome Sticken (†1449) or Katharina van Naaldwijk (†1443). Moreover, another cycle of *viten* can be distinguished in the Diepenveen sisterbook which was probably created in the sixth decade of the fifteenth century. This consists of the lives of the first twelve sisters to take the veil in 1408, of whom Elsebe Hasenbroecks was the last to die, in 1458. Though it is impossible to

---

way of an old convent chronicle, which must therefore be dated to before 1320 (see Lewis 1996, 13–15 and 289).

[7] D, f. 163b mentions nineteen nuns, whereas on f. 138a–b the number of victims is given as twenty. DV, f. 81r counts eighteen dead nuns; the nineteenth victim was brother Gert Velthuus (cf. §2.1).

[8] *Die suverliken droem die suster Alijt Comhaers hadde voer hore doet, als van der groter bruloft die ten Diepenveen wesen solde* (D, ff. 145c–163c). MS D lists the victims presumably in the order in which they died. When the person in question has already been treated elsewhere, her name is mentioned nevertheless at the appropriate place; thus for example Griete Dagens (f. 146a; *vite* 127d–130b) and Liesbeth van Heenvliet (f. 147b; *vite* 70a–82b).

[9] Cf. Spitzen 1875, 179–80.

say with any certainty when the sisterbook was begun, this evidence points to a *terminus post quem* of around 1450.[10]

The sisterbook from the Meester-Geertshuis also contains evidence to support this dating. Manuscript G contains an abbreviated *vite* of the former rectrix Salome Sticken, in which the author refers to a more detailed life which apparently was also available in the Meester-Geertshuis.[11] There is no doubt that this is a reference to the life of Sticken written in Diepenveen, which was thus already present in the Meester-Geertshuis, probably within the larger context of the sisterbook in redaction *Y. De Man dates the paper upon which manuscript G is written to 1475–85: thus before 1485 a *vite* of Salome Sticken, which must have come from Diepenveen, was certainly in existence. Again, according to de Man, manuscript G is a copy of an original, now lost. Given the fact that manuscript G contains only *viten* of women who died in or before 1456, it is reasonable to conclude that the original was composed not long after 1456. It follows that the date of Salome Sticken's *vite* must be earlier than that. In all likelihood the same is true for redaction *Y, but also for *X, in as much as *Y is based on *X. Thus this complex set of indications points to 1450–60 as the period in which the Diepenveen sisterbook was created.[12]

The material for the Diepenveen sisterbook must have been largely drawn from oral tradition, though there are few direct indications of this. Nevertheless, examples like the following carry a great deal of weight. The author of the *vita* asks an older sister for information concerning Armgert van Lisse:

> I asked an older sister about her life. She answered me, saying, 'Why are you asking me about Armghert van Lissen? I know of no virtues not possessed by Armghert van Lisse.'[13]

The authors of the *viten* make regular use of the pronouns 'we' and 'us' when referring to generally known facts or when appealing to feelings shared by all. Thus we read in one sentence how 'we' began to have some little hope when Katharina van Naaldwijk recovered a little from an extended illness – alas, in vain, for Katharina died shortly thereafter.[14] The choice of narrative

---

[10] In previous publications, based on existing studies (especially Wilbrink 1939), I have cited *c*.1475 as the date of origin. This position does not, however, sufficiently take into account the very real possibility that the sisterbook came into being gradually.

[11] G, ff. 119a and 120d.

[12] MS G: Deventer, SAB, Suppl. 208 (101 F 25) (ed. de Man 1919, 1–256), containing sixty-four *viten*. A second volume of sorts probably existed, but has not survived (cf. Scheepsma 1995a, 32–5). For the dating of this sisterbook, cf. Bollman and Staubach 1998, 8 n. 15 and 19 n. 67.

[13] *Ic vraghede eenre oelder suster wat na horen leven. Doe antwaerde sie mi ende sede: 'Wat vraghe ghi mi na Armghert van Lissen? Ic en weet ghiene doghede die Armghert van Lissen niet and hadde'* (DV, f. 290r; cf. D, f. 174c).

[14] DV, f. 253v and D, f. 63a.

perspective demonstrates irrefutably that the sisterbook was not only concerned with the sisters at Diepenveen, but that it was written for a select audience, the convent of Diepenveen itself.

Sometimes the author of a *vite* will describe a situation she has experienced herself.[15] The following example illustrates the curious habit the sisters had of stealing good works from one another.

> The sisters were so devoted to the common good, that they were just as eager to perform the tasks assigned to others as they were to perform their own. And they were wont to steal the chores of one another, as happened to me once when I worked in the bakery, and I thought to sift the flour. When I turned to that task, I found the containers full of sifted flour, and it was Sister Alijt Reijners who had done this, along with some other sisters who are still alive.[16]

The infrequent references to what older sisters knew, and this kind of 'eye-witness report' or personal observation, are the only passages in the Diepenveen sisterbook that allow us to trace the origin of its narrative material. With the exception of the Bible and the liturgy, there are hardly any concrete identifiable references to written sources or the literary tradition.[17] The Diepenveen sisterbook is primarily the product of oral tradition.

Narrative material from the Diepenveen circuit not contained in the sisterbook has, by chance, come down to us. In a manuscript dated to 1487, produced in the German convent of Eldagsen, there are two exempla in Middle Low German concerning sisters from Diepenveen. The first deals with Margaretha van den Colke (Griete ten Kolke), canonness regular of Diepenveen, who suffered from severe haemoptysis (coughing up blood). This would ultimately cause her death, in 1453. She had promised her confessor – at the time Ludolf van Kampen was rector of Diepenveen – that she would appear to him thirty days after her death. And lo, on the appointed day Griete appeared before the rector. She reported that she had spent only an hour in purgatory, after which she was taken up into heaven by

---

[15] An overview of such autobiographical first-person forms is given at §6.3, n. 72.

[16] *Die susteren weren doe soe vlitich voerden ghemienen orber, dat sie joe soe vuerrich weren toe doen die dynghe die enen anderen bevalen weren als dat hem selven bevalen was. Ende sie pleghen malkanderen die warke toe stelen, alst mi noch wal ghevallen is doe ic int backhuus wonde, dat ic miende toe budelen. Als ic quam, soe vant ic die kisten vol ghebudelt, dat suster Alyt Reyners hadde ghedaen ende sommeghe anderen die noch leven* (DV, f. 289v); cf. D, f. 174b; here the comment regarding Alijt Reijners is lacking. It seems unlikely indeed that the same author lies behind these first-person references in both fragments (on the question of authorship, see further §6.3).

[17] There is a reference to the vision of Hendrik Mande in the *vite* of Stine Tolners (DV, ff. 300v–301r and D, f. 88d); Mande did indeed write a vision featuring Stine (i.e. vision 16; cf. Mertens 1986, 114–17). In the *vite* of Katharina and Griete van Naaldwijk a vision of Mande has been inserted (see below), i.e. vision 20 (Mertens 1986, 119). On Mande as a visionary, see Mertens 1989b.

God and given a place there only three levels above even St Catherine. It is not known who recorded this miracle (although the confessor is a likely candidate) nor even exactly how the story made its way to Eldagsen.[18] It suffices here to observe that stories concerning Diepenveen were disseminated well beyond the walls of that convent. At the same time it seems clear that not every remarkable event that took place at Diepenveen made it into the sisterbook.

The hour of death was one of the most impressive moments in the lives of the Windesheim choir sisters. A bell was tolled, calling the entire convent together around the bed of the dying sister.[19] The last words of the dying woman, who was after all on the very threshold of eternal life, were awaited with heightened attention. The most moving account of such an event is found in the *vite* of Gertrud van Rijssen (†1416). She had concealed a serious sin from her confessor. On her deathbed the devil confronted her with this error again and again. The *vite* gives a practically blow-by-blow account of her fearful struggle with death, for the most part in direct speech. The final words of the dying Gertrud are reproduced in such detail that it is almost inconceivable that the author of the *vite* was not working from some kind of written account of this terrifying event.[20]

There are further signs that these biographies existed in some written form before the Diepenveen sisterbook. From the very beginning it had been the custom among the inhabitants of Diepenveen to record 'good points' for their personal meditation. They could be drawn from the Bible or religious literature, but they could also come from the confessor's speeches or from spiritual conversations with the other sisters. In this context we might also mention the religious testaments left behind by some sisters from Diepenveen. When a sister lay on her deathbed, those gathered around her would often ask for a good point to remember her by. Thanks to the sisterbook we know the contents of the religious testaments of Zweder van Rechteren (†1407), Dymme van Rijssen (†1413) and her sister, Katharina van Rijssen (†1427). Among other things, Dymme van Rijssen bequeathed to her sisters the following saying: 'Obedience is the shortest path to the eternal life.'[21]

---

[18] The two *exempla* are found in MS Hannover, Niedersächsischen Landesbibliothek, MS I 237, ff. 88r–90v (Griete ten Kolke) and 90v–95v (an anonymous nun, judging by the context, also from Diepenveen). On this MS Härtel 1982, 82–4 and the two *exempla*, see Mertens 2002b.

[19] CM 2.6.27–34.

[20] The *vite* van Gertrud van Rijssen is found in DV, ff. 181r–188v and D, ff. 120c–125a. For more on this deathbed scene, see Kühler 1914, 278–80, Breure 1985b, 446–7 and Breure 1987, 185–9.

[21] *Ghehoersamheit is een coert wech totten ewighen leven* (DV, f. 181r); cf. DV, ff. 128v–129r and D, f. 31a–b (Zweder van Rechteren), DV, f. 181r and D, ff. 120b–c (Dymme van Rijssen; cf. the citation at §4.2, n. 42) and DV, f. 189v and D, f. 125d (Katharina van Rijssen). On the spiritual testament among the Modern Devout see Mertens 1989c.

Presumably many more such sayings were in circulation, not just orally, but also written down on loose pieces of paper and scrolls, i.e. in *rapiaria*.

The practice so common in Diepenveen of collecting good points is as it were reflected in the very structure of the *viten*. The virtue of the sisters is portrayed in the form of brief stories, or otherwise illustrated by means of apt sayings. In this way the sisterbook itself became a reservoir of good points. Thanks to this point-by-point narrative structure, the sisters who read or heard it could use it as a point of departure for their own meditative exercises.

The authors of the *viten* turned to hagiography for models in structuring the rich but amorphous material concerning the deceased sisters. Thanks to their daily exposure to these legends, the sisters were very familiar with this literary genre. What was more natural than to model the biographies of their fellow sisters after the saints' lives? This would also explain the appearance of all kinds of hagiographical motifs in the *viten*. But there are also important differences between the devout *viten* and the classical *vitae*. The miraculous events so characteristic of the traditional saints' lives are for the most part absent in the Diepenveen *viten*. The sisters of Diepenveen were not saints – a fact which the authors of these texts fully realised, despite their admiration for their subjects – so no miracles occur in the *viten* (though sometimes there are expressions of awe at divine intervention). Likewise no miracles take place at the graves of the deceased sisters, a motif seldom absent from the classical *vitae*. We do, however, encounter events that border on the miraculous. When some seven years after her death the grave of Stine Tolners was opened in order to bury another sister there, a sweet aroma rose from the grave and not a single bone belonging to the good sister could be found.[22]

The Diepenveen *viten* are characterised by a tripartite structure modelled broadly on the classical *vita*. Generally speaking then, three sections are to be distinguished: 'living in the world and conversion', 'life in the convent' and 'death and remarkable events thereafter'. The different sections may appear more or less fully developed in an individual biography. Usually the greatest focus is on life in the convent, the period about which the surviving sisters knew the most and which held the greatest relevance for them. In a 'model' *vite* such as Katharina van Naaldwijk's, each one of these sections is exhaustively developed.[23]

In some of the *viten* the proportions are somewhat out of balance; thus the *vite* of Gertrud van Rijssen mentioned earlier is devoted practically in its entirety to her terrifying death struggle. In the life of Katharina's cousin Liesbeth van Heenvliet, the emphasis falls almost entirely on her early

---

[22] DV, f. 302r and D, f. 89a–b. On the hagiographical elements in the Diepenveen *viten* see Jongen and Scheepsma 1993, 301–10; cf. Lewis 1996, in particular 52–4.

[23] Cf. the typology of the saint's life given by Boyer 1981 (which is much more refined and distinguishes nine components).

conversion. She had been promised to God as an oblate by her mother even before her birth. It was thus no surprise that Liesbeth felt her calling to the religious life at a very early stage. No moment of conversion is to be found in her biography; she was simply destined for a life of virtue. Even as a small child Liesbeth tried one night to run away to the convent of Warmond, but her attempt failed. She seized her opportunity when she was allowed to accompany her mother and aunt to attend the profession of her cousin, Katharina van Naaldwijk, in Diepenveen. The ten-year-old Liesbeth feigned illness and thus had to remain behind in the convent. Liesbeth van Heenvliet would never leave Diepenveen again. Her stay there apparently made less of an impression, for her *vite* has little to say about it. The author of the *vite* does mention in passing that Liesbeth was to undergo her fair share of mortification.[24]

The biographies of other devout are often incorporated into the Diepenveen *viten* without further commentary. The life of Katharina van Naaldwijk is one such story with the structure of a *vite*-within-a-*vite*.[25] To begin with, the life of her sister Griete van Naaldwijk has been incorporated into hers. Furthermore, room is made for their father, a meek and humble man. Lord Hendrik van Naaldwijk was always satisfied with humble food and while travelling provided his servants with better lodging in inns than he did for himself. When his estate of Crayenstein was struck by the St Elizabeth's day flood in 1421, he had its victims brought to his estate in Naaldwijk, where they were provided with money and land and given a fresh start.[26] Such illustrations of brotherly love are ideally suited to the sisterbook and are therefore allowed to interrupt the narrative thread of the *vite*.

From time to time distinctly different kinds of texts have been inserted into the Diepenveen corpus of *viten*. The author frequently weaves an integrated whole from fragments of diverse form and contents, in which these loose pieces take on new meaning. The *vite* of Katharina and Griete van Naaldwijk may again serve as an example of this phenomenon. Following the death of Griete on 21 October 1424, a vision experienced by the Windesheim mystic Hendrik Mande is inserted, in which he sees her, together with two other religious sisters, being brought by Mary before the Lord.[27] This vision demonstrates the efficacy of Griete's pious lifestyle and is therefore inserted into the *vite* in its entirety.

At the end of this complex *vite*, when it focuses exclusively on Katharina

---

[24] DV, f. 284r–v describes how Liesbeth had unjustly appropriated an advantage for herself. The life of Liesbeth van Heenvliet is given in DV, ff. 266v–287r and D, ff. 70a–82b; her youth and entry into the convent are treated in DV, ff. 266v–278v and D, ff. 70a–77b.
[25] Cf. Jongen and Scheepsma 1993, 301–2.
[26] DV, ff. 238v–239v and D, f. 53a–d.
[27] DV, ff. 245r–247v and D, ff. 57c–59a; cf. n. 17.

van Naaldwijk, a rather lengthy allegorical text has been inserted. As a result of the schism of Utrecht, i.e. the struggle for the see of Utrecht (1425–32), the Pope pronounced an interdict against the bishopric, which, among other things, meant that with the exception of feast days, no masses could be celebrated. Despite a papal bull allowing mass to be celebrated in the Windesheim convents in the bishopric, there were nevertheless severe restrictions even there, and communion was celebrated much less frequently than usual.[28] During this difficult time Katharina van Naaldwijk had trouble falling asleep on St Agnes's eve (20 January) – no year is given. In Diepenveen the new sisters were veiled on the evening of the name day of the convent's patron saint: Katharina thought all the sisters of the convent should be allowed to celebrate communion on this feast day in particular, in order to commemorate the day upon which they donned their spiritual bridal dress. She easily won Salome Sticken over to her plan, and together they were able to convince the rector, Egbert van Lingen, to celebrate mass. These two fervent sisters created an elaborate allegory of the marriage with Christ, which was then expounded upon to the entire convent, gathered in the chapter house. This wedding allegory constitutes the conclusion of Katharina's *vite* in the sisterbook. Apparently this story and the manner in which it happened were thought to be so characteristic of Katharina's lifestyle that it was added to her biography.[29]

By way of concluding this section, something should be said about the selection of sisters who were deemed worthy of a *vite*. The sisterbook of the Meester-Geertshuis is likely to have been conceived of as a kind of 'book of the dead', in which was entered a brief biography of each of the deceased. After all, manuscript G organises its sixty-four *viten* according to the year of death. As far as can be determined, the sisterbook of Diepenveen was never intended to have such a structure, even though it contains the cycle of sisters who perished in the epidemic of 1452. A quick glance at the 'necrology' of Diepenveen bears this out: none of the following canonesses who died in 1433, Gertrud ten Voerde, Elseken van Steenren, Liesbeth van Snellenberg and Katrijne van Steenbergen, were immortalised with a *vite*.[30] Thus a selection of noteworthy sisters was made for the Diepenveen sisterbook. The most important criterion was undoubtedly how far the deceased sister had been an exemplary model for those who survived her. But if appearances do not deceive, rank and status also play a role here. The sisterbook takes a

---

[28] Cf. Post 1968, 351–3; for Diepenveen, Kühler 1914, 117–19.

[29] The wedding allegory is found in DV, ff. 257r–266v (ed. Raue 1996, 365–75) and D, ff. 64d–70a.

[30] The necrologium of Diepenveen is contained in MS Deventer, SAB, I, 23 (101 D 11), which also contains the cartularium. It covers the period up to and including the year 1472 (ed. van Slee 1908, 323–40; here p. 325). This is not, however, a true necrology or obituary (cf. Huyghebaert 1972, 35); rather it is a straightforward list of the dead.

particular interest in sisters of high social status and if a sister had rich parents never neglects to mention it. Rejecting worldly fame and wealth was, after all, a virtue in and of itself.

6.2 Learning Virtues

The biographies of the nuns of Diepenveen are referred to once by the phrase, 'the legends of the sisters'.[31] Yet both the authors of the *viten* and the community of Diepenveen were very much aware of the fact that these were not true saints' lives. The Diepenveen *viten* are not concerned with exceptional figures from far-off lands and times past, but deal instead with recently deceased sisters from their own convent. The people described in the *viten* have relevance for their audience, in terms of time, place and situation. The spectacular events described in saints' lives leave the believer astonished at the power of God. But the *vitae* afford hardly any opportunity for audience identification. The Diepenveen *viten*, on the other hand, are designed expressly to provide models for the living. Time and again the exemplary nature of a sister's actions is emphasised. Such is the case, for example, with Daya Dierkens, who was not re-elected prioress in 1478 because she was too strict, but who afterwards bore no resentment and lived on in virtue: 'In this honest piety she lived a full thirteen years after she was deposed, and her firmly devout lifestyle was a good example to us all.'[32] Daya Dierkens's example was designed for all members of the Diepenveen community to follow.

The intended audience of the sisterbook was the convent of Diepenveen. The work would have been used at plenary gatherings in particular: early in the morning in the chapter house, in refectory and perhaps during special gatherings on Sundays or feast days. The sisterbook chronicled the tradition for every sister in which they were all rooted. Every member of the community could identify with the glorious history of Diepenveen, just as each of them would have had a favorite among the deceased sisters, whose example she would strive to emulate. Diepenveen's past is portrayed in the sisterbook as a time in which the old ideal was given almost perfect expression. It was the task of the current sisters to continue that ideal. The sisterbook would have been of particular significance for the novice nuns, who, along with other new sisters, would not have been familiar either with the history of the convent or with the words and deeds of their great predecessors. The sisterbook provided them not only with historical information, but also with models for honest convent life in the Diepenveen tradition.[33]

---

[31] *Die legenden der susteren* (DV, f. 46v).
[32] *In deser eerlicker goddiensticheit levede sie noch wal dartijn jaer na dat sie ofghesat was, ende gaf ons allen een goet excempel mit hore stichtiger devoter wanderinghen* (DV, f. 412v).
[33] Cf. the *Hic aliqua sequuntur* manuscript from the brotherhouse of St Gregory at

The passage dealing with Daya Dierkens leaves the precise nature of her virtue somewhat up in the air. The prologue to manuscript DV, however, leaves little room for doubt.

> In the name of the Father, the Son and the Holy Spirit, I have taken it upon myself to write a little and to collect information on the life and death of our reverend father Lord Johannes Brinckerinck, as well as on those of some of the devout plants that have grown and flourished in his orchard. And because it would be impossible for me to record their every virtue, I have taken some pains to make selections from a great abundance, so that we may emulate their virtue and example – for St Paul says, 'For what things soever were written, were written for our learning' (Rom. 15:4) – and [I offer this] for correction by others who are wiser and more discerning than I am, so that all who read this may say a brief prayer for me, for I hope with this to arouse others somewhat to devotion.[34]

The *viten* in the sisterbook are, then, primarily lessons in virtue. In the epilogue the author again stresses the fact that she wanted to write about the virtues of the sisters of Diepenveen (cited at §6.3). The most important goal of the sisterbook is *paraenesis*: the *viten* are intended to exhort the sisters of Diepenveen to virtue.[35]

The lives of the Diepenveen sisters were dominated entirely by the *profectus virtutum*, or progress towards virtue. Johannes Brinckerinck compares the sisters to bees, who gather honey in the summer against the severe winter soon to come.[36] And yet the sisterbook is no systematic cata-

---

Emmerich, in which disparate anecdotes from the brotherbook of the Heer-Florenshuis are arranged according to the virtues they deal with. Van Engen 1988b, 187–94 shows that the purpose of this book was to instruct the young monks in the brotherhouse at Emmerich in the virtues, based on the example of Geert Grote, among others. See also §3.8, n. 137.

[34] *Inden namen des vaders, des soens ende des hillighen ghiestes heb ic voer mi ghenamen een weinich toe scriven ende toe vergaderen vanden leven ende starven onses eerwerdighen vaders heer Johan Brinckerincks, ende van sommighen devoeten planten die ghewassen ende opgheghaen sint in sinen bomgoert. Ende want mi onmoghelick weer al die dogheden toe scriven, soe heb ic opghesat een weynich toe vergaderen uut vollen, op dat wy hoer dogheden ende exempelen na mochten volghen-want sancte Pauwel secht: 'Al dat ghescreven is, dat is ghescreven tot onser leren'* (Rom. 15:4) *– ende tot verbeterynghe andre die wyser ende subtilre van sijnne sijnt dan ic sy, op dat voer my sollen bidden een cort ghebedeken alle die dit lesen of horen lesen, want ic hape hier sommighe mede tot devocien toe te verwecken* (DV, f. 1r).

[35] The prologue and epilogue do not occur in manuscript D, possibly because they are later additions to manuscript DV (cf. §6.3), but perhaps also because the nuns were not seen as immediate models for the sisters of the Meester-Geertshuis. Manuscript G of their own sisterbook does contain an extensive prologue, in which the virtues of the early sisters are extolled in similar fashion (G, f. Ca–Dd; translated in van Engen 1988a, 121–3).

[36] *Collatie I*, 112.

logue of virtues. A number of set virtues emerge from the biographies of the sisters of Diepenveen, but in addition most of them excelled in one or more other areas. Jutte van Culemborg, for example, was not in the least fastidious at table: she did not notice if the butter had gone bad or the bread was stale. This virtuous attitude becomes all the more impressive when we learn that in the outside world Jutte had had such refined tastes that the liver was the only part of a chicken she would eat.[37] Seldom absent from the spectrum of virtues of the Diepenveen sisters are the two main pillars of spirituality of the women of the Modern Devotion: obedience and humility.[38]

The virtue of *humilitas* ('humility, meekness') is highlighted in the sisterbook repeatedly and in numerous variations.[39] According to Gerard Zerbolt, humility was Christ's greatest virtue; his incarnation was the most important proof of this.[40] If a devout sister wished to be worthy of her spiritual betrothal to him, then she must be willing to be just as humble as her groom. Christ humbled himself symbolically by washing his disciples' feet. Katharina van Naaldwijk took this example so literally that she, a woman of the highest social status, kissed the feet of her fellow sisters in refectory.[41] All of the efforts of the exemplary sisters of Diepenveen were directed to being the least and the lowest. In the sisterbook, humility constitutes the essence of spirituality.

The internal poverty of the sisters was symbolised externally by the humble state of their habits. Johannes Brinckerinck taught the nuns of Diepenveen to strive to be the lowest and the least in their clothing, too, traditionally the area in which women could distinguish themselves.

> And he said that he did not want us to lavish much care on our clothes, but that we should cut them round and poorly and sew them together as if they were a covering made from two sides of bacon. And he wanted our cloaks to be extremely tattered, so that he might see us go about in them, all threadbare, and it was his custom to teach and tell us things whereby one could recognise his humble nature.[42]

When Katharina van Naaldwijk took the veil, the rector forced her to tread upon her splendid fur-lined cloak, which she had just cast off for ever and

---

[37] DV, ff. 381v–382r.
[38] Cf. van Engen 1988a, 25–35.
[39] On humility among the Modern Devout, see van Engen 1988a, 32. Johannes Brinckerinck's *Collatie IV* is devoted in its entirety to humility.
[40] Gerrits 1986, 110–11.
[41] DV, f. 241v and D, f. 55a.
[42] *Ende hie sede dat hie wolde datmen ghiene grote const en beseghede tot onsen clederen toe maken, meer datmen sie ront ende slicht snede ende makede, recht of twi sijde specks toe samen ghestolpet weren. Ende hie wolde dat onse mantelen zeer versletten weren opdat hie ons daer mede mochte sien ghelappet ghaen, ende volle dierghelike punten plach hie ons toe segghen ende toe leren, daermen sijnen oetmodigen gront uut mochte marken* (DV, f. 46r).

which now lay on the steps before the altar.[43] The influence of Johannes Brinckerinck's lessons on Katharina van Naaldwijk and her sister Griete is apparent from the way they treated their clothing.

> So long did they keep their clothes and everything that was given to them – that is, their shoes, socks, shawls – that they wore them out to the point where they looked more like knotted nets than garments, good for nothing more than to be thrown out.[44]

The prioress regularly scolded both sisters because their garments were utterly dirty from overuse. Sister Griete wore a thick fur, the leather of which had been rather crudely worked by the sisters themselves.[45]

The second chief virtue preached in the sisterbook follows naturally from humility. When they took their vows, the nuns and *conversae* of Windesheim made a pledge to live in obedience, chastity and poverty. Keeping the latter two vows would seem to have cost them the least effort, relatively speaking, for chastity and poverty seldom receive individual attention in the sisterbook. But remaining obedient to monastic authority, and in so doing ignoring their own will, was for many of the sisters a daily struggle.[46] The sisterbook contains numerous stories of the impressive deeds of sisters who obeyed absolutely the orders of their superiors. Thus it was that Jutte van Ahaus drowned her two lapdogs when Johannes Brinckerinck ordered her to do so. 'This was a good beginning to true obedience', says the sisterbook, with approval.[47] Living according to the principles of the Modern Devotion meant complete obedience to the brothers and sisters to whom authority had been entrusted. It is not surprising, then, that obedience is a recurrent theme in the writings produced by this movement. It is more or less the main theme of the collations of Johannes Brinckerinck, but Salome Sticken, too, attached a great deal of significance to this virtue.[48]

When every sister strove to achieve absolute obedience, awkward consequences could result. It happened once that an unidentified sister had asked Salome Sticken for a certain object she needed. The sister subsequently appeared before the procuratrix Elsebe Hasenbroecks, but failed to mention

---

[43] DV, ff. 234r–v; cf. D, f. 51b.

[44] *Soe nauwe waerden sie hoer cleder ende al dat hem ghegheven was toe ghebruken-dat was van scoen, voetdoken, snuteldoken-die versletten sie selven soe degher dattet beet scenen ghecnupte netten toe weesen dan doecken, dat sie narghent toe en dochten dan onwech toe warpen* (DV, ff. 240v–241r; cf. D, f. 54c–d).

[45] DV, f. 243v; D, f. 56b.

[46] For the Dominican Canonesses in the *Schwesternbücher*, too, the vow of obedience was the most difficult to follow (Lewis 1996, 249–50).

[47] *Dit was een goet beghin waerachtigher gehoersamheit* (DV, f. 131r–v; cf. D, f. 33b).

[48] On obedience see for example Gerrits 1986, 307–8 and van Engen 1988a, 32–3. Johannes Brinckerinck's *Collatie III* deals with obedience; cf. Brinckerinck's *vite* in DV, f. 40v.

that she had already received permission to collect it. The procuratrix adamantly refused her request, as she did not wish to set a precedent. Only then did the sister in question inform her that she had already asked permission from the prioress. Elsebe Hasenbroecks became so upset by this that she called the sister by name, something which the Modern Devout only very rarely did. The procuratrix's anger was occasioned by the fact that she had initially refused to carry out an order issued by the prioress. She had thus fallen short of absolute obedience. Consequently her wrath in this instance is to be interpreted as an expression of virtue.[49]

This accumulation of virtues led in Diepenveen to a practice which in our eyes seems excessive, namely the 'stealing of good works'. Manual labour was an integral part of the religious life in the Windesheim convents, but to many it was not their favourite activity. The performance of all kinds of extra chores was thus regarded as a virtue at Diepenveen. The sisters went so far as to relieve their fellows of humble works by rising at night to perform the tasks of the following day. The champions in the purloining of virtuous works were Armgert van Lisse, Stine Groten and Souke van Dorsten.

> And at night Sister Stine Groten and Sister Souke, together with others whom they recruited for that purpose, were wont to rise and do their work. When the other sisters arrived, intending to see to their chores, they found them already finished: the churning, the baking and the slaughtering – it was their custom to kill and slaughter the sheep within the walls – and all of these things they had done during the night, everything was finished, with the exception of the sausage-making. And they also did the washing at night. They were indeed eager to perform all kinds of humble works at all times.[50]

Rather curious is the detail about sausage-making. Apparently that task did not lend itself to nocturnal operations!

The collection of virtues was an absolute priority for the nuns of Diepenveen: if necessary, they would 'steal' them from their fellow sisters. On purpose, the sisterbook makes no mention of the conflicts that undoubtedly arose from this practice. One can imagine, for example, that there were sisters who needed their sleep, but wished nevertheless to do their fair share

---

[49] DV, ff. 214r–v; cf. D, ff. 15b–c.
[50] *Ende des nachtes pleghen suster Stine Groten ende suster Souken mit sommighen die sie daer toe beden optestaen ende pleghen die warke des nachtes toe done. Als die susteren quemen ende mienden die dynghe toe doen, soe vonden siet ghedaen, als carnen, backen, slachten – ende men plach doe die scape bijnnen toe steken ende uut toe stoten-ende dat hadden sie dan des nachtes ghedaen ende alle dynghe bereit, op dat worsten na. Ende ock pleghen sie des nachtes toe wasschen. Ende altoes weren sie bereit tot allen oetmodighen warken* (DV, f. 373r–v); cf. DV, f. 289r–v (cited at §6.1) and D, f. 174a–b (Armgert van Lisse) and DV, f. 413v and D, f. 190d (Stine Groten).

of the manual labour. They were thus denied an important opportunity to perform good works.

The characterisation of the *viten* of the Modern Devotion has proven an extremely problematic task. Jan Romein writes the following about manuscript D (he was not aware of the existence of manuscript DV) in his overview of northern Netherlandish historiography:

> No matter how important they may be for the cultural history of the northern Netherlands in the later Middle Ages, the edifying biographies of a total of some fifty nuns who lived during the first century of the convent of Diepenveen, founded in the fourteenth century, should not be included in the record of history unless, for the sake of contrast, the lives of the nuns before their entrance into the convent are also treated, no matter how briefly; a circumstance which, despite their hagiographical nature, gives them a place among the oldest northern Netherlandish biographies extant.[51]

A connection is made here with three more or less related genres: hagiography, historiography and biography. Romein really did not know what to do with the Diepenveen sisterbook (or the other collections of *viten* produced by the Modern Devotion). In the end he included them in his compendium because they contain some amount of historical data. The problem is most readily resolved by regarding the *viten* as a subgenre of religious literature with some historical content. If one recognises that the devout *viten* were composed primarily to edify, then the historical data they contain can be more accurately assessed.[52]

The description and categorisation of the corpus of devout *viten* might have gone more smoothly had more religious reform movements been active in the northern Netherlands. It might then have been more obvious that many late medieval reform movements made use of the biographies of important figures as the flag-bearers of a common ideal.[53] A well-known example is Konrad von Eberbach's (†1221) *Exordium magnum cisterciense*, in which the lives of Bernard of Clairvaux (†1153) and his fellow brothers are recorded.[54] And the female religious movement, too, has left its literary

---

[51] Romein 1932, 194.
[52] Cf. Romein 1932, 161–211, 'De kring der Moderne Devotie' and the supplement Bruch 1956, 64–5. The anthologies of *viten* are also treated in the repertorium of medieval historical sources by Carasso-Kok 1981. For the question of genre, see Jongen and Scheepsma 1993, especially 299–301.
[53] In the biographies of the monastic reformers, their authors almost always draw upon the *Vitae patrum* and the early Christian tradition. For more on the devout *viten* see for example van Engen 1988b, 181–5, van Engen 1992, 10 and 20–1, Jongen and Scheepsma 1993, 310–14 and Mertens 1994a, 232–6.
[54] On Konrad and the *Exordium* see for example Worstbrock 1985, especially 158–9; on the influence of the *Exordium* on the brother- and sisterbooks of the Modern Devout see van Engen 1988b, 183. Bernard and his brothers are referred to twice in the

legacy in the form of biographies of important women. Famous are the thirteenth-century Latin *vitae* of the religious women from Brabant, some of whose amazing biographies were recorded by the learned Dominican Thomas of Cantimpré; among those credited to him are, for example, the lives of Christina Mirabilis (†1224) of St Truiden and Lutgard van Tongeren (†1246).[55]

The sisterbook of Diepenveen, and other devout sisterbooks in the vernacular, are fairly removed from these Latin women's *vitae*, which were for the most part recorded by male religious. The genre does, however, exhibit striking similarities with the female variant of Dominican historiography, the *Schwesternbuch*. *Schwesternbücher* were compiled by nuns in no fewer than nine Dominican convents in southern Germany and Switzerland in the first half of the fourteenth century.[56] The similarities between this genre, consisting of a mixture of convent historiography, hagiography and nuns' *viten*, and the devout sisterbook are so striking that one is compelled to consider a common source, though thus far it has not been possible to establish a direct link.[57] Perhaps we should instead think in terms of a more or less identical historical situation, giving rise, as it were, to this type of literature naturally.

In the comparison of *Schwesternbuch* and sisterbook, there are two important differences. In the lives of the Dominican canonesses there is a fairly strong emphasis on their intellectual qualities, whereas these play a subordinate role in those of the Windesheim sisters. In the Dominican order, with great figures such as Thomas Aquinas and Albertus Magnus, study and learning were important components of spirituality, and nuns were no exception.[58] A second distinction lies in the frequency with which visions, miracles

---

Vivendi formula (see §5.1). Bethanië in Mechelen owned a translation of the *Exordium* (MS Brussels, KB, 12.166 (3875); see Deschamps 1972, no. 62 and cf. no. 63). Comparable are the 'Franciscan treatises', containing among other things the *vite* of Francis of Assisi; cf. Ruh 1980; for the manuscripts see Kruitwagen 1905, Ruh 1956, 217–39 and Deschamps 1976.

[55] On the *viten* of women in Brabant see for example Peters 1988, 9–39, Ruh 1990-9, vol. 2, 81–110 and McGinn 1991-8, vol. 3, 153–98.

[56] On this genre see Lewis 1996; cf. Peters 1988, 101–10 and 129–35. Bibliographical information on the *Schwesternbücher* is found in Lewis, Willaert and Govers 1989, especially 289–316 (where eight specimens are discussed); cf. Lewis 1996, 10–31 (nine specimens). Lewis 1996 publishes the extant editions again in microfiche; Meyer 1995 provides a new edition of the *Schwesternbuch* from St Katharinental.

[57] According to Lewis 1996, 53–4 the *Vitae fratrum praedicatorum* by Gerard of Frachet (†1281) provided the model for the *Schwesternbücher*: at the behest of his order, Gerard collected the biographies of noteworthy Dominicans. We may assume that the Modern Devout knew the Dominican tradition of the lives of the brothers (cf. van Engen 1992, 10 and 21); the *Vitae fratrum praedicatorum* is mentioned in the meditation scheme of *c*.1450 from the Heer-Florenshuis (Obbema 1996, 141 no. 31).

[58] Lewis 1996, 263–83.

and charismatic experiences occurred in the lives of the nuns in question.[59] To the Dominican nuns of the fourteenth century, such experiences were proof that a sister was blessed. One of the important functions of the *Schwesternbuch* was mystagogical: with the example of their predecessors before them, the young nuns became familiar with the mystic consciousness that played such a central role in the lives of the Dominican canonesses.[60] Mystic phenomena are only very rarely mentioned in the sisterbook of Diepenveen, and even then barely touched on (see §6.3).

In this way the sisterbook gives expression to a new and altered attitude about what the goals of female religious should be. Up until the fourteenth century it had been the *mystica*, the women with a special sensitivity for the divine experience, who constituted the ideal. In the course of the fifteenth century, the Modern Devotion distanced itself more and more from the mystical path, which came to be regarded as too disorganised. The sisterbook of Diepenveen is one exponent of this development. The mystagogical element is entirely absent from the *viten*, which does not necessarily mean that no traces of the mystical way of life are to be found in Diepenveen (see especially §9.3).[61] The lessons which the Diepenveen sisterbook offers its audience are geared, however, towards the practical and ascetic virtues. Both *Schwesternbuch* and sisterbook have a didactic purpose, but the 'lessons' differ considerably.

6.3 The Work of Griete Essinchghes

The authors of devout *viten* almost never identify themselves. Although we do know the names of a couple of male *viten* authors, this is usually thanks to their own biographies, which often show an interest in bibliographical information.[62] Only the author of the sisterbook from the St Agnes convent in Emmerich signed her work, with the letters S. V. W., but it is impossible to know what these letters stand for.[63] The authors of the *viten* remain anonymous because they regarded themselves as the scribal voice of the entire community. Boasting about the authorship of these biographies would go against the devout pursuit of humility. Here the sisterbook contrasts significantly with the German *Schwesternbücher*, in which the female authors frequently and rather more consciously step to the fore, often mentioning their own names.[64]

---

[59] Lewis 1996, 76–127.
[60] Ringler 1980, especially 13–15 and 352–6.
[61] See Koorn 1992, 100–5 and Mertens 2002a, 81–6 on mysticism in the sisterbooks of Diepenveen and the Meester-Geertshuis; cf. Breure 1985a, Scheepsma 1996a, 167–8 and M. van Dijk 2002, on the female aspects of Devout spirituality.
[62] Cf. for example the passage in the Latin *vite* of Johannes Brinckerinck on the editing of eight collations of diverse material (§5.4).
[63] Cf. Bollmann and Staubach 1998, 14.
[64] Cf. Lewis 1991 and Lewis 1996, 32–5 and 272–7.

At least three different authors contributed to the Diepenveen sisterbook, but they, too, failed to reveal their identity.[65] There can be no doubt that they came from the circle of Diepenveen. Who else could possess such detailed information about life within the convent walls? The possibility that the authors of the Diepenveen *viten* were confessors cannot be discounted, but it is not likely. The rectors, after all, lived outside the walls and were thus removed from the community of sisters, while it is the latter who are continually and directly addressed by the sisterbook.[66]

Both extant manuscripts of the Diepenveen sisterbook do mention the name of the scribe. Manuscript D was written by Griete Koesters, apparently a sister from the Meester-Geertshuis. For some inexplicable reason her name has been crossed out in red ink.[67] There are indications that Griete Koesters's role was not limited to that of scribe, and that she left her own mark on this redaction of the sisterbook. The *vite* of Johannes Brinckerinck, for example, has been left out of manuscript D, even though it is referred to elsewhere in the text. Further research may determine what might have motivated Griete Koesters to do this.

The scribe of manuscript DV is also known by name. On the pastedown she wrote: 'Griete Essinchghes wrote and completed this book on the Feast of the Exaltation of the Holy Cross, 14 September 1524.'[68] Like the other, anonymous, authors of the *viten* of the older redactions, Griete Essinchghes must have been a nun from Diepenveen. Further biographical details concerning her are lacking, however.[69] The 'writing' referred to in the colophon may be interpreted more broadly than merely 'copying', for Essinchghes produced a

---

[65] Cf. Jongen and Scheepsma 1993, 297–8.

[66] Rudolf Dier van Muiden did, however, compose the *vite* of Lutgert van Buderick (†1453) of the Meester-Geertshuis. That this was an exceptional case is clear from the fact that special attention is called to it here in manuscript G. It is possible that Rudolf laid the foundations for the sisterbook with this *vite* (cf. Scheepsma 1996a, 223–4 and Scheepsma 1996b, 157). On the *vite* of Lutgert van Buderick see Carasso-Kok 1981, no. 360; ed. de Man 1919, ff. 133c–137c (Middle Dutch) and Kühler 1910, 32–45 (Latin).

[67] The colophon, crossed out, is found in D, f. 197r, the reference to Brinckerinck on f. 114b.

[68] *Dit bock heeft ghescreven suster Griet Essinchghes ende gheendet op des hillighen cruces dach exaltacio anno domini MVc XXIIII* (DV, f. IIr).

[69] DV, f. 383r makes mention of a certain sister Truke Essinchghes, who was present at the death of Jutte van Culemborg in 1503; was she related to Griete? A Latin Book of Hours is preserved in the Deventer library whose provenance is somewhere in the Diepenveen area: MS SAB, I, 12 (101 E 1). It contains among other things the obituaries of mother Gerbergis (1466), father Hilbrandus (1467) and brother Hilbrandus Essink (1478). Were they perhaps relatives of Truke Essinchghes? It seems unlikely that they would be the parents of Griete Essinchghes, given the fact that she was still alive in 1524. Griete Essinchghes is absent from the Diepenveen list of names of 1592 (Dumbar 1731–88, vol. 2, 7).

distinctively personal redaction of the Diepenveen sisterbook by means of diverse interventions.

Through close scrutiny of manuscript DV it is sometimes possible to catch a glimpse of Essinchghes at work. A prologue precedes the first *vite*, Johannes Brinckerinck's, in manuscript DV, in which a first-person author addresses the audience (cited at §6.2). This first-person perspective manifests itself even more strongly in the epilogue.

> Likewise no one may think or suppose that we believe that none but those whose lives are written here were worthy of being recorded. There are very many devout sisters who have passed away and enough still alive who possess such virtues and even more. If I were to record the virtues of all the sisters, I daresay I would not accomplish it in a hundred years. But allow me to set forth this much, then, as an example of how to conduct our lives and consider it enough to follow in accordance with our shortcomings. Thus I offer this book as a testament to all those who are here now and will follow afterwards and I pray in God's name for mercy, despite my negligent life. And may God grant that I better myself and that the labour for this book be in compensation for my sins, for it has frequently and sorely tested me.[70]

This first-person narrator was very much aware of her role as creator of this redaction of the sisterbook. She even left her work behind as a testament for her fellow sisters.[71]

The epilogue follows immediately after the double-*vite* of Fye (†1504) and Cecilia van Marick (†1503), the last deceased sisters of Diepenveen to be commemorated in a *vite*.[72] This *vite* does not appear in manuscript D, nor, moreover, do the prologue and epilogue. Griete Essinchghes could have taken the prologue and epilogue from her exemplar – presumably manuscript *X – but the placement of the epilogue after the *vite* dating to 1503–4 renders this unlikely. More likely is that the epilogue was a later interpolation in redaction DV. And given the fact that the first-person narrator in this

---

[70] *Item niemant en darf dencken of mienen dat wi vermoden dat daer niemant goet gheweest en is dan daer wy hoer leven van ghescreven hebben. Deer synt alte volle devoter susteren ghestorven ende der leefter noch ghenoch die dusdane dogheden hebben ende meer dogheden daer toe. Solde ic alder suster dogheden scriven, ic en vermetes mi in hondert jaren niet toe doen. Meer laet ons dit weijnich voer ons setten, als een excempelaer daer na toe leven ende dencken ons dit ghenoch toe wesen na onser crancheit na toe volghen. Soe sette ic dit boeck toe testemente alden ghenen die hier nu synt ende namaels comen solt ende bid om Gades wyllen ene cleine almisse voer myn versumende leven. Ende God moet gheven dat ic mi noch beteren moet ende dat den arbeit van desen boke mi moet staen voer al myn sunden, want het is mi dicke zuer gheworden* (DV, ff. 387v–388r).

[71] Cf. the spiritual testaments composed by some of the Diepenveen nuns (§6.1).

[72] Oddly enough manuscript DV continues after this epilogue with the *vite* of Mette van Linbeck (ff. 388r–390v) and a history of the reforms at Hilwartshausen (ff. 391r–414v).

epilogue should logically be the same as in the prologue, the latter should also be considered a later interpolation.

The way in which the first-person forms have been adapted in DV provides further grounds for this theory. A comparison of both redactions of the sisterbook reveals that most such references in D have been converted to the third-person in DV. In addition, the editor of DV added new first-person references, in which she herself gives witness to the virtue of certain sisters. This is particularly the case in *viten* that do not appear in D. The following example concerns Beatrix van der Beeck (†1500), who even at her advanced age was a mentor to the younger nuns, even though this meant that her own internal exercises were disrupted. 'She was old and could hardly walk, but I never in my life heard of her complaining that it [i.e. a visit with one of her mentees] lasted too long or happened too frequently, no matter what time of day it was.'[73] The editor of DV has fairly consistently intervened in her exemplar wherever the author's first-person view conflict with her own. This makes it reasonable to assume that behind the first-person perspective in manuscript DV there is the voice of a single person.[74]

The next question to consider is whether it is possible that Griete Essinchghes might have been this person, i.e. the editor of manuscript DV. An important piece of evidence for this is provided by the *vite* of Stine Tolners (ff. 295v–302r). When this *vite* was copied, the scribe initially began transcribing the biography of Lubbe Snavels included there. As work progressed, however, it was decided that a separate *vite* should be devoted to Lubbe. In redaction DV the full *vite* of Lubbe Snavels follows immediately after Stine Tolners's (ff. 302r–305r). The leaf on which a portion of the

---

[73] *Sie was olt ende konde quelke over wech comen, meer ic en hoerde ny myn leven dat sie claghede dat hoer dat toe langhe of toe vake viel, tot wat tyde dat ock was* (DV, f. 340v).

[74] Wilbrink 1939, 160–4 provides an overview of the first-person forms in D, van der Veen 1976, 35–7 does the same for DV. The folios in question are f. 1r (prologue; cited at §6.2), 285r (Liesbeth van Heenvliet; see text), 289v–290v (Armgert van Lisse; cited at §6.1), 317v (Salome van den Wiel the younger), 340v (Beatrix van der Beeck; cited in text), 369v–370r (Liesbeth van Arden, which contains two interesting scribal errors, which lead one to suspect a misinterpretation of the exemplar), 384v–385r (Fye van Marick) and 387v–388r (epilogue; cited in the text). In general all the first-person pronouns in DV have been changed to the third person. Twice first-person pronouns have been left out in DV: D, f. 18b (in DV, f. 219r changed to *een suster* ('a sister')) and f. 147b (Liesbeth t'Overlaeck; not included in DV). A clear exception to this is the *vite* of Armgert van Lisse, in which the first-person pronouns have been systematically retained (cf. D, ff. 174b–c and 175a and DV, ff. 289v–290v). One explanation for this is that the compiler of DV knew Armgert personally. Finally, the passage on D, f. 89a, *Ende die dit van hoer geschreven heeft roeket oeck* ('And those who wrote this concerning her smelled it, too') pertains in DV, f. 302r to all the nuns in general (cf. on this Jongen and Scheepsma 1993, 469 n. 25). The first-person plural forms have not been systematically altered in DV; cf. for example D, f. 63a (DV, f. 253v) and D, f. 122c (DV, f. 184r), f. 123a (DV, f. 185r), f. 124b (DV, f. 186v); the statement in DV, f. 187r has no parallel in D, f. 124d.

biography of this intelligent nun from Zwolle had been written was later removed (f. 299), thus interrupting the narrative of Stine's *vite*.⁷⁵ This intervention, the decision for which was taken as the copying progressed, must almost certainly have been initiated by the scribe of this manuscript, Griete Essinchghes.

In the 'old' *vite* of Liesbeth van Heenvliet there also appears a phrase that must have been inserted by Sister Griete. This phrase looks ahead to the biography of Cecilia van Marick, who died in 1503, 'whose life I hope to touch on briefly elsewhere'.⁷⁶ One can hardly take this in any other way than to mean that Griete Essinchghes wrote the *vite* of Cecilia van Marick (and her sister Fye). Did she also write other 'late' *viten* that do not appear in manuscript D, such as those of Mette van Linbeck (†1479), Souke van Dorsten (†1480), Liesbeth van Arden (†1485), Salome van den Wiel the younger (†1490), Truke (†1469) and Beatrix van der Beeck (†1500), and Jutte van Culemborg (†1503)? It would seem certain at any rate that Griete Essinchghes was more than just the scribe.

Further comparison of redactions D and DV shows interventions in DV at other levels.⁷⁷ The cluster of *viten* concerning the nuns who fell victim to an epidemic in 1452 was discussed earlier (§6.1). In redaction D these *viten* constitute a textual unit (ff. 145c–163c). While some of these sisters are discussed elsewhere, for instance Liesbeth van Heenvliet (ff. 70a–82b), in the account of the Great Wedding her *vite* in particular is singled out (f. 147b). This group of *viten* has been broken up in manuscript DV. All the *viten* of the victims of 1452 are included, but they have been dispersed throughout the manuscript. The extremely brief reports of the last words of Gertrud Boeckmans, Alijt Ooms, Liesbeth t'Overlaeck and Gijsel ter Aves are not mentioned at all in DV. In fact, the 'wedding of 1452' is no longer a theme in manuscript DV, though Alijt Comhaer's prophetic dream is still briefly alluded to in her *vite*.⁷⁸ Given the fact that manuscript D represents in all likelihood an older arrangement of the *viten*, we must assume that their order has been rearranged in DV. The most likely candidate to have done this is again Griete Essinchghes.

At the textual level, too, a number of possible interventions have taken place. Comparison here is largely difficult, for manuscript D contains *viten* which are usually about one third shorter than those of DV. (It is also striking to see the remarkable differences in choices of words the two redactions use

---

⁷⁵ The transposition of a significant part of the text (an entire quire?) in the *vite* of Trude van Beveren, relative to manuscript D (cf. DV, ff. 163r and 168v), is another indication that no draft version preceded DV.

⁷⁶ *Welker leven ic een weinich hape toe ruren op een ander stede* (DV, f. 285r).

⁷⁷ Alterations have also been made in the order of the *viten*; for instance, a number of nuns from Holland and Zeeland have been included as a group at this point (cf. Scheepsma 1997, 241–2).

⁷⁸ DV, ff. 80v–81r.

to tell the same story.) Moreover, the *vite* of Elsebe Hasenbroecks (†1458), singled out for further scrutiny as a test case, is on the whole thirty per cent longer in redaction DV.[79] Nevertheless, the D version is in fact in some places the more complete one. This is the case, for example, with sister Elsebe's amazing experience, recounted below.

> It happened once that that ardent flame stood in the choir with spirit uplifted to the Lord, and she considered with great thankfulness the blessings the Lord had bestowed upon her. And as she stood thus, she was transported. And then she saw in the spirit the blessed heart of our Lord, and around that heart there was a splendid band of gold, and that band was very beautiful in the most marvellous fashion. And in that sweet, living heart she saw an open wound, but no blood flowed from it. And she noticed that there was writing on the golden band that enclosed the heart. Then she was addressed as with a living voice: 'With eternal love I have loved you; out of concern for you I have brought you before me.' This speech increased her fervour and gratitude towards the Lord, which was well borne out by her life and deeds. That sweet, blessed heart of our Lord looked just like a human heart, but it was broader and less pointed at the bottom, more round, and broad and open at the top, for the sweet heart of our Lord is always open and broad for the salvation of mankind.[80]

> Once, in the time of Father Ludolphus, when she stood in the choir, a voice spoke to her, 'With eternal love I have loved you; out of mercy for you I have brought you to me.' This was very comforting and pleasing for her to hear.[81]

---

[79] It is in the description of Elsebe's life in the world in particular that a great deal of information has been left out in D, such as the advice of her brother Johan van Delden, Carthusian at Monnikhuizen near Arnhem, to look for another husband (cf. DV, f. 94r–v). At the end of the *vite* the order is changed radically compared to DV. There too we find most of the passages that are more extensive in D.

[80] *Op een tijt stont die vurige vlamme in den choer myt enen op ghevenen gemoede in onsen lieven heren ende over dachte die grote waldaden die hoer onse lieve here gedaen hadde mit groter dancberheit. Ende doe sie aldus stont, quam sie mydallen van hoer selven. Ende doe sach sie inden geeste dat gebenedyde herte ons lieven heren, ende omme dat herte genck een schone gulden bant, ende die bant was seer claer in wonderliker manieren. Ende in dat suete mynlike herte sach sie een apene wonde, mer daer and genck geen bloet uut. Ende sie merckte dat in den gulden bant die om dat herte genck wat geschreven was. Doe waert hoer toe gespraken als myt eenre levendiger stemmen: 'In ewiger mynnen heb ic dy gemynt; daer omme dijnre ontbarmende heb ic dy tot my getagen'. Van deser toesprekinge waert sie noch vuriger ende dancbare onsen lieven heren, als hoer leven ende wanderinge wal bewees. Dat suete gebenedyde herte ons lieven heren dat liet recht als een menschen herte, mer het was brieder ende ock niet so scharp beneden, mer wat ront ende baven breet ende apen, want dat suete herte ons lieven heren is altoes apen ende breet tot zalicheit der menschen* (D, ff. 116d–117b).

[81] *Sonderlinghe by pater Ludolphus tijt, doe sie stont inden choer, waert hoer eens toe ghespraken 'Van ewigher mynnen hebbe ic u ghemijnt; daer om ontfarmende hebbe ic di tot my ghetaghen', dat zeer troestlick ende ghenochlich was toe horen.* (DV, f. 105r).

Manuscript DV, then, is much more concise: it reduces this vision of sister Elsebe to an address by the Lord, in which it is the comforting aspect of the message in particular that receives emphasis. At the same time it adds some information about Father Ludolf van Kampen, rector of Diepenveen from 1449 to 1455.

It is not likely that this vision is a later interpolation in manuscript D. How would Griete Koesters, the scribe of manuscript D, have come by information like this from Diepenveen in 1534? It is much more likely that she took the complete passage from her presumed exemplar, manuscript *Y. This would indicate that here we have an intentional intervention in manuscript DV, for if the account of Elsebe's vision appeared in *Y, then it must have been present in *X as well, which itself was in all likelihood the model for DV. The reasons for this intervention are nowhere given, but it is reasonable to look for them in the move, cited earlier, to eliminate the culture of mysticism at Diepenveen, a move that resulted in ecstatic experiences being played down. The 'dismantling' of the conglomerate group of *viten* concerning the victims of the epidemic of 1452 in redaction DV, based as it was on a prophetic dream, may also be traced to this mistrustful attitude. Moreover Diepenveen was never known to be a convent whose inhabitants were particularly interested in the supernatural. Katharina van Naaldwijk appears after her death to a monk in Gouda (Holland), for, she says, in Diepenveen 'they regard revelations as nothing but fantasies and sickness of the head'.[82]

The examples of changes, expansions and traces of adaptation discussed here illustrate how the DV redaction of the Diepenveen sisterbook assumed a character of its own. It is very likely that Griete Essinchghes was the force behind this redaction, although she would certainly have consulted others (the prioress, perhaps, or the rector?). Griete emerges as someone who approached her subject and materials actively. She did not copy her exemplar slavishly, but instead edited her sources sometimes radically, arranged them differently, and wrote at least one, but quite probably ten, new *viten*. Griete Essinchghes was thus not merely the scribe of manuscript DV, but the author – now compiling, now creating new material – of a new redaction of the sisterbook of Diepenveen. The devout genre of *viten* may be seen at its most highly perfected form in the Diepenveen sisterbook. What is true for Griete Essinchghes's redaction is true as well for the other surviving redactions of the Diepenveen sisterbook (D and B), and probably for the now-lost manuscripts *X and *Y too. Whenever a new version of the sisterbook was made the current one served as the model, to be sure, but it was adapted by the editor(s) according to a more or less established pattern.

---

[82] *Daer holtment al voer fantasien ende crancheit des hovedes dat daer gheapenbaert woert* (DV, f. 256v). Cf. Mertens 2002a, 89–92.

6.4 *The* Kroniek Bethanië

In 1486 Liesbeth van Bergen, prioress of the convent of Bethanië in Mechelen from 1482 to 1503, gave one of her nuns the task of writing a convent chronicle. The convent in Brabant had been in existence at the time for about sixty-five years. The chronicle itself reports briefly on this event.

> In the year 1486 just cited, this chronicle was first collected and compiled by one of the poor sisters, a professed nun, in this house of God, who was very hard pressed and hampered by a great illness. Nevertheless, because she had always held this house of God of Bethanië in such high esteem, she eagerly and willingly performed this labour at the behest of our reverend prioress, Liesbeth van Bergen – described above – even though it proved a difficult thing, in that past events were many and greatly obscured by the long interval before the task was begun and the fact that many people had died. Therefore she prays humbly that any and all who find anything inaccurate here will correct it, and finally she asks fervently for all those who read or hear this to say an Ave Maria for her, that her name may be written in the Book of Life along with all of the names contained in this book. Amen.[83]

This anonymous nun probably received her special task because of her physical infirmity, which would have prevented her from participating in daily physical labour. It would seem that she is speaking about her own work here in the third person, a common phenomenon in medieval prologues. Whether this is truly the case is difficult to determine. The manuscript containing the medieval portion of the chronicle of Bethanië is written in a single hand, which continues to around 1580. This hand cannot possibly be that of the infirm chronicle author. It is quite possible that the scribe inserted a passage dealing with the founder of the chronicle under the year 1486, or that she paraphrased a prologue-like text for her predecessor.[84]

---

[83] *Inden voorscreven jare van LXXXVI* [= 1486] *soo wert desen boeck eerst vergaedert ende ghecopuleert van een der aermer suster professie nonne in desen godtshuyse, die seer beswaert ende belast was met grooter sieckten. Nochtans want sy dit godshuys van Bethanien altyt heeft ghehadt in grooter weerden, soo heeft sy ter begheerten onser eerwerdigher priorinnen, mater Lysbeth van Berghen boven beschreven, dit werck gheerne ende willichlyck beaerbeyt, al est haer gheweest seer lastich want die voorleden dinghen waeren veel ende seer verduystert overmidts lanckheyt der tyt eermen begoste ende dat veel persoonen waren ghestorven. Daerom sy bidt ootmoedelyck dat eenen yeghelyck wil verbeteren dat hy daer in vindt incorect, ende ten lesten bidt sy oock seer hertelyck eenen yeghelycken diet sal lesen oft hooren om eenen ave maria, dat haeren naem mach werden gheschreven int boeck des levens ende oock alle der gheender namen die in dit boeck syn ghescreven. Amen* (Kroniek Bethanië, 1486).

[84] The chronicle of Bethanië, comprising three volumes, covers the period from its establishment in 1421 to the year 1765. The text dealing with the medieval period of the convent's history is in MS Mechelen, Stadsarchief, EE XXIX/1. A few fragments have been published by Cordemans de Bruyne 1896, 25–8 and 60–82. Because the

The anonymous first chronicler faced a difficult task. She laments in particular that the earliest history of the convent is shrouded in the mists of time: many of the older nuns who might have helped her had already died. The oral transmission was apparently of great importance to her, but documentary sources covering most of the convent's history must also have been available. In the entry for 1429 (cited below), the veiling of Liesbeth van Bergen, later both prioress and commissioner of this chronicle, is described in such neutral terms that it would seem as if the author of the entry knew nothing of her future. Presumably there already existed extensive records of (parts of) the early history of the convent. The chronicle of Bethanië is remarkably precise and detailed almost from the very outset, but the information covering the first few years is rather cursory. It seems that the new model of 1486 led to a more detailed recording of events than had earlier been the case.

Prioress Liesbeth van Bergen was the one who commissioned the writing of her convent's history, but the text leaves us in the dark as to her motives.[85] Internal genre indications are almost entirely lacking: only once does the text refer to itself as *deser cronyken* ('this chronicle'); elsewhere it uses the neutral *desen boeck* ('this book').[86] The chronicle of Bethanië came into being towards the end of the fifteenth century, when several historiographical texts were written in convents: not only sisterbooks, but also chronicles and numerous hybrid forms of the two. Bethanië followed this trend. Apparently the convent, or at least its prioress, possessed sufficient historical awareness to appreciate the value of a written history. Every once in a while it is made clear why the chronicle was written; among such passages is the account of the first prioress of Bethanië, Liesbeth Tayen from Tiel, trained at Diepenveen:

> This has been written for the following reason: in order that those who were not present at the beginning, those who are here now and those who will join us in the future, should have some knowledge of things past, and should serve all the more fervently with appropriate gratitude to God, both day and night, faithfully praying for the souls of those who have brought our house of God thus far, provided and worked for it, as will be clearly seen from the writings that follow.[87]

---

manuscript is not foliated, I have seen fit here to cite the text of the *Kroniek Bethanië* under the year of any given entry.

[85] The chronicle is not mentioned in Liesbeth's biography (*Kroniek Bethanië*, 1503). If she had donated money or resources for its writing, it would undoubtedly have been reported among her other material accomplishments.

[86] *Kroniek Bethanië*, 1522 (on the occasion of the one hundredth anniversary of the convent).

[87] *Dit es hier daerom ghescreven, op dat die ghene die inden beginne niet en waeren, nu syn ende noch comen sullen doch kennisse hebben souden vanden dinghen voorschreven, ende met werdigher danckbaerheyt Gode te vierichlycker dienen, nachte ende dach,*

This chronicle, then, was written in order to pass on certain knowledge, to inspire devotion and to exhort prayers for the sisters who had made Bethanië great.[88]

We know even less about the later authors of the chronicle of Bethanië than we do about its founder. It seems logical that the work would have been continued by other sisters, rather than by the rector or a *socius*, but as with the *viten* from Diepenveen, its authors remain anonymous. The chronicle writers from Bethanië restrict themselves to the personal and material history of the convent in particular, and take great care to record names and numbers accurately. These rather dry (but historically interesting) lists hardly afford the chronicler's personality much opportunity to emerge. Sometimes it does shine through, when for example the community loses a valued member or a confessor, and she includes a brief biography of the deceased.

The chronicle of this convent in Mechelen is in essence an annalistic one: successive authors record the most important events, year after year, according to a fixed pattern.[89] The structure of the chronicle of Bethanië is lucid and well organised. The entry for each year first notes under whose commissionership the convent was placed. In the early years this was the prior of Eemstein, later the prior of Rooklooster, and in 1438 the prior of ten Troon near Grobbendonk assumed this task. Next follow the names of the rector and the prioress. Should there in any given year be a change in one of these three offices, for example through relocation or death, then almost without exception there follows a biography of the officer in question. Furthermore the chronicle records all new veilings, professions and deaths. Finally, important events in the history of the convent are described, such as visits by the imperial family.[90]

By way of illustration the entire entry for the year 1429 is printed below.[91] At that time the convent had not been in existence for very long and the sources concerning that period were limited. So early in the convent's history there were hardly any deaths to report, and consequently no biographies.

---

ghetrouwelycken biddende voor die sielen der geender die ons godtshuys dus verre gheholpen hebben, becosticht ende beaerbeyt, soomen uut den nae beschreven schriften noch claerlycker sal moeghen bekennen (*Kroniek Bethanië*, 1432).

[88] In the biography of the second prioress Clara 's Clercx (†1463?) it reads: *Op dat die genen die sint comen ende noch comen sullen ende die geen kennis en hebben haers weerdighen persoons, dat dan uut desen schriften doch kennes moghen hebben* ('That those who are here now and those who will join us in the future and have no knowledge of her worthy person, may learn about her from these words'; *Kroniek Bethanië*, 1463). Persoons 1993c, 526–7 gives the French form of Clara's surname: *Soleres*.

[89] On this historical genre, see Schmale 1985, 105–12.

[90] *Kroniek Bethanië*, 1486 (on the arrival of the Emperor Frederick), 1525 and 1530 (the Countess van Elfsteyn, daughter of Emperor Maximilian of Austria).

[91] Cordemans de Bruyne 1896, 72–82 (even pages) provides the entire text for the year 1455.

In the year of our Lord 1429.

In this past year of 1429 the rector of this house of God was Lord Willem Berwouts, and Sister Liesbeth van Tiel, a professed nun from Diepenveen, was prioress.

Likewise in the same year of 1429, in September, at around the Mass of the Angels, the following five people received the habit of the holy order from the reverend prior of Eemstein. Three of them took the nun's habit while the two others became *conversae*.

The first was Sister Liesbeth van Croenenborch, nun.

The second, Sister Joanna Dierix, nun.

The third, Sister Margriete van Geerdege<e>m, nun.

The fourth, Sister Deliana Smolders, *conversa*; she later became a nun.

The fifth, Sister Margriete Nots, *conversa*.

Likewise in the same year of 1429, in the first days of the month of October on the morning of St Remigius' day, at low mass, the two persons listed below also received the holy habit of the order from the reverend prior of Eemstein:

The first, Sister Margriete Hannemans, nun.

The second, Sister Kunegonda van Boxtel, *conversa*.

In this same year of 1429 a damsel by the name of Katharina van Eppegheem entered into this house of God; she arrived the day after St Luke's day, in October.

Likewise in the same year of 1429 another damsel, by the name of Liesbeth van Bergen, entered into this house of God.

Likewise in the same year of 1429 another damsel, Katharina Nots, entered into this house of God.

Likewise in the same year of 1429 another damsel, by the name of Sister Joanna vanden Hoede, entered into this house of God.[92]

---

[92] *Inden jaere ons heeren MIIIIC ende XXI. In desen jaere voorschreven van XXIX soo was rector dees godtshuys heer Willem Berwouts voorschreven ende suster Lysbeth van Tyele, professi nonne uut Diepeven, was doen priorinne. Item inden selven jaere van XXIX inder maent september ontrent alder inghelendach, soo ontfinghen dese nae beschreven vyf persoonen dat abyt der heyliger religien vander hant des eerwerdighen prioer van Eymsteyn. Die dry waeren ghecleet nonne ende die twee ander conversinnen: Die eerste, suster Lysbeth van Croenenborch, nonne. Die tweede, suster Joanna Dierix, nonne. Die derde, suster Margriete van Geerdege<e>m, nonne. Die vierde, suster Deliana Smolders, conversinne; dese wert naemaels nonne. Die vyfde, suster Margriete Nots, conversinne. Item inden selven jaere van XXIX ende inden eersten daeghe der maent october op sincte Remigiusdach, soo ontfinghen oock vander hant des eerwerdighen prioer van Eymsteyn, des morgens onder een lesende misse, dat abyt der heyliger religien dese twee nae beschreven persoonen: Die eerste, suster Margriete Hannemans, nonne. Die ander, suster Kunegonda van Boxtel, conversinne. Item inden selven jaere van XXIX soo es ghecomen in desen godtshuyse van Bethanien een jonffrouwe, geheeten Katharina van Eppegheem; dese quam des anderen daechs nae sincte Lucasdach in october. Item noch inden selven jaere van XXIX soo es gecomen in desen godtshuyse een ander jonffrouwe, gheheeten Lysbeth van Bergen. Item noch inden selven jaere van XXIX soo es oock ghecomen in desen godtshuyse jonffrouwe Katharina Nots. Item noch inden selven jaere van XXIX soo es ghecomen in desen godtshuyse een jonffrouwe gheheeten suster Joanna vanden Hoede* (Kroniek Bethanië, 1429).

The authors could take somewhat more poetic license with the biographies of rectors and prioresses than they could with such lists of data and facts. The biographies concentrate on these people's performance of their office, with a strong emphasis on their contributions to the convent. Barbara van der Elst was prioress from 1475 to 1482. The chronicle briefly describes the illness that first forced her to resign and subsequently took her life. Next her spiritual stature is characterised in three sentences.

> And at all times, day and night, she led the sisters in strict observance and maintenance of the order, for she was like a mirror of humility, and an industrious bee, gathering a wealth of virtues. And she brought many people to virtue through her exemplary, virtuous life and example, her sweetly consoling and loving words. Nor did she spare herself because of old age, but rather continued most diligently in the service of God day and night up to her last illness.[93]

Next follows a much more elaborate entry, in which the great works accomplished under this prioress are discussed in greater detail. Despite the political unrest caused by the extremely strict rule of the Burgundian overlords, she managed to have a portion of the main convent building constructed, as well as a turf barn. Furthermore she had a fishpond dug, and under her leadership a portion of the wall surrounding the convent was constructed.

In the biographies of the confessors of Bethanië the emphasis also falls squarely on their physical accomplishments. The biography of rector Kerstiaen van 's-Grevensande, also known as Christianus Bloots (†1504), constitutes a special case. He was prior of ten Troon – and as such commissioner of Bethanië – but in 1487 he relinquished the priorship. The chronicle does not expand on his reasons for this unusual decision, but presumably he did so out of humility. Brother Jan van Peer, at the time rector of Bethanië, was elected prior of the convent of ten Troon, and Kerstiaen van 's-Grevensande took his place. Lord Kerstiaen made a great impression as a person and pastor; even the duke of Burgundy, Philip the Fair, expressed his great admiration for him. According to the chronicle of Bethanië Kerstiaen was possessed of an unusual number of skills and characteristics that were of service to the holy order, for he was exceptionally devout and steadfast in the celebration of the holy mass, mature and very firm in his habits, so that he was always a living example for others of the holy devout way of life, and

---

[93] *Ende sy heeft nacht ende dach, vroech ende spade den suster voor ghegaen in strengher observantien ende onderhoudinghe der ordenen, want sy heeft gheweest als eenen spiegel der oetmoedicheyt ende een neerstighe bie om te vergaederen veel schatten der doechden. Ende veel menschen heeftse ghetrocken ter doecht overmidts haeren doechdelycken voorgaenden leven ende exempel, suete troestelycken ende minnelycken woorden. Oock soo and spaerdese haer outheyt niet, maer sy vervolchden den dienst godts nacht ende dach seer neerstelyck tot haeren lesten sieckten* (Kroniek Bethanië, 1482).

moreover he was very pleasing and kind in his speech, so that religious and layfolk alike were always very much comforted by him.[94]

Judging by his career and actions, Kerstiaen was a living example of devout humility, yet the chronicle does little to bring out this aspect of his life. Particular attention is paid instead to the way in which this rector protected the convent during the political struggles of the period.[95]

The chronicle always places great emphasis on the history of construction at Bethanië. The biographies of the prioresses describe without fail and in great detail the construction and renovation projects undertaken by them. The renovation of the refectory in 1515 was carried out under the supervision of prioress Margriete Oddyns (†1541) and rector Tielman Schuermans (†1537) – the chronicle even refers to him as a *man van timmeringhe* ('a man of carpentry'). For the benefit of those who entered the convent after the renovation, there follows a description of the situation beforehand:

> Built on this very spot the refectory was very broad, but no higher than the corner of the wall itself. And above it there was an attic that served as the dormitory where the working sisters slept. And because it was so wide, there were four long beams that extended through the refectory. [. . .] and the windows were large wooden affairs without any glass panes, built according to the old ways, so that it looked more like a stall than a refectory.[96]

No trace here of extolling the old, primitive conditions, as one finds in the sisterbook of Diepenveen. On the contrary, the author is pleased with the blessings of progress and condemns the 'old ways' of ascesis and austerity. Gone are the days when 'odours of cooking (*lit*. food) hung so thickly in the air' in the refectory 'that the sisters thought they would become ill from the fumes going to their heads'.[97]

---

[94] *Sonderlinghe veele bequaemheden ende puenten die dienlyck waren der heyliger religien, want hy sonderlinghe devoet ende ghestadich was inder celebreringhe der heyligher missen, ryp ende seer ghestichtich in seeden, soo dat hy altyt toenende was voor alle menschen een devoete heylighe wandelinghe, nochtans was hy seer suet ende goederthieren in toesprake, soo dat geestelyck and werelycke persoonen seer in hem ghesticht werden* (Kroniek Bethanië, 1487).

[95] Lord Kerstiaen's performance as rector is recounted in the *Kroniek Bethanië*, 1487; in the entry for the year 1504 it is recorded how, having attended a celebration of profession at Bethanië, he was forced to remain there due to a sudden illness and died thirty days later. For more on Kerstiaen van 's-Grevensande (Christianus Bloots) and Jan (Augustijns) van Peer, see Persoons 1993b, 489.

[96] *Synde op dese selve plaetse soo was hy alsoo veer, niet hoogher dan den muer hoeck en is. Ende daer boven lach eenen solder ende was eenen dormpter daer de werck susteren sliepen. Ende want hy soo wyt is, soo stonden vier groote balcken lanckx door den refter. [. . .] Ende het waren al groote houten vensteren sonder ghelasen al nae die oude wet, soo dat hy bat ghelyckten eenen stal dan eenen refter* (Kroniek Bethanië, 1515).

[97] *Soo stercken rueck vander spysen . . . dat den susteren dochte dat sy sieck werden van dat hen die locht al int hooft sloech* (Kroniek Bethanië, 1515).

6.5 Chronicle and Sisterbook

Both the chronicle of Bethanië and the Diepenveen sisterbook record the history of a Windesheim convent, but they do this in different ways for different ends. The differences between the two are clearly revealed in the episode concerning the organisation of Bethanië by two sisters from Diepenveen, which is described in both sources. In 1424 an initiative was set in motion to bring Bethanië into the Chapter of Windesheim. Father Willem Berwouts from Groenendaal became rector and Liesbeth Tayen van Tiel (†1452) and Janne van Diest (†1444) came over from Diepenveen.[98] As prioress and procuratrix respectively, they were expected to introduce the Diepenveen way of life at Bethanië. Both of these Diepenveen nuns stayed in Mechelen from 1423 to 1432. The accounts of the success of this monastic reform in the chronicle and the sisterbook could not be more dissimilar.

Judging by the chronicle of Bethanië, Liesbeth Tayen's tenure as prioress was virtually untroubled:

> The aforementioned sister and mother superior Lysbeth was the very first ordained and confirmed prioress of the convent of Bethanië, which house of God she served very maternally, very lovingly and very faithfully, and furthermore she helped this house of God in many profitable ways at many times and in many places, as was well known among the sisters who lived with her at the time.[99]

The chronicle trumpets the praises of Janne van Diest as well. She fulfilled her task of supervising the material needs of the convent seriously, meekly and lovingly. When the Diepenveen nuns return home in 1432, the chronicle once again lauds their great virtues. In the biographies of these nuns, too, the emphasis falls on the services they performed in the expansion of the convent.

The sisterbook of Diepenveen gives a dramatically different account of this reformation. Prioress Liesbeth in particular seems to have had serious conflicts with her Brabantine subordinates.

---

[98] The biography of Liesbeth Tayen van Tiel is recounted in DV, ff. 362v–365v and D, ff. 159d–161a; see also the *Kroniek Bethanië*, 1421 and 1432. The *vite* of Janne van Diest is found in DV at ff. 366r–368r and D, ff. 161b–162c; see also the *Kroniek Bethanië*, 1421 and 1432. The sisterbook consistently refers to the latter as 'Johan'. In order to avoid confusion, I have here maintained the spelling found in the chronicle.

[99] *Dese suster ende moeder Lysbeth voorschreven is gheweest die alder eerste gheordineerde ende gheconfirmeerde priorinne dees convents van Bethanien voorschreven, den welcken godtshuyse sy seer moederlycke, seer minnelycke ende seer ghetrouwelyck ghedint heeft ende voort gheholpen in menichvuldighen profyte die sy desen voorschreven godtshuyse te menigher tyt ende plaetsen ghedaen heeft, ghelyckerwys den susteren die doen ter tyt by haer woonden wel condich was* (*Kroniek Bethanië*, 1423).

They [Liesbeth and Janne] travelled there together in obedience and out of love for God, whom they truly loved and adored. Nevertheless, they did not depart from Diepenveen without great heaviness of heart, out of both spiritual and practical concerns. This was not surprising, for what they found there was not Diepenveen. And when they arrived, they did their best to establish the customs of Diepenveen and to teach their customs, and they laboured in all ways to build a solid foundation there with the help of our Lord. When they had worked diligently and devoutly and, with God's help, had provided good leadership for nine years, the weeds of wilfulness began to spring up, in that they felt that she [Liesbeth] was too strict and too righteous; though they [the rebels] were not many in number, they developed such a dislike for her that it was all the good sister from Diest could do to calm them down and appease their anger both day and night.[100]

A group of nuns emerged who felt that the prioress was much too strict. Janne van Diest mediated between the two parties, but did not succeed in resolving the conflict. The exact circumstances surrounding the resignation of Liesbeth Tayen remain unclear. Did she of her own volition request a replacement, or was she simply not re-elected by the convent of Bethanië? The sisters of Bethanië would have liked to have had Janne van Diest as their new prioress, but she opted to accompany Liesbeth Tayen, who returned to Diepenveen.[101] From the Diepenveen perspective, then, the mission to Brabant ended in disappointment.

What we have here is an important difference in attitude between Diepenveen and some of the other Windesheim convents. By no means all the monastic reforms undertaken by Diepenveen were a success. Griete Dagens, for instance, undertook a brave but fruitless attempt to reorganise Bethanië in Arnhem according to the Diepenveen model. She found herself thwarted at every turn by the rector, who was apparently not enamoured of the strict Windesheim regime.[102] In general, Diepenveen appointed its best nuns for

---

[100] *Sie toghen toe samen heen in ghehorsamheit ende dat om die minne Gades, dien sie inder waerheyt mynden ende lief hadden. Nochtant and begheven sie Dyepenven niet sonder grote zwaerheit des harten, inwendich ende uutwendich. Dat and was niet te verwonderen, want Dyepenven and was daer niet toe wynden. Ende doe sie daer quemen, deden sie hoer beste hem Dyepenvens ghewonte in toe prenten ende hoer maniren hem te leren ende zeer daeromme arbeiden van buten ende van bijnnen om daer een goet fondament toe legghen mitter hulpe ons lieven heren. Als sie trouwelick ende goddienstlick ghearbeit hadden neghen jaer lanck ende daer een goed reyment ghemaket hadden mitter hulpe Gades, soe bestoent daer op toe spruten dat hoelt der wettentheit, alsoe dat hem dochte dat sie toe strack ende toe rechtvierdich was, meer deser and was nochtant niet volle, meer dese creghen enen helen afkier van hoer, alsoe dat die gode suster van Diest ghenoch toe done hadde sie toe vreden toe setten ende hem die passien uut toe slaen nacht ende dach* (DV, ff. 363v–364v; cf. D, ff. 160b–c).

[101] DV, f. 364v.

[102] DV, ff. 50v–52v and D, ff. 128c–129c. On these and other reforms undertaken by Diepenveen see Kühler 1914, 313–37.

this kind of endeavour. Presumably these reformers maintained high standards which they themselves could meet, but which asked too much of the average nun. The conflict between Liesbeth Tayen and the convent of Bethanië had its origins in a difference of opinion concerning the degree of strictness in monastic discipline.

Generally speaking, the atmosphere at Bethanië would have been a great deal laxer than at the almost fanatical Diepenveen. The chronicle and the sisterbook reflect this difference. A good example of this is the way both works describe the lives of various former abbesses of noble nunneries. Jutte van Ahaus (†1408), abbess of the nunnery in Vreden, has already been mentioned. She came to Diepenveen seeking to deepen her inner life. Back in Vreden, she educated her little niece Griete van Ahaus (†1458). Griete later became abbess of the Benedictines of Freckenhorst near Münster. In 1423 Griete followed the path of her aunt: because her wealth and high position stood in the way of a pure spiritual life, she too went to Diepenveen.[103]

In the course of 1455, the former abbess of the imperial abbey at Thorn, Jacoba van Loon–van Heinsberg (†1466), arrived at Bethanië.[104] It is thanks particularly to her exhorbitant gifts to Bethanië that the chronicle devotes so much space to her. She is even referred to there as its second founder, after Maria van Boutershem. Two other high-born women accompanied Jacoba van Loon from Thorn, Christine van Rijswijk and Joanna van Chaboth. The arrival of these three nuns was apparently also prompted by a desire for a pure spiritual life. Jacoba van Loon took the status of *familiaris*, which meant that she could not assume monastic office. As we have already seen, she was intensely involved in her meditative exercises. She, too, added a remarkable activity to the traditional monastic programme: she had a *formerye* or

---

[103] The biography of Griete van Ahaus appears in DV, ff. 319v–322r and D, f. 146a–d; on her position at Freckenhorst, see Kohl 1975, 318–20. Griete's step-brother, Hendrik van Ahaus, was one of the great sources of inspiration for the Modern Devotion in Germany.

[104] A recent geneaology of Loon-Heinsberg appears in Paquay 1990, 137; cf. Cordemans de Bruyne 1896, appendix X. On Jacoba's origins and her period at Thorn, see Koch 1994, disk, no. 68 (for the royal abbey of Thorn, see pp. 31–3). An account of Jacoba's life at Bethanië appears in the *Kroniek Bethanië*, 1455, ed. Cordemans de Bruyne 1896, 72–80 (no. 14). After her death an inventory of her house of mourning was made (ed. Cordemans de Bruyne 1896, 40–59 and Persoons 1980, 104–11). Jacoba came from the highest social circles. Bishop Jan van Luik was her (half)brother and her sister Maria van Loon was married to Jan van Nassau (on Maria van Loon see Paquay 1990; on her personal library see also Brinkman 1993). Maria named Bethanië in one of her wills (Paquay 1990, 189). Odilia van Loon, daughter of Maria and Jan, also arrived in Bethanië in 1455; in 1464 she made profession and in 1477 she departed to help organise the convent founded by her mother, Vredenberg te Princenhage (near Breda) (*Kroniek Bethanië*, 1455, 1464 and 1477; ed. Cordemans de Bruyne 1896, 26–7). For more on Vredenberg, which was moved to Lier in the sixteenth century, see Vanhoof 1993; on Odilia and her mother, see Vanhoof 1993, 667.

printing-press built, where religious images and texts were printed using wood-cuts. Judging by the caption of an extant *Ecce panis angelorum* print, the three sisters from Thorn were involved, along with others, in the work that went on in this press.[105] Christine van Rijswijk lived in Bethanië for twelve years as *familiaris*, but ultimately opted to become a canoness regular. But because she found the liturgical requirements of the Windesheim Bethanië too stringent, she moved to a regular convent where only the Hours of the Virgin Mary were recited.[106] Joanna van Chaboth remained in Bethanië and made profession in 1464.[107]

Jacoba van Loon's generosity is a prominent leitmotiv in her biography. Her arrival at Bethanië led to a considerable expansion of the physical complex of buildings. Jacoba had a house built for herself on the convent grounds which reverted to the convent after her death. And without exception all of her other gifts, great and small, are described. She had the choir decorated, for example, with a blue silk cloth for the altar, a large crucifix and a golden statue of the Virgin Mary. Griete van Ahaus's *vite* is remarkably vague in this regard: it restricts itself to mentioning that she gave all of her possessions away to anyone who needed them. This was sufficient within the context of the sisterbook, for in its pages there was little interest in material matters. Griete's actions demonstrate that her conversion was complete and no further details are required.

At least as remarkable are the differences in the way the chronicle and the sisterbook approach the theme of eating and drinking. The Diepenveen sisterbook describes Jutte van Ahaus's behaviour at table as follows:

> She would choose the very poorest and least savoury morsels from the dishes before anyone else saw them; no one could take her place there who was so quick as to be able to claim the unsavoury bits before she did, so that her sisters avoided sitting with her at table, for they could not bear it. And some of them could not watch for the pain it caused them in their hearts when they considered who she was and who she had been.[108]

Taking the least savoury portions of food is entirely out of keeping with the status of a former abbess, and some of the nuns seem to have had trouble

---

[105] For the most recent treatment of the press at Bethanië, see Persoons 1993c, 524 and 527. An image of this print is in Scheepsma 1997, 89.
[106] *Kroniek Bethanië*, 1455; ed. Cordemans de Bruyne 1896, 80 (cf. §3.1, n. 13).
[107] *Kroniek Bethanië*, 1455 and 1464; ed. Cordemans de Bruyne 1896, 25–6.
[108] *Sie plach dat alre snodeste ende onbequaemste uutter scottelen toe nemen eer een ander toe sach; daer and konde niemant bi comen toe sitten die soe behende was die hoer voer conde comen dat onbequaemste uutter scottelen toe nemen, dat hoer die susteren scuweden daer bi toe sitten over tafele, want siet tot horen goede niet liden and mochten. Ende sommich and mochtens niet sien van sericheit des harten als sie dachten wie sie weer ende wie sie gheweest hadde* (DV, f. 136r; cf. D, f. 36c–d).

watching her do this. But Jutte's lack of fastidiousness does show that she was capable of humbling herself utterly, which is precisely what the sisterbook seeks to illustrate. Elsewhere we learn that Jutte van Ahaus even gnawed on the remains of fishbones discarded by some workers.[109] The chronicle of Bethanië illustrates a different attitude towards the fortification of the inner woman. Jacoba van Loon is lauded because, among other things, 'even in the final hour of her life it was her wish that the sisters be well provided for with food and drink at her wake'.[110] The tone of this account suggests that the sisters of Bethanië enjoyed the meal very much indeed.

The descriptions of holiday feasts given by the chronicle of Bethanië stand in stark contrast with the austerity preached by the Diepenveen sisterbook. The celebration of feasts and jubilees seems to have increased dramatically in Bethanië in the sixteenth century.[111] It is not without some satisfaction that the chronicle notes how at these occasions the meat was roasted, or how much wine was served, or who paid for the feast, and so forth. An example:

> In that same year, on a Sunday in the octave of All Saints, a great feast was held to honour the jubilee of our beloved sister Barbara van den Dorpe. And she treated us to a sumptuous feast, and she often gave us prints as gifts, for she was always generous towards the convent.[112]

It became the custom for the celebrant – be it the rector, the prioress, a sister or *donatin* – to give the convent a meal with wine, as well as small gifts to all the nuns, devotional pictures or prints, for example.[113] Sometimes texts were read aloud on such occasions. Poems and refrains were read at the jubilee celebrations of Rector Tielman Schuermans in 1530 and Prioress Margriete Oddyns in 1539. Both were presented with a special jubilee book in which the texts delivered were recorded. Neither of these books survives, and nothing is known about their contents.[114]

The author of the chronicle describes these festivities with unmistakable pleasure. She is hardly able to conceal her anger when she reports how in

---

[109] DV, ff. 137v–138r and D, f. 37c–d.
[110] *Oock in die leste urs haers levens soo begeerden sy datmen den susteren emmer weldoen soude van spyse ende van drancke tot haeren uutvaert* (Cordemans de Bruyne 1896, 74).
[111] The earliest mention I encountered is in the *Kroniek Bethanië*, 1517.
[112] *In desen selven jare, des sondaechs binnen die octave van allen heylighen, soo hielmen groote feeste van dat jubilee van onse beminde suster Barbara van den Dorpe. Ende sy gaf ons een ryckelycke maeltyt ende beeldekens te menighen tyde, want sy was den convente altyt gunstich* (*Kroniek Bethanië*, 1519).
[113] In addition to the jubilee of Barbara van den Dorpe (1519), already mentioned, prints were distributed on the jubilees of Katharina van Giesen (1526) and Jacoba van Doenereyn (1537). In light of the preceding we might speculate as to whether the nuns printed these themselves. It is rather unlikely that the term *beeldekens* refers to statuettes, though these were known to have been present in Windesheim convents.
[114] *Kroniek Bethanië*, 1530 and 1539.

1544 the celebration of jubilees was forbidden by the Chapter General.[115] Maria de Latere, prioress from 1541 to 1573, wished to obey the Chapter – so says the chronicle – and therefore allowed a number of jubilees to go uncelebrated. She later managed to get permission to celebrate feast days somewhat more elaborately, after which they amply recovered their losses.[116] That Maria de Latere attempted to practise restraint is evident from the account of her own jubilee. The celebrant preferred to have no praise poems presented to her, to the great disappointment of the convent. But because she was not entirely sure she would live to see her jubilee, this prioress twice took an advance on her feast, so that in fact it was celebrated three times.[117]

It should of course be noted that the high ascetic accomplishments of Diepenveen took place in the fifteenth century. In 1413, for example, Katharina van Naaldwijk's mother had to ask special permission of the prior of Windesheim to offer the convent roast goose on the occasion of her daughter's profession.[118] The jubilee accounts all date to after 1500, and Bethanië would not have been the only Windesheim convent where such feasts were held. On the other hand it is true that manuscript DV, a new redaction of the sisterbook, was written at Diepenveen in 1524. At the very least, it expressed the intention that the ideal of asceticism and poverty should be kept alive at Diepenveen in the sixteenth century. Thus it is that we can identify significant differences in religious attitudes between Diepenveen and Bethanië.

It would no doubt be going too far to try to account for the Diepenveen preference for the *vite* genre by means of this difference in attitude, and yet there does seem to be a connection. The convent of Diepenveen was an important bearer of the female reformation tradition in the Modern Devotion, as was the Meester-Geertshuis. When these communities set out to record their histories, they chose a literary form that did the most justice to their religious ideals. The sisterbook illustrates strikingly how a successful spiritual community is built up by individual persons, often pioneers, who succeed in rising above themselves. Bethanië would never have developed fully without the idealism of enthusiastic individuals, though this apparently weighed much less heavily in the image that this convent had of itself or wished to present to the outside world. The chronicle of Bethanië portrays a convent community that is self-aware and proud of what it accomplished from year to year. Enthusiasm for reform was not a part of this self-awareness.

---

[115] *Kroniek Bethanië*, 1544; cf. van der Woude 1953, 148, where reference is made to the earlier proclamation of 1538. The prohibition was not directed at any one convent in particular.

[116] *Kroniek Bethanië*, 1547. The *Acta* mention no such decree.

[117] *Kroniek Bethanië*, 1557.

[118] DV, f. 238r and D, f. 52d. In the spiritual testament of Johan Vos van Heusden, prior of Windesheim from 1391–1424, the statement is often made that the consumption of roasted meat was to be abjured (Mertens 1989c, 82 n. 42).

7

Two Spiritual Friends from Facons

IN 1490, POPE INNOCENT VIII felt the need to acquaint himself with the situation at the Windesheim convent of Facons. He sent Lubbert Vyncke, abbot of the Benedictine dual monastery of Dikninge (near to the village of Ruinen in the province of Drenthe), to Antwerp as his delegate. Reports of what Abbot Vyncke found at Facons do not survive. The seventeenth-century chronicler of Facons, Rector Christophorus Caers (†1673), mentions the arrival of the abbot in 1490 only briefly. As to the reasons behind this visitation he notes only – perhaps advisedly – that the Pope had received word that life at Facons was somewhat undisciplined.[1]

Caers does mention incidents at Facons elsewhere in his chronicle that suggest a laxness in monastic discipline there. In 1451, Sister Angela van Zuylen brought with her an annuity as a gift to the convent on the occasion of her profession, which was to be used to provide the entire convent with a meal, twice a week, of 'good, freshly salted and boiled mutton, a respectable portion on every plate'.[2] And in 1460 the magistrate of Antwerp decided to absolve Facons of the obligation of paying the tax on sweetened wine. Because the nuns were often weak or ill and lived in cold lodgings,

---

[1] *Naem- en doodtboeck*, pp. 37–8 and *Register*, ff. 26v–27r; cf. Persoons 1993d, 572. The visitation by the abbot of Dikninge is closely related to a dispute going back to 1480 about the rights of visitation in the bishopric of Kamerijk/Cambrai. The new bishop of Kamerijk, Hendrik van Bergen (his tenure ran from 1481 to 1502) – he was incidentally a brother of Liesbeth van Bergen, prioress of Bethanië in Mechelen – wanted to visit Facons that year. Prims 1936, 412–13 explains that the newly chosen bishop wanted to pay a visit and expected to be received at Facons with his entire retinue in a fashion befitting his status. But there must have been more to it, given the long-lasting nature of the conflict and the many documents pertaining to it: a serious conflict concerning the judicial control of the monasteries of Kamerijk. Facons successfully appealed to the right of exemption earlier granted them by the papal edict to the Chapter of Windesheim. The visitation of Facons in 1490 was a by-product of this conflict: Pope Innocent VIII wanted to know more about the status of the monasteries in the bishopric of Kamerijk. For more on this dispute see Acquoy 1875–80, vol. 2, 139–41; cf. the summary in vol. 3, 297–300. On Lubbert Vyncke, abbot of Dikninge, see Arts 1945, 133–4.

[2] *Goet wel gelyst, nieu gesprengt ende vorgesoden scapen vleesch, in elcken schotel een goet redelyck stuck* (*Naem- en doodtboeck*, pp. 71–3).

they often had to drink mulled wine.[3] If we compare both of these instances to the prevailing indifference at Diepenveen to the quality of food consumed – which undoubtedly represents the Diepenveen ideal – then it would seem as if Facons, too, was clearly less strict in this regard. Finally, an unmistakable sign of the erosion of the spiritual life at Facons was the initiative of Catharina Steeyncx, who at her profession bought off the *wollenwerck*, or manual labour in textiles. The prior superior of the Chapter of Windesheim did, it is true, vehemently protest at this unheard of interference with the observance, but he was not successful in reversing what amounted to the undermining of one of the pillars of the Windesheim monastic way of life.

It appears, then, that the Pope had ample reason to send a visitation to Facons, for the spiritual life there was of a rather low standard. But in 1489, before Abbot Lubbert could pay his visit to Facons, it was struck by the scourge of God. Jacomijne Costers (†1503) was one of the nuns stricken by the plague, but she survived the disease, however narrowly. In a vision it was revealed to her how poorly matters stood with respect to her spiritual life and that of her fellow sisters. Jacomijne was determined to bring about a spiritual revolution at Facons. In order to convince her sisters of its necessity, she committed her hair-raising vision to parchment.

This chapter attempts to place the authorship of Jacomijne Costers within the context of the deterioration of the observance at Facons. Because next to nothing is known about her as a person, we will first present an overview of Costers's life based on the available sources (§7.1). Next follows a discussion of the vision of 1489, which occasioned such a radical change in the life of Jacomijne Costers. We shall look at the genesis of the *Visioen en exempel* ('Vision and Exemplum'), following which will be presented a summary and discussion of the vision (§7.2). The third section is devoted to the way in which this inspired nun attempted, with the help of texts, to improve the monastic life in her convent. At the same time we will take up the question of in what sense she wanted to reform Facons (§7.3). The chapter concludes with a discussion of Mechtild van Rieviren (†1497), fellow sister and confidante of Jacomijne Costers. Mechtild left behind writings that reveal her intimate relationship with Christ (§7.4).

7.1 Jacomijne Costers

In the *Register*, his chronicle of Facons, Christophorus Caers has a digression on Jacomijne Costers, despite the fact that she was but an 'ordinary' nun. This special attention is entirely due to the extraordinary event experienced by

---

[3] *Register*, f. 18; cf. Persoons 1993d, 571.

Costers in the tumultuous year of 1489. Caers first describes the plague which hit Brabant so hard that in Brussels alone there were thirty thousand victims. Next follow the trials and tribulations of Costers:

> In that same year the plague was here in the convent, and three nuns fell victim to it. Of Sister Jacomyne Ziericx, in the book of the dead called Costers, it is said that, her soul having been separated from her body, she was led by an angel before God, the True Judge, and then through the intervention of the Virgin Mary, the Mother of God, led back to her body, where the angel brought her back to life. She made her profession before this very prioress [Clara Box] and had lived at first somewhat wantonly within the order, despite performing good works every Saturday in the name of the Mother of God; this was why she [Mary] was her advocate at her time of need, on account of whom she bettered her ways and wrote many profitable things, as appears from a little book. How much of it is true I leave to the reader to decide, for I have found nothing in the books of the rectors that touches upon this.[4]

Caers gives Costers the benefit of the doubt: he is familiar with her writings from a little book that apparently still was present at the convent, but with no further corroborating evidence from his predecessors in office he remains sceptical about the authenticity of its contents.

In his *Naem- en doodtboeck* ('Book of Names and the Dead') of Facons, in which all its nuns are recorded, Caers provides a biography of Costers which is likewise longer than the typical entry.

> Sister Jacoba Kosters, otherwise known as Ziericx, made her profession in the year 1483, on 11 November. Of her it is said that, having died, she was brought for judgement before the throne of God and would have been damned by him for her wanton life were it not that the Holy Mother of Mercy Mary had intervened through prayer on her behalf, in whose name she [Jacomijne] had been wont to perform some good work every Saturday. After some hours her soul returned to her body and by bettering her ways and leaving these good writings behind she demonstrated that she had

---

[4] *Int selve jaer was hier int cloester oyck de peste, waer van datter dry susteren sterven. Als doen seyt men dat suster Jacomyne Ziericx, int doodtboeck genompt Costers, soude verscheyden geweest hebben vanden lyve ende haer ziele soude vanden engel geleyt syn geweest voor Godt, der rechtveerdigen rechter, dan door voorspraeck vande maget Maria, moeder Godts, is weder gekeert naer haer liechaem, dat den engel interim hadde geroert oftet leefden. Sy was recht voor dese priorinne [Clara Box] geproffessit ende leefde int eerste seer roeckeloos inde ordre, niet tegenstaende dede alle saterdagen eenige goede wercken ter eeren van de heilige moeder Godts, waerom sy oyck haer advocaterse in haeren uyttersten noodt is geweest, naer den welcken sy haer leven heeft gebetert ende veele schoone leringe heeft geschreven, soe uyt een boecxken daer af gemaect is te sien. Watter vande waerheyt is laete een igelyck vry te oordeelen, door dien ick hier van in geene boecken van de rectoren iet bevinde geschreven oft geruert* (Register, f. 28r–v).

experienced something wonderful, and she blissfully passed away on 28 April in the year 1503.[5]

It would seem that Caers is mistaken about her Christian name, as all other sources speak of 'Jacomijne', even his own *Register*. As far as her surname is concerned, we encounter the combinations Jacomijne Costers and Jacomijne Ziericx. In order to avoid confusion, we use the name Jacomijne Costers throughout.[6]

The biography of the visionary of Facons can be augmented by information from manuscript Vienna, Österreichische Nationalbibliothek, s.n. 12.827. This codex is of crucial significance for the transmission of the work of Jacomijne Costers (as well as that of Mechtild van Rieviren). The Vienna manuscript dates to the seventeenth century, 1651 to be precise. De Vooys justly calls it an important source of medieval exempla, but it is first and foremost an anthology of texts relating to the history of the convent of Facons (though the texts themselves are exemplary in nature). It is significant that the manuscript opens with Costers's *Visioen en exempel*; apparently this was considered an important point in the convent's history. Distributed throughout the manuscript are several other texts from her hand. The scribe of this manuscript must have drawn heavily from the book containing Costers's works, to which Rector Caers refers in his *Register*. All sorts of citations, sayings and text-fragments from this exceptional denizen of Facons have been incorporated into the biography of Costers that follows the vision. This leads one to suspect that the scribe/author of the Vienna manuscript may have had access to personal notes by Costers, and quite likely also to her *rapiarium*.[7]

According to the introduction to her *Visioen en exempel*, Jacomijne Costers was stricken by the plague at the age of twenty-seven.[8] She would therefore have been born in 1462 or 1463. Costers made her profession when she was twenty, in 1483, but according to her own testimony, she did not take life in the convent seriously at first. In 1489, then, Costers contracted the plague. She appeared doomed to die, but her soul returned to her seemingly lifeless body after a journey to the next world. This near-death experience changed the

---

[5] *Suster Jacoba Kosters, diemen anders nompt Ziericx, professide anno 1483, den 11. novembris. Van dese wort geseyt als datse, gestorven synde, is gebrocht voor den rechterstoel Godts ende soude vanden selven om haer roecloos leven verdompt syn geworden, ten waere de heilige moeder der genade Maria haer hadde verbeden, tot wiens dinst sy alle saterdagen iet goets pleeg te doen. Naer ettelycke uuren is de siele weder in haer liechaem gekeert ende heeft met beternisse van haer leven ende goede schriften diese achtergelaten heeft getoont dat haer iet wonders overkomen was ende is salichlyck gestorven anno 1503, den 28. april* (Naem- en doodtboeck, p. 84 no. 104).

[6] In addition to the works of Christophorus Caers, Costers's name is found in MS Vienna, f. 1r, 63v en 82r, and in MS Brussels, KB, IV 50, on the flyleaf.

[7] On the Vienna MS see e.g Menhardt 1961, 1529–30 and Scheepsma 1997, 247–9.

[8] *Visioen en exempel*, l. 20.

direction of Costers's life. According to her biography she never laughed again after her vision, and she cried all the more frequently. She also retained from that illness a constantly festering wound just above her heart, placed there as a reminder of her frightening experience.[9] In all likelihood this life-changing event marks the beginning of Costers's activities as a writer of spiritual texts.

Following her vision Costers tended to retreat from the community. She led a reclusive life, and had more visions. The Vienna manuscript describes a revelation in which Christ explains to her the purpose of suffering, and Costers herself recounts the appearance of St Anne in a letter (for more on this, see §7.3).[10] She had a spiritual friend at Facons with whom she shared numerous 'secrets and visions'; there can be no doubt that this confidante was Mechtild van Rieviren. During the last fourteen years of her life, Costers's ascetic way of life was an example for her fellow sisters. Ultimately she probably did fall victim to the plague: in 1503 this terrible disease struck Facons once again, killing eleven nuns and eight *donatinnen*. Jacomijne Costers died on 28 April of that year.[11]

7.2 An Account of a Journey through Hell

The prologue of Costers's *Visioen en exempel* confronts us immediately with the complicated issues of transmission so typical of medieval vision-literature.

> This is the vision and exemplum of the blessed sister Jacomijne Costers, also known as Zirix, a nun of our convent, and it happened in the year of our Lord 1489. She wrote it herself, as commanded by the Holy Trinity upon pain of eternal damnation, and she wrote her account as if it had happened to someone else. And this has been copied from it; it is most worthy and of great profit to everyone.[12]

These are the words of someone writing at some remove in time from Costers; in all probability this is her seventeenth-century 'publisher', but it could also have been an earlier editor. We know hardly anything about how Costers's visionary experience was transformed into the vision text as we

---

[9] MS Vienna, f. 31r–v.
[10] MS Vienna, f. 44r–v for the vision of suffering.
[11] *Register*, f. 29r.
[12] *Dit is het visioen en exempel vande gelucksalige religieuse suster Jacomijne Costers, met bij naem Zirix, een religieus van ons clooster, en tis geschiet int jaer ons heeren 1489. De religieus hevet self geschreven, wantet haer vande heilige drijvuldicheijt bevolen was op haer eeuwige verdommenis, en sij schreef dat al oftet aen een ander gebeurt waer. En dit is daer uut geschreven; het is seer notabel en profijtelijck voor alle menschen* (Visioen en exempel, lines 1–6).

know it.[13] Theoretically it is possible that *Visioen en exempel* was not written until the seventeenth century, based on personal notes left by Costers. But because the contents of this text are tailored to conditions at the end of the fifteenth century, this does not seem likely. I assume therefore that Costers wrote this text herself – perhaps several years after receiving the vision in 1489 – and that *Visioen en exempel* is a copy of it, though we do not know the extent of the editing it underwent.[14]

In the prologue of *Visioen en exempel* cited above we may observe further characteristic features of the medieval vision. To begin with, it contains the divine exhortation to write, here performed by the Holy Trinity, which ultimately led to the recording of the vision.[15] In this way Jacomijne Costers legitimised her role as author and as bearer of perhaps less than welcome news. Within the institutional structures of the Church, women could exert very little real power. With the help of visions and other supernatural experiences many of them managed to acquire a certain degree of authority in spiritual matters.[16]

Moreover, it is striking that the narrative point of view in *Visioen en exempel* has been shifted to the third person. In so doing Jacomijne Costers was able to distance herself to an extent from her terrifying experience. For her audience this shift meant that they could separate the vision from the person of Costers. And perhaps Costers was influenced a little by the prohibition against writing of 1455, which after all forbade the choir nuns of Windesheim to write down visions originating in their own experience.

The dual genre – *visioen en exempel* ('vision and exemplum') – indicated in the exordium of Costers's work is remarkable, but also extremely apt.[17] In this way the vision focuses attention on the example afforded by this weak sister, who acknowledges her sinfulness, repents and converts to a more worthy lifestyle. The Modern Devotion had its share of exemplary figures, as witnessed by the brother- and sisterbooks. The form chosen by Costers for her exemplum is, however, unique, at least for the Windesheim choir nuns. She illustrates her exhortation to the pure spiritual life with the aid of the motif of a journey through heaven, hell and purgatory.

The classic texts in the medieval genre of eschatology include *St Patrick's*

---

[13] On the religious phenomena and experiences upon which vision literature is based, see Dinzelbacher 1991, 16–27. On the difference between the visionary experience and the visionary text, see for example Mertens 1986, 102–4 and Mertens 1989b, 108.

[14] On the complex process whereby mystic texts by women came into being, cf. for example Peters 1988, 100–88 and Dinzelbacher 1991, 42–58.

[15] *Visioen en exempel* lines 112–15 refer to yet another divine command to write.

[16] For more on this see for example Jantzen 1995.

[17] In the Middle Ages the vision genre is usually referred to with the term *visio* or *revelatio*. For a typology of the medieval vision see Dinzelbacher 1991; the genre designations are on p. 37.

Purgatory and *The Vision of Tundale*. It is certain that Jacomijne Costers knew at least the latter work quite well; it provided the structure for her own journey to the afterlife, and morever she borrowed motifs and situations from *The Vision of Tundale*. The Irish knight Tundale was allowed – compelled – to view all of mankind in the various levels of the afterlife. In her *Visioen en exempel*, Costers restricted herself to her own class of religious. Moreover she reports almost exclusively on religious who find themselves in hell or purgatory. Regarding heavenly bliss, she refers for the sake of brevity to Tundale's narrative, which was apparently available at Facons: 'But I shall pass this by, for it is clearly described in *The Vision of Tundale*'.[18] Costers's *Visioen en exempel*, together with the paintings of Hieronymus Bosch, is one of the most important witnesses to the reception of *The Vision of Tundale* in the Low Countries.[19] Also the life of St John, Apostle and Evangelist, contained in Jacobus de Voragine's *Legenda aurea* inspired her to write her vision.[20]

In order to guarantee the authenticity of Jacomijne Costers's experience, the events leading up to the vision are recounted in the Vienna manuscript in as much detail as possible. The plague that struck the southern Netherlands in 1489 reached the convent of Facons in August of that year. On the octave of St Lawrence – i.e. the eighth day following his feast (17 August) – Costers realises that she, too, has contracted the disease. Looking death itself in the face, the young nun realises how poorly she had led her life up till then. On her deathbed she makes the first honest confession of her life, motivated though it be by fear of death, rather than upright contrition. The disease progresses so swiftly that within days Costers's confessor decides that the next day, on St Bernard's day (20 August), he will administer the last sacraments to her. Awaiting the last rites and death, Costers lies languishing in bed the entire night, anxiously reviewing in her mind her sinful life. Suddenly the devil appears before her in the form of a giant toad. He appears to have a special mission: 'I am the one who tricks religious in particular into breaking their vows and keeping their ordinances poorly and into leaving

---

[18] *Maer ick gaen dat cortelijck voorbij, want het staet clarelijck int visioen van Tondalus* (*Visioen en exempel*, lines 816–17).

[19] A synoptic edition of the Dutch version of *The Vision of Tundale* incorporating five redactions is Verdeyen and Endepols 1914–17, vol. 2; on its dissemination see furthermore Palmer 1982. The torments of religious who have broken their vows, Costers's main theme, constitute the seventh circle of hell in *The Vision of Tundale* (Verdeyen and Endepols 1914–17, vol. 2, 80–90). For more on this, see Scheepsma 1996c, esp. 158–9. An English translation of the Latin version is found in Gardiner 1989, 149–95

[20] This *vita* contains an episode in which John brings a young man back from the dead, who then recounts what he has seen there for two unbelievers (cf. Ryan 1995, vol. 1, 52–3). Cf. Scheepsma 2003, 276–77.

many bad examples behind.'[21] This sets the tone for the vision. Following the toad a more horrible monster reveals itself, a fire-breathing dragon.

> And this devil brought with him a great book in which were recorded all of the sins she had committed either by words, deeds or thoughts, for which this unfortunate creature had deserved eternal damnation.[22]

Costers is forced to conclude that she cannot be saved. She hears the other sisters gathered about her deathbed, speaking of the mercy of God, but she cries out in her mind that their good words are useless.

At this point the narrative perspective of the vision shifts for a while from third person to first person. Now that things are becoming excited, Jacomijne Costers – or could it be the scribe? – addresses her audience directly:

> Oh, hearken now, my beloved sisters in Christ, to a wondrous thing that has not often been heard nor shall be again, which with the help of God I write down in highest honour of him and to his eternal glory, and for my own ultimate salvation, and for the ultimate betterment of my fellows and for their continued progress in virtue and the salvation of their souls.[23]

Striking here is the phrase 'progress in virtue' (*voortganck in deuchden*), an idea so very prominent in the Modern Devotion. Costers clearly wants to exhort her sisters to virtue. She follows this with a well-intended warning:

> I pray and desire that no one read what follows who is of little faith or who does not believe that God is all-powerful, so that they may not sin thereby and anger God greatly, but I hope and trust in the goodness of God and the Holy Trinity that no one shall read the text that follows who will not be improved by it afterwards – and that shall come to pass. He need not believe it as he does our Christian faith, for he should take care lest he do harm to himself thereby, and become upset and suffer a blow to his virtue.[24]

---

[21] 'Ick ben die gene die sonderlinge geestelijcke menschen treck om haer beloften te breken en haer ordinantien qualijck te houden en veel quade exempelen achter te laten' (*Visioen en exempel*, lines 55–7).

[22] *En desen vijant brocht met hem eenen grooten boeck inden welcken stonden allen haer sonden die sij met woorden, wercken en gedachten gedaen hadde, met de welcke desen onsaligen mensch die eeuwige verdommenis verdint hadde* (*Visioen en exempel*, lines 73–6).

[23] *Och nu hoort, mijn beminde susteren in Christo, den wonderlijck dinck dat niet veel gehoort en is noch en sal worden, d'welck ick nu meijn metter hulpen Godts te schrijven tot sijnder hoochster eeren en eeuwiger lof en tot mijnder aldermeester salicheijt en tot mijns even smenschen aldermeeste stichtinge en tot voortganck in deuchden en tot hunder sielen salicheijt* (*Visioen en exempel*, lines 100–4).

[24] *Ick bidde en begeer dat niemant dit naer geschrift en sal lesen die cleijn is van betrouwen oft dien Godt niet allen dingen mogelijck en dunckt, op dat sij daer niet door en sondigen en Godt grootelijckx vertoornen, maer ick hope en betrouwe op de goetheijt Godts en der heijliger drijvuldicheijt dat niemant dit naer geschrift lesen en sal, hij en sals naermaels te beter hebben – en dat moet oock sijn. Niet en moet hijt gelooven als ons christen geloof, maer hij sal hem sonderlinge hoeden dat hij daer sijn schade niet mede en doet, op dat hij daer niet*

The vision proper is introduced with another precise time reference. On the eve of St Bernard's day (19 August), at seven o'clock in the morning, the soul of Jacomijne Costers was torn from her body by the devil and led to judgement before the Lord. The vision lasted three hours, 'beginning at seven and lasting till ten, whereupon she returned to her body'.[25] Her soul finds itself at the foot of a crucifix, surrounded by howling devils who level charges against her. The accusations are that she had broken her monastic vows, failed to observe her hours of prayer and spoken ill of her superiors. In short, this soul has provided a *quaet exempel* ('evil example') of spiritual living for the rest of the convent.

The crucified Christ turns his back on the sinful soul. Despairing, she now wonders aloud if there is anyone from whom she can expect help. St John the Evangelist is her patron saint, it is true, but she has paid him hardly any special devotion. Then she remembers that, despite her laxness, she did pray to Mary every day from her psalter and in her honour observed an extra period of silence. Immediately the Mother of God appears before her in all her glory, flanked by Sts John and Augustine, the patron saint of Facons. Costers's weekly prayers have reached Mary after all, who thus is willing to intercede on behalf of this doomed soul.

At first Christ is unmoved by Mary's pleas:

> Oh, mother mine, do not pray to me on behalf of this soul, for I am not bound or obliged to show her any mercy, in as much as she has acted contrary to her three vows, as well as the Rule and its statutes, and she has frequently broken those three vows which she promised me she would keep on behalf of my heavenly Father and the Holy Trinity, and she has broken her faith to me which she was bound to keep. And because she has done all of this and has in no way been faithful to me, I am not obliged to show her any mercy, but justice alone. And now, dear mother, the time of justice, not mercy, has come for her.[26]

Only after a passionate plea by Mary, in which she brings her maternal love in particular to bear, is the Lord willing to acknowledge some small virtue on

---

in geergert en worde en hem een letsel worde totter deucht (*Visioen en exempel*, lines 119–26).

[25] *Beginnende vanden sevenen totten tinen, doen quamp sij weder in haer lichaem* (*Visioen en exempel*, lines 151–2).

[26] '*O mijn moeder, en wilt mij toch voor dese siel niet bidden, want ick en ben niet gehouden noch schuldich haer eenige ontfermherticheijt te bewijsen, want sij tegen haer drij beloften heeft gedaen en tegen den regel en de statuten, en heeft die drij beloften dick gebroken datse mij gesworen en belooft heeft te houden voor mijnen hemelschen vader en voor den heijlige geest, en heeft haer trouw gebroken diese mij schuldich was te houden. En want sij dit altemael heeft gedaen en mij in geen dingen getrouw en heeft geweest soo en ben ick haer niet schuldich eenige bermherticheijt maer alle rechtveerdicheijt. En, mijn lieve moeder, het is nu tijt met haer van rechtveerdicheijt, en niet van bermherticheijt*' (*Visioen en exempel*, lines 286–95).

the part of this faithless soul. Costers had recited the Lord's Prayer once on the occasion of the moment when Christ's soul left his crucified body. Her prayer had not been especially passionate – she herself speaks of a *snode dinst* ('a miserable prayer') – but here apparently the power of the primal Christian prayer asserts itself. The balance is tipped in favour of the soul, but only just. She receives one more chance to better her ways. Moreover, says Mary, Costers will be in a position to help the nuns of Facons to abandon the broad way and follow the straight and narrow instead.

Now Costers's guardian angel appears on stage, to lead her to heaven. Once there, her soul is allowed to gaze upon Mary, bathed in a light 'that was indescribably strong and bright, a thousand times brighter than the sun'.[27] In her turn Mary leads her soul to the Cross, upon which Christ hangs, 'so cruelly stretched out upon it that it cannot be described in speech or in writing, nor can painters depict the misery of it'.[28] The dismissive attitude of the King of Heaven has now been transformed to one of love. Costers is allowed to approach and view from close by the wounds he must suffer in part on her account. The soul is prepared for her role as reformer of Facons. She gains insight into the spiritual status of all of her fellow sisters: almost all of them are doomed and will be stricken by the plague! Again thanks to the intercession of the heavenly mediatrix, the passionate plea which the soul makes on behalf of her fellow nuns is successful.

The guardian angel next leads the soul on a tour of hell, purgatory and the earthly paradise. In a steaming, smouldering cauldron full of pitch and sulphur, in which the souls of religious are being tormented, she sees to her horror a familiar face bob to the surface. It is the former chambermaid of the convent's mother superior, who frequently tattled on her sisters to the prioress. This is why as an added punishment she bears a red-hot tongue that stretches to the floor. In purgatory too the soul encounters familiar faces, among them a former prioress of Facons. Her name is not given, but perhaps it is Elisabeth van Daesdonck (†1486) being referred to here, who held the office from 1477 to 1486. Costers was there, after all, during her tenure.[29] The soul asks the prioress why it is that she is still in purgatory.

> She answered: 'I was prioress and that is why I am here, because I was not fair in my judgements, for out of awe of some people I often brought injus-

---

[27] *Dat onspreckelijck groot en claer was, boven dusent claerheden der sonnen* (*Visioen en exempel*, lines 417–18).

[28] *Alsoo vreedelijck [. . .] uutgereckt dattet niet te seggen noch te schrijven en is, noch geen schilders en connen dat soo mismaeckt schilderen* (*Visioen en exempel*, lines 469–71). Vandenbroeck's (1994a) exhibition catalogue offers a wide range of pitiable images of the Man of Sorrows.

[29] Christophorus Caers mentions hardly any particulars about the tenure of Elisabeth van Daesdonck (*Register*, f. 21r and *Naem- en doodtboeck*, pp. 36–7); cf. Persoons 1993d, 571.

tice down upon those who were not guilty, even when I knew them to be innocent. And those who were guilty I left unpunished because I was in awe of them, and feared that they might do me harm, and this is the reason that I have wandered here for so long.'[30]

Here Costers provides a lesson for the prioresses of Facons, who were, after all, responsible for the spiritual life of the convent. She goes on to add that this particular prioress admitted postulants based on their gifts to the convent and not because of any particular suitability for the monastic life.[31]

The amazing journey ends in heaven, where the soul is allowed to see Christ. Because she has now been purified, she may kiss his feet. Christ requires penance of her in the form of a comprehensive programme of prayer exercises. Next the soul takes leave of her guardian, Mary, who asks for prayers from her as well. The soul must recite the Ave Maria three times a day in honour of the meekness of the Mother of God. She is also to recite the Magnificat three times a day. When Mary created this prayer, she was filled with the Holy Spirit, which lent the prayer great efficacy and power. Having given her this task, the Mother of God sends the soul back to her body.

7.3 Reform through Literary Means

Jacomijne Costers addressed her *Visioen en exempel* to the entire community of Facons, even though the convent is nowhere mentioned by name. The vision constitutes an attack from within on the lax monastic discipline at Facons. In Costers's view Christ was punishing his unfaithful brides by sending the plague to Facons. Thanks to her plea before Mary there were only three victims. One may only speculate whether this marvellous tale of her journey through hell was received by everyone with the same degree of enthusiasm. 'There were religious there who did not wish to believe what had happened and who mocked it, and that is why she wrote it as if it had happened to someone else, for the benefit of many.'[32] The status of mediatrix between Facons and heaven assumed by Costers was by no means recognised by everyone.[33]

---

[30] *Sij antworden: 'Ick was overste en daerom ben ick hier, om dat ick niet in allen dingen gelijck en oordeelden, want uut ontsach van sommige menschen soo liet ick dickmael dat onrecht comen op den genen die niet schuldich en was, nochtans dat ickt wel wist dat hij onschuldich was. En die sculdich was, liet ick ongecorigeert, om dat ick hun ontsach oft vreesden dat sij mij eenich verdriet aendoen mochten, en dit is de oorsaeck dat ick hier soo lange heb gaen doolen' (Visioen en exempel*, lines 796–803).

[31] Cf. Johannes Brinckerinck's initial refusal of Katharina van Naaldwijk because of her wealth (§2.2).

[32] *Daer waren doen religieusen dies niet en wouden gelooven datter geschiet was en hilden hunnen spot daer mede, en daerom heeft sijt self geschreven als oftet aen een ander gebeurt waer, tot troost van veel* (MS Vienna, f. 36v).

[33] Cf. MS Vienna, f. 36v; even Christophorus Caers had his doubts about what had really happened (see the citation at §7.1).

And yet at Facons there were 'devout persons' who urged Costers to commit her experience to writing.[34] The prioress or the rector must have been among them; it would have been virtually impossible for Costers to publish *Visioen en exempel* internally without the permission of her superiors. Moreover we read that she was in the habit of confiding her visionary experiences to her confessor.[35] Father Johannes Ooms from Korsendonk was confessor at Facons from 1485 to 1494, the period during which both the vision and the visitation by the abbot of Dikninge took place. At the time Clara Box was prioress; she held office from 1487 to 1504. Caers says nothing of any reform initiatives undertaken by the rector Ooms or Prioress Box around 1490.[36] It is therefore very likely that Costers was allowed to carry on with her reform efforts, but also that the reformation of Facons was at first essentially the private undertaking of this inspired nun.

Her superiors at Facons could afford to give Costers free rein in this respect, for she was not advancing any dangerous or controversial ideas. The *Visioen en exempel* seeks to be nothing other than a weapon in the struggle against the deterioration of monastic discipline at Facons. The nuns are accused of having broken their monastic vows, and of having ignored the Rule and statutes. The purpose of the *Visioen en exempel* emerges most clearly when Christ tells Costers the five abuses at Facons which grieve him the most.

> Now soul, hearken to me. I shall tell you five things that anger me daily, and if they do not correct them, I shall chastise them more heavily, without hope of respite.
>
> The first abuse is that my hours are so poorly recited, as well as those of my mother, and that they are read at the wrong time or sometimes not at all, and that not everyone participates and those that do are often inattentive, especially during mass and in my temple, where I am present together with all of my saints; this angers me greatly.
>
> The second abuse is that it displeases me that they are difficult and obstreperous towards their superiors. They ought to obey them as they would me, and the religious who are thus difficult and obstreperous towards their superiors and not obedient, their prayers I shall not answer

---

[34] *Visioen en exempel*, line 115.

[35] The text of one of Costers's letters is found on ff. 28v–31r of the Vienna manuscript. On ff. 29r and 31r is described how through a vision Jacomijne received the command from Christ to confide in her confessor. Unfortunately this vision is not datable. During Costers's stay at Facons the following men were confessors, in order of succession: Johannes van Eyck (1480–5), Johannes Ooms (1485–94), Gisbertus Simoens (1494–5), Nicolaas van Oosterwijk or Sterts (1495–1502), Cornelius Beeke (1502) and Thomas Vermoelen or Bel (1502–4).

[36] On Johannes Ooms see *Naem- en doodtboeck*, p. 15 and *Register*, f. 21r–v; cf. Persoons 1993a, 470 and Persoons 1993d, 571–2. On Clara Box see *Naem- en doodtboeck*, p. 37 and *Register*, ff. 26v–29r; cf. Persoons 1993d, 572.

and I shall be their harshest punishment in their hour of need and on the Day of Judgement.

The third abuse is that they pass their time so poorly with vain words, deeds and thoughts, for nothing is more precious than time, and nothing is more despised by mankind than time and death.

The fourth abuse that displeases me greatly is that during religious meetings they are so contentious among themselves and full of complaints, and especially that they agitate against their superiors, and create discord between those where there was none before by means of evil behaviour.

The fifth abuse is fleshly love, that they love one another so much that they forget me, and this sensual love is often a great cause of their falling into sin, which angers me most of all. And this displeases me the most when it concerns religious, and for that reason I frequently send great plagues upon them.[37]

The contents of this reform programme are thoroughly monastic in nature. According to Costers the abuses at Facons could best be rectified by returning to the Rule of St Augustine and the statutes of Windesheim.

She also recommends almost exclusively orthodox remedies for the improvement of the interior life of the nuns. In *Visioen en exempel* Costers attributes great power to such traditional prayers as the Hail Mary and the Lord's Prayer. So, for example, she encounters in her journey through purgatory a sister from Facons who contends that many more prayers need to be said for the souls in purgatory. Recited intensely, one prayer by a fellow nun can relieve her of ten years of torment.[38] Significantly Costers ends her vision

---

[37] 'Nu siele, hoort naer mij. Ick sal u seggen vijf punten door welcke ick dagelijckx vertorent woorde, ende en willen sij hun daer niet af beteren soo sal ickse noch swaerder plagen sonder eenich verbidden.' 'Dat eerste punt is dat mijn getijden soo qualijck betaelt woorden en de getijden van mijn lieve moeder, en dat sij die soo ongetijdelijck lesen en somtijts altemael achter laten en niet met allen en lesen en die oock lesen sonder aendacht, sonderlinge inden dinst Godts en in mijnen tempel, daer ick en alle mijn heijligen tegenwoordich ben; daer ick seer in vertorent woorde. Dat 2 punt is dat mij in hun mishaecht dat sij haer oversten soo hert en swaer sijn die mijn stede besitten. En men behoort die te hooren gelijck mij, en die religieusen die aldus haer oversten swaer en hert sijn en niet gehoorsaem en sijn, die en sal ick niet verhooren in haer gebeden en ick sal hun herten straf syn in hun uutterste en inden dach des oordeels.Het derde punt is datse haren tijt soo qualijck overbrengen met ijdel woorden, wercken en gedachten, want geen dinck en is costelijcker dan den tijt, en geen dinck en wort vande menschen min geacht dan den tijt en doet Dat 4 punt is dat mij seer mishaecht onder geestelijcke vergaderingen datse soo twistichachtich sout sijn onder malcanderen en vol murmuratien, en dat sonderlinge tegen haer oversten verweckende ondermalcanderen, en maecken onminne die goede minne samen hebben overmits quaet verdrach. Dat 5 punt is minne der creatueren, datse die een den anderen soo sijn beminnende datse mijns sijn vergetende, en dese sinnelijcke liefde is dickmael een saecke van groote val inde sonden te vallen, daer ick aldermest in vertorent woorden. En meest mishaecht mij dat van geestelijcke persoonen, daer ick dickmael groote plagen om sijnde' (*Visioen en exempel*, lines 550–75).

[38] *Visioen en exempel*, lines 734–40.

with a scene in which Jesus and Mary assign her a number of devout exercises consisting of sequences of fixed prayers. The penance given by Christ consists of reciting the Lord's Prayer fifteen times a day for a year. This is a classic late medieval exercise: thus during the course of the year every wound of Christ (365 × 15 = 5475) would receive one prayer.[39] In addition Costers is to recite the fifteen prayers of the wounds of the Cross, composed by St Bridgitte, every day for a year.[40] Finally, the Lord commands her to recite the Lord's Prayer, which he taught his disciples, with much more conviction. Next the Mother of God asks in turn that she constantly repeat the familiar prayers to Mary. The recitation of such series of prayers became very popular in the Middle Ages; the phenomenon is known as the 'piety of sums'. In the eyes of many, including Costers, this form of prayer constituted a sure path to salvation.

Costers recounts her marvellous experiences in the *Visioen en exempel* with the clear intention of improving the spiritual lives of her fellow nuns. How far she actually succeeded in changing the atmosphere at Facons is of course difficult to say. If we are to trust the sources, then Costers does seem to have influenced the lives of individual nuns. Though she led the life of a recluse, she did share her interior experiences with a few confidantes, among them Mechtild van Rieviren. After 1489 Costers appears to have become something of a spiritual oracle for the sisters at Facons. All kinds of wise sayings and advice she gave her fellow sisters in this regard are recorded in her biography.

The Vienna manuscript contains three shorter texts written by Costers which, like the *Visioen en exempel*, were designed to improve the monastic life of the individual or the community. Costers seems to have written these texts for her fellow nuns. The *Bereijdinghe tot het Heijlich Sacrament* ('Preparation for the Holy Sacrament') teaches the nuns how to prepare for Holy Communion. They are presented with a list of seven points, the first of which reads as follows: 'First you will cleanse yourselves of all sins and impurities, for if you would join the ranks of the most pure, then no blemish or flaw may be found upon you.'[41] Following these seven brief points, Costers delves more deeply into the meaning of Christ's sacrifice for mankind, which cannot be overestimated. Alas, says Costers, we allow ourselves to be distracted from the

---

[39] For more on this exercise, see Stracke 1943, especially 75–85; cf. Angenendt, Braucks, Busch *et al.* 1995, 45–6.

[40] This cycle of fifteen prayers had been in existence for some time, but in the fifteenth century it was attributed to St Bridgitte of Sweden. On this meditation of the Passion, see especially Stracke 1943, 133–40 (with an edition of three manuscripts); cf. Meertens 1931, 15–26 and Oosterman 1993, 441 n. 39.

[41] *Ten eersten suldy u suijvermaken van alle sonden en vlecken, want suldij den alderpuersten woorden toe gevoecht, soo en mach in u geen vlecke noch smette gevonden worden* (*Bereijdinghe*, f. 63v).

highest good. We occupy ourselves with insignificant things, and when we pray, our hearts and souls are often not in it. It is of the utmost importance to experience Christ's sacrifice intensely ourselves, for by doing so our sins and faults will be cleansed.

The treatise *Van de perfectie* ('On Perfection') is likewise composed of series of points, a structuring technique often employed by Costers. She also uses it in her treatise on meditation exercises, the *Previlesien van Sint Joannes*, discussed at §4.3).[42] The believer is obliged in all ways to pursue perfection, represented by Christ. The experienced sister Costers explains that there are three types of daily sins that can hinder the pursuit of perfection. There are of course also the mortal sins, but they are not discussed here. The first type of daily sin is committed more or less consciously; these burn like logs in the fires of purgatory, i.e. for a long time. The second type involves sins committed subconsciously. This kind of sin smoulders in purgatory, like hay. Lastly there are the sins committed through weakness, because against his better judgement the sinner has again allowed himself to be carried away by his natural urges. These sins burn like straw and turn relatively quickly to ash. From the way Costers structures her typology of sins, it is clear that this latter category is the least serious of all.

Now that the nuns are familiar with the most important pitfalls, *Van de perfectie* offers a series of twelve points, each one of which is designed to aid one in achieving perfection. Significantly enough, Costers gives poverty pride of place: one must be willing to give up certain material pleasures in the name of Christ. The second point says 'that we should recite our hours earnestly and that we must read and sing with our mouths so that we may contemplate it in our hearts'.[43] The third focuses attention on obedience to one's superiors, and so on. Assuming that Costers wrote this treatise with an eye towards the reformation of Facons – compare the similarities with the abovementioned five points from the *Visioen en exempel* – then what we have here is perhaps a list ordered according to the relevance of the abuses that obtained there. Following this series of twelve points there is another of seven, which also have as their subject the achievement of perfection. Point seven states that we must continually renew our resolutions to do good and that we must progress in virtue. Convents, after all, are to be regarded as schools where virtues can be learned.

The third treatise, entitled *Van de drij beloften der religieusen* ('On the Three Vows of Religious'), is closely related to the first two. It deals with the monastic vows – which incidentally featured as the third point in the series of seven just discussed, *Van de perfectie*. Costers has relatively little to say about chastity. She puts a much greater emphasis, on the other hand, on the vow of

---

[42] Cf. §8.2, n. 24.
[43] *Dat wij ons getijden met aendacht sullen betalen en dat wij metten mont lesen oft singen, dat wij dat metter herten sullen aendencken* (*Van de perfectie*, f. 83v).

poverty, which was also touched upon in *Van de perfectie*. This vow implies that one should not become attached to material goods.

> You shall not busy yourselves with curiosities and vain things or spend your valuable time on them, such as the making of objects or crafts out of vanity, like excerpts from St John or diaries or other such trinkets to give your friends.[44]

After all, a nun cannot give anything to anyone, for she has no possessions.

Next Costers discusses the vow of obedience, on which she also placed great emphasis in *Vande perfectie*. A truly obedient person profits more by sleeping than a disobedient one does with all sorts of devout works. Finally, she reminds the superiors of their duties. A good prioress is not lenient, nor is she hard-hearted in dealing out the necessary punishments and reprimands. Her model is after all that of the Good Shepherd. The abuses discussed in *Van de drij beloften* and *Van de perfectie* are the same ones as appear in Costers's vision.

In addition to all kinds of anecdotes and citations, two lyrical texts, apparently written by Costers, are included in her biography. The first is a prayer to Christ of twenty-four lines, in rhymed couplets.[45] Here follow the first six lines:

> O, my one and only Beloved
> Without you all things say 'No'
> For you alone remain my eternal 'Yes'
> Firmly and otherwise not at all.
> Therefore all things must be silent in me
> In order that I may attain that single One.[46]

Thus Costers composes verses on the One, to whom she wishes to devote herself utterly. *Och, laet mij u kiesen / En niet verliesen* ('O, let me choose you and not lose you'), she finally sighs. This text would have had its primary function in personal meditation, initially for Costers herself, but later perhaps for some of her fellow nuns. Could the Vienna manuscript be citing Costers's *rapiarium* here?[47]

---

[44] *Gij en sult niet staen naer curiose oft sinnelijcke dingen en daer uwen edelen tijt mede over brengen, als met iet propers te maken oft te pronselen uut sinnelijckheit, als sint Jans leskens oft registeren oft ander ploncelinge om u vrinden te geven* (*Drij beloften*, ff. 86v–87r).

[45] For more on the genre of the Middle Dutch rhymed prayer, see Oosterman 1995, 17–44.

[46] *O mijns herten lief eenich een / Sonder u soo sprecken alle dingen neen / Aen u alleen blijft mij eeuwich jae / Vast en anders nergens nae / Daerom moeten alle dingen in mij swijgen / Op dat ick dat een mach vercrijgen* (*Mijns herten lief*, f. 35r).

[47] A similar reception history may be assumed for the *Previlesien van Sint Joannes Evangelist*. This exercise for Jacomijne Costers's patron saint would also have benefited the other nuns (see §4.3). Cf. Scheepsma 2003, 279–80.

The second lyrical work is introduced as a 'refrain'. Its first line reads: *Die op lanck leven stelt al sijn hopen* ('He who puts all hope in a long life'). Because it is composed in the simplest of rhyme schemes, aabbcc, and because the usual refrain and envoi are absent, we may surely ask whether this may be regarded as a true refrain.[48] The contents of this sixty-line poem hinge upon a consciousness of the transitory nature of life, as appears immediately from the opening lines:

> He who puts all hope in a long life,
> Even though he be exhorted to follow it,
> He does not do so, but lets it pass him by,
> Heeding instead the lesson of the crow
> Who cries out: '*cras, cras:* tomorrow, tomorrow'
> Not knowing how long God will grant him.[49]

A second important lesson is that one should not put too much store in worldly friendships. The 'refrain' concludes with a lament on the state of the world: whereas in the past there was justice and compassion for one's fellow man in the world, now the courts of rulers are governed by scheming and deceit, and men slay each other for a crust of bread. Compared to the rest of Costers's oeuvre this text is remarkable for its non-monastic contents and its higher literary quality. Is it possible that Costers adapted here a poem she knew from her previous life in the outside world? Against the backdrop of the predilection for worldly pleasures exhibited at Facons at the end of the fifteenth century, the function of this poem seems clear. It was the younger sisters in particular – she addresses her remarks specifically *gij, jongers* ('To you, the young ones'; *Lanck leven*, line 19) – whom she wished to convince, by means of fine, rhyming lines, that the choice for the monastic life was ultimately the most rewarding one.

Presumably Costers maintained contacts outside Facons as well, which must as a matter of course have been accomplished through letters. The Vienna manuscript paraphrases the contents of just such a letter (ff. 28v–31r), unfortunately without providing the name of the addressee (who could well have been a nun at Facons). Costers writes to a *beminde suster* ('beloved sister') concerning a miracle she has experienced and which up until then she had only revealed to her confessor. During a period of serious doubt, it seemed to Costers a futile thing to keep visiting and greeting the image of the

---

[48] Roose's edition (1958, 38–40) is far from flawless; therefore my citations here are directly from the manuscript. On the genre designation see Roose 1958, 36–7; cf. van Elslander 1953, 90, who questions whether texts consisting of rhyming couplets can be considered refrains.

[49] *Die op lanck leven stelt al sijn hopen / Al heeft hij van sijn contientie nopen / Hij en volchtse niet, maer laetse ontwaeyen / Aenhoorende die lesse vander craeijen / Die al roept: 'Cras, cras: morgen, morgen' / Niet wetende hoe lanck hem Godt sal borgen* (*Lanck leven*, lines 1–6).

Blessed Virgin Mary. When next she looked at the image she saw tears streaming from her eyes. The next night the pusillanimous sister slept fitfully, and therefore she rose early to pray to St Anne. When she was on her way to the chapel, Mary's mother appeared to her and told her that she should continue her devotions to Mary. Costers rushed to the priory church and said her usual prayer to the Blessed Virgin Mary. Thereupon Jesus appeared before her and consoled her and – again – urged her to reveal her experience to her confessor. Costers wrote all of this to her friend so that she could aid her giving thanks to the Lord, his blessed Mother and St Anne. This letter, therefore, has more to do with a spiritual friendship than it does with a focused attempt at reform.

Further traces of her correspondence may been preserved, but with Costers as recipient. In manuscript Brussels, Koninklijke Bibliotheek, IV 50, dated to the sixteenth century, Elisabeth van Couwerven (†1678) from Facons notes, among other things, the following: 'This little book was written by our beloved sister Jacomyne Costers herself.'[50] The first and quite possibly the second treatise is the product of a spiritual correspondence between an experienced nun and a novice concerning the love for Christ. The first text bears the somewhat indecipherable inscription *Dit is van Magrie<te> <b?>yen lee<r>inge*. This suggests that a Margriete – perhaps with the surname *Bijen* – was the author of the letters, which were apparently excerpted later on by the addressee.[51] Was Costers this addressee, and did she copy the most important passages from this treatise, with its mystical meanings, into her own book? Costers may well have had to seek inspiration for her conversion outside the walls of her own uninspired convent. It may be the case that she wrote her letter about St Anne's miracle to her mystical mentor.

Despite her sincere efforts it is quite possible that Costers received her greatest recognition only a century and a half after her death. The Vienna manuscript of 1651 situates her prominently at the head of what must have been intended as a spiritual chronicle of Facons. Her vision lays the groundwork, as it were, for a long series of miracles and other wondrous events in this convent in Antwerp, events which are unmistakable indications of God's blessing.

> Afterwards there were very many good and holy religious in that convent. Some have been exalted above St Agnes and some of them fairly flew through purgatory while others travelled to heaven directly, as it has been revealed to many enlightened people. For many took to heart the example

---

[50] *Dit boeckxken heeft self gheschreven onse beminde medesuster suster Jacomyne Costers.*
[51] An overview of mystic authors is found in Dinzelbacher 1991, 89–108 and lists a considerable number of female mystics by the name of Margaretha, none of whom, however, have a surname even remotely resembling *Byen*. Our Magriete is in all likelihood an unknown nun who left no visions or other literary works behind.

of the aforementioned religious and did not wish to experience what she went through.[52]

Next follow stories about Mechtild van Rieviren (†1497), Barbara van Achterhout (†1576) and an entire series of other exceptional nuns.[53] From a sixteenth-century viewpoint, Costers's *Visioen en exempel* was the spiritual turning point at Facons. That her history was still generally known at the time is demonstrated by Elisabeth van Couwerven's colophon, cited above.

The spiritual chronicle of Facons has as it were a 'counterpart' in the 'official' chronicle begun (together with the *liber memorialis*) by Christophorus Caers at the same time. The contrasting perspectives of rector and nuns in the seventeenth century are striking. Caers maintained a certain degree of scepticism regarding the veracity of Costers's vision, but the author of the Vienna manuscript – in all likelihood a woman – regarded her as the undisputed founder of renewed spiritual zeal at Facons.

7.4 Mechtild van Rieviren and Her Comforting Conversations with Christ

The series of exemplary nuns who according to the Vienna manuscript followed in Jacomijne Costers's footsteps begins with Mechtild van Rieviren (†1497).[54]

> Concerning some of the religious who followed thereafter in sanctity. First, concerning a nun who lived with her and was called Sister Mechtild van Rieviren. They loved each other in God and were close confidantes, telling each other many secrets and visions. She died in the year of our Lord 1497, on the feast of the Exaltation of the Cross [= 14 September], blissfully, as is described in what follows.[55]

The 'her' here can refer to none other than Jacomijne Costers, as up to this point she is the featured protagonist of the codex. As we know, Costers led a

---

[52] *Daer naer syn in dat selve clooster seer veel goede en heilige religieusen geweest. Sommige syn verheven boven sint Agneet en sommige en vlogen maer doort vagevier en sommige sijn van mont ten hemel gevaren, alst aen veel verlichte persoonen is geopenbaert. Want veel dat exemplaer vande voorseijde religieus wel ter herten namen ende en wilden niet verwachten dat haer gebeurt was* (MS Vienna, f. 45r).

[53] On Barbara van Achterhout, who made her profession in 1518, see *Naem- en doodtboeck*, p. 100 no. 183 and MS Vienna, f. 57r–v.

[54] In the seventeenth-century sources we find her name written in different ways: Mechtildus/Mechtildis/Machtildis van/vander Rieviren/Ryvieren. I have opted here for the form Mechtild van Rieviren.

[55] *Van sommige religieusen die daer naer tot heilicheit comen sijn. Ten eersten van een nonneken die met haer geleeft heeft en was genoemt suster Mechtildus van Rieviren. Sy beminden malcanderen in Godt en waren vrij tegen een, seggende malcanderen veel secreten en visioenen. Sy is gestorven int jaer ons heeren 1497, op den heilige cruijsverheffinge dach seer salichlijck, gelijck hier volcht* (MS Vienna, ff. 45v–46r).

reclusive life after her journey through hell, but according to her biography she had one confidante among the nuns of Facons. 'She retreated from all persons, with the exception of one religious who was her confidante. They loved each other for God and in God.'[56] In the light of the above, it is not difficult to identify this special friend as Mechtild van Rieviren.

Van Rieviren has thus far never been cited in scholarship, either in surveys of the Modern Devotion or in literary histories. Nevertheless she left behind a small yet intriguing spiritual oeuvre, presumably preserved exclusively in the Vienna manuscript. In approximately twelve folios of this manuscript a picture is painted of a very humble nun who possessed exceptional spiritual qualities (ff. 45v–57r). This 'biography' of van Rieviren is constructed predominately of accounts, written by her, of ecstatic experiences and a few separate anecdotes. Here and there the author of the Vienna manuscript furnishes these texts with commentary, which frequently amounts to praise of the exemplary nature of van Rieviren's monastic lifestyle. Christophorus Caers did indeed include her in the Facons book of the dead, but he provides no biographical particulars: 'Sister Machtildis vander Ryvieren died in the year 1497 on 13 September.'[57] For biographical information we are dependent on the spiritual chronicle of Facon, which is unfortunately rather sparse when it comes to historical detail.

At the end of the section dealing with van Rieviren her 'biographer' takes the initiative. What follows is a fairly detailed deathbed scene, which as far as attention to detail is concerned is reminiscent of the account of Gertrud van Rijssen's (of Diepenveen) deathbed. Were deathbed accounts recorded at Facons that could be drawn upon in the seventeenth century? Here follows the entire narrative:

> From the great familiarity of this bride of Christ with her beloved Bridegroom one may discern how saintly and pure was her life. She was entirely unknown to others, for she kept to herself as a simple religious. Just how saintly a death she experienced may be seen from the following, when she was in her final illness and was on the verge of death and had received her last rites. She showed extreme joy, so much so that the priest asked her how she could be so happy, and whether she was afraid of death. To this she replied with great courage: 'Why, not at all, for I know that I must die in order to live.' At that he asked her: 'Daughter, are you not afraid of the pain of death?' She replied: 'I have helped my Beloved bear his suffering. I hope that he will bear mine, in turn.' A third time he asked her if she were not fearful of the terribly severe judgement of God. To this she replied passion-

---

[56] *Sij trock haer van alle menschen, alleenelijck wasser een innige religieus daer sy vrij tegen was. Sij beminden malcanderen om Godt en in Godt* (MS Vienna, f. 36v).

[57] *Suster Machtildis vander Ryvieren sterf anno 1497 den 13. septembris* (Naem- en doodtboeck, p. 74 no. 58). The Vienna manuscript puts the date of her death on the feast of the Exaltation of the Cross, i.e. 14 September 1497 (see the citation, above). It is impossible to determine which reading is the correct one.

ately: 'Oh, father, why should I be fearful? My Beloved is my judge. I love him and he would do me an injustice not to love me in return. Therefore it will be a soft judgement in which beloved shall pass judgement on beloved and in which beloved shall be judged by beloved.' And having said this she died and went to enjoy her eternal reward. Oh, blessed soul! Pray for us that we may follow in your holy footsteps, especially in great humility and simple obedience and in passionate love, so that we may live eternally with you and all the saints. Amen.[58]

Van Rieviren is portrayed here as the epitome of the honest and sincere religious life, characterised by three devout virtues: humility, obedience and passionate love. After more than a century and a half she is still an example for her successors in the convent of Facons.

For the author of her biography, the most intriguing quality of van Rieviren is her intimate relationship with Christ.

> She was loving and friendly in conversation externally, but internally she was very intimate with her beloved Jesus, having received many revelations and visions from him, some of which follow below, from which one may see how loving a bride of God this woman was.[59]

The Vienna manuscript provides a fairly full account of these revelations, apparently without intending to be exhaustive. In general it may be said that even in these visions van Rieviren is above all else humble, as well. Here one will search in vain for radical ideas, apocalyptic images or mystical specula-

---

[58] *Uut alle dese groote familiariteijt van dese bruijt Christi met haren beminden bruijdegom Jesum canmen bemercken hoe heijlichlijck en suijverlijck sy geleeft heeft. Sy was vande menschen heel onbekent, want sy haer hielden als een simpel eenvoudige religieus. Hoe salichlijck sy gestorven is bemercktmen hier uut, doen sy in haer leste sieckte was en nu tot het uutterste gecomen synde en nu tot het uutterste ontfinck haer heilige rechten. En sy toonden een groote blijschap, alsoo dat den pater haer vraechden hoe datse soo blij cost syn en oft sy haer niet en ontsach te sterven? Doen antwoorden sy met een groote coragie: 'Och neen ick, want ick weet dat ick moet sterven, soude ick leven.' Doen vraechden hij haer: 'Dochter, en ontsiet gij u niet voor die pijne des doots?' Sy antwoorden: 'Ick heb mijnen beminden syn lijden helpen dragen. Ick hoep dat hij d'mijn oock dragen sal.' Ten derden vraechden hij haer oft sij haer niet en verveirden voor dat grouwelijck streng oordeel Godts. Doen antwoorden sy seer virichlijck: 'O pater, waerom soude ick mij verveiren? Mijnen wel beminden is mijnen rechter. Ick hebbe hem lief en hij soude mij onrecht doen dat hij mij niet weder en beminden. Daerom het sal een saecht oordeel sijn daer lief over lief sal oordeelen en daer lief van lief sal geoordeelt woorden.' En dat seggende is sij gestorven om haren alderliefsten eeuwelijck te genieten. O geluckige siele, bidt voor ons, opdat wij u heijlige voetstappen wel mogen naer volgen, principalijck in een grondige ootmoedicheijt en in een simpel gehoorsaemheijt en in een virige liefde om met u en met allen heijligen eeuwelijck te leven. Amen* (MS Vienna, f. 56r–v).

[59] *Sij was minnelijck en vrindelijck van conversatie van buijten, maer van binnen was sij seer familiaer met haren alderliefsten Jesum, hebbende veel revelatien en visioenen van hem, alsser hier een deel volgen, waer aen men mercken can wat een amoeureuse bruijt van Godt dit heeft geweest* (MS Vienna, f. 46r).

tions. As with so many female religious in the late Middle Ages, she seeks consolation in resignation.[60]

A significant portion of van Rieviren's account consists of conversations between this mystically talented nun and her spiritual bridegroom.[61] An example:

> My Beloved told me to clothe my naked soul in his pure virtues and that I should change garments as often as I wished, now wearing one virtue, now another, now wearing humility and then meekness, now patience and then so on with all the other virtues. This is so that I should strive to recognise these virtues and try according to my meagre abilities to follow them, and to strive assiduously to acquire the ones I lack from him, and to offer them to the heavenly Father. And he will receive them lovingly as if they came from me.[62]

Just how we are to imagine these 'conversations' remains unclear. According to medieval belief, Christ could address the faithful both through the written word and through a preacher. The reference to her many revelations and visions, however, leads one to suspect that van Rieviren was in contact with the Lord internally, conversing intimately with him on spiritual subjects. The selection provided shows the relative innocence of her mystical practice: she speaks of a kind of vision of Christ, but in terms of contents she receives little more than a traditional lesson in virtue.

The silent sister from Facons does at times become involved in an exceptionally intimate relationship with the heavenly persons. One example should suffice here, the Christmas vision van Rieviren had after a meditation on the scene in the manger in Bethlehem.

> She said once: 'One Christmas day, when I contemplated the birth of the sweet baby Jesus as best I could, it seemed to me that Mary put the child in my arms, saying that I could do with him as I pleased. And as often as I approached the crib, so often did she give him to me to embrace and cradle in my lap, and especially on Candlemas [= Purification of the Blessed Virgin, 2 February]. And she commanded me to give him my interior breasts, which she had rendered full that night. Then, when I did so as best I could, my Beloved said to me: "Give me your breasts that I may drink your

---

[60] On 'consolation through resignation' see Willeumier-Schalij 1990 and Mertens 1995b, 131–2, where Mechtild is discussed.

[61] Cf. Dinzelbacher 1991, 19, on *auditiones*.

[62] *Mijnen beminden heeft mij geseyt dat ick mijn naeckte siel suijverlijck soude cleeden met sijn deuchden en mij soo dick soude vercleeden als ick woude, nu metter eender deucht en dan metter ander, nu met ootmoedicheijt en dan met saechtmoedicheijt, met verduldicheijt en met allen ander deuchden desgelijckx. Dat is dat ick mij soude pijnen dese deuchden aen te mercken en naer mijn arm vermogen die pijnen naer te volgen en al daer mij ombreckt dat ick dat met de syne die soude pijnen te vervullen en den hemelschen vader die opofferen. En hij salse minnelijck ontfangen als oft ickse self gedaen hadde* (MS Vienna, f. 49r).

love for me, and I will give you my wounded heart, so that you may drink from it my love for you." '[63]

This image of van Rieviren and the Christ child exchanging bodily fluids may be a startling one, but such graphic descriptions are not unusual in the Middle Ages. It is women in particular who go to great lengths in their identification with Christ, whose suffering provides the only example worthy of emulation. The drinking of milk and blood serves in this case as a metaphor for the fluid transformation from the human to a higher state.[64]

Usually van Rieviren addresses the adult, suffering Christ. She may turn to him with all her cares and difficulties.

> When I looked back in sorrow at the time I had lost, he said to me: 'Take all the time that I lived most gloriously on earth and offer it to the heavenly Father for all of your lost time.'[65]

For all of its brevity, this passage portrays clearly the relationship between the two spiritual lovers. Van Rieviren experiences a certain degree of difficulty in the physical life and explains this in an interior conversation with Christ, following which the latter provides a concrete solution. In this case she is to meditate on Jesus's life on earth, which after all was one of pain and suffering. We may imagine that van Rieviren was reassured once she had received this interior message. This would certainly have been the case following another vision, in which she learned that she could obtain forgiveness for her sins in her lifetime.

> My Beloved promised me forgiveness of all my sins as long as I forgive all trespasses against me and love those who have oppressed, offended or gossiped against me.[66]

---

[63] *Sij seijde eens: 'Op eenen kersdach, doen ick mij keerden totter geboorten van dat soet kindeken Jesus soo ick best cost, soo docht mij dat Maria mij dat kint gaf in mijn armen, seggende dat ick daer mede doen soude dat ick woude. En soo dickmael als ick aende cribbe quamp, soo gaf sy mij hem om hem te omhelsen en te laten rusten in mijnen schoot, sonderlinge tot lichtmis toe. En sij hiet mij dat ick hem soude geven syn inwendige borsten, want sij hadde die vruchtbaer gemaeckt in dier nacht. Daer naer doen ick mij daer toe gaf soo ick best cost, doen seijde mijnen beminden tot mij: "Geeft mij u borstiens dat ick daer uut suygen mach u minne tot mij, en ick geve u mijn doorwont hert, dat gij daer uut moecht suijgen mijn minne tot u" '* (MS Vienna, ff. 46r–v).

[64] Cf. Vandenbroeck 1994b, in particular 50–6, who delves more deeply, from a psychological point of view, into the identification of women with the suffering Christ.

[65] *Doen ick eens met leetwesen docht op mijnen verloren tijt, soo seijde hy mij: 'Nemt al mijnen tijt die ick alder glorioestelijckxt op der aerden heb geleeft en offert hem den hemelsche vader voor al uwen verloren tijt'* (MS Vienna, f. 48v).

[66] *Mijnen beminden heeft mij gelooft vergiffenisse van alle mijn sonden, ist dat ick vergeve al dat mij misdaen is en die gene minne die mij bedruckt, beswaert oft beclapt hebben* (MS Vienna, f. 47r).

These visions and revelations will undoubtedly have provided her with a great deal of consolation in this difficult earthly existence.

Despite her humility van Rieviren's exceptional talents did not go unnoticed in the small community of Facons. The other nuns knew about her blessed life and some of them were rather envious of her. It is not difficult to imagine the despair, for example, of a certain Sister Janneke, who never once received any such consoling experience.[67] Mechtild mediated for her on a couple of occasions; she would present Janneke's problems to their bridegroom on her behalf.

> It happened once that my beloved sister [= Janneke], who was always ill or in a state of spiritual dryness and desolation, and frequently suffered temptation as she served God, beseeched me urgently, saying: 'Beloved sister, if our dearest Beloved once again comes to you, please ask him to grant me, unworthy as I am, a crumb of that with which he nourishes you so copiously, for I receive nothing but suffering and sorrow from God and mankind, without any consolation whatsoever.'[68]

Van Rieviren resolves this situation elegantly by telling Sister Janneke a splendid story, the only one, incidentally, corroborated in another source.[69] In a vision Christ shows her a tree in which a bird sits on a branch, singing. That is Sister Mechtild herself. Janneke, on the other hand, is represented by an entire forest of beautiful trees, populated by entire flocks of warbling birds. The Lord directs van Rieviren to tell her sister that for her to receive a portion of God's grace here and now is simply not part of the divine plan. Janneke's consolation must be that in the afterlife her joy will be greater than that of her mystically talented sister. 'That is good, my Lord, that is good: something now and something later', is van Rieviren's resigned comment at this point, for thanks to this vision she learns what her place in the afterlife will be.[70]

---

[67] According to a passage on folio 51r of the Vienna manuscript, Mechtild asked Christ whether he would help sister Janneke rise for the nightly celebration of matins (cited at §3.1). From the context it would seem that she is to be identified with the same unnamed nun mentioned here. In the absence of a surname it is not possible to identify her with any person listed in the *Naem- en doodtboeck*.

[68] *Het is noch eens gebeurt dat mijn beminde medesuste, die altoos in groote dorricheijt en gelatentheijt was oft in sieckten, in lijden oft in temtatien Godt dinden, mij hertelijck badt, seggende: 'Mijn beminde suster, als onsen alderliefsten wederom bij u comt, bidt toch dan eens voor mij dat hij mij, onweerdige, toch oock een cruijmken geve vant gene daer hij u soo overvloedich mede voedt, want ick niet en crijgen dan lijden en verdriet van Godt en vande menschen, sonder eenige consolatie'* (MS Vienna, f. 51r–v).

[69] The story also appears in the Middle Dutch translation of the *Liber specialis gratiae* by Mechthild von Hackeborn (cf. Scheepsma 1997, 250–1) and Alijt Bake also uses it in her exemplum concerning the virgin Machtelt and the anonymous anchoress (§8.3).

[70] Cf. for example Bynum 1982, 247–56, on the mediating role assumed by some nuns

Sometimes interesting theological questions are explained to her in her visions.[71] Christ himself explained to her the meaning of one of his most important biblical statements: 'I am the way, and the truth, and the life' (John 14:6).

> My Beloved has granted me some understanding of the words he spoke when he lived in the world: *Ego sum via, veritas et vita*, so that I would know that he was the way of love upon which he came to us and upon which we are to travel if we are to come to him. And in order to make it attractive to us, he has lined it with lovely flowers, such as the violets of humility, the roses of martyrdom, the lilies of purity, and so on, of all the virtues. By this means he has made this path, which he himself is, appealing and pleasing to all loving hearts, for he is the foundation and the root of all virtues. This he has proved in his life and words, his works and exempla, and whoever travels this path faithfully and follows him in virtue, to him shall be clearly revealed the truth which he himself is. For through no craft or subtlety of nature may one know the real truth except through the infusion of the Holy Spirit, to which one may aspire by means of the path of love, which he is. And through fervent love the mind is enlightened and enabled to see the truth in all things. And to the extent that one is able to see, love and experience the truth clearly in all things, to that extent one is able to achieve the true life, which is God himself. Thus these words *Ego sum via, veritas et vita* encompass the beginning, the progression and the perfection of the spiritual being. For the beginning must be the access to the virtues, so that we may thus progress to knowledge of the real truth and, loving and experiencing these, that we may achieve the true life which is God himself.[72]

---

of Helfta (Gertrud the Great, Mechthild of Hackeborn), and of course the case of Jacomijne Costers.

[71] Cf. MS Vienna, f. 47r, where in a vision Christ provides a gloss to his own words.

[72] *Mijnen beminden heeft mij wat verstants gegeven van die woorden die hij sprack doen hij op aertrijck wandelden: 'Ego sum via, veritas et vita', als dat ick soude mercken dat hij was den wech der minnen daer hij door tot ons was gecomen en daer wij door moesten wandelen, souden wij tot hem comen. En omdat ons dien genuchelijck soude wesen, soo heeft hij dien met lieffelijcke blommen beset, als met violetten der ootmoedicheijt, met de roosen der martelien, met de lelien der suijverheijt, en soo van alle deuchden. Waer mede hij desen wech, die hij self is, alle minnende herten lustelijck en bequaem gemaeckt heeft, want hij is den gront en den wortel van alle deuchden. Dat heeft hij bewesen in syn leven met woorden, met wercken en met exempelen, en soo wie desen wech trouwelijck wandelt en hem wel naervolcht inder deuchden, die sal alder clarelijckste die waerheijt bekennen die hij selver is. Want met geen vernuft noch subtijlheijt der natueren en machmen de warachtige waerheijt bekennen sonder invloeijen des heiligen geest, daermen toe comt door den wech der minnen die hij self is. En naer viricheijt der minnen wordet verstant verlicht en verclaert in alle dingen die waerheijt te bekennen. En alsoo veel alsmen de waerheijt clarelijck bekent, bemint en beleeft in alle dingen, alsoo veel machmen oock comen tot het warachtich leven dat Godt self is. Dus is in dese woorden Ego sum via, veritas et vita besloten dat begin, den voortganck en die volmaecktheijt van een geestelijck mensch. Want dat begin moet sijn eenen toeganck tot de deuchden, op dat wij alsoo al voortgaende mogen comen totter kennisse der warachtiger waerheijt en die minnende en belevende mogen geraken tot het warachtich leven dat Godt self is* (MS Vienna, ff. 52v–53r).

Here van Rieviren harmonises the theme of the love for God with the devout doctrine of humility. Her insights may not be exceptional, but they do demonstrate her theological insight. The way in which at the end of her exposition van Rieviren connects the biblical text with the three stadia of the spiritual path, all three of which are defined again, in a different context, in the commentary that follows, leads one to suspect she was a very well-read nun, and perhaps an experienced writer. Or did she insert here an existing biblical commentary into her own vision?

All that survives of van Rieviren's visions and other writings is written in the first person, and the author never addresses a particular audience. This justifies the assumption that the seventeenth-century compiler of the Vienna manuscript drew primarily upon this spiritually gifted nun's personal spiritual diary, presumably preserved in the convent library. One may therefore wonder whether van Rieviren wrote down her experiences initially for her own private use, and whether they only became publically known after her death. According to her biography in the Vienna manuscript, she was a rather shy person.

Nevertheless it is not out of the question that the visions of van Rieviren may have played an admittedly modest but not unimportant role in the spiritual life of Facons. We know that she and Jacomijne Costers, and perhaps a few other nuns, shared this kind of intimate spiritual experience with one another. Apparently there arose something approaching a small mystic circle in Facons – whereby Facons took a decidedly different direction from the trend-setting Diepenveen. Costers wrote a letter to a friend in which she described one of her supernatural experiences. It is not impossible that Mechtild may have been prompted by a similar correspondence to start writing down her visions, so that they then became more widely known. Exactly who belonged to this circle we do not know, but it is likely that it contained nuns such as Sister Janneke. Perhaps van Rieviren wrote her vision of the trees and the birds in part for the benefit of her fellow sister, desperate as she was for some form of consolation. Also, in her commentary on the scriptural passage *Ego sum via*, it would seem that the author was interested in more than just explaining the meaning of Christ's words to herself. This exegesis could well have been intended for a number of sincerely reformed nuns interested in the remarkable interior life of Mechtild van Rieviren.

And yet the differences between van Rieviren and Jacomijne Costers remain significant: the latter's work is permeated with exhortations to reform directed at the entire community of Facons, whereas the writings of Mechtild are aimed mainly at the individual. During van Rieviren's lifetime her writings would have played only a marginal role. But appreciation for them increased with time. In the Vienna manuscript, her seventeenth-century successors at Facons placed Mechtild van Rieviren on an almost equal footing with her friend, Jacomijne Costers.

8

Alijt Bake, a Woman with a Mission

IF THERE WAS any nun in the Chapter of Windesheim who made a conscious choice for this order in particular, it was Alijt Bake (†1455). She entered the convent of Galilea in Ghent at a relatively late age, and once there began to have serious doubts about the wisdom of her decision. Ultimately the religious atmosphere of the Modern Devotion and the Windesheim lifestyle must have seemed ideal in her eyes for realising a deep interior spiritual life. Bake remained at Galilea and was elected prioress by her fellow sisters in 1445. It was then that the path lay open to her to expand opportunities for the mystic life – which to her represented the highest ideal – at Galilea. But in 1455 the Chapter General of Windesheim intervened heavy-handedly: Bake was deposed and banished. Ultimately, then, the Chapter of Windesheim did not meet Bake's expectations at all; it would not give her the space she demanded.

To Bake reading, and later writing, was almost a matter of life and death. Even in her early years she was capable of intense concentration when it came to religious works. Books were for her the means to learn about the experiences of her great spiritual predecessors. As Bake gained greater insight into spiritual matters and her own special vocation, she began writing herself. At first her notes were meant just for herself. They helped her understand what was going on around her and God's intentions for her. Once she had become prioress, Bake began to write down her spiritual doctrine for the benefit of her fellow sisters. That Bake wrote so exhaustively concerning her interior life was clearly not well received by the authorities of the Chapter of Windesheim. It was in the year of her death that the 'prohibition against writing' was issued, forbidding nuns to write down visions and similar experiences.

This chapter is primarily concerned with the role spiritual literature played in the life of Alijt Bake, and only analysis of her teachings, relevant in that context, will be brought into the discussion. The chapter begins with a sketch of Bake's life; this is brief, as this is widely available in other places (§8.1).[1] Following this we shall examine the way Bake approached the literary

---

[1] Alijt Bake was mentioned for the first time in scholarship by Lieftinck 1936, 370, and subsequently by Axters 1956, 166–8, who delved more deeply into her life and works. Lievens 1958b comprises a biography, a list of works and a discussion of the

tradition (§8.2). Her personal contribution to spiritual literature will receive the greatest attention. Bake's works were composed in three phases: shortly after her election as prioress in 1445, in the years 1451-2, and in the period following her banishment from Galilea in 1455 (§8.3). Finally, an attempt will be made to determine the audience for whom she wrote and the extent to which her writings were actually disseminated (§8.4).

8.1 Biography

Alijt Bake was probably born on St Lucia's day (13 December) in 1415. Based on her connections with the town of Utrecht – see further below – it is usually assumed that she came from there, or at least from the region around Utrecht, though the sources do not state this explicitly. Nothing is known about Bake's parents and other family members. Given the normal profile of the Windesheim nuns and taking into consideration her later election as prioress, her origins were probably in the upper ranks of society.

Bake describes how, when she was still living in the world, she would often attend crowded feasts and even there she would feel herself ineluctably drawn to thoughts of the Passion and death of Christ.[2] Such outbursts of brief and superficial joy would have convinced Bake that the world was not the place for her. She was destined for the religious life, but how, and where?

In her autobiographical *Mijn beghin ende voortganck* ('My Beginning and Progress') Bake recounts in detail her quest for the religious way of life that would suit her best. Among other things, she writes that she has sought out the loneliness of the cell in order to lie there at the feet of Christ, like Mary Magdalene before her. To the best of our knowledge Bake was never enclosed as an anchoress. But she did have a spiritual friend who was a recluse in Utrecht, whose name she unfortunately fails to mention. This anchoress was one of Bake's most important teachers in spiritual matters. From her Bake learned how she could be commune with Christ internally and lose herself in him. In the many hours she spent in or near the cell in Utrecht, the youthful Bake probably gained a good idea of what this solitary life entailed.[3] Another

---

transmission of Bake's writings, whereas Spaapen published the bulk of her oeuvre in his series of articles 'Middeleeuwse passiemystiek' ('Medieval Passion Mysticism') in *OGE* (1966-9). Dresen 1990 investigates Bake's convictions from the perspective of feminist theology. Van Dijk 1992 considers her in the context of the medieval female religious movements, and van Dijk and van den Berg 1997 provide a translation into modern Dutch as well as an in-depth analysis of *Mijn beghin ende voortganck*. Ruh 1990-9, vol. 4, 252-67 devotes a whole chapter to Bake. John van Engen (Notre Dame) is preparing an English translation of a number of her most important works.

[2] *Mijn beghin ende voortganck* 23, lines 806-16.
[3] On Bake's attraction to the cell, see *Mijn beghin ende voortganck* 23, lines 816-19; on the anchoress from Utrecht, see chapters 16 and 17; cf. Mulder-Bakker 1996, 155-7.

friend from Utrecht was a nun in a hospital, probably that of St Barbara and St Lawrence. Through this nun Bake came into contact with the life of brotherly love in practice at the hospital. We gain the impression that this life appealed to her less than the contemplative life of the anchoress.[4] Via her friends in Utrecht, then, Bake was introduced to two different forms of semi-religious lifestyle. Presumably after consultation with her experienced mentors, she chose the classic religious life of the enclosed nun.

In 1440 Bake decided to become a postulate in the Windesheim convent of Galilea, in Ghent. She was already twenty-five, relatively old for a Windesheim nun. For reasons that can no longer be recovered, Bake chose the convent of Galilea in Ghent, which was founded in 1431 by the wealthy Jan Eggaert (†1452), lord of Purmerend and Spaarnland. Jan Eggaert was the son of Willem Eggaert (†1417), a merchant from Amsterdam who had risen to the post of treasurer of Willem VI, count of Holland. His son Jan held important posts at the court of Jacoba of Bavaria in Holland, but when she came under increasing pressure from her opponents, Eggaert fled to the safe haven of Ghent, where he subsequently devoted himself to spiritual matters.[5] He not only founded the convent of Galilea, but became an important patron of the Windesheim convent of canons regular of Onze Lieve Vrouw ten Walle in Elzegem, just south of Ghent. Under the leadership of his son, Jan Eggaert (his tenure ran from 1447 to 1473), ten Walle experienced its period of greatest prosperity.[6] Between 1436 and 1438 they managed to have Galilea accepted into the Chapter of Windesheim, despite the incorporation of convents having in the meantime been forbidden by papal bull. Henceforth the prior of ten Walle had governance over the convent, though the rectors came mostly from Groenendaal. Among the first nuns of Galilea were two of Jan Eggaert the elder's daughters, Wilhelmina and Johanna. That Katharina of Burgundy, the natural daughter of Duke Philip the Good, became prioress of Galilea in 1480, speaks volumes for the high regard in which this convent was later held.[7]

No doubt Bake had high expectations for the enclosed life under the regular observance of the Chapter of Windesheim. She was to be sorely disappointed in Ghent, however. She quickly discovered that life in Ghent was entirely devoted to what she describes as 'external' piety. Long before this, she herself had discovered the path of interior, mystic spirituality, which she had no intention of abandoning. With characteristic fervour – and

---

[4] For the nun in the hospital, see *Mijn beghin ende voortganck* 16 and 17.
[5] On Jan Eggaert's connection with the foundation of Galilea and ten Walle, see among others Cassiman 1952, 146–7 and 159–61, van Mingroot 1984a, especially 692–3 and van Mingroot 1984b, 768–9.
[6] On the convent of ten Walle at Elzegem see van Mingroot 1984a; on Jan Eggaert jr, pp. 696–700.
[7] For more on Galilea, see van Mingroot 1984b.

because she did not yet realise that the nuns in Ghent were not familiar with the interior life – the freshly arrived sister informed the prioress in no uncertain terms what she thought of the situation at Galilea. She even threatened to inform the prior superior of Windesheim how inadequately, in her eyes, the constitutions were observed there.

At that time the very reverend Hille Sonderlants of Diepenveen was prioress. She was an older nun who had already successfully reformed several convents and had been sent in 1439 to direct the transition of Galilea to the Chapter of Windesheim.[8] It is quite understandable that this veteran reformer did not accept Bake's criticisms of the Diepenveen ascetic lifestyle, the efficacy of which had been proven there and elsewhere, and she reprimanded the postulant sharply.

During this period of misunderstanding – even her fellow nuns considered her self-willed and overambitious – Bake fell prey to a deep spiritual crisis, which she recounts in detail in *Mijn beghin ende voortganck* (see §8.3). She wondered in despair whether she should not change the course of her life yet again by leaving Galilea. Bake had several options: she could return to the familiar Utrecht, but she could also ask to be transferred to another Windesheim convent. She even seriously considered joining the order of the reformed Poor Clares of Coleta of Corbie (†1447). At about this time Coleta had successfully reinstated the observance of Clare of Assisi's ideal of poverty, and to that end founded a number of new convents. One of them was the convent of Bethlehem in Ghent, founded in 1442, although its construction was begun two years earlier. The saintly Coleta died at the convent of Bethlehem in 1447 and was buried there.[9]

Bake would have heard this sad news, for in 1447 she was still in Ghent. But it was 1440 – for Bake in many ways a pivotal year – that saw her make her definitive decision. A variety of forces had been mobilised to advise her. She makes mention of one or more letters from 'devout men' who gave her advice, advice which she could not, however, follow.[10] In the end it was Jan

---

[8] The life of Hille Sonderlants is recounted in DV, ff. 47r–48r and D, ff. 126b–127a. She was at first rectrix of Diepenveen from 1408–12, but was not the first elected prioress of her convent. Instead Hille became prioress of Mariënveld in Amsterdam, from 1412–24. Following a stay at Diepenveen she attempted to reform the Cistercian convent of Klaarwater in Hattem in 1435, not altogether successfully. Thereupon Hille departed with the other like-minded nuns for the Cistercian convent of Nijeklooster (Aula Dei) near Scharnegoutum in Friesland. She was the only one to remain faithful to the order of canonesses, and once Nijeklooster was established, she returned to Diepenveen. It was then that she assumed the priorate over Galilea in Ghent, which lasted from 1439 until her death on 25 January 1445 (cf. n. 13).

[9] On Coleta of Corbie see Ruh 1990–9, vol. 4, 209–11. On Alijt Bake's associations with Coleta see Spaapen 1967a, 239 note 16e and van Dijk and van den Berg 1997, 14 and 142–6.

[10] *Mijn beghin ende voortganck* 16, lines 531–4.

Eggaert, the founder of Galilea, who came forward with a good plan. He dispatched several messengers to Utrecht through whom Bake could send letters to her spiritual friends, asking them for their judgement in the matter. When she was still waiting for the messengers to return, it was the Lord himself who informed Bake, by means of a vision, what she was to do. Galilea was the place in which she was to fulfil a sacred task. Within the foreseeable future she would become prioress and direct the reforms of the spiritual life there, at first only in Galilea, but thereafter also within her order. Then she would be able to teach her fellow nuns about the internal relationship with Christ. When the messengers returned with the response from the nun at the hospital – the anchoress had apparently passed away in the meantime – it agreed precisely with what Bake had already experienced mentally.

Now that the decision had been made – this would have been in early December of 1440 – events followed in quick succession. The vision of Christ and the letter from Utrecht confirmed what Bake wanted in her heart of hearts: to remain at Galilea and to bring about there a radical reform of the spiritual life. She devoted herself even more fervently to meditation on the Passion and prepared herself to take the veil, which she did at Christmas 1440. The intense spiritual exercises she performed during her novitiate led to a spiritual breakthrough at the Ascension day celebration of 1441. In a vision the Lord gave her insight into the way in which she could follow him. Bake describes these four paths of the Passion in great detail in her important treatise, *De vier kruiswegen* ('The Four Paths of the Cross'). The first two, the contemplation of and actual immersion in the life of Christ, were already familiar to her from her own experience. In her Ascension day vision she learned about the two highest paths, the beholding of Christ – the third path – and the fourth and final path, unification with her Lord. Bake now experienced for herself what the mystics traditionally termed 'resignation': a person must let go of everything that binds him to himself and endure in resignation whatever it is God intends for him.[11] In this, too, Christ is the greatest model. In the garden of Gethsemane he did not pass the cup of suffering, but rather did what his Father intended for him. The loneliness experienced there by Christ is the ultimate form of resignation. Bake often refers to this detachment with the terms *laten ende liden* ('resignation and suffering'), which is characteristic of her teachings. She compares the resigned person to a ball: whoever wishes to play with Christ (*werreballen*) must be a ball (*sollebal*) and allow himself to be tossed back and forth without resisting.[12]

At Christmas 1441, Bake made her profession at Galilea, thus officially entering the order of the canonesses regular of the Chapter of Windesheim.

---

[11] On resignation, see for example Völker 1972 and Mertens 1995b, 131–2.
[12] *Louteringsnacht*, lines 708–10. Over *laten ende liden* as the central tenet of Bake's doctrine, see Spaapen 1967a, 8–12, Scheepsma 1992, 159–64 and Scheepsma 1994, 107 note 7.

With her strong personality and exceptional spiritual talents, she must gradually have been able to win over her fellow nuns. When the prioress Hille Sonderlants died on 25 January 1445, the convent of Galilea elected Bake as her successor.[13] The *Constitutiones monialium* calls for a new prioress to be appointed within forty days, so Bake must have been inaugurated as the second prioress of Galilea before 6 March 1445.[14] Following Hille Sonderlants of Diepenveen, who had taken the safe path of ascesis, Galilea now chose a prioress who could lead the convent on a higher, but also riskier, path to the interior life.

For ten years the inspired Alijt Bake provided leadership for the spiritual life in the community of Galilea, until the visitation from the Chapter General of Windesheim put an end to her leadership in 1455. Bake was treated with exceptional harshness: she was not only deposed, but banished to a convent in Antwerp as well, most probably Facons.[15] Apparently there was a desire to cut the convent of Galilea off entirely from the dynamic influence of its mystical leader. Having been treated with such contempt, this disdain for what she saw as her highest calling and truth must have been too much for Bake. She died a short while later, in exile, on 18 October 1455. She was only forty years old.

8.2 Reading, Writing and Erasing

In several of her works Bake expressed her relationship with religious literature in words like these:

> I never studied any other book than the loving open heart of our beloved Jesus Christ or of his mother Mary, nor did I ultimately seek consolation or advice from anyone else but God, for his advice served me best on my path to ultimate salvation.[16]

This sounds strange coming from the mouth of someone who by medieval

---

[13] Cf. van Mingroot 1984b, 769–70.
[14] Cf. van Dijk and van den Berg 1997, 20–1; on p. 185 it is suggested that Bake was elected prioress by acclamation. The authors fail to mention that Alijt Bake had to have been thirty years old to be elected prioress (*CM* 1.2.52–4). If she was indeed born on 13 December 1415, as is generally assumed, then she would have been too young in early 1445 to have been considered for that office.
[15] Cf. Spaapen 1967b, 351 and van Dijk 1992, 130–1. Incidentally, Christophorus Caers does not mention Alijt Bake's stay at Facons in his *Register*.
[16] *Ick en studierde nye ander boec dan dat minnende open herte ons liefs heren Jhesu Cristi of synre liever moeder Marien, noch nye en ginc ick om troost noch om raet tot yemant eyndelick dan tot Gode, want die raet diende mi best totter hoechster salicheit* (*Memorie*, lines 2–5). See also *Mijn beghin ende voortganck* 14, lines 427–30, *Brief* 9, lines 256–60 and *Vier kruiswegen* 21, lines 253–9; cf. furthermore *Louteringsnacht*, lines 151–75 and the epilogue to *Merkelike leeringhe* (ed. Lieftinck 1936, 21).

standards (and a woman, no less) had not only read an entire library's worth of books, but had added a number of 'books' by her own hand to the corpus of religious literature. This apparently paradoxical view was, however, a widespread phenomenon in religious circles, especially the Modern Devotion. Such statements were intended to clarify what the proper function of reading was: a book was not an end, but a means. Reading just to satisfy curiosity or for study simply to increase one's knowledge distracts from what is really important. Only by experiencing internally what is read can one arrive at a proper understanding of texts. This kind of experiential knowledge, which preceeds a true understanding of a text, was the only worthwhile kind for Bake.[17]

Even in her interest in religious literature Bake shows herself to be an exponent of the Modern Devotion. Her erudition is great, especially for a choirnun from Windesheim. She knew the Holy Scriptures very well indeed, as is apparent from her many references to more and less familiar passages. Bake was also familiar with the story of the fall of Jerusalem, presumably via Jacob van Maerlant's *Wrake van Jerusalem* ('Revenge of Jerusalem'). It is not clear whether she received any kind of formal grounding in theological matters. In her own works Bake mentions a considerable number of spiritual authors or writings which in one way or another she managed to become familiar with: Augustine, Bernard, Dionysius (the Areopagite), Richard of St Victor, Johannes Tauler, Jordan of Quedlinburg, Jan van Ruusbroec, Jan van Leeuwen and Rulman Merswin, and possibly Origen. Naturally she was well versed in hagiography: she refers explicitly to events from the lives of Catherine of Siena, Clare of Assisi, Francis of Assisi, Jerome, Jan van Ruusbroec, Lame Margaret of Magdeburg, Mechthild of Magdeburg and Nicolas of Myra. Bake is the only Windesheim nun of whom it is known for sure that she was in any way familiar with the rich tradition of medieval female mysticism. This is especially evident from her reference to the German Beguine Mechthild of Magdeburg; likewise it is assumed that she was familiar with the works of Hadewijch.[18]

Strictly speaking the nuns of Windesheim had little time or opportunity for private spiritual reading, on average no more than an hour per day. In *Mijn beghin ende voortganck* Bake illustrates how in a very brief span of time she was able to digest the contents of an entire book.[19] On the Sunday before Christmas in that year of years, 1440, which fell on 18 December, she got hold of a copy of the *boecxken dat heet van de neghen velden* ('the book of the nine fields') for a couple of hours. This somewhat misleading title is actually the *Neun Felsen Buch* ('Book of the Nine Crags') by the banker and 'Gottesfreund'

---

[17] Cf. Mertens 1989a, and incidentally Staubach 1991, especially 418–28, on the connection between pragmatic use of texts and empirical knowledge.

[18] For more on Bake's sources see Scheepsma 1997, 260–4.

[19] This paragraph is based on *Mijn beghin ende voortganck* 68.

from Strasburg, Rulman Merswin (†1382).[20] Apparently Bake did not know his name, but she had heard a lot about the *Boek van de negen velden*, from which we may conclude that in her circle religious books were a topic of discussion. Bake describes how at her request – and we must not forget that at the time she was merely a postulant – a copy of the *Boek van de negen velden* was procured.[21] For unspecified reasons the book in question had to be returned to its owner the very same day. Feverishly Bake set about reading the entire book in the two to three hours at her disposal. Although she read all sorts of passages that caught her attention and that she would have loved to contemplate further, she denied herself that luxury. Her goal was to commit the *Neun Felsen Buch* to memory as best she could in the brief time at her disposal.

The medieval mind was trained to systematically absorb texts during the reading process, so that afterwards they could be easily memorised. That Bake had thoroughly mastered this skill is apparent from the following account.[22] On Wednesday, 21 December, three days after she had read the translation of Rulman Merswin's *Neun Felsen Buch*, Bake found herself in the spinning house with the rest of the convent. The monotonous labour provided an ideal opportunity for meditative contemplation, 'for she then had sufficient time to cast her mind inwards'.[23] She called up the contents of the *Boek van de negen velden*, so recently read, before her mind's eye and attempted to fathom its meaning. Bake's method of 'word-processing' makes it clear why so many religious texts – including, for example, Jacomijne Costers's *Previlesien* – are structured numerically or allegorically. The series of nine crags is used by Merswin as a mnemonic device to represent the same number of stages on the spiritual path. Several days later Bake was able to recall with reasonable accuracy which characteristics belonged to which crag.[24]

Spinning and meditating, Bake eventually arrived at the eighth crag. This passage had caught her attention three days before, when she had read it for the first time, but only then did she find the opportunity for a deeper contem-

---

[20] On Rulman Merswin see Steer 1987b.
[21] The phrase *Doen soo gaft sijt wederom thuijs te draghen daert behoorde* ('Then she gave up the book so it could be returned to where it belonged'; *Mijn beghin ende voortganck* 68, lines 319–20) suggests that the book was on loan, perhaps from another convent. The contents of the famous Rooklooster catalogue, which frequently noted those who possessed texts not available in its own library, suggests that there existed a kind of inter-library loan system among (Windesheim) convents (for more on this see Obbema 1996, 103–20).
[22] This paragraph is based on *Mijn beghin ende voortganck* 68 and 72.
[23] *Want sij doen bequamen tijt hadde om haer inwaert te keeren* (*Mijn beghin ende voortganck* 68, lines 326–7).
[24] The use of series, numbers and images improved the 'learnability' of the spiritual material (see Angenendt, Braucks, Busch et al. 1995, 62–9).

plation of it. 'And though she had read it, she did not then properly understand how what God showed and commanded of her was to be brought about, therefore she was compelled to ascend.'[25] The deeper meaning of the text that had been occupying her for a couple of days had now sunk in in full force. She recognised all too well the eighth crag, characterised by the life of external poverty and penitence: it represented the spiritual level she had already achieved. That there was a ninth level above that one was something Bake had not previously realised. This ninth crag was characterised by inner poverty, in which a person renounces all individuality. Merswin calls this stage 'nakedness'. What Bake had not realised during her intial reading was now made clear through divine intervention: she had to ascend yet another crag, so that she could come as close to God as was possible for her to do.[26]

Illustrative of Bake's attitude and her approach to meditation is the decision she made as the clock struck the hour and the nuns were to leave the spinning house. She prayed to the Lord and asked what she was to do: remain in her heart with the nine crags during the divine office, or recite it in earnest as a good Windesheim nun should. She received instructions to stick with the *Boek van de negen velden*, to remain, that is, with what moved her most. In so doing Bake in fact defied the vow of obedience; she remained faithful, however, to what she considered in her heart to be the truth.[27]

In *Mijn beghin ende voortganck* Bake also refers to the works of the mystics from Groenendaal, Jan van Ruusbroec and Jan van Leeuwen. During her novitiate in 1440-1, Christ taught her the two highest ways of the Passion. In order to clarify the fourth way, which presupposes a life of resignation and devotion to God, Bake refers to van Ruusbroec and his good cook, van Leeuwen. Both authors wrote about resignation, but she finds in neither of them an adequate description of the deep feelings of desolation and abandonment by God that also constitute an element of this state.[28] Bake wrote her autobiography more than ten years after her first experiences with resignation. Thus it is possible that she became familiar with van Ruusbroec and van Leeuwen only afterwards. But apparently their works were available in the library of Galilea around 1450, making it possible for Bake to refer to literature that could clarify, for herself and others, the spiritual state in which she lived. Here we see medieval religious literature in its prime function: van

---

[25] *En als sijt al ghelesen hadde, sij en verstont noch doen niet te rechte waerin dat het volbracht mochte worden, waer dat het haer Godt toinde en eijsschende van haer, daer sij door opclemmen saude* (*Mijn beghin ende voortganck* 72, lines 429–32).

[26] This paragraph is based on *Mijn beghin ende voortganck* 72. There, presumably from memory, Bake paraphrases a passage on the ninth crag.

[27] On this dilemma see *Mijn beghin ende voortganck* 68, lines 334 to 69, lines 342. Lewis 1996, 250 gives the example of a Dominican nun from the fourteenth century who interrupted a vision in order to say matins; obedience went before all else for these nuns, too.

[28] Cf. Ruh 1990–9, vol. 4, 256.

Ruusbroec and other mystic leaders wrote about the spiritual life from their own experience, and capable readers such as Bake were adept at finding in their writings that which was relevant to their experience.[29]

An author in whom Alijt Bake found support during this same difficult period, even though she does not mention him by name in her autobiography (though she does mention him in her *Van die memorie der passien ons heren* ('On the Commemoration of Our Lord's Passion')), was the Dominican preacher Johannes Tauler. Around 1440 Jan Eggaert gave the convent a manuscript containing a large number of his sermons.[30] In a survey of her models Bake praises him the most of all, because in her view Tauler understood best how a person can become internally like Christ.

> Oh, I know of only one master of divinity who teaches this, the devout Tauler; he says more about this than I had previously seen done in any treatise. And yet he does not explain how one is to arrive at this state, for that was impossible for him to express with the written word. But he knew intimately the ways in which it is properly and truly constituted.[31]

Even though the state of true resignation cannot be described in writing, Bake had found in Tauler an author who was on the same track as she was. In this case, too, she compared the spiritual or mystical tradition to her own experience, an approach that was essential for her. She did not, indeed, read simply to acquire useless knowledge, but immersed herself with great intensity in writings that could deepen her insight into the spiritual way of life.

In *Mijn beghin ende voortganck* Bake describes almost exclusively her period of postulancy and novitiate, in the years 1440 and 1441. It is only for this brief period, then, that we have information concerning her reading and writing. Based on this, and despite the absence of concrete comparative evidence, it must be assumed that in the context of the Chapter of Windesheim, Bake was an exception to the rule. The normal programme of reading for novices consisted primarily of instructions on life in the convent such as the *Profectus religiosorum* by David of Augsburg and other such ascetic works. Bake, on the other hand, read pure mystic literature even before she officially took the veil. She had probably already been exposed to it during her Utrecht period. She is able to apply the contents of Rulman Merswin's *Neun Felsen Buch* precisely to her own spiritual situation: even before she took the habit of a nun, she had already achieved the eighth stage. No wonder that her fellow sisters were at

---

[29] This paragraph is based on *Mijn beghin ende voortganck* 63.
[30] MS Brussel, KB, 2283–4; cf. Stooker and Verbeij 1997, vol. 2, no. 458.
[31] *Och, alleen ken ic een meester inder godheit die daer of leert, die devote Thauler, die gaet hem naere dan ic ye hoerde in enigen scriften. Nochtans en verclaert hi niet hoemen daer toe coemt, want dat was hem onmogelic mit woerden der letteren te verclaren. Mer hi wist die wegen alre naest daert properlic en eygentlic in staet* (Memorie, lines 140–4).

first somewhat suspicious of this self-assured postulant. They had learned as novices that the essence of the monastic life was humility and obedience.

The initial lack of sympathy from the nuns of Galilea resonates in a passage in which Bake describes how with great effort she attempted to meditate on the Passion. Because it was so difficult for her to concentrate solely on the Passion, she forced herself to speak continuously to the Lord. And because they saw her constantly mumbling, the sisters accused her of reading too much. For them this mumbling by their new fellow nun meant that she was continuously contemplating recently read texts. Bake does, in fact, deny the charge, but here, too, where there is smoke, there is probably fire. She probably read much more, and certainly more intensely, than most of her fellow sisters. This zealous reading was directly related to Bake's life of prayer, which was also much more penetrating than that of her fellow nuns.[32]

It was during this period of intense meditation and concentration that Bake's authorship gradually began to take form. By means of the meditation technique of *ruminatio*, among other things, she achieved a greater degree of inner peace.

> But our Lord, who recognised my simple intentions and desires, my great effort and diligence in how eagerly I helped myself, came at last to my aid, and matters improved somewhat, so that I began not only to speak, but also to contemplate and consider internally, which is what I should have been doing before.[33]

Her spiritual life was enriched by this meditation, which grew constantly deeper, and she gained new insights. This brought the youthful Bake joy, but also great confusion. It was in this period that she discovered the ideal aid to organising her inner life: writing.

> And all that I learned in this way I wrote down, so that I would not forget it. Thus I spent my time all the while speaking and contemplating and learning and writing and erasing and writing again, and in that way I forgot all those other cares.[34]

---

[32] This paragraph is based on *Mijn beghin ende voortganck* 27; the text cited is found at lines 971–2. Spaapen 1967a, 258 note 27a takes *lesen* to mean 'prayer'. The term combines the senses of reading and praying more or less simultaneously, for the contemplation of spiritual texts was for the Modern Devout a form of meditation (see §4.1 and 2).

[33] *Maer onsen lieven heere, die mijn goede, simpel meininghe ende begheerte aensach, mijnen grooten aerbeijt ende neerst<i>cheijt hoe gheeren ick mij selven gheholpen hadde, die quam mij ten lesten te hulpe, alsoo dat wat beterde, alsoo dat ick bij tijden ende stonden daer wel bij bleef niet alleene sprekende, maer oock peijsende ende leerende van binnen wat ick daer vooren oock doen soude* (*Mijn beghin ende voortganck* 27, lines 999–6).

[34] *Ende wat ick aldus leerde dat schreef ick al op, dat ick niet vergheten en soude. Ende aldus al segghende ende al peijsende ende al leerende ende al schrijvende ende wederuutplanerende*

In this period she had such intense experiences of the divine that she had to work hard to make sense of them all. Describing her experiences as best she could was her way of attempting to maintain a grip on her interior life.

During that first year at Galilea, like other Windesheim postulants and novices, Bake would have learned how to enrich one's meditation by maintaining a *rapiarium*. This reading and writing technique stood her in good stead during this period of great confusion. But in Bake's case, writing as a form of support for her interior life took a different turn. Whereas the approach of the other choir nuns was entirely passive, with perhaps the exception of Jacomijne Costers and Mechtild van Rieviren, Bake began to cast her own experiences in written form. The aspect of coming to terms with herself is clearly present in her writings. Bake was deluged with awe-inspiring experiences and deep emotions and attempts through writing and rewriting to gain insight into her situation. Her notes, which she repeatedly erased, served in this period exclusively as a means of coming to grips with her interior life, the same function, in fact, as the *rapiaria* fulfilled for the other nuns. Here, however, the seed of authorship was planted that made Bake's priorate so special.[35]

8.3 Three Moments in the Literary Career of Alijt Bake

Having started out as a strong-willed novice, mistrusted by everyone, the zealous Alijt Bake gained the trust of the community of Galilea in 1445. By electing her as their spiritual leader, the nuns of Galilea opted firmly for Bake's mystical lifestyle. That a significant cultural shift took place in the convent in Ghent is clear from the sharp criticism Bake directs at her predecessor's regime in *Mijn beghin ende voortganck*. During that period, Galilea 'was nothing short of a nest of devils, hiding its unworthy nature under a thin veil of a religious life based only on appearances'.[36] Her *Van die memorie der passien ons heren* offers a passage in which Bake explains her position more clearly:

> Thus this way, like the way of letting go, requires a separation of virtuous works, emptiness and openness to God and with earnest feelings of

ende noch weder schrijvende brocht ick emmer mijnen tijt over, dat ick die ander sonderlinghe ghepeijsen vergat (*Mijn beghin ende voortganck* 27, lines 7–11).

[35] In Bake's oeuvre the technique described here is frequently discernible, for example in the recurring treatment of the series 'resignation, suffering and love', as well as in the semi-concentric structure of her works (cf. Scheepsma 1992, 159–66).

[36] *Mijn beghin ende voortganck* 26. I see Bake's criticism of life at Galilea in the periculous context of the contrast between the interior and the exterior life. It might well have been the case, however, that Hille Sonderlants was no longer able to maintain monastic discipline in the convent, perhaps because of her advanced age (cf. Kohl, Persoons and Weiler 1976–84, vol. 3, 258–9).

remorse, in which a person must experience tender resignation and suffering in simple faith and loving trust of God that God will not abandon him.[37]

Although Hille Sonderlants advocated the path of asceticism and virtue, the norm for all Windesheim convents, to Bake this was no more than a lower stage. She and her followers wanted to tread the path of the interior life, one consequence of which could be that the pursuit of virtue would be placed in a quite different light. Complete surrender to God's intentions for a person in this life transcended the performing of good works.

The new prioress did not wish to deny her followers access to the texts that had proved so beneficial to her. During her priorate, then, a programme of mystical reading came into existence. This is apparent, for example, from Bake's description of how the nuns had mistrusted her and thought that 'I might have been or become one of those false spirits of whom Jan van Ruusbroec writes'.[38] This allusion illustrates how van Ruusbroec's mysticism had become part of the entire community's frame of reference.[39] Unfortunately too little of the convent of Galilea's library survives to allow us to form an accurate picture of its holdings.[40]

It is no longer possible to tell whether Bake's activities also led to an increase of books through purchase or copying, though the number of sources she is able to mention does point in that direction. Perhaps, faced with lack of appropriate materials, Bake may have attempted to augment the library of the young convent on her own. At any rate, it is possible for us to follow the development of Bake as spiritual author from the moment she became prioress. Her role as an author cannot be separated from her office. As prioress, she was in a position where the natural authority which she undoubtedly possessed was formally validated by her rank. As the spiritual leader of Galilea she had the opportunity to make her ideas public. She would have delivered the great majority of her lessons orally, for example at

---

[37] *Alsoe sal dese wech, als die wech des afterlatens, eyschen een afgesceyden der duechdelicker wercken, in ledicheit van allen toekeer ende in swaren berespen der consciencien, daer een mensche in sachtmoedigen laten ende liden doer gaen moet in een simpel gelove ende minlic betrouwen tot Gode dat God hem niet laten en sal* (Memorie, lines 83–7).

[38] *Dat ick emmer een van die bedroghen gheesten sijn soude oft werden, daer heer Jan Ruijsbroeck af schrijft* (Mijn beghin ende voortganck 3, lines 54–5).

[39] This issue is taken up in *Vanden vier becoringhen* (Jan van Ruusbroec 1981–, vol. 10, 256–317), and also at the end of the second part of *Die geestelike brulocht* (Jan van Ruusbroec 1981–, vol. 3).

[40] Galilea is often singled out as a centre of interest for its mysticism; see, among others, Lieftinck 1936, especially 133–4, 149 and 369–71, Ubbink 1978, 135–41 and 158–60, Willeumier-Schalij 1981, 298–303 and Ubbink 1985, 162–3. This is due in large part to MS Brussels, KB, 643–4 (see text), which contains the works of Tauler, Eckhart and Alijt Bake, but which was not produced at Galilea. For the manuscripts at Galilea see Stooker and Verbeij 1997, vol. 2, no. 458–63.

the communal gathering in the chapter house at prime, but some of them were also committed to writing.

In Bake's life there are three particular moments in which she is seen to take up her pen. It is perhaps no coincidence that these three 'writing moments' coincide with high and low points in her life. The first one comes at the beginning of her priorate, when God keeps his promise and Bake is indeed elected prioress of Galilea, and she is free to begin her task of reform in earnest. We encounter Bake as author again in 1451, when her spiritual leadership has climbed to even greater heights. She writes a spiritual autobiography in order to show her followers how God can be active in a person's inner being. The final 'writing moment', in 1455, is without a doubt a low point in her career. Bake is deposed and banished to Antwerp. One last time she launches a written offensive in an attempt to win her case, but as far as is known, she did not succeed in gaining satisfaction.[41]

Bake would have started writing fairly soon after her inauguration as prioress. We know this because of the important colophon in MS Brussels, KB, 643–4:

> Pray for the one who composed and wrote this,
> For she remained poor in the name of God.
> Fourteen hundred years
> After Jesus was on the Cross
> And forty-six more, or thereabouts,
> Was this composed in Ghent
> By Sister Alijt, prioress
> Of Galilea, may God secure her soul.[42]

This shows, then, Bake wrote one or more works in or around the year 1446. Yet this rhyming colophon raises a number of further questions. It is sufficient to note here that the codex from Brussels was not, despite what others initially thought, Bake's autograph manuscript. This not only brings the authenticity of the colophon into question: it makes it harder to assess the book's contents.[43]

Because the status of the colophon is not entirely clear, it is not easy to determine precisely which of the texts in this manuscript were written by Bake herself. The colophon concludes a rather long section of text written in the same hand (ff. 114ra–198va). This section begins with a series of a few

---

[41] An overview of Bake's works is found in Scheepsma 1997, 252–3 and Ruh 1990–9, vol. 4, 255–6.

[42] *Bidt voor diet maecte ende heeft ghescreven / Want zij arm door Gode es bleven / Doe men M vierhondert screef / Na dat Jhesus ant cruce bleef / Ende XLVI ofte daer omtrent / Soe was dit eerst ghemaect te Ghent / Van zuster Alijt, der priorinnen / Van Galileen, God wille haer ziele gewinnen* (MS Brussels, KB, 643-4, f. 198va).

[43] The colophon is cited after Scheepsma 1995b, 224, cf. 234; on its interpretation, see pp. 224–6.

dozen sermons for Sundays and feast days, composed predominantly by her teacher Johannes Tauler, though the odd sermon by Meister Eckhart and a few anonymous sermons are included as well (ff. 114ra–154va). We shall pass over the question of whether Bake may have been responsible for compiling this corpus of texts, in which Tauler features so prominently, though it is firmly likely.[44] Instead we share focus on the next section of text (ff. 154va–198va), in which Bake's hand is unmistakably present. Here the prime questions are how, and with what intentions, Bake set to work on her writing.[45]

Bake first emerges as author in the Brussels codex in a prologue on f. 154va, in which she introduces two sermons on the Gospel for Palm Sunday, both by Jordan of Quedlinburg (†1380). This Augustinian hermit composed an impressive corpus of sermons, the *Opus postillarum*, for every Sunday and feast day, based on the lection of the day.[46] The lection for Palm Sunday read: 'And a very great multitude spread their garments in the way: and others cut boughs from the trees, and strewed them in the way' (Matt. 21:8); or, in Middle Dutch, according to the rubrics in the Brussels manuscript: *Een groete scare stroyden haer cleederen inden weghe*. In her prologue Bake explains how she would read five additional sermons on the lection for Palm Sunday, crumbs, as it were, fallen from the table of the *wise eersaem leerare Jordanus* ('wise, reverend teacher Jordan').[47]

In her own 'sermons' Bake gives a thorough explication of Jordan of Quedlinburg's commentary. Moreover, she adds her own insights from time to time. It is striking, to say the least, that in the middle of the fifteenth century and within the circle of influence of the Modern Devotion, a woman should be glossing the commentary of a highly respected theologian such as Jordan of Quedlinburg. None of the scholars who have studied Bake's 'sermons' closely has succeeded in distinguishing five distinct texts. Lievens found only three; he categorises them as 'monastic lessons', and thus not true homiletic texts.[48] Spaapen, who published the edition of Bake's teachings, distinguishes four texts, which he even provided with titles: *De louteringsnacht van de actie*, *De weg der victorie*, *De weg van de ezel* and *De lessen van Palmzondag* ('The Purifying Night of Action', 'The Path of Victory', 'The Path of the Ass' and 'The Lessons for Palm Sunday'). The last he splits into two texts in order to arrive at a total of five.

We turn to *De louteringsnacht van de actie*, Bake's first monastic lesson, in

---

[44] See on this question Scheepsma (forthcoming).
[45] A recent description of MS Brussels, KB, 643–4 is found in Deschamps and Mulder 1998, 2–7; cf. Stooker and Verbeij 1997, vol. 2, no. 659 and Scheepsma (forthcoming).
[46] On Jordan of Quedlinburg see Zumkeller 1983, on his influence in the Low Countries, see Lievens 1958a.
[47] The prologue in question is edited in Lieftinck 1936, 18–19, Lievens 1958a, 189–90 and Spaapen 1968b, 225.
[48] Lievens 1958b, 134–8.

order to illustrate her *modus operandi*. In his sermons, Jordan of Quedlinburg speaks of three groups of people who accompanied Jesus on his entry into Jerusalem. In front were the teachers and authorities, behind Jesus there was a large group of followers and next to Jesus were his disciples (the later Apostles). According to Jordan, monks should identify themselves with this last group, because their contemplative lifestyle grants them the highest state of spiritual life. Bake provides a characteristic nuancing of the learned Jordanus' categories. Religious belong indeed in close proximity to Jesus, but it is those who (should) take the step from the contemplative to the apostolic life who are closest to him. This is true, for example, of the disciples – those who are closest to him in the procession – who received from their master the task to spread his word far and wide. In this lesson Bake defends the argument that actions are more important than contemplation.[49]

Bake mentions a number of saintly examples whose lives illustrate her position, among whom are a strikingly high number of women. The first woman she mentions is Mary Magdalene, who, according to legend, as an anchoress initially lived the contemplative life, but who eventually followed in the footsteps of the Apostles. She set out to preach the gospel and went as far as Provence. Catherine of Siena also had an apostolic mission: she showered the Pope in Avignon with proposals for church reform. Bake also mentions 'Mechtild and Margaret the Lame', presumably the beguine writer Mechtild of Magdeburg and Margaretha Contracta from Magdeburg. Further on in the Brussels manuscript an exemplum has been inserted about a virgin Machtelt and an anonymous anchoress, which probably refers to them. Their spiritual friendship is strongly reminiscent of the relationship between Bake and her mentor from Utrecht.[50]

Bake shared the opinion of this anonymous recluse from Utrecht that she was destined for a life of works. She explains in *De louteringsnacht van de actie* what the life of works consists of. Bake uses the image of a knight sent by his lord in search of adventure. The nuns of Galilea would have experienced no difficulty in recognising in that knight their new prioress, whose quest it was to reform their interior lives.[51] One might observe that Alijt Bake had no need to work all of this out in writing for herself, for she had already received the interior call to action in 1440. She did, however, have matters to explain to her followers, the nuns of Galilea. As prioress she possessed formal authority

---

[49] The focus here is quite emphatically on being chosen: in *Louteringsnacht*, lines 137–60 Bake shows how poorly things turn out for those who imagine they have been sent by God. In this respect Bake's vision is reminiscent of Meister Eckhart, who also put action before contemplation (cf. for example Mieth 1986, 52–64), but even more so of Jordan of Quedlinburg (cf. Saak 1996, 322–4).

[50] The female examples in *Louteringsnacht* are at lines 199–206 and 639–70. The identification of Margaretha Contracta and Mechtild of Magdeburg is given at Mulder-Bakker 1996, 155–7 (cf. Mulder-Bakker 1995) and Ruh 1990–9, vol. 4, 264–5.

[51] On spiritual knighthood among women see M. van Dijk 2000, especially 150–2.

over Galilea, but the higher spiritual leadership she claimed for herself demanded further explication. Her monastic lessons appear to have been intended to instruct the convent of Galilea in the power relationships within a mystic community. And yet one may also detect in *De louteringsnacht van de actie* a note of surprise at her own role. It is as if she has to convince *herself* that she must follow the example of Mary Magdalene.

The third monastic lesson, only partially edited, bears the title *De weg van de ezel*.[52] Here Bake explains, in six points, what lessons the ass upon which Jesus rode into Jerusalem can teach us. The fifth point consists of the fact that the ass has a cross between its shoulders. Likewise the believer should always carry the cross with him or her. Following a brief allusion to Jordan, the complete text of Bake's chief work has been inserted: *De vier kruiswegen*.[53] Here she discusses the four ways of passion – the four ways in which a person can embrace the Cross – into which she was granted deep insight through her Ascension day vision of 1441. Thus by around 1446 Bake had fully formed her spiritual doctrine. Having first set out her own position for her followers, she then presents them with her doctrine of the interior life.

Of central importance to this philosophy of life is the act of experiencing Christ's suffering. *De vier kruiswegen*, for example, describes four ascending stages at which a person can embrace the Cross of Christ. In the structure of the compilation left by Bake in Brussels manuscript 643–4, Holy Week is the spiritual backbone. The series begins with commentaries on the Gospel readings for Palm Sunday, the beginning of Christ's suffering. Following this block of 'sermons' is a text entitled *Een merkelike leeringhe* ('A Remarkable Lection'). It has not yet been determined whether this can be ascribed to Bake, but it certainly has close ties to her work.[54] This treatise deals with the seven interior garments that a person must cast off while standing at the foot of Christ's Cross. They stand for such interior characteristics as self-love and stubborness, which distract from the divine. This theme is connected to Good Friday, the day when Christ's suffering was completed.[55]

This at first sight impenetrable collection of texts from the Brussels manuscript exhibits more than just a strong cohesion in its contents. From the moment when Bake begins to respond to the sermons of Jordan of Quedlinburg, she constantly refers back and forth among the various texts in this manuscript, establishing links between them. The entire compilation may be regarded as a statement of her position, with firm awareness of her formal

---

[52] Cf. Ruh 1990–9, vol. 4, 261–6.
[53] Cf. Ruh 1990–9, vol. 4, 256–61.
[54] Ruh 1990–9, vol. 4, 255 n. 6 considers the text, which he refers to as *Boexken vander passien* ('Book of the Passion'), as an authentic work by Bake.
[55] Van Dijk and van den Berg 1997, 179–81 show that Alijt Bake did indeed have an eye for such symbolism: *Mijn beghin ende voortganck* presents a 'model of spiritual transformation' based on the cycle of the liturgical year.

and spiritual leadership. She intended to make the most of her task as monastic reformer. And because Bake sought the salvation of herself and her community in an immersion in the interior life, her writings of 1446 constitute a clear mystic manifesto.

We may ask ourselves why Bake thought it necessary to commit her ideas to writing. Her work probably derived from the oral exhortations she delivered regularly before the community at prime and during the chapter of faults. Bake herself provides a partial answer in the prologue to *Een merkelike leeringhe*.

> Now I shall give you the highest, most valuable and noble point that you have ever heard. And because I feared that you would not understand it or remember it even though I told it to you, I have written it down for you, so that you may always find it again should you ever forget it.[56]

Bake wanted to preserve her fleeting words, apparently without the express intention of spreading her doctrine; they were primarily a *vade mecum* for the inexperienced nuns of Galilea. Bake must certainly have assumed that her fellow sisters would study her lessons, as she had done with the *Boek van de negen velden*. But where she had been forced to return that manuscript after a short while, her convent would always have a written reminder of her lessons.

But Bake also gives the impression that she wished to leave a spiritual testament behind for her followers, as if she had already foreseen her deposition. This is particularly evident in the short treatise, *De trechter en de spin* ('The Funnel and the Spider'), which concludes the Brussels compilation and which directly precedes the aforementioned colophon. Bake once again addresses the relationship between the mystic leader and her followers. Here it is apparent how aware she is of the unpredictability of being God's chosen one. She characterises her role using the metaphor of the funnel, through which divine grace may pass more easily into the narrow throats of her yet ignorant followers.

For she is nothing more than a funnel between the barrel and the wine. Because the opening in the barrel is narrow and the wine cannot be had without pouring, a funnel must be used.[57] But a funnel is nothing more than a tool, something that Bake knew all too well. 'And when at last it is worn out,

---

[56] *Nu willic u gheven dat alderhochste, weerdichste ende dat edelste poent dat ghij noch gehoort hebt. Ende om dat ic duchte dat ghijs niet te rechte verstaen en sout noch onthouden, al seidict hu metten monde, daer omme hebbict u gescreven, op dat ghijt dan altoes weder vinden moeght als ghijt verloren hebt* (Merkelike leeringhe, f. 181va). This prologue is edited in Lieftinck 1936, 20 and Lievens 1958a, 192.

[57] *Want ic en ben anders niet dan een trechterkin datter dient tusschen den dranc ende dat vat. Om dat vat nauwe es ende den dranc niet ontfanghen en mach sonder storten, soe moetmen den trechter hier toe oorboren* (Trechter en spin, lines 32–5).

it is discarded and tossed into a corner and a new one is sought, and this is the reward for its good work.'[58] The same thing could happen to her. It would have served as some consolation to Bake that by 1446 she had already provided the convent with a substantial written legacy.

A few years into her priorate, Bake added a new and lengthy work to the library of Galilea. In the form of a spiritual autobiography, she describes how her transition to the mystic way of life had come about. The use of forms of address such as *alderliefste* ('dearest beloved') or *lieve kinderen* ('dear children') are indications that Bake wrote her biography for the community of Galilea.[59] A passage that deals with Hille Sonderlants's position on the spiritual life proves this definitively:

> Oh, if I had followed them, how I would have missed my true path and wandered aimlessly. And if I were not to have found this blessed way, I would not have received this great good. Oh, dear children, how harmful this would have been for me and for the Holy Church and in particular for you who are in this house, how harmful if I had done that.[60]

Thanks to Bake's tenacity the sisters of Galilea are now in a position to become familiar with the interior life, by which they may come closer to perfection.

When she was first prioress, Bake would have found it difficult to present her own life story to her followers as an example to follow. However, it seems her confidence and authority increased dramatically, perhaps alongside the comprehension of her circle. Bake wrote her autobiography approximately six years after she took office, as is shown by time references in *Mijn beghin ende voortganck*:

> And it is now eleven years ago at Christmas that this took place, when I was twenty-six years old. And now on the very day that I write this, namely St Lucia's day [13 December], I am thirty-six years old.[61]

---

[58] *Ende ten lesten alst versleten es, dan soe werptmen wech uut den weghe in eenen hoec ende men siet om eenen anderen, ende dit es sijn loen van sinen arbeide* (*Trechter en spin*, lines 42–4).

[59] See for example *Mijn beghin ende voortganck* 8, line 199 and 25, line 907, and 8, line 203 and 21, line 773.

[60] *Och, oft ick hun gevolcht hadde, hoe hadde ick mijn weghen ghemist en verdoolt. Och, soo en waer ick tot desen salighen wech niet ghecommen, noch oock dit groot goet niet vercreghen. Och, lieve kinderen, hoe schaedelijck hadde dit voor mij en de heijlighe kercke en besonderlijck u lieden, die hier sijt in desen huijse, schaedelijck gheweest, hadde ick dat ghedaen* (*Mijn beghin ende voortganck* 8, lines 200–6); cf. *Mijn beghin ende voortganck* 19, lines 675–7.

[61] *Ende dit is nu ter tijd van kersdach XI jaer gheleden dat dit gheschiede, ende doen ick 26 jaeren effen out was. Ende nu op desen selven dach dat ick dit schreef, welck is op Sinte Luciendach [13 December], ben ick nu 36 jaeren out* (*Mijn beghin ende voortganck* 19, lines 671–5).

Bake refers here to the remarkable blessings she received around Christmas in 1440. Her account dates from eleven years later, i.e. 1451. Given the size of this text, she would hardly have completed it in just one day. We can therefore cautiously date the composition of *Mijn beghin ende voortganck* to the winter of 1451–2.

The only manuscript containing Bake's autobiography is Ghent, UB, 3854, dated to 1705 and written by Augustina Baert, a nun from Galilea. She did not work directly upon Bake's autograph copy, but rather upon a transcript made by Jacobus Isabeels, rector of Galilea (1611–13), made in 1613 from an exemplar which even then was no longer complete.

The exordium of the autobiography in the Ghent manuscript reads as follows: 'Here begins another book concerning my origins and progress.'[62] From what follows it becomes clear that this 'other book' must have comprised the first volume of Bake's autobiography. Unfortunately it has been lost, and it is the second volume that we know as *Mijn beghin ende voortganck*. Here Bake recounts how twice in the course of her life she was seriously tested by God. (The shift in narrative perspective to the third person is due to one of the text's intermediaries.)[63]

> Behold, thus has the Lord subjected her [Alijt Bake] to two tests and stages which transcend anything I have ever heard written down. The first one occurred in her early years, during her period of tribulation. I shall tell you the second one according as God grants me grace for the task.[64]

The account of the first period of testing is recorded in *dat boeck der tribulatien* ('the book of tribulation'), the first section of Bake's autobiography. As mentioned above, *Mijn beghin ende voortganck* constitutes the second part of this work. The prioress of Galilea organised her biography, then, around two spiritual crises she had experienced.

Thanks to references in *Mijn beghin ende voortganck* we are able to catch a glimpse of the contents of the now lost *Boeck der tribulatien*.[65] It dealt with the period preceding Bake's entry into the convent of Galilea. By this time she had already achieved an exceptional, intimate relationship with Christ and she practised the first two paths of the Passion: contemplation and immersion. She learned to give herself over to the Lord entirely and in the process

---

[62] *Hier beghint dat ander boecxken van mijn beghin ende voortganck* (*Mijn beghin ende voortganck* 1, lines 10–11).

[63] On this see Scheepsma 1994, 113.

[64] *Siet, aldus heeft haer den heere ghestelt in twee preuven ende graeden die boven alle schryfturen sijn die ick oijt hoorde. Die eerste ghesciede in haer beghin, daer inden tijt der tribulatien. Die ander sal ick u segghen, naer dat dat mij Godt gracie hiertoe gheven sal* (*Mijn beghin ende voortganck* 72, lines 407–11).

[65] This reconstruction is based on *Mijn beghin ende voortganck* 2, lines 13–30, 15, lines 450–5, 23, lines 819–25, 31, 33, 38, lines 408–10, 64, lines 151–5, and 72, lines 409–10; cf. Spaapen 1967a, 218 note 2b and 338 note 72b.

learned more about the spiritual life. In this period Christ forgave her all of her sins, on the condition that Bake did public confession, which, however, provoked only surprise and annoyance. Afterwards Bake realised that the mocking and contempt she suffered at the time, and would endure again later on, were essential elements of the path of passion. Through her *Boeck der tribulatien*, she showed the first stages of the mystical ascent.

The second part of the autobiography describes her second trial, which essentially comprises her period as postulant and novitiate (1440–1). During these two defining but difficult years, Bake experienced a spiritual development which allowed her to follow the two highest paths of the Cross. In *Mijn beghin ende voortganck* she presents a detailed and accessible account of her experiences. The *structure* of her narrative is more difficult to follow, however; it is the recurring meditations on the different paths of the Passion that cause particular difficulty. In his analysis of this text van Dijk shows that Bake nevertheless hit upon a different way of structuring a complex narrative. She draws steadily closer to the core of her message, as it were, by tracing continually tighter concentric circles, and in so doing she gives her audience the opportunity to follow her in the process of mystical transformation. She wrote *Mijn beghin ende voortganck* from a personal perspective based on her own experience, which not only lends it great spontaneity, but makes her experiences immediately recognisable. Bake's great desire to reveal her experiences of the spiritual path made up for her lack of formal training in composing a carefully structured theological treatise.[66]

Bake chose the spiritual crisis she experienced in 1440 as the point of departure for her narrative. At the time the big question for her was whether she would stay on at Galilea, where the level of the spiritual life was so disappointing. She was faced with three dilemmas. First, there was her conflict with Hille Sonderlants and her novice mistress Yde, who wanted to impose upon her an ascetic lifestyle, although she yearned for the interior, mystical life. Was she to obey her unknowing superiors, or should she follow her heart and continue down the interior path? One possible solution was to leave Galilea and search for another convent within the Chapter of Windesheim where her convictions would find more fertile ground: this was her second dilemma. The third was whether she should leave Windesheim altogether and follow instead the path of Coleta of Corbie and her Poor Clares.[67]

Through these three dilemmas Bake shows what the life of resignation and suffering (*laten ende liden*) is like. Even in the darkest of times one must remain faithful to what one feels is the truth. Slander and contempt from outsiders constitute an integral part of the process. During this difficult

---

[66] For an exhaustive interpretation of *Mijn beghin ende voortganck*, from which I learned a great deal, see van Dijk and van den Berg 1997, 120–78.

[67] These three dilemmas are developed in *Mijn beghin ende voortganck*, 1–11, 12–18 and 19–21, respectively; see also van Dijk and van den Berg 1997, 130–46.

period Bake tried hard to remain close to Christ. Sometimes she would stand with arms outstretched in order to feel the pain of the crucified one, and she tried to meditate as often and as intensely as she could. In *Mijn beghin ende voortganck* Bake openly recounts the way in which she was close to the Lord. She provides exhaustive accounts of her inner, often passionate prayers and recounts countless interior dialogues with Christ. In this way Bake shows those sisters not yet experienced in the mystic life how a life committed to interior devotion is to be conducted. On the one hand there is suffering, despair and the lack of understanding, on the other hand there is always consolation in the Lord.

Two important visionary experiences are treated at some length. Around Christmas of 1440, when Bake had decided to remain in Galilea after all, she received 'such great grace and knowledge of the truth that I simply had to believe it'.[68] During the night of 25 December Bake had a vision in which she shed the fourteen garments of interior and exterior subjectivity, a theme developed in great detail in *Een merkelike leeringhe*. Moreover, at each of the three masses celebrated at Christmas – the midnight mass, the mass at dawn, and the day mass – she got a nosebleed during the exaltation of the host. Bake took this as a sign of the presence of the Father, the Son and the Holy Spirit, mentioned by John the Evangelist in his Epistle (1 John 5:7–8).[69] It was then that she knew she was worthy of the monastic habit. Having made confession as required by the *Constitutiones monialium*, which in Bake's case was an exceptionally drawn-out affair, lasting seven hours, she was admitted to the novitiate on Christmas of 1440.[70]

Even more important was the vision that Bake received during the Ascension day vigil in 1441.[71] It was then that all four paths of the Passion were revealed to her, the first two of which she had already been practising for some time. The two higher stages, beholding God and becoming one with the Lord, were traditionally only undertaken by strong men. Bake pleaded with the Lord to grant her this deeper insight. Did not the strong men also derive their strength from God? It was then that she received the coveted insight that women, too, could gain knowledge of the secrets of the highest paths of

---

[68] *Soo groote gratie ende kennisse d<e>r waerheijt dat ickt wel ghelooven moest* (*Mijn beghin ende voortganck* 18, lines 639–41). On the events surrounding Christmas, see *Mijn beghin ende voortganck* 18, 19 and 20. Spaapen dates the Christmas vision to both 1440 (Spaapen 1967a, 246 note 19e and 19f, 249 note 21b and 250 note 21d) and 1441 (Spaapen 1967a, 248 note 19s). The analysis of *Mijn beghin ende voortganck* by van Dijk and van den Berg 1997, would suggest that it took place in 1440.

[69] For the Christmas vision, see *Mijn beghin ende voortganck* 19. Based on this passage, Axters 1956, 164–5 identifies Alijt Bake as one of the few women of her day for whom trinitarian imagery plays a role in the spiritual life.

[70] For Alijt Bake's confession, see *Mijn beghin ende voortganck* 38 and 39.

[71] For the facts of the case, see especially *Mijn beghin ende voortganck* 40 and 47 and *Brief* 7.

the Cross. So she taught the sisters of the convent of Galilea that women, too, could live the mystic life, following the example provided by such men as Tauler and van Ruusbroec.[72]

The Ascension day vision was of central importance in the life of Bake and constitutes the key to her oeuvre. She had already explained what the paths of the Passion entailed in *De vier kruiswegen*. The autobiographical *Mijn beghin ende voortganck* should be considered an illustration of the argument put forth there. Bake shows how she fared in following the life of the paths of the Cross. She recounts her own life experiences in order to provide her pupils with an anchor in their difficult endeavour. By dividing her autobiography in two parts, Bake follows the tradition of other medieval female religious who recorded their interior spiritual experiences in order to provide other women with an example.[73]

The visitation that was to have such painful consequences for Alijt Bake took place some time in the autumn of 1454 or early 1455. Hardly anything is known about the events leading up to the unexpected actions of the inspectors, who came annually to Galilea. They must have known for some time about the curious behaviour of its prioress, but more than ten years passed before anything was done about it. The inspectors did not stop at deposition, either, but banished Bake to the convent of Facons in Antwerp. Thanks to a letter written by her during her period of exile, we do at least have her perspective on these humiliating events. It goes without saying that her deposition and exile were unjust, as the inspectors did not acknowledge what she experienced as an interior truth. Bake could not herself go to Windesheim to defend her stance, not least because women were not allowed into meetings of the Chapter. So she wrote a response to the Chapter General, which convened on the third Sunday after Easter (18 April) in 1445. Her account would have been presented by the rector of Galilea, who was apparently one of Bake's most important confidants. This was in all likelihood Nicolaas van Duvendyc.[74]

In early 1455, Bake sent a draft, a so-called 'minute', of her defence to the rector. The text of this defence has not been preserved; unfortunately only the text of the letter that accompanied it has come down to us. A copy of this *Brief uit de ballingschap* ('Letter from Exile') is contained in MS Ghent, UB, 3854, which also contains *Mijn beghin ende voortganck*. This letter is the most moving

---

[72] See especially *Mijn beghin ende voortganck* 59.
[73] Such interior experiences were often the only means for women to acquire spiritual authority (cf. §7.2, on the vision of Jacomijne Costers).
[74] Nicolaas van Duvendyc is the first known rector of Galilea; he appears for the first time in the sources on 10 February 1455 (van Mingroot 1984b, 771). Although his successors usually came from Groenendaal, it is not clear whether he was a native. He does not appear in that convent's obituarium (ed. Dykmans 1941; cf. Scheepsma 1995b, 227).

extant text of Bake's. Although elsewhere her writing is sometimes prolix and unstructured, here she gets straight to the point and her tone is uncommonly fierce. She might have been formally deposed, but her will was far from broken.

Bake's letter opens with a few friendly words for the rector. She thanks her 'reverend and most beloved father' for his efforts on her behalf.[75] Because he had faith in her, she now wants to tell him about her interior life, with more frankness than she had done with anyone up till then. Next Bake asks the rector's advice as to how she should proceed; to whom should she address the letters in which she pleads her case? There is an indication here of the existence of a small circle of insiders, 'my dear chosen friends and those privy to my interior life'.[76] Bake asks the rector not to reveal her plans concerning the Chapter General to most of the others, because they might wish to stop her. Likewise the new prioress of Galilea, Katharina van Gheldere, and the other nuns were not to be informed of her undertaking, for they might not be able to deal with the consequences. Apparently drastic measures against her followers had been considered, and Bake gives the impression that she is protecting them. This could be the reason for her failure to mention any names in this letter.[77]

The *Brief uit de ballingschap* changes gradually in tone. It begins as a personal request of the rector, but then develops into an impressive apology. Bake explains ostensibly for the rector, but in fact for her entire mystical circle, 'my reasons for and views on this case and what compels me to undertake it'.[78] In the first place she realises that man cannot himself fully achieve the state of perfection. Only God can purify the soul, by imposing supernatural challenges on it, thus transforming it into the purest and most refined gold. Bake regarded her composition of an explanation for the Chapter General as a trial, and sought by that means to purify her soul. Secondly, she sought to teach a lesson to the devil and his minions – the leaders of the Chapter of Windesheim! – by showing them that their evil intentions had no effect on her. Just as St Lawrence taunted his persecutors from the grill upon which they roasted him, so too she saw herself as mocking her tormentors: Christ himself said that one should turn the other cheek to one's enemy. They took away her good name and her honour; now, like a true martyr, she would sacrifice her body. It would seem, then, that Bake's early death in 1455 is to be attributed to severe self-castigation.[79]

---

[75] *Eerweerdighen ende seer gheminden pater* (*Brief* 1, line 4).
[76] *Mijn lieve uutvercoren vrienden en die medeweters van mijn inwendicheijt* (*Brief* 3, line 67–8).
[77] For scholarship on this letter see especially van Dijk and van den Berg 1997, 186–91 and the annotations accompanying the translation.
[78] *Wat mijn cause ende meijninghe van dese saeke is ende wat mij hiertoe praemt* (*Brief* 4, line 74–5).
[79] Bake speaks of *mijn nature te quellen* ('perturbing her nature'; *Brief* 5, line 147), that is to say that she was physically weakened.

Everything points to the fact that Bake identified strongly with Christ, who was not only her great model, but also her confidant. Looking back on her life she observes that it was played out according to a fixed plan.

> Observe, my beloved ones, how everything that has befallen me resembles his experience. For we [= Christ and Alijt] arranged all of this together years ago and decided that matters would fall out in this way.[80]

The rejection and contempt that she was subjected to were comparable to the scorn experienced by Christ. Unlike her role model though Bake rose up in protest against those who wished to crucify her, for she engages her accusers in debate. It can be argued that she wished to increase her suffering in order to be more closely united with the Lord.

Bake informs the rector that her deposition and banishment have had hardly any effect on her personally, so thoroughly has she succeeded in destroying her own self. Sometimes she feigns anger or sadness, but that is only because it is expected of her. But she finds assurance in the realisation that God has something special in mind for her, even though she knows that there is a great deal of misunderstanding surrounding this.

> Oh, beloved friends, what has happened seems to many people to be wondrous and of great import. And this is true, if only they knew how these things had come to pass. If one considers this case rationally and justly, according to what is contained and prescribed in the Scriptures as well as in our own rule and statutes, it would surely be an error and truly remarkable how our spiritual, wise and learned men should have arrived at this foolish and irrational idiocy, were it not that God permitted it.[81]

The Jewish high priest Caiaphas said at the trial of Christ that it was better for one man to die than that an entire people should perish. Similarly, Bake protects her followers by sacrificing herself.

In the above quotation, written perhaps in the heat of anger, Bake expresses harsh criticism of the learned men who led the Chapter of Windesheim, but have no idea of what God can do for the interior life. They have no faith in the exceptional knowledge Bake was privy to, and that prompted her to behave the way she did. That her claim was not recognised

---

[80] *Siet nu, o beminden, aldus alle dinghen op mij commen naer sijns selfs ghelijcheijt. Ende wij hebben dit te saemen aldus langhe jaeren te vooren gheschickt ende ghesloten dat dit aldus gheschien saude* (Brief 8, line 226–9).

[81] *Och, beminde vrienden, veel menschen dunckt hun dat wat wonderlijckx ende wat groots gheschiet is. Ende dat is waer, wisten sijt hoe dat alle dinghen gheschiet sijn. Die dit merckte naer rechte reden ende bescheijdentheijt, naer dat die ghemeijne schrijften ende oock onsen regulen ende statuten beschrijven ende uutwijsen, soo ist seker wel een abus ende wel seer te verwonderen hoe dat onse gheestelijcke, wijse ende gheleerde mannen tot dese onwijse ende onbescheijden sotheijt ghecommen sijn, en waert niet dat toelaten Godts* (Brief 6, line 160–8).

by the authorities of the Chapter of Windesheim is undoubtedly true, but it is not true to say that they acted against the letter of the rule and statutes. The measures taken by the inspectors who carried out the visitation to Galilea were unusual, but not without precedent.[82]

Towards the end of the letter we receive a somewhat clearer insight into the events that precipitated the whole affair. The deposed prioress asks the rector to defend her position before the Chapter and to explain to the wise fathers in what way she had 'enchanted' him with the truth concerning the mystical way of life.

> In this, when you come before the Chapter, please be true to me, so that they may know what sort of magic I have worked upon you. For to my mind it is none other than the glory of God, the bliss of all the angels and the saints, and my own ultimate salvation. And if our order is to profit at all from this, then this is how it is to be, and not through observable signs and miracles, which they greatly prefer. But the true, supernatural virtues, which one must practise beforehand, cannot convert the learned. The signs and miracles will not convert them, for the true virtues themselves are much more certain than the signs of the virtues.[83]

The leaders of the Chapter of Windesheim are blind to a virtue that is readily observable and moreover constantly demonstrate to in, for example, the sisterbook of Diepenveen. To Bake such ascetic accomplishments are nothing more than the external signs of virtue, whereas she knows from her own experience the kind of inner richness that can also be achieved through the imitation of Christ.

The final words in this letter from exile are addressed to Bake's followers, whom she continues to refer to as her 'children'. If she had had only herself to consider, she would have told the priors of the Chapter of Windesheim the unadulterated truth.

> But for the sake of my poor, frail children and all my chosen friends, who would have to share in the suffering and who, I fear, would not be strong enough to bear it, for them I dared not act without your advice. Therefore

---

[82] On the legal aspects of Alijt Bake's deposition, see van Dijk 1992, 130–2 and van Dijk and van den Berg 1997, 182–6.

[83] *Hierom, ist dat ghij ten capittel comt, soo sijt mij hierin ghetrauwe, opdat sij daerdoor moghen kennen wat tooverije ick u ghedaen hebbe. Want het is, naer mijn goetdincken, de glorie Godts, de blijtschap van alle de engelen en heijlighen ende mijne hoochste salicheijdt. Ende saude onse oorden eenighe vrucht of salicheijt hieraf hebbe, soo moet dit aldus geschieden ende niet met sinnelijcke teecken ende mirakelen, daer sij seer naer staen. Maer de waerachtighe, overnaturelijcke deuchden, die men tevooren oeffenen moet, kan hun niet bekeeren die gheleert sijn. De teeckenen ende mirakelen en sullen hun niet bekeeren, want het is veel sekerder de waerachtighe deuchden dan de teeckenen der deuchden* (Brief 10, lines 288–99).

discuss this together, my dear friends, and advise me in God and as best you can.[84]

We do not know what advice the rector gave Bake. Perhaps he recognised the hopelessness of the situation and advised her to give up her brave attempt. This could explain why her written defence does not survive and also why the *Acta Capituli Windeshemensis* make no mention of this remarkable case. All that remains is the prohibition against writing of 1455, which proves that the Chapter authorities wished to silence nuns like Bake, who thus made their experiences of the interior life public.

8.4 Audience and Dissemination

In the prologue of *De trechter en de spin*, written around 1446, Bake addresses her readers and listeners as follows:

> Oh, dearest beloved brothers and sisters and beloved children to whom I wish to give renewed birth in the living interior of our dear Lord Jesus Christ, so that he once again is transformed within your interior lives.[85]

From this we may make some general deductions about the audience for whom Bake primarily wrote her texts. The term *susteren* must refer to the nuns and *conversae* of the convent of Galilea, as became apparent in the previous section. If we take *gheminde kinderen* literally, then it must refer to the novices or perhaps a small group of young children who were being schooled at Galilea. But a figurative sense is more likely here, especially given what follows. After all, as the new prioress of Galilea Bake presents herself as the spiritual mother of her subjects and, alluding to biblical imagery, sets for herself the ambitious role of giving birth again to her children.[86]

The size of Bake's primary audience can be determined with a fair degree

---

[84] *Maer om mijn arme, crancke kinderen ende alle mijne uutvercoren vrienden, die de vervolghinghen mede lijden moeten ende daervan mede deelen, die, ick vrese, noch niet sterck ghenoech en sijn, hierom en darve ick het niet wel doen sonder uwen raet. Hierom soo spreeckt te saemen, mijn lieve vrienden, ende raet mij dat beste in Godt, ende dat soo ghij best cont* (*Brief* 10, lines 320–6).

[85] *Ach, alderliefte broederen ende susteren ende gheminde kinderen dien ic anderwerven begheere te baren in die levende binnenste ons liefs heren Jhesu Cristi tot datti weder in u levende binnenste getransformeert werde* (*Trechter en spin*, lines 1–3). This citation corresponds almost exactly with the opening of the epilogue of *Een merkelike leeringhe*, f. 197va (ed. Lieftinck 1936, 21; cf. Scheepsma 199b, 230 n. 4).

[86] Cf. the imagery of motherhood in the epilogue of *Een merkelike leeringhe* (ed. Lieftinck 1936, 21; cf. Peeters 1968, 43). This imagery must have been borrowed from Paul, who-as a man-speaks in similar terms in Gal. 4:19. On the image of Christ's innermost self, see Axters 1958, especially 232–3; on spiritual motherhood and other typically female images in Alijt Bake's work, see Dresen 1990, m.n. 93–131.

of accuracy. Despite the fact that at its enclosure in 1437 the convent of Galilea was restricted to no more than sixteen nuns, in the period 1455–60 approximately one hundred people lived in the convent. Whether or not this steady stream of new nuns had anything to do with Bake's priorate is, unfortunately, impossible to know. We may, however, conclude that she initially wrote for an audience of some one hundred women.[87]

The most striking thing about the passage just cited is the fact that Bake also considers the *broederen* to be her children: she may be referring to the odd *conversus* or lay-brother who would presumably have lived in the convent in order to perform the heavy manual labour. Just as likely, however, is that Bake is here addressing the rector and his *socii*. From the *Brief uit de ballingschap* it is clear that the *gheminden pater* ('beloved father') – probably Nicolaas van Duvendyc – was at any rate on her side around 1455. It would appear that during her priorate she had been able to convince him or one of his predecessors of her spiritual leadership. Moreover the letter suggests that the circle of like-minded brothers had been even larger. She asks the rector not to tell 'our good prior, the subprior and the procurator' about the written defence she intended to address to the Chapter General. She is probably referring here to the authorities of the convent of ten Walle in Elzegem, whose prior held the commissionership over Galilea. This also explains why she refers to him as 'our prior'.[88] Jan Eggaert, the son of the founder of Galilea, had been prior of ten Walle since 1447; apparently his relationship with Bake was a good one. We may therefore assume that over the course of time Bake had managed to draw a number of male Windesheimers into her circle.

There are fairly strong indications that with the help of these influential friends Bake enthusiastically sought a wider audience for her spiritual doctrine. In the years 1454–6 three sisterhouses in East Flanders adopted the Augustinian Rule: St Barbara in Ghent, Sion in Oudenaarde and St Margaret in Deinze. The involvement of Jan Eggaert and Nicolaas van Duvendyc in the reformation of these three houses is attested in charters. Galilea is also mentioned a number of times, on account of its observance serving as a benchmark for the new convents. The prior of ten Walle was given responsibility over the three Flemish convents of canonesses regular in East Flanders. Although her name is nowhere mentioned, it is probable that Bake was one of the driving forces behind these foundations. After all, Christ had set her the task, as he had done Coleta of Corbie, of bringing about a reformation towards the interior life not only in her own convent, but within the entire order.[89]

---

[87] For the figures, see van Mingroot 1984b, 769 and 773.
[88] *Brief* 3, lines 45–6. For this identification, cf. van Dijk and van den Berg 1997, 111.
[89] For further information on these three convents see Cassiman 1952, 156–9 and van Simaey 1984 (Sint-Barbara), Cassiman 1952, 150–2 and Nuyttens 1984 (St Margaret)

Without the help of like-minded people in key positions Bake would never have been able to see this reform through, bound as she was to her own convent by the terms of enclosure. But given her strong personality and fervour for reform, it is unimaginable that she would not have been involved in the development of the spiritual life in these new convents. For the practical execution of the reforms she would have had to rely on Jan Eggaert, Nicolaas van Duvendyc and other male friends, who could attend to the organisational and legal issues involved. Nuns from Galilea may have been installed in the new convents to help introduce the new spiritual way of life and to instruct the new canonesses, just as Hille Sonderlants had been sent from Diepenveen to Ghent. Through them the mystical doctrine of the four paths of the Cross may have been transplanted elsewhere, although we possess little concrete evidence to support this. But if Bake wanted to be even more directly involved in the spiritual reformation of the new convents, which, given her enthusiasm, seems likely, then the written word would have provided her with the means. It is therefore not unlikely that works by Bake were used to structure the spiritual life in the convents of St Barbara, St Margaret and Sion. But outside Galilea there is no firm evidence for this.[90]

In 1455, at the meeting where Bake's position was to be defended by Nicolaas van Duvendyc, the Chapter General of Windesheim issued a proclamation forbidding writing by nuns. From this it is apparent not just that the initiative led by the former prioress and the rector had failed – even assuming they were able to put their plan into practice – but also that the leaders of the Chapter would not tolerate the production of mystical or theological literature by Windesheim canonesses. It is remarkable that the writings of Bake have been preserved at all, given that both the inspectors and the prior superior had the right to confiscate any suspect writings.[91] The fortunes of the important Bake codex, Brussels, KB, 643–4 is a case in point. The manuscript probably originated at Groenendaal, the convent which usually produced the rectors of Galilea. After the five teachings and *Een merkelike leeringhe* the colophon discussed earlier appears, in which Bake's authorship is revealed. The hand responsible for the text that follows, and which added Willem Jordaens's *Mystieke mondkus* ('The Mystic Kiss') to the manuscript, crossed out Alijt's name, convent and function in the colophon. In all probability her name was regarded as suspect, due to her deposition and banishment.[92] Remarkably, though, Bake's writings were left untouched in this large (220 × 150 mm) and elegant manuscript. It suggests that there was some admiration

---

and Cassiman 1952, 149–50 and van der Donckt 1984 (Sion); cf. van Mingroot 1984a, especially 699, and van Mingroot 1984b, 771–2.

[90] Cf. the less than optimistic overviews of the manuscript holdings in these convents by van Simaey 1984, Nuyttens 1984 and van der Donckt 1984.

[91] Cf. van Dijk and van den Berg 1997, 191–2.

[92] On the erasures in the colophon, see Peeters 1968, 42 and Scheepsma 1995b, 228.

for her mysticism, as her works are preserved alongside those by such important men as Johannes Tauler, Jordan of Quedlinburg and Willem Jordaens.

The transmisson history of the works of Bake is so complicated that we cannot be entirely sure precisely where the Brussels manuscript is to be situated. It is certainly the oldest Bake manuscript, and the works it contains were the most widely disseminated ones. The latter always occurred, incidently, anonymously; the use of Bake's name was apparently not regarded as a recommendation. Bake's most popular work was the treatise on the Passion, *De vier kruiswegen*, of which no fewer than five manuscripts, dating to the fifteenth and the beginning of the sixteenth century, are known. It can be no coincidence that this text usually accompanies the didactic *De weg der victorie* or *Een merkelike leeringhe*, that also provide guidance for emulating the Passion of Christ. If Bake should prove to be the author of the latter treatise, and not the scribe or adapter of an older work – which in my view is by no means impossible – then her influence was unexpectedly far-reaching in terms of both time and space. Material from this work was incorporated into the *Boecxken van den inwendighen navolgen des levens ende des cruces ons heren* ('The Book of the Interior Emulation of the Life and Passion of Our Lord'), which was published in Antwerp in 1514 and went through several editions thereafter. The Franciscan Frans Vervoort incorporated it into his *Bruygoms mantelken* ('The Bridegroom's Cloak') in 1554, giving the Passion material it contained an even wider audience. And Vervoort's *Mantelken* served in turn as a source for the blind French mystic Jean de Saint-Samson, whose mysticism influenced the sixteenth-century reform movement of the Carmelites. Thus it is possible that Alijt Bake's mystic reform initiatives had a greater influence than she herself ever could have imagined.[93]

---

[93] An in-depth overview of the transmission of Alijt Bake's works is to be found in Scheepsma 1997, 252–9.

9

Literature and the Choir Nuns of Windesheim

WE BEGAN THIS study by situating the Modern Devotion in the larger context of medieval reform movements, as outlined by Grundmann. The Modern Devotion does indeed fit well into the pattern of successive reform movements, but its rise and flourishing too have their own dynamic. The reform movement of the northern Low Countries arose from circumstances similar to earlier movements, but developed its own ideal of the return to the roots of Christian spirituality. The same holds true for the women of the Modern Devotion. The second movement of female religious bears many similarities to the first, but it was certainly not spawned directly from it. Here, too, we may speak of a movement developing independently with its own characteristic features.

In a sense the nuns of Windesheim constitute the core of the second movement of female religious, in that from the very beginning they embodied the monastic way of life that represented the ideal for the bulk of the female devout. The choir nuns of Windesheim have left behind a fairly extensive corpus of writings. Grundmann argues that this, too, is a hallmark of late medieval reform movements.[1] These authors did not write because the production of texts held any intrinsic value for them. For the nuns of Windesheim writing always served a higher purpose, the improvement of the religious life, and through their work we can gain insight into their spiritual lives. Nowhere else is the voice of the choir nuns of Windesheim so clearly heard as in their writings. The disciplines of philology and literature therefore can also be valuable in studying the minds and attitudes of these women.

This concluding chapter attempts to construct a coherent picture of the spirituality of the nuns of the Chapter of Windesheim, and determine the place occupied by texts within that spirituality. A number of threads developed in the previous chapters are gathered together here and where possible related to one another. Of central importance are questions concerning the significance texts and writings had for the nuns of Windesheim. There are three main themes here. First, the place occupied by study and literature in

---

[1] Grundmann 1977, 452–75.

the daily lives of the Windesheim nuns will be discussed (§9.1). The following section deals with the role of the pastors of Windesheim: did they write texts especially for the women, and what was their role when the nuns began to write themselves (§9.2)? Finally, the authors themselves are highlighted. We will explore what prompted them to write, what message they wished to convey and what their position was with regard to the mystic tradition (§9.3).

9.1 Language and Literature in Daily Life

In the fifteenth century numerous women decided to leave the turbulence of the world behind and devote their lives to God. Many women found refuge in the convents of Windesheim. They utterly rejected the outside world, and adopted a way of life that took the form of strict enclosure. The convents tried to be as self-sufficient as they could. They often kept their own livestock, grew their own vegetables and fruit and had their own fishponds. Thus a Windesheim convent was a world unto itself. Within the walls of the convent the nuns and the *conversae* formed a religious community. They sought in each other the inspiration necessary for realising their religious ideal. The spiritual core of the monastic life was comprised of the eternal celebration of the liturgical hours in Latin. Responsibility for carrying out this chief task lay with the choir nuns. They had the time to devote themselves entirely to the services, thanks mainly to the efforts of the working members of their communities, the *conversae* and, in some cases, the lay sisters, who performed the domestic duties. Education was not required of the *conversae*; their job demanded physical exertion. But the nuns' work did require a certain degree of literacy, as celebrating the divine office was one of their main tasks. Our comments here will be restricted to the choir nuns.

Whereas in the fifteenth century many convents and (former) sisterhouses used an abridged Latin service, or even Geert Grote's Windesheim version of the Middle Dutch Book of Hours, the nuns of Windesheim continued to celebrate the classic monastic liturgy in its unabridged Latin form. The Chapter authorities took it for granted that the choir sisters followed the official Windesheim liturgy as it had been established in 1395 by a special commission. Prospective nuns were therefore expected to be able to read and sing in Latin. For many of the women this meant that they had only a partial understanding of what they were singing. And yet knowing the language of the Church and using it as often as possible was a matter of pride for them. In convents where the religious spirit was strong, new initiatives were regularly mounted for improving the inmates' Latin.

In the choice between Latin and the vernacular, the Modern Devotion assumed a pragmatic position. The goal was to seek salvation for as many souls as possible, including simple and uneducated ones. The Devout vigorously defended the right of those who could not read Latin to have access to religious literature in the vernacular, subject to only simple and safe material being made available in translation. The canonesses regular of the Chapter of Windesheim, too, fell initially into the category of the unlearned. Though in some convents attempts were made to improve the nuns' Latin – Otto Poten's activities at Diepenveen come to mind – a thorough course of training was not part of the programme.[2] In practice, therefore, most of the nuns of Windesheim continued to have serious problems with Latin.

The use of the vernacular in all but the liturgical celebrations was thoroughly entrenched in the Chapter's convents. This is apparent at a glance from the surviving booklists, which show a preponderance of Middle Dutch.[3] It would be going too far to assume, however, that the Latin books were read and used only by the rector and other priests. Presumably every convent had a couple of learned sisters who were well versed in Latin. The dominant status of the vernacular in the daily life of the Windesheim convents is also apparent from the writings of the choir nuns themselves, which were practically always composed in Middle Dutch. Naturally the authors, who in the main addressed their fellow sisters or other female religious, wished to reach the widest possible audience, and therefore used the vernacular. The language situation may be summarised as follows: for the nuns of Windesheim Latin was the ideal, but the vernacular was usually the reality.

The choir nuns carried out a number of communal spiritual activities in which texts played roles of varying importance. To begin with, there were of course the daily celebrations in the chapel, during which the liturgical texts were solemnly recited and sung. The church calendar, with its feast and holy days, lent structure to the lives of the nuns. During the daily gatherings in refectory, at which the *conversae* were also present, the consumption of food and drink was accompanied with spiritual sustenance. The nuns of Windesheim listened mostly to sermons and hagiographical literature at table; presumably the goal was to link the reading to the season in the liturgical calendar. Once a week, on Fridays, the nuns came together for the chapter of faults. The prioress would first address the entire community with a general admonition, after which the nuns would be admonished individually. Finally, at Diepenveen, and possibly other convents too, there were regular collations by the rector. Presumably he, too, provided the sisters with particular advice on how to deepen their spiritual lives, though he would probably also have read and commented on passages from scripture.

Every bit as important as the communal life was the way in which the

---

[2] In the fourteenth century education and study were important elements of the monastic life for nuns of the Dominican order (Lewis 1996, 263–83; see also §6.2).

[3] In the fifteenth century there remained convents with a strong Latin culture. The canonesses regular of the St Margaretha convent in Gouda (Holland) seem to have attained a higher level in this regard than the average Windesheim convent, given the extant booklist which shows no fewer than 80 religious works in Latin (ed. Meinsma 1902, 257–60; see Gumbert 1990, 56–8).

sisters organised their own personal spiritual lives. Like all the Modern Devout they strove constantly to reform their own religious persona. External impulses played a role in this, of course, for example when they pointed out their shortcomings to each other in the chapter of faults. But the interior transformation was primarily a process initiated and maintained by the individual, although this could not, of course, take place without divine inspiration. By constantly keeping in view how strongly man was governed by his own needs and desires, and then measuring this against the selfless example of Christ, the sisters endeavoured to emulate him as closely as they could. This ideal is splendidly epitomised by the most important book produced by a Windesheimer, *De imitatione Christi*, by Thomas a Kempis.

In this process of transformation, which is so characteristic of the Modern Devotion, spiritual literature fulfilled an important function. The devout strove towards an inner imitation of God. To that end it was first necessary to become familiar with one's sinful nature. Through intensive meditation the devout would then strive to focus continuously on the divine and thus keep evil at bay. This interior contemplation was systematically helped by the reading of edifying literature in which good was given verbal expression in a variety of ways. In order to remember this material for meditation, the devout would record important excerpts in his *rapiarium*. Reading, writing and meditation are thus inextricably connected in the development of the religious person.

The process of religious transformation among the choir nuns of Windesheim was a less intellectual one than that of their brothers, the monks. Every day the canons retreated to their cells for a few hours of reading and meditation. In theory they all maintained a *rapiarium*. The nuns had far less time for reading than their male counterparts, and writing as an auxiliary to meditation was much less widespread among them. In so far as it is possible to form a picture of the situation, the *rapiaria* of the nuns do not show systematic extracts from religious literature. The sisters eagerly recorded good points, but while writing as an *aide mémoire* did not play a large role in their daily lives, intellectually gifted sisters such as Katharina van Naaldwijk and Alijt Bake set much store in writing as an aid to meditation, and while they were not prevented from doing so, their activities did make them somewhat atypical.

At the end of the day the nuns of Windesheim were in general better educated than, for example, the Sisters of the Common Life, but little attention was devoted to learning. It was enough for the nuns to be able to read their choir books in Latin and religious literature in Middle Dutch. It was only those nuns who were involved in book production as fulfilment of their manual labour who spent extended hours with spiritual texts.

There was very little free time for recording one's own ideas and experiences of the spiritual life. The sisters who wished to do this presumably had to find time for it during their 'free' hours on Sundays and feast days. And yet there were a few independently minded nuns who wrote. Given the general Windesheim lifestyle, one would expect that these authors would write texts that would be of immediate use in their own meditation; this seems the reason for writing for the authors among the canons regular of Windesheim – note for example Gerlach Peters, Hendrik Mande or Jan Mombaer. Yet the authors among the canonesses did not usually write their texts for themselves, but rather for the community to which they belonged. They reached for the pen when they felt that the spiritual life needed to be reformed in one way or another.

Only a few texts written by Windesheim nuns were intended expressly for meditation survive. Presumably more once existed, but personal texts stood little chance of survival. Two such meditation exercises have come down to us because they found a place in the larger context of the sisterbook of Diepenveen. Just why the exercises of Katharina van Rijssen were included in their entirety remains a mystery. Their content is anything but striking, and the fact that van Rijssen meditated in Latin appears not to have been exceptional. The allegory of the wedding used by Katharina van Naaldwijk (and Salome Sticken) is, on the other hand, unusual. Not for the theme itself, for the theme of the heavenly wedding resonates throughout the sisterbook, but rather because the allegory in this case is so thoroughly developed. That this is actually a meditation exercise is shown by the recommendation with which it ends: every reader should adapt and improve this exercise as she sees fit. The third meditative text is Jacomijne Costers's *Previlesien van Sint Joannes Evangelist*, which provides the opportunity of contemplating the memorable deeds of St John. Costers presumably wrote this text for her own use, as an aid to the veneration of her patron saint.

The authors among the sisters of Windesheim wrote almost entirely in prose. We rarely encounter rhyming texts, and these hardly deserve the label 'poetry' from an aesthetic point of view. The pieces in question are a few short rhymes by Salome Sticken, a rhyming prayer by Jacomijne Costers and the 'refrain' attributed to Costers. In all three cases the rhyme scheme has been used as a mnemonic device, and not to make the text more elegant. Once again the pragmatism of the Modern Devotion comes to the fore. In the same way religious songs can fulfil an important function during meditation, as, after all, is familiar. We know that songs were regularly sung by the nuns at Diepenveen, in which the emphasis was on singing devoutly, as opposed to loudly.[4] Although there are a number of surviving songbooks from the circles of Modern Devout women, none of them can be connected to the Windesheim convents. As far as is known, then, the authors among the nuns did not themselves embrace the lyric form.

Finally, the large number of letters written (and received) by the

---

[4] DV, f. 40r (Johannes Brinckerinck) and 370r (Liesbeth van Arden); both passages are cited in van Buuren 1992, 248.

Windesheim nuns is striking.⁵ Written correspondence was, it is true, one of the few means of maintaining contact with the world outside the convent; but the coming and going of mail was also strictly controlled. Letters whose content was too wordly were intercepted or censored. This explains in part why practically all the known letters are concerned with religious issues; a second reason for this is that personal or business letters were generally too ephemeral to be worthy of preservation. The Windesheim nuns tried to aid their fellow sisters in a spiritual sense, to convince their families that their choice of the monastic life was the correct one, or to exhort people living in the world to act in a more Christian way. It is striking that letters are often involved in the conversion of the nuns. For example, Johannes Brinckerinck regularly wrote to Jutte van Ahaus in the two years before she decided to go to Deventer to live under his leadership.⁶ The intensive correspondence among the nuns of Windesheim is proof of the increasing role of writing in the late medieval reform movements.⁷

9.2 The Role of the Pastors

According to Grundmann's thesis, wherever reform-minded priests and theologians come in contact with well-educated women with religious ambitions, religious literature in the vernacular appears.⁸ In a number of ways these conditions certainly obtained within the monastic union of Windesheim. But did this lead to a flourishing of vernacular literature? I use Grundmann's view as a point of reference for the study of the case of Windesheim. We also need to take into consideration criticism of this thesis, especially that offered by Peters. In her view the role of the pastors in the literature of female religious has been strongly exaggerated. While the medieval texts themselves often claim to be the result of cooperation between priests and female mystics, this is an expression of the ideal rather than the reality. According to Peters, the literature of the female mystics is largely the result of the efforts of the women themselves.⁹

The attitude of the Chapter of Windesheim is characterised primarily by a vigorous striving towards uniformity, to which individual interests had to yield. The relationship between the canons and the canonesses was determined by obedience. As priests the canons represented the authority of the Chapter and the nuns were obliged to acknowledge this fact. This one-sided

---

⁵ Scheepsma 1997, 235–9 provides an overview of all the letters and references to letters from the milieu of the Windesheim choir nuns.
⁶ DV, ff. 230v–131r and D, ff. 32c–d.
⁷ Cf. Schreiner 1992, 72–3.
⁸ Grundmann 1977, 457.
⁹ Peters 1988. One objection one might levy against Peters's approach is that in her attempts to undermine existing and influential theories she frequently oversimplifies them (cf. Wehrli-Johns 1990 and Küsters and Langer 1991).

power structure is strikingly illustrated in their respective constitutions. The *Constitutiones Capituli Windeshemensis* are cast in the first person plural, as a sign that the brothers are aware that they must honour their statutes collectively. In the *Constitutiones monialium*, on the other hand, the third person is used. The brothers are the ones who tell the sisters how *they* are to live. The pronoun 'we' here is used exclusively in constructions like 'we determine that . . .'.[10] Within this strict hierarchical power structure one would expect that the monks would prescribe the nuns' reading. The question remains whether they did so or not.

The extant manuscript collections from the thirteen convents provide us with an initial indication, despite the fact that there are large gaps in the transmission. The literature read by the nuns of Windesheim to develop their spiritual lives can be divided into three groups: patristic (Augustine, Jerome, John Chrysostom), works from the heyday of mysticism (Bernard of Clairvaux – but only his least mystical writings – Francis of Assisi, Richard of St Victor, Tauler) and authors from their own circle (Jan van Ruusbroec, Jan van Leeuwen, Gerard Zerbolt, Jan van Schoonhoven). If general guidelines for the composition of libraries in the convents were ever drawn up by the Chapter General, no trace of them remains. And yet it seems striking that the mystics of the first movement of female religious are missing entirely, at least in the surviving collections. It is hardly conceivable that the nuns of Windesheim would have had no interest in what these women had to say. But the question remains whether they actually knew about the mystics of previous centuries.[11] We must not discount the possibility that this literature was intentionally kept out of the libraries of the Windesheim convents.

Among the Windesheim brothers who worked as pastors it is the rectors and *socii* who are most likely to have played a role in providing the nuns with literature. There were three possible ways of doing this, in order of importance: copying existing texts, translating them from Latin, and composing entirely new ones. There are examples of copying done by pastors in the circles of the Modern Devotion, but no pastor or rector hailing from Windesheim is known to have copied books for the convents of the Chapter. There was little need for this, after all, as the nuns of Windesheim were perfectly capable of producing their own books.

Rather strange in this context are the actions of Father Johannes van Eyck, who, when he returned to his mother convent Korsendonk in 1489, took with him the books he had acquired (and copied?) while in the service of the convent of Facons, a treasure-trove *dier wel thien was grooter gebonden boecken* ('of fully ten large, bound books'). To mollify the nuns somewhat, an indignant Christophorus Caers tells us, the prior of Korsendonk – the commissioner of Facons, after all – finally had four old books, and copies at that, sent

---

[10] Mertens 1987, 284–5.
[11] Cf. my forthcoming article (Scheepsma, forthcoming 2).

from his library to the disappointed convent. The books in question were a paper manuscript of the *Legenda aurea*, a *Vitae patrum* on parchment, an old *Liber de apibus* (Thomas of Cantimpré's 'Book of Bees') and a cycle of sermons pertaining to the proper of the saints. According to Caers the books were intended to be used by the priest in his studies. This explains to some extent his agitation – Caers himself was a rector – and perhaps too the behaviour of the rector and prior. Presumably those in Korsendonk were of the opinion that the nuns of Facons would not have known what to do with these Latin books.[12]

The translation of literature suitable for the nuns could be a fitting augmentation of the pastoral tasks of the more enthusiastic pastors. There is but one, late example of a Windesheimer who was engaged in such work. Nicolaas de Dinter (†1518), canon regular of Grobbendonk and *socius* at Bethanië in Mechelen, regularly translated Latin homilies into Dutch, so that the nuns could read them in refectory. At the request of the nuns he also translated the hours of certain saints and prayers into the vernacular.[13] Before we accuse the Chapter of Windesheim of dereliction of duty in this regard, it should be noted that a substantial body of translations was produced in the milieu of the Modern Devotion: the *Profectus religiosorum* by David van Augsburg, Thomas of Cantimpré's *Liber de apibus*, certain works by Geert Grote, Gerlach Peters, Jan van Schoonhoven, and others. These translations were warmly welcomed by the nuns of Windesheim. To give but one example: both Mariënburg in Nijmegen and Mariënveld in Amsterdam possessed a manuscript copy of the *Liber de apibus* in Middle Dutch.[14] It would seem, then, that the Modern Devotion made a substantial body of literature accessible to women, although this was apparently done at a higher organisational level within the movement. This planned approach had the advantage that many more like-minded people could make use of the same translation. Given its significant contribution to the *cura monialium* during the fifteenth century, it seems obvious to attribute a leading role in this effort to the Chapter of Windesheim, but so far concrete evidence is lacking.

Nor did the Windesheimers write much by way of texts specifically aimed at a female audience. Under the auspices of the Chapter only the *Boecken van den inwendighen gheestelike oefeninghe ende uutwendeghen lichameliken oefeninghen* ('Book of Interior Spiritual Exercises and External Physical Exercises'), which was begun in 1429 at Barberendaal, was produced. It is possible that the text was originally intended for that convent, but as far as we know

---

[12] *Register*, f. 21r.
[13] *Kroniek Bethanië*, 1518, partially cited at §3.6. On Nicolaas see Dykmans 1941, 97 n. 2.
[14] On the *The Book of Bees* in Middle Dutch translation see Stutvoet-Joanknecht 1990; on the manuscripts from Mariënveld and Mariënburg, respectively, see 85*–87* (MS The Hague, KB, 135 F 11) and 88*–90* (Copenhagen, KB, Thott N 314² fol.).

this book was not available at Barberendaal or any other Windesheim convent.[15] Perhaps the centrally organised Chapter of Windesheim did not allow its rectors and priors to write texts for the nuns. There are a few examples of texts produced by confessors for people other than the Windesheim female devout, of which I would name only Jan Bellens (†1483) here. While rector of the canonesses regular of the convent of Jericho in Brussels, he wrote the *Tractaet op den pater noster* ('Treatise on the Lord's Prayer') at the request of a *suster van Limborch* ('sister from Limburg'). Both the extant manuscripts were produced at Jericho, a clear example of 'Hausüberlieferung' ('in-house production').[16]

The role played by the Modern Devotion and the Chapter of Windesheim in the production of religious literature by and for women is placed into somewhat greater relief when we compare it to that of earlier periods and movements. The roots of the literature generally referred to as 'medieval female mysticism' are to be found in the first half of the thirteenth century. The impression made by this new phenomenon is reflected in the following frequently cited verses from the *Tochter Syon* ('Daughter of Sion'), written by Lamprecht of Regensburg in 1252 (he restricts his remarks to the German-speaking areas):

> This art was brought into existence
> Among our women here
> In Brabant and Bavaria.
> Lord God, what kind of art is that
> That an old woman understands
> Better than a wise man?[17]

By 'art', Lamprecht means the mystic sensitivity of women. Because of their softer heart, their more jovial nature and their greater simplicity they have easier access to the highest inner wisdom than learned men do.[18] This excerpt reflects a great respect for women's experience-oriented religious nature, which was first discovered in this time. It was certainly not universally accepted by male clergy, and yet many remarkable relationships were struck

---

[15] For more on the *Boecken* see Stooker and Verbeij 1997, vol. 1, 243.

[16] For Jan Bellens and his treatise, see Warnar 1995, in particular 186, note 89; on Jericho see Despy-Meyer 1971. Jan Bellens also wrote the first part of the chronicle of the convent of St Agnes in Ghent, where he also served as rector (for both convent and chronicle, see Goossens, Trio and van Mingroot 1989).

[17] *Diu kunst ist bî unsern tagen / In Brâbant und in Baierlanden / Undern wîben ûf gestanden. / Herre got, waz kunst ist daz, / Daz sich ein alt wîp baz / Verstêt dan witzige man?* (ed. Weinhold 1880, 431, lines 2838–43). *Tochter Syon* is a translation in High German of a Latin treatise originating in Cistercian circles, in which the mystic interpretation of the Song of Songs is dicussed in great detail.

[18] I follow here the reading offered by Willaert, Kors and Vekeman 1992, 6 and 7 note 16, but this passage can also be read ironically (cf. McGinn 1991–8, vol. 3, 174).

up between spiritually gifted women and clergymen. A well-known example is the friendship between Jacques of Vitry (†1240), later bishop of Acco and Tusculum, and Mary of Oignies (†1213). It was he who recorded her remarkable biography, just as so many other *vitae* of female religious were written by clergymen in the region of Brabant and Liège during this era.[19]

After a while the Church attempted to annex the women's movement, now growing unchecked, with its new and sometimes threatening spirituality. In the fourteenth century the Dominican order committed outstanding pastors and theologians such as Eckhart, Seuse and Tauler to the *cura monialium*. This shows not only that the religious needs of women were recognised, but also that there was a perceived need to point the spirituality of the nuns in the right direction. And yet the fourteenth century in southern Germany, for example, presents us with a lively picture of intense relations between pastors and religious women.

One remarkable example is that of the secular priest Heinrich von Nördlingen, a pioneer of the 'Friends of God' in Basel and Strasburg and a kindred spirit of Johannes Tauler. Heinrich befriended Margaretha Ebner, from the Dominican convent of Medingen. He wrote her some fifty-six letters, in which he speaks very openly about his interior life. Von Nördlingen appears there both as the spiritual mentor that, being a priest, he was, and also as Margaretha's student. Heinrich introduced her to Mechthild of Magdeburg's book *Das fließende Licht der Gottheit* ('The Flowing Light of the Godhead') which he, perhaps with Tauler, translated into High German for Margaretha and her fellow sisters. Von Nördlingen maintained relationships with other female religious, of whom Christine Ebner is the most famous. Prioress of the Dominican convent of Engelthal, she is the author of its *Schwesternbuch*, and of a rather difficult complex of texts containing autobiographical messages, visions and all manner of other revelations. Von Nördlingen is thus an example of a fourteenth-century religious who maintained friendships with spiritual sisters, corresponded with them about spiritual literature and made the works of female mystics accessible for them.[20]

By comparison the Modern Devotion's movement of the fifteenth century seems rather meagre, despite the fact that it was of the utmost significance for women who wished to live the spiritual life. In the collations of the standardbearer of the movement of the female devout, Johannes

---

[19] See for example Ruh 1990-9, vol. 2, 81-110; on Mary of Oignies and Jacques of Vitry, see pp. 85-90 and McGinn 1991-8, vol. 3, 32-41.

[20] For a brief treatment of Heinrich von Nördlingen, see Weitlauff 1981; on his connection with Margaretha Ebner Weitlauff 1988 and Schmidt 1993. For the translation of *Das fließende Licht der Gottheit*, see among others Gnädinger 1993, 37-9. On the autobiographical work of Christine Ebner, see Peters 1988a, especially 169-76 (she discusses the literary cooperation between Heinrich von Nördlingen and Christine (and Margaretha) Ebner). On Christine as author of the *Schwesternbuch* see Ringler 1980, 88 and Lewis 1996, 19.

Brinckerinck, we find only a faint reflection of Lamprecht van Regensburg's admiration when he acknowledges that women receive grace more frequently and easily than men. But in his collations he particularly stresses monastic virtues like humility and obedience, a message repeated over and over again. In the case of Margaretha Ebner and Heinrich von Nördlingen we may well wonder who is leading whom; with Johannes Brinckerinck and the other Modern Devout there are no such doubts. The priests take the lead and the women are obliged to follow. Brinckerinck is rarely seen to have a warm relationship with a religious sister, even though he did everything in his power to ensure their spiritual salvation. He maintained the distance he felt was appropriate and advisable for a priest and shepherd.

Beerte Swijnkes, the rectrix of the Meester-Geertshuis, saw the face of her rector for the first time only when he lay in his coffin.[21] Brinckerinck's fear of women is praised as a virtue in his *vite*, presumably because caution was advised when dealing with those who were the cause of original sin. There are situations in Windesheim circles that can only be characterised as straightforward examples of misogyny. Wilhelmus Zegers (†1481) was rector of Facons from 1464 to 1467, but considered himself extremely fortunate that he was elected prior of the canons of Korsendonk, 'for he could hardly bear the phantasies and troubles of women here; [he] has prayed annually that the Lord would remove him from among such remarkable monsters'.[22] Though Zegers was certainly not the only monk to have such feelings, the aloofness towards the sisters maintained by the Windesheimers may not be explained simply by hatred of women. There were after all Windesheim monasteries like Gaesdonck and Bethlehem which made the *cura monialium* their main concern. No doubt most of the brothers of Windesheim fulfilled their pastoral duties in a worthy and conscientious fashion. That their actions were also very much appreciated by the nuns is irrefutably demonstrated by the fact that countless convents requested Windesheim priests as their confessors. In the eyes of the female devout of this period, too, the lifestyle laid out for them by the Chapter of Windesheim apparently offered the best guarantee for their salvation.

The Windesheimers' aloofness from the movement of female religious is not easily explained. The Modern Devotion constitutes a temporary highpoint in the historical development in the later Middle Ages after which less and less autonomy was granted to religious women to order their lives as they saw fit.[23] A number of factors contributed to this situation. First, the poli-

---

[21] Dumbar 1719, 16l; cf. Kühler 1914, 166 n. 1.
[22] *Want seer quaalyck hier konnende verdragen de vrouwelycke phantesyen ende ongerustheden; heeft jaerlyck den heere gebeden dat hy hem van sulcke wonderlycke monsters soude wech nemen* (*Naem- en doodtboeck*, p. 13; cf. *Register*, f. 16r).
[23] The Dominican order, too, opted for the safer path in the fifteenth century. Johannes Meyer (†1485), the great reformer of the Dominican nuns in Germany,

cies of the Church, which violently persecuted unorthodox doctrines and practices, were reason enough to exercise caution. Given that it was frequently the women who were accused of heresy (the Beguines come to mind), it was up to the leaders of the Modern Devotion to steer their sisters away from these dangerous waters. A second factor was the Modern Devotion's quest to win as many souls as it could. The great influx of less talented women led to a certain decline in its intellectual and spiritual levels, because these women had to be offered a spiritual way of life that was achieveable by all. This meant that the more talented women had to adapt to the situation, which it would seem that most did – with the notable exception of Alijt Bake. A third factor is that the devout consistently chose the surest path, that of monastic virtue and asceticism, instead of the path of contemplation and mysticism, which may have led to greater heights, but was unpredictable at best. In general the Modern Devotion exhibited an increasing desire for safety and security.

The question remains as to how the nuns of Windesheim felt about the patronising behaviour of their severe brothers. Did they accept their humble position or were they privately assured of their own strength? Thanks to the spiritual works written by some of them, we do have some insights into these questions. Their literature demonstrates as well the great reserve of the Windesheim pastors. There are no known instances of close literary cooperation between a Windesheim nun and monk of the kind we are familiar with from earlier centuries. In all likelihood the nuns who wrote did so on their own initiative, without their confessors being much involved. The latter might have provided encouragement, as was the case with the visions of Jacomijne Costers. But the writings of the Windesheim nuns appear mainly to confirm Peters's theory concerning the genesis of medieval woman's literature.

9.3 The Windesheim Choir Nuns as Authors

There are a number of reasons why the nuns of Windesheim produced a fairly extensive body of literature. The nuns were among the most highly educated female religious of their day. As canonesses they dealt with the sacred texts on a daily basis, which gave them ready access to the spiritual tradition. A nun with literary talent would find relatively favourable working conditions in a convent of the Chapter of Windesheim. But above all she would have had to have possessed a strong urge to write. There was after all very little room for the writing of texts in the daily schedule of the nuns. The

> drew upon the mystic tradition (he edited a number of *Schwesternbücher* and wrote a number of new *vitae* of nuns), but treats mysticism with a great deal of reserve. A summary of his life and works is given in Fechter 1987, especially 474–89; cf. Williams-Krapp 1990 and 1993.

author usually wrote because of a desire to reform the spiritual life in her own or another convent. Apart from the chronicle of Bethanië and the works of Mechtild van Rieviren, the writings of the nuns of Windesheim may be characterised as literature of reform.

In the Windesheim convents the writing increased when change was required. But the nuns did not all have the same goal in mind when they undertook their reform initiatives. The writings of the Windesheim nuns demonstrate a characteristic development in the second movement of female religious. Each one of them determined in her own way her place in the area of tension between 'mystical culture' and 'convent culture' (the tendency towards institutionalisation, whose outlines become more clearly discernable as the fifteenth century progresses).[24] The dominant theme in the lives and literature of female religious in the Middle Ages is, after all, almost always the mystic experience. A brief chronological review of the writings of the Windesheim canonesses can best illustrate what each one's position was.

The *Devote epistelen* (1418–20), addressed to the sisters of Jeruzalem in Utrecht, are the oldest known writings from the milieu of the Windesheim choir nuns. They were presumably written by a nun from Diepenveen, perhaps by the prioress Salome Sticken. In order to instruct the new nuns in Utrecht, she drew upon the works of Jan van Ruusbroec and Hendrik Mande, which were apparently closely read at that time at Diepenveen. Although they could hardly be considered daring works of mysticism, it is significant that it is precisely these authors who were cited so extensively in the context of the reformation of a new Windesheim convent. This may be an indication of a fairly vibrant mystic culture in the first quarter of the fifteenth century in some of the convents of Windesheim.

The only work by a Windesheim nun written at the request of – but not in collaboration with – a Windesheim canon regular is Salome Sticken's *Vivendi formula* (1435–9). Hendrik van Loder was deeply involved in the female devout movement in Westphalia. For help in setting up the spiritual lifestyle in a new sisterhouse he sought out Sticken, who at first refused humbly, but in the end acquiesced. Van Loder's request constitutes an acknowledgement of Sticken's authority. He recognised that women were in need of a special kind of religious leadership that he could not provide. He therefore asked Sticken to write a rule for the sisterhouse, from the perspective of the rectrix and the nuns. She emerges from the *Vivendi formula* as a Modern Devout who preferred to keep both feet firmly on the ground. Like Johannes Brinckerinck, she considered obedience and humility to be the most important virtues. She prescribed ascetic exercises and contemplation of the Passion for the interior lives of the sisters. If they performed with conviction, they might receive God's grace and experience his presence. This is in fact the only reference to

---

[24] I use the term 'mystical culture' as formulated by Mertens 1995b (cf. §1.2).

the mystical experience as a coherent theme in the entire rule. This says little about Sticken's own thoughts on the matter, however, for the *Vivendi formula* was intended for women at the beginning of the spiritual path, and who, moreover, would become (only) Sisters of the Common Life.

Salome Sticken herself must almost certainly have been familiar with the mystic life. One could almost deduce her possible authorship of the *Devote epistelen* from her choice of subject matter. Furthermore it is striking that her *vite* in the Diepenveen sisterbook exhibits the greatest use of mystic language. The first prioress is compared to a seraph, burning with divine love, and a dream is described in which a nun sees the face of Mother Superior Salome in a flame.[25] Her fellow sisters, then, associated the first prioress of Diepenveen with visionary phenomena. The most striking thing about this is that the others did not really know what to make of her blessings. This becomes apparent when the sisterbook describes how the former prioress collapsed after being severely admonished during the chapter of faults.[26] In earlier centuries such an event would have been seen as an ecstatic experience of God's presence, but the sisterbook does not dare to draw this conclusion. Sticken herself remains anxiously cautious. Despite being in all likelihood familiar with the mystic union from her own experience, she hardly mentions it. From her actions (or their representation?) it would appear that she places her trust primarily in discipline, ascesis and humility. This is not to deny that experiences of divine blessing did indeed play a role in the spiritual lives of the nuns in Sticken's Diepenveen. It is important to note that during this period it is possible to speak of a mystic circle of sorts in the mother monastery of Windesheim, to which the prior Johan Vos van Heusden also belonged. It is quite possible that as prior superior of the Chapter he exercised a certain degree of tolerance in this regard.

But the mystic life in Diepenveen did not reach a very ecstatic or speculative level. The inmates sent to other convents primarily conveyed the message of ascesis. Thus it was that Alijt Bake discovered in her conflict with Hille Sonderlants (1440–1) that she had little tolerance for nuns possessed of mystic talent. Bake herself is the only one of the choir nuns of Windesheim who longed explicitly for the interior (mystic) life, and wished furthermore to steer the spirituality within her order in that direction. For her, the inner experiences were the most important touchstone for her spiritual life, and she dared to draw the obvious conclusions from them. Based on her exceptional talents, Bake assumed a measure of spiritual authority; and moreover, she wrote about her experiences in order to show her successors the mystic path, just as many of her predecessors had done before her. Like those women,

---

[25] DV, ff. 206r–208v and D, ff. 10a–11d; cf. DV, f. 219v and D, f. 18b. See also DV, ff. 196r–v and D, ff. 4b–c, on Elsebe Hasenbroecks, who saw fiery, multicoloured rays of light emerge from the mouth of the praying Salome Sticken.

[26] DV, f. 212v (cited at §3.2) and D, f. 14a.

Alijt was able to convince a number of male religious of her truth, such as the rector Nicolaas van Duvendyc and the prior of Elzegem, Jan Eggaert the younger. But this group was so small the it could not successfully defend her.

Bake's unconventional behaviour forced the Chapter of Windesheim to assume an entirely new orientation. One may well ask why the Chapter authorities gave her free reign for ten years. It is possible that there was a perceived need for personalities of Alijt Bake's calibre in a monastic organisation that had lost the *élan* of its early years. But as prioress Alijt Bake had begun to behave in a way that was inappropriate in the brief Windesheim tradition. A figure of no less impressive stature, Salome Sticken, did not appoint herself as a spiritual authority, but instead acknowledged the authority of the Chapter General. The direct impetus for Alijt Bake's deposition and banishment, and the prohibition against writing, which all took place in 1454, may well be due to the arrival of a new prior superior of the Chapter of Windesheim, Jan van Naaldwijk. Perhaps he wished to take immediate action against a situation that for some time had been considered undesirable.[27] But it is also possible that steps were taken to restrain Bake because it was during this period that she began to get involved in the reformation of a number of convents in the area. Whatever the case may be, from 1455 on, the theme of 'nuns and mysticism' was kept under a much tighter reign in the Chapter of Windesheim.

It would be too easy to accuse the Chapter of Windesheim of being simply misogynistic, despite the fact that administrators like Jan van Naaldwijk can hardly be praised for their sensitivity. Willeumier-Schalij justly points out that the 'prohibition against writing' was also designed to protect the sisters from themselves, in that their expectations for the powers of mysticism were too high.[28] An example from the Diepenveen sisterbook illustrates this (as does the story of the unfortunate sister Janneke of Facons). Sister Liesbeth van Delft (†1423) often burst into tears during her meditations; this gift of tears was generally considered to be a sign of grace.[29] Her fellow sisters also yearned for grace, but seldom received it. They therefore suspected Sister Liesbeth of keeping certain interior exercises from them.[30] The sisters in Diepenveen failed to grasp that mystic talent is a gift which God can never be compelled to bestow. Even in a convent like Diepenveen, where the level of spirituality was high, such misconceptions about mysticism could and did exist. The firm intervention of the Chapter General in 1455 can therefore also be interpreted as an expression of pastoral concern. By taking Alijt Bake –

---

[27] On Jan van Naaldwijk see Kohl, Persoons and Weiler 1976–84, vol. 3, 504 and 511. The visitation by the papal emissary Nicholas of Kues (cf. §5.3) may also have been a factor in the drastic decision of the Chapter of Windesheim.
[28] Willeumier-Schalij 1981, 300.
[29] For more on this, see Lewis 1996, 81–2 ('gift of tears').
[30] DV, ff. 58r–v.

who knew very well what the mystic way of life was all about – out of circulation to stop a precedent being established, an attempt was made to ensure that the nuns of Windesheim concerned themselves only with spiritual ideas that could not be misinterpreted.[31]

The 1455 prohibition against writing had a definitive effect, for thereafter the nuns of Windesheim never again took up mystic literature. Not long after the proclamation of this prohibition the foundation for the sisterbook of Diepenveen was laid, a work that like no other from this milieu propagates strict ascesis and practical virtue. It seeks, among other things, to bring about internal reform by revealing to the contemporary nuns the deeds of their predecessors, who had made Diepenveen great. The *viten* present women who serve to exemplify the epitome of the Windesheim monastic ideal. These are exemplary *monastic* sisters, who place themselves at the service of the community of Diepenveen and do not take it upon themselves to follow their own spiritual paths. The sisterbook is the result of a strong cooperation among the women of Diepenveen who wrote down the history of their convent and their fellow sisters as an inspiration to one another, though the rector and the members of the visitation would have monitored it. And yet the *viten* provide a particular female view of the spiritual life, a life that appears not to have diverged much from what the Chapter authorities had in mind. This leads to the tentative conclusion that most of the sisters at Diepenveen embraced the same ideal of ascesis and virtue.

In the final years of the fifteenth century literature flourished briefly at Facons, in Antwerp, as a reaction to the decline of the preceding years. To bring about this much-needed turn around, Jacomijne Costers employed the traditional female genre of the vision. By doing so she in fact violated the prohibition against writing. But Costers had but one aim with her *Visioen en exempel*: to bring Facons back to the Windesheim observance. No delegate from the Chapter could object to such a high purpose. It is quite possible that the rector encouraged Jacomijne to commit her experience to writing, but it is her vision that shines through in this work. In her vision as well as her other works she argues for strict adherence to the rule and the constitutions. And although she herself was the recipient of God's grace and a witness to it – apparently mysticism was less controversial at Facons than at Diepenveen – she advised her fellow sisters first and foremost to recite such traditional prayers as the Ave Maria and the Lord's Prayer.

Mechtild van Rieviren was perhaps the most mystical author after the prohibition against writing. She had an intimate relationship with Christ, with whom she frequently spoke, just as Alijt Bake had done. But Mechtild did not assume a leadership role, and from a literary perspective she did little more than commit a number of her interior experiences to writing. By writing

---

[31] See Willeumier-Schalij 1981, *passim*, Willeumier-Schalij 1990, and Mertens 1995b.

down her mystic experiences and the insights they provided her with, she enabled other nuns to learn something about the interior life, which may well have raised the spiritual level at Facons. But in the works of Mechtild van Rieviren we cannot detect the kind of concrete ambitions for reform held by Alijt Bake and Jacomijne Costers.

The sixteenth century produces one last Windesheim nun who undertook an ambitious literary project. Presumably on behalf of the entire convent of Diepenveen, Griete Essinchghes completed a new redaction of the sisterbook in 1524. The stories concerning the exemplary sisters from the early years still enjoyed enormous appeal. The time-honoured monastic ideal was still current, judging by the newly added *viten*, in which sisters from Diepenveen stand out once again in practical virtue. In the older *viten* one detects a tendency to push the supernatural (even further) into the background. Apparently these relics of a mystical tradition did not fit well into the vision of Griete Essinchghes and those who may have supported her in her work, thus leading them to place a greater emphasis on the classical monastic virtues.

There are two more or less oppositional forces vying for dominance in the literature of the Windesheim nuns. The first is constituted by the personal religious experience. Time and again the point of departure for the nuns who wrote is what they themselves experienced in their spiritual lives. In this respect these writings fit in well with the mystic women's literature of the Middle Ages. But unlike the female mystics of previous eras, they have difficulties interpreting what they find, and they derive much less confidence in the spiritual realm from what they know internally. This uncertainty is connected to the second force, namely the fear of God, which became increasingly more dominant among the Modern Devout. The fear of displeasing God in one way or another became greater than the joy in divine grace. It is for this reason that the sisters sought solace in the peaceful and regulated communal life devoid of exceptional behaviour, under which category mysticism was certainly classified. The constant exhortations to obedience, the warnings against backbiting and overly intimate friendships and other such things give expression to this attitude. In the early days of enthusiasm and the construction of the Windesheim convents the personal input of pioneering sisters could have a significant effect, but in the period of stabilisation and institutionalisation that followed, it was the communal ideal that was emphasised.

Alijt Bake undertook a courageous attempt to breathe new life into the mystical culture that had been incorporated into the Chapter of Windesheim via Groenendaal, but which had thereafter lost much of its influence. But Bake's initiative came at the wrong moment. The Chapter of Windesheim had every reason to consider itself a successful religious movement and took steps to preserve what it had built up. In this tradition there was no room for women who wrote visions and paraded themselves as spiritual leaders. The nuns of Windesheim were expected to live in humility and devotion.

BIBLIOGRAPHY

Acquoy, J. G. R., 1875–80, *Het klooster te Windesheim en zijn invloed*, 3 vols., Utrecht (repr. Leeuwarden, 1984).
van Aelst, J. J., 1997, 'Suffering with the Bridegroom. The *Innighe sprake* of the Utrecht Recluse Sister Bertken', *OGE* 71, 228–49.
Aercke, K. (ed.), 1994, *Women Writing in Dutch*, New York, Women Writers of the World.
Alberts, W. J., 1958, 'Zur Historiographie der Devotio Moderna und ihrer Erforschung', *Westfälische Forschungen* 11, 51–67.
—— 1961, 'Middelnederlandse heiligenlevens uit de kring van de Devotio Moderna', *Bijdragen en mededelingen van het Historisch Genootschap* 75, 13–61.
—— and A. L. Hulshoff, 1958, *Het Frensweger handschrift betreffende de geschiedenis van de Moderne Devotie*, Groningen, Werken Historisch Genootschap, 3rd series, 82.
Ampe, A., 1945, 'Orde en wanorde in Ruusbroec's XII Beghinen', *OGE* 19–II, 55–82.
Andriessen, J., P. Bange and A. G. Weiler (eds.), 1985, *Geert Grote en Moderne Devotie. Voordrachten gehouden tijdens het Geert Grote congres, Nijmegen 27–9 september 1984*, Nijmegen, MSt 1. (Also in *OGE* 59 (1985), no. 2–3.)
Angenendt, A., T. Braucks, R. Busch *et al.*, 1995, 'Gezählte Frömmigkeit', in *Frühmittelalterliche Studien* 29, 1–71.
Arts, A. J. M., 1945, *Het dubbelklooster Dikninge*, Assen.
Axters, S. G., 1956, *Geschiedenis van de vroomheid in de Nederlanden*, vol. 3, *De Moderne Devotie 1380–1550*, Antwerp.
—— 1961, 'Joannes Tauler in de Nederlanden', in E. Filthaut (ed.), *Joannes Tauler, ein deutscher Mystiker. Gedenkschrift zum 600. Geburtstag*, Essen, 348–70.
—— 1967, 'Inleiding tot een geschiedenis van de mystiek in de Nederlanden', in *Verslagen en mededelingen van de Koninklijke Vlaamse Academie voor Taal- en Letterkunde*, Ghent, 165–306.
—— 1970, *Bibliotheca dominicana neerlandica manuscripta 1224–1500*, Leuven, Bibliothèque de la Revue d'histoire ecclésiastique 49.
de Baere, G., 1993, 'Ruusbroecs "Spieghel" in de Latijnse vertaling van Geert Grote', in T. Mertens *et al.*, 156–70 and 413–19.
Bange, P., 1996, 'De hervorming van de Saksische vrouwenkloosters als verhaald door Johannes Busch in boek II van zijn "Liber de reformatione monasteriorum" ', in A. J. Hendrikman, P. Bange, R. T.M. van Dijk *et al.* (eds.), *Windesheim 1395–1995. Kloosters, teksten, invloeden*, Nijmegen, MSt 12, 143–53.

Barthelmé, A., 1930, *La Réforme dominicaine au XVe siècle en Alsace et dans l'ensemble de la province de Teutonie*, Strasburg.

Basse, M., 1920–1, *Het aandeel der vrouw in de Nederlandsche letterkunde*, 2 vols., Ghent, Uitgave van het Willems-Fonds 157–8.

Becker, P., 1980, 'Benediktinische Reformbewegungen im Spätmittelalter. Ansätze, Entwicklungen, Auswirkungen', in *Untersuchungen zu Kloster und Stift*, Göttingen, Veröffentlichungen der Max-Planck-Institut für Geschichte 68, Studien zur Germania sacra 14, 167–87.

Bell, R. M., 1985, *Holy Anorexia*, Chicago.

van Bemmel, H. C., 1999, *Catalogus van de handschriften aanwezig in de Bibliotheek Arnhem*, Hilversum.

Bemolt van Loghum Slaterus, A. J., 1938, *Het klooster Frenswegen*, Arnhem.

Bénédictins du Bouveret, 1976, *Colophons de manuscrits occidentaux des origines au XVIe siècle*, vol. 4, *Colophons signé L-O*, Fribourg, Spicilegii Friburgensis subsidia 5.

Bollmann, A., and N. Staubach, 1998, *Schwesternbuch und Statuten des St. Agnes-Konvents in Emmerich*, [n.p.].

Borchling, C., 1914, *Mittelniederdeutsche Handschriften in den Rheinlanden und in einigen anderen Sammlungen. Vierter Reisebericht*, Berlin, Nachrichten von der Königlichen Gesellschaft der Wissenschaften zu Göttingen, Philologische-historische Klasse, 1913 (Beiheft).

Bos, E. P., and G. Warnar, 1993, *Een claer verlicht man. Over het leven en werk van Jan van Ruusbroec (1293–1381)*, Hilversum, MStB 38.

Bot, P., 1990, *Tussen verering en verachting. De rol van de vrouw in de middeleeuwse samenleving 500–1500*, Kampen.

Boyer, R., 1981, 'An Attempt to Define the Typology of Medieval Hagiography', in H. Bekker-Nielsen, P. Foote, J. H. Jørgensen et al. (eds.), *Hagiography and Medieval Literature. A Symposium*, Odense, 27–36.

Breure, L., 1985a, 'Männliche und weibliche Ausdrucksformen in der Spiritualität der Devotio Moderna', in P. Dinzelbacher and D. Bauer (eds.), *Frauenmystik im Mittelalter*, Ostfildern bei Stuttgart, 231–55.

—— 1985b, 'Het devote sterven als menselijke ervaring', *OGE* 59 (1985), 435–46. (Also in Andriessen, Bange and Weiler 1985, 323–44.)

—— 1987, *Doodsbeleving en levenshouding. Een historisch-psychologische studie betreffende de Moderne Devotie in het IJsselgebied in de 14e en 15e eeuw*, Hilversum.

Brinkerink, D. A., 1902, 'De "Vita venerabilis Iohannis Brinckerinck" (in MS No. 8849–59 in de Koninklijke Bibliotheek, Brussel)', *NAKG* 1, 314–54.

—— 1904, *Van den doechden der vuriger ende stichtiger susteren van diepen veen ('Handschrift D'). Eerste gedeelte – De tekst van het handschrift*, Leiden.

—— 1907, 'Devote epistelen (in MS No. 133 F 22 in de Koninklijke Bibliotheek, den Haag)', *NAKG* 4, 312–38 and 388–409.

Brinkman, H., 1993, 'The Composition of a Fifteenth-Century Aristocratic

Library in Breda: The Books of John IV of Nassau and Mary van Loon', *Quaerendo* 23/3, 163-83.

Bromberg, R. L. J., [n.d.], *'Het boek der bijzondere genade' van Mechtild van Hackeborn*, 2 vols., Zwolle, Zwolse drukken en herdrukken voor de Maatschappij der Nederlandse Letterkunde te Leiden 51.

Bruch, H., 1956, *Supplement bij 'Geschiedenis van de Noord-Nederlandsche geschiedschrijving in de Middeleeuwen' van dr. Jan Romein*, Haarlem.

de Bruin, C. C., 1944-5, 'De Dietse oertekst van de anonieme "Epistola de vita et passione domini nostri Ihesu Christi et aliis devotis exercitiis" ', *NAKG* 34, 1-23.

—— 1984, 'De spiritualiteit van de Moderne Devotie', in C. C. De Bruin, E. Persoons and A. G. Weiler, *Geert Grote en de Moderne Devotie*, Zutphen, 102-44.

de Bruin, M., and J. Oosterman, 2001, *Repertorium van het Nederlandse lied tot 1600*, 2 vols., Ghent and Amsterdam.

van Buuren, A. M. J., 1992, ' "Soe wie dit liedtkyn sinct of leest". De functie van de laatmiddelnederlandse geestelijke lyriek', in F. Willaert *et al.*, *Een zoet akkoord. Middeleeuwse lyriek in de Lage Landen*, Amsterdam, NLCM 7, 223-4 and 399-404.

—— 1993, ' "Wat materien gheliken op sonnendage ende hoechtijde te lesen". Het Middelnederlandse collatieboek van Dirc van Herxen', in T. Mertens *et al.*, 245-63 and 444-7.

—— 1995, ' "Want ander konsten sijn my te hoghe". De stadsschool in de Nederlanden in de late Middeleeuwen', in R. E. V. Stuip and C. Vellekoop (eds.), *Scholing in de middeleeuwen*, Hilversum, Utrechtse bijdragen tot de mediëvistiek 13, 221-38.

Bynum, C. Walker, 1982, *Jesus as Mother. Studies in the Spirituality of the Middle Ages*, Berkeley.

—— 1987, *Holy Feast and Holy Fast. The Religious Significance of Food to Medieval Women*, Berkeley.

Byvanck, A. W., and G. J. Hoogewerff, 1922-5, *Noord-Nederlandsche miniaturen in handschriften der 14e, 15e en 16e eeuwen*, 3 vols., The Hague.

Carasso-Kok, M., 1981, *Repertorium van verhalende historische bronnen uit de middeleeuwen. Heiligenlevens, annnalen, kronieken en andere in Nederland geschreven verhalende bronnen*, The Hague.

Caron, M. L., 1985, 'Het beeld van Christus in de vrouwenkloosters en bij de zusters van het gemene leven', *OGE* 59, 457-69. (Also in Andriessen, Bange and Weiler 1985, 345-57.)

Cassiman, A., 1952, 'De Moderne Devotie van Geert Grote in Vlaanderen', in *OGE* 26, 145-86.

Christ, K., 1942, 'Mittelalterliche Bibliotheksordnungen für Frauenklöster', in *Zentralblatt für Bibliothekswesen* 59, 1-29.

Cockx-Indestege, E., J. Deschamps, F. Hendrickx *et al.* (eds.), 1990, *Spiritualia Neerlandica. Opstellen voor dr. Albert Ampe*, Antwerp.

Constable, G., 1976, *Letters and Letter-Collections*, Turnhout, Typologie des sources du moyen âge occidental 17.

Cordemans de Bruyne, H., 1896, 'Bibliographie Malinoise. Histoire de l'art typographique à Malines et bibliographie raisonnée de ses productions. 1. Quinzième siècle', in *Bulletin du cercle archéologique, litteraire et artistique de Malines* 6, 1–111.

Costard, M., 1992, 'Predigthandschriften der Schwestern vom gemeinsamen Leben. Spätmittelalterliche Predigtüberlieferung in der Bibliothek des Klosters Nazareth in Geldern', in V. Mertens and H.-J. Schiewer (eds.), *Die deutsche Predigt im Mittelalter. Internationales Symposium am Fachbereich Germanistik der Freien Universität Berlin vom 3.–6. Oktober 1989*, Tübingen, 194–222.

—— 1995, 'Zwischen Mystik und Moraldidaxe. Deutsche Predigten des Fraterherren Johannes Veghe und des Dominikaners Konrad Schlatter in Frauenklöstern des 15. Jahrhunderts', *OGE* 69, 235–59.

Daniëls, L. M. F., 1937–9, *Dirc van Delf, 'Tafel van den kersten ghelove'*, 4 vols. in 3, Antwerp, Tekstuitgaven van *OGE* 5–8.

Deblaere, A., 1980, 'Mombaer (Jean; Mauburnus, de Bruxelles)', in *DS* 10, 1516–21.

Debongnie, P., 1927, *Jean Mombaer de Bruxelles, abbé de Livry. Ses écrits et ses réformes*, Leuven, Recueil des travaux publiés par les membres des conférences d'histoire et de philologie II–11.

—— 1937, 'Busch, Jean', *DS* 1, 1983–4.

Defoer, H. L. M., A. S. Korteweg and W. C. M. Wüstefeld, 1989, *The Golden Age of Dutch Manuscript Painting*, Stuttgart.

Degler-Spengler, B., 1984, 'Die religiöse Frauenbewegung des Mittelalters. Konversen–Nonnen–Beginen', *Rottenburger Jahrbuch für Kirchengeschichte* 3, 75–88.

—— 1985, ' "Zahlreich wie die Sterne des Himmels". Zisterzienser, Dominikaner und Franziskaner vor dem Problem der Inkorporation von Frauenklöstern', *Rottenburger Jahrbuch für Kirchengeschichte* 4, 37–50.

Deschamps, J., 1967, 'Handschriften uit het Sint-Agnesklooster te Maaseik', in *Album Dr. M. Bussels*, Hasselt, 167–94.

—— 1972, *Middelnederlandse handschriften uit Europese en Amerikaanse bibliotheken*, Tentoonstellingscatalogus, 2nd revised edition, Leiden.

—— 1976, 'Middelnederlandse vertalingen van levens en legenden van de H. Franciscus van Assisi. Handschriften en drukken', *Franciscana* 31, 59–73.

—— 1989, 'De Middelnederlandse vertalingen en bewerkingen van de "Hundert Betrachtungen und Begehrungen" van Henricus Suso', *OGE* 63, 309–69. (Also in Cockx-Indestege, Deschamps, Hendrickx *et al.* 1990, 193–253.)

—— and H. Mulder, 1998, *Inventaris van de Middelnederlandse handschriften van de Koninklijke Bibliotheek van België (voorlopige uitgave)*, Brussels.

Despy-Meyer, A., 1971, 'Prieuré de Notre-Dame de la rose de Jéricho, à Bruxelles', *MB* IV–5, 1247–71.
van Dijk, M., 2000, *Een rij van spiegels. De Heilige Barbara van Nicomedia als voorbeeld voor vrouwelijke religieuzen*, Hilversum, MStB 71.
—— 2002, 'En zuster Jutte lachte ... Vroom en vrouwelijk in het zusterboek', in W. Scheepsma (ed.), *Het ootmoedig fundament van Diepenveen. Zeshonderd jaar Maria en Sint-Agneskloster 1400–2000*, [n.p.], 95–112, 143–5 and 167–9.
van Dijk, R. T. M., 1984, 'De onvoltooide weg van Geert Grote', *Benediktijns tijdschrift* XLV, 100–11.
—— 1985, 'Het probleem van de "Cura monialium" ', *OGE* 59, 225–37. (Also in Andriessen, Bange and Weiler 1985, 113–25.)
—— 1986, *De constituties der Windesheimse vrouwenkloosters vóór 1559. Bijdrage tot de institutionele geschiedenis van het Kapittel van Windesheim*, 2 vols., Nijmegen, MSt 3–1 and 3–2.
—— 1987a, 'De Middelnederlandse vertalingen van de vrouwelijke versie der Windesheimse kloosterwetgeving', in E. Cockx-Indestege and F. Hendrickx (eds.), *Opstellen voor dr. Jan Deschamps ter gelegenheid van zijn zeventigste verjaardag*, Leuven, Mediaevalia Neerlandica 2, 109–20.
—— 1987b, 'De bestuursvorm van het Kapittel van Sion. Hollands verzet tegen het Windesheims centralisme', *AGKKN* 29, 166–91.
—— 1988, 'Windesheimse observantie in na-middeleeuwse vrouwenkloosters. Verschuivingen in de beleving van de beslotenheid', in P. Bange, C. Graafland, A. J. Jelsma *et al.* (eds.), *De doorwerking van de Moderne Devotie. Windesheim 1387–1987. Voordrachten gehouden tijdens het Windesheim Symposium Zwolle/Windesheim 15–17 oktober 1987*, Hilversum, 253–65.
—— 1990, 'Het getijdenboek van Geert Grote. Terugblik en vooruitzicht', *OGE* 64, 156–94. (Also in Cockx-Indestege, Deschamps, Hendrickx *et al.* 1990, 456–94.)
—— 1992, 'De mystieke weg van Alijt Bake (1415–55)', *OGE* 66, 115–33.
—— 1993, 'Methodologische kanttekeningen bij het onderzoek van getijdenboeken', in T. Mertens *et al.*, 210–29 and 434–7.
—— 1994a, 'Die Devotio Moderna als geistlicher Raum des Klosters Frenswegen', in H. Voort (ed.), *Kloster-Leben. Vom Augustinerchorherrenstift zur ökumenischen Begegnungstätte*, Nordhorn, Das Bentheimer Land 131, 7–32.
—— 1994b, 'Windesheim', in *DS* 16, 1457–78.
—— 2002, 'Het vrouwenklooster Diepenveen in zijn historische context', in W. Scheepsma (ed.), *Het ootmoedig fundament van Diepenveen. Zeshonderd jaar Maria en Sint-Agneskloster 1400–2000*, [n.p.], 15–39, 131–6 en 149–62.
—— and M. K. A. van den Berg, 1997, *Alijt Bake. Tot in de peilloze diepte van God. De vrouw die moest zwijgen over haar mystieke weg*, Kampen, Mystieke teksten en thema's 12.
—— and A. J. Hendrikman, 1996, 'Tabellarium chronologicum Windeshemense. De Windesheimse kloosters in chronologisch perspectief', in A. J. Hendrik-

man, P. Bange, R. T.M. van Dijk *et al.* (eds.), *Windesheim 1395–1995. Kloosters, teksten, invloeden*, Nijmegen, MSt 12, 186–210.

—— and T. Mertens, 1993, 'Termen uit het kerkelijk leven van de late middeleeuwen', in T. Mertens *et al.*, 341–59 and 490–2.

Dinzelbacher, P., 1991, *Revelationes*, Turnhout, Typologie des sources du Moyen Âge occidental 57.

—— 1994, *Christliche Mystik im Abendland. Geschichte von den Anfängen bis zum Ende des Mittelalters*, Paderborn.

Dols, M., 1941, *Bibliographie der Moderne Devotie*, 3rd edn, Nijmegen.

van der Donckt, R., 1984, 'Prieuré de Sion à Audenaerde', in *MB* VII–4, 859–77.

Donndorf, J., 1929, *Das 'Rosetum' des Johannes Mauburnus. Ein Beitrag zur Geschichte der Frömmigkeit in den Windesheimer Klöstern*, Halle.

Dresen, G., 1990, *Onschuldfantasieën. Offerzin en heilsverlangen in feminisme en mystiek*, Nijmegen.

Dumbar, G., 1719, *Analecta, seu vetera aliquot scripta inedita ab ipso publici juris facta*, vol. 1. Deventer.

—— 1731–88, *Het kerkelyk en wereltlyk Deventer, behelzende eene uitvoerige beschryving van stats oirsprong, gelegenheit, enz. Als ook een omstandigh verhaal der beurtenissen van ouden tyden af haer betreffende*, 2 vols., Deventer. Ex Leiden, UB, 448 a 2.

Dykmans, M., 1941, *Obituaire du monastère de Groenendael dans la Forêt de Soignes*, Brussels, Publications de la Commission royale d'histoire Belgique, série in-8°.

van Eeghen, I. H., 1941, *Vrouwenkloosters en begijnhof in Amsterdam van de 14e tot het eind der 15e eeuw*, Amsterdam.

Elm, K. (ed.), 1980a, *Ordensstudien. I Beiträge zur Geschichte der Konversen in Mittelalter*, Berlin, BHS 2.

—— 1980b, 'Verfall und Erneuerung des Ordenswesen im Spätmittelalter. Forschungen und Forschungsaufgaben', in *Untersuchungen zu Kloster und Stift*, Göttingen, Veröffentlichungen des Max-Planck-Instituts 68, 188–238.

—— 1985, 'Die Bruderschaft vom gemeinsamen Leben. Eine geistliche Lebensform zwischen Kloster und Welt, Mittelalter und Neuzeit', *OGE* 59, 470–96. (Also in Andriessen, Bange and Weiler 1985, 358–84.)

—— (ed.), 1989, *Reformbemühungen und Observanzbestrebungen im spätmittelalterlichen Ordenswesen*, Berlin.

—— and P. Feige, 1981, 'Reformen und Kongregationsbildungen der Zisterzienser im Spätmittelalter und früher Neuzeit', in *Die Zisterzienser. Ordensleben zwischen Ideal und Wirklichkeit*, Bonn, Schriften des Rheinischen Museumamtes 10, 243–54.

van Elslander, A., 1953, *Het refrein in de Nederlanden tot 1600*, Ghent.

Eman, S., 2002, 'De kloostergebouwen van Diepenveen, in het bijzonder de kapel met het nonnenkoor', in W. Scheepsma (ed.), *Het ootmoedig*

fundament van Diepenveen. Zeshonderd jaar Maria en Sint-Agnesklooster 1400–2000, [n.p.], 41–62.
Enenkel, K. A. E., 1987, 'Der andere Petrarca: Francesco Petrarca "De vita solitaria" und die "Devotio Moderna" ', *Quaerendo* 17, 137–47.
van Engen, J., 1988a, *Devotio Moderna. Basic Writings*, New York, The Classics of Western Spirituality.
—— 1988b, 'The Virtues, the Brothers, and the Schools', *Revue bénédictine* 98, 178–217.
—— 1992, 'A Brabantine Perspective on the Origins of the Modern Devotion: The First Book of Petrus Impens's "Compendium decursus temporam monasterii christifere bethleemitice puerpere" ', in W. Verbeke (ed.), *Serta devota in memoriam Guillelmi Lourdaux*, vol. 1, *Devotio Windeshemensis*, Leuven, Mediaevalia Lovaniensia I-20, 3–78.
—— 1993, 'Late Medieval Anticlericalism: The Case of the New Devout', in P. A. Dykman and H. Oberman, *Anticlericalism in Late Medieval and Early Modern Europe*, Leiden, 19–52.
—— 1999, 'The Work of Gerlach Peters (d. 1411), Spiritual Diarist and Letter-Writer, a Mystic among the Devout', *OGE* 73, 150–77.
Epiney-Burgard, G., 1970, *Gérard Grote (1340–84) et les débuts de la Dévotion moderne*, Wiesbaden, Veröffentlichungen des Instituts für europäische Geschichte Mainz 54.
Everts, W., 1866, 'De stichting des kloosters "Jerusalem" te Venray', *De Dietsche warande* 7, 27–39 and 105–16.
Ewerhart, R., 1955, *Die Handschrift 322/1994 der Stadtbibliothek Trier als musikalische Quelle*, Regensburg, Kölner Beiträge zur Musikforschung 7.
Fechter, W., 1987, 'Meyer, Johannes OP', in *VL* 6, 474–89.
Feismann, R., 1994, *Das Memorienbuch des St. Michaeliskonventes zu Lübeck. Zwei Handschriften aus den Jahren 1463 und 1498*, [Lübeck], Veröffentlichungen zur Geschichte der Hansestadt Lübeck, herausgegeben vom Archiv der Hansestadt B–24.
Foncke, R., 1932, 'Werk van Jan van Ruusbroec in het voormalig klooster van Bethaniën te Mechelen', *Mechlinia* 9, 129–30.
Franke, H. M., 1981, *Der 'Liber Ordinarius' der Regularkanoniker der Windesheimer Kongregation*, Leverkusen, Studia Vindesemensia. Beiträge zur Erforschung der Devotio Moderna und des Kanonikalen Lebens II–1.
Gardiner, E., 1989, *Visions of Heaven and Hell before Dante*, New York.
Gehl, P. F., 1987, ' "Competens silentium". Varieties of Monastic Silence in the Medieval West', *Viator* 18, 125–60.
Geirnaert, D., and J. Reynaert, 1993, 'Geestelijke spijs met zalige vermaning. Verspreiding, overlevering en receptie van Jan van Leeuwen', in T. Mertens *et al.*, 190–209 and 426–34.
Gerrits, G. H., 1986, *'Inter timorem et spem'. A Study of the Theological Thought of Gerard Zerbolt of Zutphen (1367–98)*, Leiden, Studies in Medieval and Reformation Thought 37.

Gnädinger, L., 1993, *Johannes Tauler. Lebenswelt und mystische Lehre*, Munich.
Goossens, J., P. Trio and E. van Mingroot, 1989, 'Prieuré de Sainte-Agnes à Gand', in *MB* VII-5, 799–828.
Goossens, L. A. M., 1952, *De meditatie in de eerste tijd van de Moderne Devotie*, Haarlem.
Goossens, M., 1980, 'Meditation au Moyen Âge. II. Les méthodes dans la spiritualité chrétienne. 1 La "Devotio Moderna" ', in *DS* 10, 914–19.
Goudriaan, K., 1995, 'Willem Clinckaert en de eerste jaren van het klooster Den Hem', in *Het klooster Sint Michiel in Den Hem buiten Schoonhoven*, Schoonhoven, 85–113.
—— and T. Mertens (eds.), 2000, *De Derde Orde van Sint-Franciscus in het bisdom Utrecht. Lezingen van het symposiumop 8 oktober 1999 te Amersfoort georganiseerd door de mediëvistenkring van de Vrije Universiteit Amsterdam*, *OGE* 74, vols. 1–2.
Grijp, L. P., 1997, 'Zingend de dood in', in Frank Willaert (ed.), *Veelderhande liedekens. Studies over het Nederlandse lied tot 1600. Symposium Antwerpen 28 februari 1995*, Leuven, Antwerpse studies over Nederlandse literatuurgeschiedenis 2, 118–48.
Grube, K., 1886, *Des Augustinerpropstes Iohannes Busch 'Chronicon Windeshemense' und 'Liber de reformatione monasteriorum'*, Halle, Geschichtsquellen der Provinz Sachsen und angrenzender Gebiete 19.
Gruijs, A., 1974, 'Jean de Schoonhoven', in *DS* 8, 724–35.
Grundmann, H., 1977, *Religiöse Bewegungen im Mittelalter. Untersuchungen über die geschichtlichen Zusammenhänge zwischen der Ketzerei, den Bettelorden und die religiösen Frauenbewegung im 12. Und 13. Jahrhundert und über die geschichtlichen Grundlagen der deutschen Mystik*, Anhang: *Neue Beiträge zur Geschichte der religiösen Bewegungen im Mittelalter*, 4th edn, Darmstadt.
—— 1978, 'Die Frauen und die Literatur im Mittelalter. Ein Beitrag zur Frage nach der Entstehung des Schrifttums in der Volkssprache', in H. Grundmann, *Ausgewählte Aufsätze*, vol. 3, *Bildung und Sprache*, Stuttgart, Germaniae Historica 25–3, 67–95. (Also in *Archiv für Kulturgeschichte* 26 (1935), 129–61.)
—— 1995, *Religious Movements in the Middle Ages*, Notre Dame, Indiana.
Gumbert, J. P., 1988, *Manuscrits datés dans les Pays-Bas / Catalogue paléographique des manuscrits en écriture latine portant des indications de date*, vol. 2, *Les manuscrits d' origine néerlandaise (XIVe–XVIe siècle) et supplément au tôme premier*, 2 vols., Leiden.
—— 1990, *The Dutch and Their Books in the Manuscript Age*, [London], The Panizzi Lectures 1989.
Harper, J., 1991, *The Forms and Orders of Western Liturgy from the Tenth to the Eighteenth Century. A Historical Introduction and Guide for Students and Musicians*, Oxford.
Hascher-Burger, U., 1998, 'Zwischen Apokalyps und Hohemlied. Brautmystik in Gesängen aus der Devotio Moderna', *OGE* 72, 246–61.

—— 2002, *Gesungene Innigkeit. Studien zu einer Musikhandschrift der* Devotio Moderna *(Utrecht, Universiteitsbibliotheek, ms. 16 H 34,* olim *B 113). Mit einer Edition der Gesänge*, Leiden, Studies in the History of Christian Thought 106.

Hasebrink, B., 1996, 'Tischlesung und Bildungskultur im Nürnberger Katharinenkloster. Ein Beitrag zu ihrer Rekonstruktion', in M. Kintzinger, S. Lorenz and M. Walter (eds.), *Schule und Schüler im Mittelalter. Beiträge zur europäischen Bildungsgeschichte des 9. Bis 15. Jahrhunderts*, Cologne, 187–216.

Hedberg, L., 1954, *'Epistola de vita et passione Domini nostri' und 'Regula Augustini' in mittelniederdeutschen Fassungen Diözesanarchiv, Trier, Ms. 45*, Lund.

Hedlund, M., 1975, *'Epistola de vita et passione Domini nostri'. Der lateinische Text mit Einleitung und Kommentar*, Leiden, Kerkhistorische bijdragen 5.

van Heel, D., 1939, 'De tertiarissen van het Utrechtse Kapittel', *AGAU* 63, 1–382.

—— 1953, 'Het Kapittel van Zepperen', *Bijdragen voor de geschiedenis van de provincie der Minderbroeders in de Nederlanden* 12–14.

Hermans, J. M. M., 1987, 'Elf kisten boeken uit het gouvernementsgebouw te Maastricht. Lotgevallen van de Limburgse handschriften en oude drukken, gevonden in 1839', in E. Cockx-Indestege and F. Hendrickx (eds.), *Opstellen voor dr. Jan Deschamps ter gelegenheid van zijn zeventigste verjaardag: Bio-bibliografie, Handschriftenkunde, Miniatuurkunst*, Leuven, Mediaevalia Neerlandica 1, 105–43.

van Herwaarden, J., 1982, 'Geloof en geloofsuitingen in de veertiende en vijftiende eeuw. Eucharistie en lijden van Jezus', in J. D. Janssens (ed.), *Hoofsheid en devotie in de middeleeuwse maatschappij. De Nederlanden van de 12e tot de 15e eeuw. Handelingen van het wetenschappelijk colloquium te Brussel 21–4 oktober 1981*, Brussels, 174–207.

——, D. de Boer, F. van Kan et al., 1996, *Geschiedenis van Dordrecht tot 1572*, Hilversum, Geschiedenis van Dordrecht 1.

Hinz, U., 1997, *Die Brüder vom Gemeinsamen Leben im Jahrhundert der Reformation. Das Münstersche Kolloquium*, Tübingen, Spätmittelalter und Reformation, n.s. 9.

Hofmeister, P., 1941, 'Die Verfassung der Windesheimer Augustinerchorherren-Kongregation', *Zeitschrift der Savigny-Stiftung für Rechtsgeschichte* 41 / Kanonistische Abteilung 30, 165–270.

van den Hombergh, F. A. H., 1967, *Leven en werk van Jan Brugman O.F.M. (± 1400–73) met een uitgave van twee van zijn tractaten*, Groningen.

—— 1985, 'Brugman en de broeders', *OGE* 59, 357–70. (Also in Andriessen, Bange and Weiler 1985, 245–58.)

Hövelmann, G., 1971, 'Das Emmericher Süsternbuch. Eine verlorengeglaubte Hauptquelle zur Geschichte der Devotio moderna', in *Thomas van Kempen. Beiträge zum 500. Todesjahr 1471–1971*, [Kempen], 43–62.

Hüffer, M., 1922, *De adellijke vrouwenabdij van Rijnsburg 1133–1574*, Nijmegen.
Huyghebaert, N., 1972, *Les Documents nécrologiques*, Turnhout, Typologie des sources du Moyen Âge occidental 4.
Hyma, A., 1921, 'Is Gerard Zerbolt van Zutphen the Author of the "Super modo vivendi"?', *NAKG* 16, 107–28.
—— 1924, 'Het "Tractatus de quatuor generibus meditationum sive contemplationum" of "Sermo de navitate domini", door Geert Grote', *AGAU* 49, 296–326.
—— 1926, 'Het tractaat "Super modo vivendi devotorum hominum simul commorantium" ', *AGAU* 52, 1–100.
—— 1950, *The Brethren of the Common Life*, Grand Rapids.
—— 1965, *The Christian Renaissance. A History of the 'Devotio Moderna'*, 2nd edn, Hamden, Connecticut.
Incunabula in Dutch Libraries. A Census on Fifteenth-Century Books in Dutch Public Collections, 1983, Nieuwkoop.
Iserloh, E., 1983, 'Busch, Johannes', in R. Auty *et al.* (eds.), *Lexikon des Mittelalters* 2, 1115–16.
Jan van Ruusbroec, 1944–8, *Werken. Naar het standaardhandschrift van Groenendaal uitgegeven door het Ruusbroecgenootschap*, 4 vols., Tielt.
—— 1981–, *Opera omnia*: vol. 3, *Die geestelike brulocht*, Tielt, 1988, Studiën en tekstuitgaven van *OGE* 20.3; vol. 7, *Vanden XII beghinen*, Tielt, 2000, vol. 1, *Prolegomena*, vol. 2, *Text and Apparatus*, Studiën en tekstuitgaven van *OGE* 20.7–7a/Corpus christianorum, continuatio mediaevalis 107a–b; vol. 10, *Vanden blinckenden steen, Vanden vier becoringhen, Vanden kersten ghelove, Brieven/Letters*, Tielt, 1991, Studiën en tekstuitgaven van *OGE* 20.10/ Corpus christianorum, continuatio mediaevalis 110.
Jan van Ruusbroec 1293–1381, 1981. Catalogue. Brussels.
Jantzen, G., 1995, ' "Cry out and write": Mysticism and the Struggle for Authority', in L. Smith and J. H. M. Taylor (eds.), *Women, the Book and the Godly. Selected Proceedings of the St. Hilda's Conference, 1993*, vol. 1. Cambridge, 67–76.
Jonckbloet, W. J. A., 1851–5, *Geschiedenis der Middennederlandsche dichtkunst*, 3 vols., Amsterdam.
Jongen, L., and W. Scheepsma, 1993, 'Wachten op de hemelse Bruidegom. De Diepenveense nonnenviten in literairhistorisch perspectief', in T. Mertens *et al.*, 295–317 and 467–76.
Keller, H., K. Grubmüller and N. Staubach (eds.), 1992, *Pragmatische Schriftlichkeit im Mittelalter. Erscheinungsformen und Entwicklungsstufen*, Münster, Münstersche Mittelalter-Schriften 65.
Koch, A. C. F., 1985, 'De collecties van de Athenaeumbibliotheek in historisch perspectief', in J. C. Bedaux, A. C. F. Koch, D. A. S. R. P. Heikens *et al.* (eds.), *Stads- of Athenaeumbibliotheek Deventer 1560–1985*, Deventer.
Koch, E., 1994, *De kloosterpoort als sluitpost? Adellijke vrouwen langs Maas en Rijn tussen huwelijk en convent, 1200–1600*, Leeuwarden.

Kock, T., 1999, *Die Buchkultur der Devotio Moderna. Handschriftenproduktion, Literaturversorgung und Bibliotheksaufbau im Zeitalter des Medienwechsels*, Frankfurt am Main, Tradition – Reform – Innovation. Studien zur Modernität des Mittelalters 2.

Kohl, W., 1968, *Das bistum Münster*, vol. 1, *Die Schwesternhäuser nach der Augustinerregel*, Berlin, Germania sacra. n.s. 3, Die Bistümer der Kirchenprovinz Köln.

—— 1971, *Das bistum Münster*, vol. 2, *Die Klöster der Augustiner-Chorherren*, Berlin, Germania sacra, n.s. 5, Die Bistümer der Kirchenprovinz Köln.

—— 1975, *Das bistum Münster*, vol. 3, *Das freiweltliche Damenstift Freckenhorst*, Berlin, Germania sacra, n.s. 10, Die Bistümer der Kirchenprovinz Köln.

—— 1980, 'Konversen und verwandte Gruppen in den Klöstern der Windesheimer Kongregation', in K. Elm (ed.), *Ordensstudien. I Beiträge zur Geschichte der Konversen in Mittelalter*, Berlin, BHS 2, 67–91.

—— 1989, 'Die Windesheimer Kongregation', in K. Elm (ed.), *Reformbemühungen und Observanzbestrebungen im spätmittelalterlichen Ordenswesen*, Berlin, 83–108.

——, E. Persoons and A. G. Weiler (eds.), 1976–84, *Monasticon Windeshemense*, Brussels: vol. 1, *Belgien*, 1976; vol. 2, *Deutsches Sprachgebiet*, 1977; vol. 3, *Niederlande*, 1980; vol. 4, *Register*, 1984, ABB extra number 16.

de Kok, D., 1939, 'De Keulse Tertiarissencongregatie', *Franciscaans leven* 22, 73–7, 153–7 and 217–21.

Koldeweij, A. M, 2000, 'Lijfelijke en geestelijke pelgrimage: materiële "Souvenirs" van spirituele pelgrimage', in Veelenturf 2000, 222–52.

Koorn, F. W. J., 1981, *Begijnhoven in Holland en Zeeland gedurende de middeleeuwen*, Assen, Van Gorcum's historische bibliotheek 97.

—— 1985, 'Ongebonden vrouwen. Overeenkomsten en verschillen tussen begijnen en de zusters des gemenen levens', *OGE* 59, 393–402. (Also in Andriessen, Bange and Weiler 1985, 281–90.)

—— 1986, 'Women without Vows. The Case of the Beguines and the Sisters of the Common Life in the Northern Netherlands', in E. Schulte van Kessel [ed.], *Women and Men in Spiritual Culture XIV–XVII Centuries. A Meeting of South and North*, The Hague, 135–47.

—— 1992, 'Hollandse nuchterheid? De houding van de Moderne Devoten tegenover vrouwenmystiek en -ascese', *OGE* 66, 97–114.

—— 2002, 'Was Diepenveen te koop? De verwerving van het goederenbezit van Diepenveen en de rol van de zusters hierbij', in W. Scheepsma (ed.), *Het ootmoedig fundament van Diepenveen. Zeshonderd jaar Maria en Sint-Agnesklooster 1400–2000*, [n.p.], 63–76, 138–41 and 164–5.

Kors, M. M., 1991, *De Middelnederlandse brieven van Gerlach Peters (†1411). Studie en tekstuitgave*, Nijmegen.

—— 1993, 'Epistolaire aspecten van de geestelijke brief (ca. 1350–1550)', in T. Mertens *et al.*, 52–69 and 380–8.

—— 1996, *Gerlaci Petri Opera omnia*. Turnhout, Corpus christianorum, continuatio mediaevalis 155.
Korteweg, A. S. (ed.), 1992, *Kriezels, aubergines en takkenbossen. Randversiering in Noordnederlandse handschriften uit de vijftiende eeuw*, The Hague.
Kronenberg, H., 1917, 'Deventer vrouwenkloosters', in *Verslagen en mededeelingen van de vereeniging tot beoefening van Overijsselsch regt en geschiedenis* 34, 57–68.
Kronenberg, M. E., 1917, *Catalogus van de incunabelen in de Athenaeum-Bibliotheek te Deventer*, Deventer.
Kruitwagen, B., 1905, 'De Middelnederlandse handschriften over het leven van Sint Franciscus en zijn eerste gesellen', *De katholiek* 128, 151–91.
—— 1907, 'Het schrijven op feestdagen in de middeleeuwen', *Tijdschrift voor boek- en bibliotheekwezen* 5, 97–120.
—— 1914, 'Het "Breviarium Windeshemense", Gerard Leeu, 1488 15 October', *Het boek* 3, 193–203.
Kühler, W. J., 1909, 'De "Vita magistri Gerardi Magni" van Petrus Horn (in MS No. 8849–59 van de Koninklijke Bibliotheek te Brussel)', *NAKG* 6, 325–70.
—— 1910, 'Levensbeschrijvingen van devote zusters te Deventer', *AGAU* 36, 1–65.
—— 1914, *Johannes Brinckerinck en zijn klooster te Diepenveen*, 2nd edn, Leiden.
—— 1932, 'De betrouwbaarheid der geschiedschrijving van Thomas a Kempis', *NAKG* 25, 49–68.
Küsters, U., and O. Langer, 1991, Review of U. Peters, *Religiöse Erfahrung als literarisches Faktum*, Tübingen, 1986, *Arbitrium* 9, 37–41.
Kwakkel, E., 1999, 'Ouderdom en genese van de veertiende-eeuwse Hadewijch-handschriften', *Queeste* 6, 23–40.
Langer, O., 1987, *Mystische Erfahrung und spirituelle Theologie. Zu Meister Eckharts Auseinandersetzung mit der Frauenfrömmigkeit seiner Zeit*, Munich, MTU 91.
Latomus, J., and J. Hoybergius, 1664, *Corsendonca sive coenobii canonicorum regularium ordinis S. Augustini de Corsendoncq origo et progressus*, Antwerp, Hieronymus Verdussius. Ex Antwerp, Ruusbroecgenootschap, 3028 C 4.
Ledeboer, A. M., 1867, *Notices bibliographiques des livres imprimés avant 1525 conservés dans la Bibliothèque Publique de Deventer*, Deventer.
Leesch, W., E. Persoons and A. G. Weiler, 1979, *Monasticon fratrum vitae communis*: vol. 1, *Belgien und Nordfrankreich*, Brussels, 1977; vol. 2, *Deutschland*. Brussels, ABB extra number 18, vol. 3, *Niederlande*, forthcoming.
Lentes, T., 1993, 'Die Gewänder der Heiligen. Ein Diskussionsbeitrag zum Verhältnis von Gebet, Bild und Imagination', in G. Kerscher (ed.), *Hagiographie und Kunst. Der Heiligenkult in Schrift, Bild und Architektur*, Berlin, 120–51.
[de Leu, J. B.], 1885, 'De origine monasterii Viridisvallis una cum vitis B.

Joannes Rusbrochi primi prioris hujus monasterii et aliquot coætaneorum ejus', in *Analecta Bollandiana* 4, 257–334.

Lewis, G. Jaron, 1991, 'Die Verfasserinnen der Schwesternbücher des 14. Jahrhunderts', in *Begegnungen mit dem 'Fremden'. Grenzen – Traditionen – Vergleiche'. Akten des VIII. Internationalen Germanisten-Kongress, Tokyo 1990*, Munich, 201–11.

―― 1996, *By Women, for Women, about Women. The Sister-Books of Fourteenth-Century Germany*, [Toronto], Studies and Texts 125.

――, F. Willaert and M.-J. Govers, 1989, *Bibliographie zur deutschen Frauenmystik des Mittelalters. Mit einem Anhang zur Beatrijs van Nazareth und Hadewijch*, Berlin.

Lieftinck, G. I., 1936, *De Middelnederlandsche Tauler-handschriften*, Groningen.

―― 1964, *Manuscrits datés dans les Pays-Bas / Catalogue paléographique des manuscrits en écriture latine portant des indications de date*, vol. 1, *Les Manuscrits d'origine étrangère (816–c.1550)*, Amsterdam.

Liesen, B., 1891, *Zur Klostergeschichte Emmerichs bei Beginn des XVI. Jahrhunderts. Beilage zum Osterprogramm des Königlichen Gymnasiums zu Emmerich*, 435, Emmerich.

Lievens, R., 1958a, *Jordanus van Quedlinburg in de Nederlanden. Een onderzoek van de handschriften*, Ghent, Koninklijke Vlaamse Academie voor Taal- en Letterkunde Reeks 6, 82.

―― 1958b, 'Alijt Bake van Utrecht (1415–55)', *NAKG* 42, 127–51.

Lingier, C., 1993, 'Boekengebruik in vrouwenkloosters onder invloed van de Moderne Devotie', in T. Mertens *et al.*, 280–94 and 454–66.

Liturgisch woordenboek, 1965–8, 2 vols., Roermond.

Liturgische handschriften uit de Koninklijke Bibliotheek. Middeleeuws manuscripten voor religieus gebruik, 1983, Tentoonstellingcatalogus, The Hague.

Löffler, K., 1930, *Quellen zur Geschichte des Augustinerchorherrenstifts Frenswegen (Windesheimer Kongregation)*. Soest, Veröffentlichungen der Historischen Kommission des Provinzialinstitutes für Westfälische Landes- und Volkskunde.

Lourdaux, W., 1974, 'Het boekenbezit en het boekengebruik bij de Moderne Devoten', in *Studies over het boekenbezit en boekengebruik in de Nederlanden vóór 1600*, Brussels, ABB extra number 11, 247–325.

―― and E. Persoons, 1964, 'De statuten van de Windesheimse mannenkloosters in handschrift en druk', *AGKKN* 6, 18–224.

―――― 1968, *Petri Trudonensis "Catalogus scriptorum Windeshemensium"*, Leuven, Universiteit te Leuven. Publicaties op het gebied van de geschiedenis en de filologie, 5th series 3.

Mahieu, J. (ed. and trans.), 1941, *Gerard Zerbolt van Zutphen, 'Van geestelijke opklimmingen'*, Brugge.

Mak, J. J., 1935, 'Christus bij de Moderne Devotie', *OGE* 9, 105–66.

de Man, D., 1919, *Hier beginnen sommige stichtige punten van onsen oelden zusteren. Naar het te Arnhem berustende handschrift uitgegeven*, The Hague.

—— 1926, 'Vervolgingen, welke de Broeders en Zusters des gemenen Levens te verduren hadden', *Bijdragen voor de vaderlandsche geschiedenis en oudheidkunde* 6th series 4, 283–95.

—— 1937, 'Uit twee Middelnederlandse handschriften', *AGAU* 61, 559–69.

Sr Marie Josepha: see G. G. Wilbrink.

Martimort, A. G., 1991, *Les 'Ordines', les ordinaires et les cérémoniaux*, Turnhout, Typologie des sources du Moyen Âge occidental 56.

—— 1992, *Les Lectures liturgiques et leurs livres*, Turnhout, Typologie des sources du Moyen Âge occidental 64.

Martin, H., 1885–99, *Catalogue des manuscrits de la Bibliothèque de l'Arsenal*, 11 vols., Paris, Cataloque général des manuscrits des bibliothèques publiques de France.

McGinn, B., 1991–8, *The Presence of God. A History of Western Christian Mysticism*, New York: vol. 1, *The Foundations of Mysticism. Origins to the Fifth Century*, 1991; vol. 2, *The Growth of Mysticism. Gregory the Great throughout the Twelfth Century*, 1994; vol. 3, *The Flowering of Mysticism. Men and Women in the New Mysticism – 1200–1350*, 1998.

Meertens, M., 1931, *De godsvrucht in de Nederlanden naar handschriften van gebedenboeken der XVe eeuw*, vol. 2, *Lijdensdevoties*, [n.p.], Historische bibliotheek van godsdienstwetenschappen.

Meinsma, K. O., 1902, *Middeleeuwsche bibliotheken*, Amsterdam.

Menhardt, H., 1961, *Verzeichnis der altdeutschen literarischen Handschriften der Österreichische Nationalbibliothek*, vol. 3. Berlin, Deutsche Akademie der Wissenschaften zu Berlin. Veröffentlichungen des Instituts für deutsche Sprache und Literatur 13.

Mertens, T. F. C., 1986, *Hendrik Mande (?–1431). Teksthistorische en literairhistorische studies*, Nijmegen.

Mertens, T., 1987, Review of R. T. M. van Dijk, *De constituties der Windesheimse vrouwenkloosters vóór 1559. Bijdrage tot de institutionele geschiedenis van het Kapittel van Windesheim*, Nijmegen, 1986, *OGE* 61, 284–6.

—— 1988, 'Rapiarium', in *DS* 13, 114–19.

—— 1989a, 'Lezen met de pen. Ontwikkelingen in het laatmiddeleeuws geestelijk proza', in F. P. van Oostrom and F. Willaert (eds.), *De studie van de Middelnederlandse letterkunde: Stand en toekomst*, Hilversum, 187–200.

—— 1989b, 'Hendrik Mande als visionair', *Millennium* 3, 106–14.

—— 1989c, 'Geestelijke testamenten in de laatmiddeleeuwse Nederlanden. Een verkenning van het genre', in G. R. W. Dibbets and P. W. M. Wackers (eds.), *'Wat duikers vent is dit!' Opstellen voor W. H. M. Hummelen*, Wijhe, 75–89.

—— 1989d, *Preken met de pen en lezen met de pen. Moderne Devotie en geestelijke literatuur*, Deventer.

—— 1990, 'Epistolaire aspecten van Ruusbroecs Brieven', *OGE* 64, 53–69. (Also in Cockx-Indestege, Deschamps, Hendrickx *et al.* 1990, 353–69.)

—— 1991, 'De geestelijke literatuur tussen theologie en filologie', in F. P. van

Oostrom et al., *Misselike tonghe. De Middelnederlandse letterkunde in interdisciplinair verband*. Amsterdam, NLCM 5, 130–41 and 218–24.

—— (ed.), 1992, *Vrouwen en mystiek in de Nederlanden (12de–16de eeuw). Lezingen van het congres 'Van Hadewijch tot Maria Petyt', Antwerpen, 5–7 september 1989*, Antwerp, OGE 66, nos. 1–2.

—— 1993, 'Boeken voor de eeuwigheid. Ter inleiding', in T. Mertens et al., 8–35 and 361–72.

—— 1994a, 'The Devotio Moderna and innovation in Middle Dutch literature', in E. Kooper (ed.), *Middle Dutch Literature in Its European Context*, Cambridge, Cambridge Studies in Medieval Literature, 226–43.

—— 1994b, 'Texte der modernen Devoten als Mittler zwischen kirchlicher und persönlicher Reform', in *Niederdeutsches Wort* 34, 63–74.

—— (ed.), 1995a, *'Siet de brudegom comt'. Facetten van 'Die geestelike brulocht' van Jan van Ruusbroec (1293–1381)*, Kampen.

—— 1995b, 'Mystieke cultuur en literatuur in de late middeleeuwen', in F. van Oostrom, J. Goossens, P. Wackers et al., *Grote lijnen. Syntheses over Middelnederlandse letterkunde*, Amsterdam, NLCM 9, 117–35 and 205–17.

—— 1996a, 'De "Apocalyps" van Hendrik Mande', in K. Porteman, W. Verbeke and F. Willaert (eds.), *Tegendraads genot. Opstellen over de kwaliteit van middeleeuwse teksten*, Leuven, 131–8.

—— 1996b, 'Postuum auteurschap. De collaties van Johannes Brinckerinck', in A. J. Hendrikman, P. Bange, R. T.M. van Dijk et al. (eds.), *Windesheim 1395–1995. Kloosters, teksten, invloeden*, Nijmegen, MSt 12, 85–97.

—— 1996c, 'Collatio und Codex im Bereich der Devotio Moderna', in C. Meier, D. Hüpfer and H. Keller (eds.), *Der Codex im Gebrauch*, Münster, Münstersche Mittelalter-Schriften 70, 163–82.

—— 2002a, 'Het Diepenveense zusterboek als exponent van gemeenschapstichtende kloosterliteratuur', in W. Scheepsma (ed.), *Het ootmoedig fundament van Diepenveen. Zeshonderd jaar Maria en Sint-Agnesklooster 1400–2000*, [n.p.], 77–94.

—— 2002b, 'Middelnederduitse exempelen over verschijningen te Diepenveen', *OGE* 76, 99–115.

—— (in press), 'Ein Prediger in zweifacher Ausführung. Die Kollationen des Claus von Euskirchen', in V. Mertens, H.-J. Schiewer and W. Schneider-Lastin, *Predigt im Kontext. Internationales Symposion am Fachbereich Germanistik der Freien Universität Berlin. vom. 5.–8. Dezember 1996*.

—— et al., 1993, *Boeken voor de eeuwigheid. Middelnederlands geestelijk proza*, Amsterdam, NLCM 8.

Mertens, V., 1979, 'Verslegende und Prosalegendar. Zur Prosafassung von Legendenromanen in "Der Heiligen Leben" ', in V. Honemann, K. Ruh, B. Schnell et al., *Poesie und Gebrauchsliteratur im deutschen Mittelalter*, Tübingen, 265–89.

Meuthen, E., 1982, *Nikolaus von Kues 1401–64. Skizze einer Biographie*, 5th edn, Münster, Buchreihe der Cusanus-Gesellschaft.

Meyer, R., 1995, *Das 'St. Katharinentaler Schwesternbuch'. Untersuchung, Edition, Kommentar*, Tübingen, MTU 104.
Mieth, D., 1986, *Meister Eckhart. Einheit im Sein und Wirken*, Munich, Serie Piper 523.
van Mingroot, E., 1984a, 'Prieuré de Ten Walle à Elsegem', in *MB* VII–4, 677–730.
—— 1984b, 'Prieuré de Galilée à Gand', in *MB* VII–4, 761–94.
Miquel, P., and M. Dupuy, 1990, 'Silence', in *DS* 14, 829–59.
Moderne Devotie. Figuren en facetten, 1984, Nijmegen.
Mol, J. A., 1992, 'De grauwe begijnen van Leeuwarden', *Leeuwarder historische reeks* 3, 61–106.
Moll, W., 1854, *Johannes Brugman en het godsdienstig leven onzer vaderen in de vijftiende eeuw, grootendeels volgens handschriften geschetst*, 2 vols., Amsterdam.
—— 1866a, 'Johannes Brinckerinck. Acht collatiën', *Kerkhistorisch archief* 4, 99–167.
—— 1866b, 'De boekerij van het St. Barbara-klooster te Delft in de tweede helft der vijftiende eeuw. Eene bijdrage tot de geschiedenis der middeneeuwsche letterkunde in Nederland', *Kerkhistorisch archief* 4, 209–85.
—— 1864–71, *Kerkgeschiedenis van Nederland vóór de Hervorming*, 2 vols., Arnhem and Utrecht.
Mulder, W., 1933, *Gerardi Magni Epistolae*, Antwerp, Textual publications of *OGE* 3.
Mulder-Bakker, A., 1987, 'Heilige maagden aan de Maas', in B. Ebels-Hoving, C. G. Santing and C. P. H. M. Tilmans, *Genoechlicke ende lustige historiën. Laatmiddeleeuwse geschiedschrijving in Nederland*. Hilversum, MStB 4, 121–39.
—— 1995, 'The Reclusorium as an Informal Centre of Learning', in J. W. Drijver and A. A. MacDonald (eds.), *Centres of Learning. Learning and Location in Pre-Modern Europe and the Near East*, Leiden, 245–54.
—— 1996, 'Lame Margaret of Magdeburg. The Social Function of a Medieval Recluse', *Journal of Medieval History* 22, 155–69.
Nauwelaerts, N., 1980, 'Scholen en onderwijs', in *Algemene geschiedenis der Nederlanden*, vol. 4, *Middeleeuwen*, Haarlem, 366–71.
Nichols, J. A., and L. Thomas Shank (eds.), 1995, *Hidden Springs. Cistercian Monastic Women. Medieval Religious Women 3*, 2 vols., [n.p.], Cistercian Studies Series 113.
Nijsten, G., 1989, ' "Vanden gestant des Heiligen Landes". Op zoek naar een vijftiende-eeuwse auteur en zijn publiek', in P. Bange and P. M. J. C. De Kort, *'Die fonteyn der ewiger wijsheit'. Opstellen aangeboden aan prof.dr. A. G. Weiler ter gelegenheid van zijn 25-jarig jubileum als hoogleraar Algemene en Vaderlandse Geschiedenis van de Middeleeuwen aan de Katholieke Universiteit Niemegen*, Nijmegen, MSt 5, 82–96.

—— 1992, *Het hof van Gelre. Cultuur ten tijde van de hertogen uit het Gulikse en Egmondse huis (1371–1473)*, [Kampen].

Nübel, O., 1970, *Mittelalterliche Beginen- und Sozialsiedlungen in den niederlanden. Ein Beitrag zur Vorgeschichte der Fuggerei*, Tübingen, Schwäbische Forschungsgemeinschaft bei der Kommission für bayerische Landesgeschichte 4–14 / Studien zur Fuggergeschichte 23.

Nuyttens, M., 1978, 'Couvent de Sion à Courtrai', in *MB* III–4, 1179–90.

—— 1984, 'Prieuré de Sainte-Marguerite dit Bethléem à Deinze, puis à Gand', in *MB* VII–4, 845–58.

Obbema, P. F. J., 1985, 'Brinckerinck en Jan van Schoonhoven', in C. De Backer, A. J. Geurts and A. G. Weiler (eds.), *Codex in context. Studies over codicologie, kartuizergeschiedenis en laatmiddeleeuws geestesleven, aangeboden aan Prof. Dr. A. Gruijs*, Grave, Nijmeegse codicologische cahiers 4–6, 277–88.

—— 1996, *De middeleeuwen in handen. Over de boekcultuur in de late middeleeuwen*, Hilversum.

Ochsenbein, P., 1992, 'Latein und Deutsch im Alltag oberrheinischer Dominikanerinnenklöster des Spätmittelalters', in N. Henkel and N. Palmer, *Latein und Volkssprache im deutschen Mittelalter 1100–1500. Regensburger Colloquium 1988*, Tübingen, 42–51.

Oosterman, J. B., 1993, 'Om de grote kracht der woorden. Middelnederlandse gebeden en rubrieken in het Brugge van de vroege vijftiende eeuw', in T. Mertens *et al.*, 230–44 and 437–44.

—— 1995, *De gratie van het gebed. Overlevering en functie van Middelnederlandse berijmde gebeden*, vol. 1, *Studie*, vol. 2, *Repertorium*, Amsterdam, NLCM 12.

van Oostrom, F. P., 1985, 'Schetskaart of geschiedverhaal? Over methode en praktijk van (een) geschiedenis van de Middelnederlandse letterkunde', in A. M. J. van Buuren, H. van Dijk, O. S. H. Lie and F. P. van Oostrom (eds.), *Tussentijds. Bundel studies aangeboden aan W. P. Gerritsen ter gelegenheid van zijn vijftigste verjaardag*, Utrecht, 198–216.

—— *et al.*, 1987, 'Dirc van Delft en zijn lezers', in W. van den Berg and J. Stouten (eds.), *Het woord aan de lezer. Zeven literatuurhistorische verkenningen*, Groningen, 49–71.

Overvoorde, J. C., 1896, 'Het regularissen-klooster van Sint Agnes te Dordrecht', *Bijdragen voor de geschiedenis van het bisdom van Haarlem* 21, 49–86.

Palmer, N. F., 1982, '*Visio Tnugdali*'. *The German and Dutch Translations and Their Circulation in the Later Middle Ages*, Munich, MTU 76.

Paquay, V., 1990, 'De laatste Vrouwe van Breda op Huize Valkenbergh: Maria van Loon-Heinsberg (†1502)', *Jaarboek van de Geschied- en Oudheidkundige kring van Stad en Land van Breda 'De Oranjeboom'* 43, 135–206.

Peeters, G. J., 1968, *Frans Vervoort O.F.M. en zijn afhankelijkheid*, Ghent,

Koninklijke Vlaamse Academie voor Taal-en Letterkunde, 6th series – Bekroonde Werken – 99.

Peristiany, J. G. (ed.), 1966, *Honour and Shame. The Values of Mediterranean Society*, Chicago.

Persoons, E., 1976, 'Prieuré de Sainte-Agnes, à Maaseik', in *MB* VI, 283–91.

—— 1980, 'Lebensverhältnisse in den Frauenklöstern der Windesheimer Kongregation in Belgien und in den Niederlanden', in *Klösterliche Sachkultur des Spätmittelalters. Internationaler Kongress an der Donau 18. Bis 21. September 1978*, Wenen, Österreichische Akademie des Wissenschaften, phil.-hist. Klasse, Sitzungsberichte 367, 73–111.

—— 1984, 'De verspreiding der Moderne Devotie', in C. C. De Bruin, E. Persoons and A. G. Weiler, *Geert Grote en de Moderne Devotie*, Zutphen, 57–100.

—— 1993a, 'Prieuré de Korsendonk à Oud-Turnhout', in *MB* VIII–2, 459–74.

—— 1993b, 'Prieuré du Trône-Notre-Dame à Grobbendonk', in *MB* VIII–2, 479–90.

—— 1993c, 'Prieuré de Béthanie à Malines', in *MB* VIII–2, 521–33.

—— 1993d, 'Prieuré de Mariendaal à Anvers', in *MB* VIII–2, 563–79.

Peters, L., 1900, 'Den beginne des Cloesters Jerusalem, 1422, tot Venraij', *Limburg's Jaarboek voor geschiedenis, taal en kunst* 7–I, 260–90.

Peters, U., 1988, *Religiöse Erfahrung als literarisches Faktum. Zur Vorgeschichte und Genese frauenmystischer Texte des 13. und 14. Jahrhunderts*, Tübingen, Hermaea, Germanistische Forschungen n.s. 56.

Phillipart, G., 1977, *Les Légendiers latins et autres manuscrits hagiographiques*, Turnhout, Typologie des sources du Moyen Âge occidental 24–5.

Pohl, M., 1922, *Thomae Hemerken a Kempis opera omnia*, vol. 7, Freiburg im Breisgau.

Post, R. R., 1952, 'De statuten van het Mr. Geertshuis te Deventer', *AGAU* 71, 1–46.

—— 1954a, *Kerkelijke verhoudingen in Nederland vóór de Reformatie van ± 1500 tot ± 1580*, Utrecht.

—— 1954b, *Scholen en onderwijs in Nederland gedurende de Middeleeuwen*, Utrecht.

—— 1957, *Kerkgeschiedenis van Nederland in de Middeleeuwen*, 2 vols., Utrecht.

—— 1968, *The Modern Devotion. Confrontation with Reformation and Humanism*, Leiden, Studies in Medieval and Reformation Thought 3.

Prims, F., 1936, '48. Valkenbroek in de XVe eeuw', *Antwerpiensia* 10, 406–14.

—— 1944, *De kloosterslot-beweging in Brabant in de XVde eeuw*, Antwerp, Mededeelingen van de Koninklijke Vlaamsche Academie voor Wetenschappen, Letteren en Schoone Kunsten van België 6.

Raue, S., 1996, *Een nauwsluitend keurs. Aard en betekenis van 'Den triumphe ende 't palleersel van den vrouwen' (1514)*, [n.p.].

Rayez, A., 1974, 'Jean Cele', in *DS* 8, 326–7.

Rehm, G., 1985, *Die Schwestern vom gemeinsamen Leben in nordwestlichen*

Deutschland. Untersuchungen zur Geschichte der Devotio Moderna und des weiblichen Religiosentums, Berlin, BHS 11, Ordensstudien 5.

Ringler, S., 1980, *Viten- und Offenbarungsliteratur in Frauenklöstern des Mittelalters. Quellen und Studien*, Munich, MTU 72.

Romein, J., 1932, *Geschiedenis van de Noord-Nederlandsche geschiedschrijving. Bijdrage tot de beschavingsgeschiedenis*, Haarlem.

van Rooij, T. M. M., 1936, *Gerard Zerbolt van Zutphen*, I, *Leven en geschriften*, Nijmegen.

Roose, L., 1958, 'Het "Refreyn" van Jacomijne Costers', *Jaarboek de Fonteine 1948–9* [Ghent], 36–40.

Rousse, J., H. J. Sieben and A. Boland, 1976, 'Lectio divina et lecture spirituelle', in *DS* 9, 470–510.

Ruberg, U., 1978, *Beredtes Schweigen in lehrhafter und erzählender deutscher Literatur des Mittelalters. Mit kommentierter Erstedition spätmittelalterlicher Lehrtexte über das Schweigen*, Münster, Münstersche Mittelalters-Schriften 32.

Rudy, K. M., 2000a, 'Laat-middeleeuwse devotie tot de lichaamsdelen en bloedstortingen van Christus', in Veelenturf 2000, 111–33.

—— 2000b, 'Den aflaet der heiliger stat Jherusalem ende des berchs van Calvarien. Indulgenced Prayers for Mental Holy Land Pilgrimage in Manuscripts from the St. Agnes Convent in Maaseik', *OGE* 74, 211–54.

Ruf, P., 1939, *Mittelalterlicher Bibliothekskataloge Deutschlands und der Schweiz*, vol. III–3, *Bistum Bamberg*, Munich.

Ruh, K., 1956, *Bonaventura deutsch. Ein Beitrag zur deutschen Franziskanermystik und -scholastik*, Bern, Bibliotheca Germanica 7.

—— 1979, 'Geistliche Prosa', in W. Erzgräber (ed.), *Europäisches Spätmittelalter*, Wiesbaden, Neues Handbuch der Literaturwissenschaft 8, 565–605.

—— 1980, ' "Franziskanische Traktate" ', in *VL* 2, 845–7.

—— 1990–9, *Geschichte der abendländische Mystik*, Munich: vol. 1, *Die Grundlegung durch die Kirchenväter und die Mönchstheologie des 12. Jahrhunderts*, 1990; vol. 2, *Frauenmystik und Franziskanische Mystik der Frühzeit*, 1993; vol. 3, *Die Mystik des deutschen Predigerordens und ihre Grundlegung durch die Hochscholastik*, 1996; vol. 4 *Die niederländische Mystik des 14. Bis 16. Jahrhunderts*, 1999.

—— 1997, 'Die Schwesternbücher der Niederlande', *Zeitschrift für deutsches Altertum und deutsche Literatur* 126, 166–73.

Rüther, A., and H.-J. Schiewer, 1992, 'Die Predigthandschriften des Straßburger Dominikanerinnenklosters St. Nikolaus in undis. Historischer Bestand, Geschichte, Vergleich', in V. Mertens and H.-J. Schiewer (eds.), *Die deutsche Predigt im Mittelalter. Internationales Symposium am Fachbereich Germanistik der Freien Universität Berlin vom 3.–6. Oktober 1989*, Tübingen, 169–93.

Ryan, William Granger, 1995, *Jacobus de Voragine: The Golden Legend*, 2 vols., 5th printing, Princeton, NJ.
Saak, E. L., 1996, ' "Quilibet christianus": Saints in Society in the Sermons of Jordan of Quedlinburg, OESA', in B. M. Kienzle, E. Wilks Dolnikowski, R. Drage Hale, *et al.* (eds.), *Models of Holiness in Medieval Sermons. Proceedings of the International Symposium (Kalamazoo, 4–7 May 1995)*, Louvain-la-Neuve, Textes et études du Moyen Âge 5, 317–38.
Salmon, P., 1947, 'Le Silence religieux. Prâtique et théorie', in *Mélanges Bénédictins, publiés a l'occasion du XIVe centenaire de la mort de Saint Benoît par les moins de l'abbaye de Saint-Jerôme de Rome*, Wandrille, 11–57.
Scheepsma, W. F., 1992, 'Twee onuitgegeven traktaatjes van Alijt Bake', *OGE* 66, 145–67.
—— (trans.), 1993, *Hemels verlangen*, Amsterdam, Griffioen.
—— 1994, ' "Van die memorie der passien ons heren" van Alijt Bake', *OGE* 68, 106–28.
—— 1995a, ' "For hereby I hope to rouse some to piety". Books of Sisters from Convents and Sister-Houses Associated with the "Devotio Moderna" in the Low Countries', in L. Smith and J. H. M. Taylor (eds.), *Women, the Book and the Godly, Selected proceedings of the St Hilda's conference*, Cambridge, 1993, vol. 1, 27–40.
—— 1995b, 'De trechter en de spin. Metaforen voor mystiek leiderschap van Alijt Bake', *OGE* 69, 222–34.
—— 1996a, 'Verzamelt de overgebleven brokken, opdat niets verloren ga. Over Latijnse en Middelnederlandse levensbeschrijvingen uit de sfeer van de Moderne Devotie', in P. Wackers *et al.*, *Verraders en bruggenbouwers. Verkenningen naar de relatie tussen Latinitas en de Middelnederlandse letterkunde*, Amsterdam, NLCM 15, 211–38 and 334–46.
—— 1996b, 'Zusterboeken. Bijzondere bronnen voor de Moderne Devotie', in C. van Eijl, M. Everard, M. Hellevoort *et al.* (ed.), *Het zaad der middeleeuwen*, Amsterdam, Jaarboek voor vrouwengeschiedenis 16, 153–70.
—— 1996c, 'De helletocht van Jacomijne Costers (†1503)', *OGE* 70, 157–85.
—— 1997, *Deemoed en devotie. De koorvrouwen van Windesheim en hun geschriften*, Amsterdam, NLCM 17.
—— (ed.), 2002, *Het ootmoedig fundament van Diepenveen. Zeshonderd jaar Maria en Sint-Agneskloosster 1400–2000*, [n.p.].
—— 2003. 'Illustere voorbeelden. De invloed van de *Legenda aurea* op de geschriften van de koorvrouwen van Windesheim', in A. Berteloot, H. van Dijk and J. Hlatky (eds.), *'Een boec dat men te Latine heet Aurea Legenda'. Beiträge zur niederländischen Übersetzung der* Legenda aurea. Münster, Niederlande-Studien 31, 261–82.
—— (forthcoming) 'Alijt Bake (1415–55) und die deutschen Prediger des 14. Jahrhunderts', in V. Mertens, H.-J. Schiewer and W. Schneider-Lastin (eds.), *Predigt im Kontext. Internationales Symposium am Fachbereich*

Germanistik der Freien Universität Berlin vom 5.–8. Dezember 1996, Niemeyer, Tübingen.
—— (forthcoming 2) 'Mystical Networks in the Middle Ages? On the First Women Writers in Dutch and Their Literary Connections', in P. Broomans, S. van Dijk, J. F. van der Meulen and P. van Oostrum (eds.), *The Muse from Abroad*.
—— and J. J. T. M. Tersteeg, 1992, *Cartularium van O. L. Vrouweklooster te Renkum 1383–1609*, [Arnhem], Werken uitgegeven door 'Gelre', Vereeniging tot beoefening van Geldersche geschiedenis, oudheidkunde en recht 40.
Schiewer, H.-J., 1993, 'Die beiden Sankt Johannsen, ein dominkanischer Johannes-Libellus und das literarische Leben im Bodenseeraum um 1300', *Oxford German Studies* 22, 21–54.
Schmale, F.-J., 1985, *Funktion und Formen mittelalterlicher Geschichtschreibung. Eine Einführung*, Darmstadt.
Schmidt, M., 1993, 'An Example of Spiritual Friendship. The Correspondence between Heinrich of Nördlingen and Margaretha Ebner', in U. Wiethaus (ed.), *Maps of Flesh and Light. Religious Experience of Medieval Women Mystics*, Syracuse (New York), 74–92.
Schmitz, P., 1953, 'Châpitre des coulpes', in *DS* 2, 483–8.
Schneider, K., 1983, 'Die Bibliothek des Katharinenklosters in Nürnberg und die städtische Gesellschaft', in B. Moeller, H. Patze and K. Stackmann (eds.), *Studien zum städtischen Bildungswesen des späten Mittelalters und der frühen Neuzeit. Bericht über Kolloquien der Kommission zur Erforschung der Kultur des Spätmittelalters 1978 bis 1981*, Göttingen, Abhandlungen der Akademie der Wissenschaft in Göttingen. Philologisch-historische Klasse 3–137, 70–82.
—— and H. Zirnbauer, 1965, *Die Handschriften der Stadtbibliothek Nürnberg*, vol. 1, *Die deutschen mittelalterlichen Handschriften*, Wiesbaden.
Schoengen, M., 1941, *Monasticon Batavum*, vol. 1, *De Augustijnsche orden, benevens de broeders en zusters van het gemene leven*, Amsterdam, Verhandelingen der Nederlandsche Akademie van Wetenschappen, Afdeeling Letterkunde, nieuwe reeks 45.
Schreiner, K., 1992, 'Verschriftlichung als Faktor monastischer Reform. Funktionen von Schriftlichkeit im Ordenswesen des hohen und späten Mittelalters', in H. Keller, K. Grubmüller and N. Staubach (eds.), *Pragmatische Schriftlichkeit im Mittelalter. Erscheinungsformen und Entwicklungsstufen*, Münster, Münstersche Mittelalter-Schriften 65, 37–75.
Sherley-Price, L. (trans.), 1952, *The Imitation of Christ / Thomas a Kempis*, Harmondsworth and Baltimore.
van Simaey, C., 1984, 'Prieuré de Sainte-Barbe dit Joris Vrancx à Gand', in *MB* VII-4, 829–44.
van Slee, J. C., 1908, 'Het necrologium en cartularium van het convent der Reguliere kanunnikessen te Diepenveen', *AGAU* 33, 317–485.

Spaapen, B., 1966, 'Middeleeuwse Passiemystiek, II. De vier kruiswegen van Alijt Bake', *OGE* 40, 5–64.

—— 1967a, 'Middeleeuwse Passiemystiek, III. De autobiografie van Alijt Bake', *OGE* 41, 209–301 and 321–50.

—— 1967b, 'Middeleeuwse Passiemystiek, IV. De brief uit de ballingschap', *OGE* 41, 351–67.

—— 1968a, 'Middeleeuwse Passiemystiek, V. De kloosteronderrichtingen van Alijt Bake, 1 De weg van de ezel', *OGE* 42, 5–32.

—— 1968b, 'Middeleeuwse Passiemystiek, V. De kloosteronderrichtingen van Alijt Bake, 2 De lessen van Palmzondag', *OGE* 42, 225–61.

—— 1968c, 'Middeleeuwse Passiemystiek, V. De kloosteronderrichtingen van Alijt Bake, 3 De louteringsnacht van de actie', *OGE* 42, 374–421.

—— 1969, 'Middeleeuwse Passiemystiek, V. De kloosteronderrichtingen van Alijt Bake, 4 De weg der victorie', *OGE* 43, 270–304.

Spitzen, O. A., 1875, 'Het leven der eerwaardige moeder Andries Yserens, overste van het Lammenhuis te Deventer, overleden in den jare 1502', *AGAU* 2, 178–216.

Staubach, N., 1991, 'Pragmatische Schriftlichkeit im Bereich der Devotio Moderna', *Frühmittelalterliche Studien* 25, 418–61.

—— 1994, 'Von der persönlichen Erfahrung zur Gemeinschaftsliteratur. Entstehungs- und Rezeptionsbedingungen geistlicher Reformtexte im Spätmittelalter', *OGE* 68, 200–28.

Steensma, R., 1970, *Het klooster Thabor bij Sneek en zijn nagelaten geschriften. Een inleiding en inventarisatie*, Leeuwarden.

Steer, G., 1985, 'Textgeschichtliche Edition', in K. Ruh (ed.), *Überlieferungsgeschichtliche Prosaforschung. Beiträge der Würzburger Forschungsgruppe zur Methode und Auswertung*, Tübingen, 37–52.

—— 1987a, 'Geistliche Prosa', in I. Glier (ed.), *Die deutsche Literatur im späten Mittelalter 1250–1370*, vol. 2, *Reimpaargedichte, Drama, Prosa*. Munich, Geschichte der deutschen Literatur von den Anfangen bis zur Gegenwart 3–2, 306–70.

—— 1987b, 'Merswin, Rulman', in *VL* 6, 420–42.

Stooker, K., and T. Verbeij, 1993, ' "Uut Profectus". Over de verspreiding van Middelnederlandse kloosterliteratuur aan de hand van de "Profectus religiosorum" van David van Augsburg', in T. Mertens *et al.*, 318–40 and 476–90.

—— 1997, *Collecties op orde. Middelnederlandse handschriften uit kloosters en semi-religieuze gemeenschappen in de Nederlanden*: vol. 1, *Studie*; vol. 2, *Repertorium*, Leuven, Miscellanea Neerlandica XVI.

Stracke, D. A., 1943, 'De origineele tekst der XV Pater Noster op het lijden des Heeren en diens latere lotgevallen', *OGE* 17, 71–140.

Strubbe, E. I., and L. Voet, 1960, *De chronologie van de middeleeuwen tot de moderne tijden*, Antwerp.

Stutvoet-Joanknecht, C. M., 1990, *'Der byen boeck'. De Middelnederlandse vertalingen van 'Bonum universale de apibus' van Thomas van Cantimpré en hun achtergrond*, Amsterdam.

Tiecke, J. G. J., 1941, *De werken van Geert Grote*, Utrecht.

Tummers, H., Review of J. E. Ziegler, 1995, 'Sculpture of Compassion: The Pietà and the Beguines in the Southern Low Countries c.1300–c.1600', *Millennium* 9, 75–8.

Ubbink, R. A., 1978, *De receptie van meister Eckhart in de Nederlanden gedurende de Middeleeuwen*, Amsterdam.

—— 1985, 'Meister Eckhart bij de Moderne Devotie', *OGE* 59, 154–71. (Also in Andriessen, Bange and Weiler 1985, 42–59.)

Vandenbroeck, P. (ed.), 1994a, *Hooglied. De beeldwereld van religieuze vrouwen in de Zuidelijke Nederlanden, vanaf de dertiende eeuw*, with contributions by L. Irigaray, B. Pelzer and J. Kristeva, Brussels.

—— 1994b, ' "Dit raken van mij die onraakbaar ben . . ." ', in P. Vandenbroeck (ed.), *Hooglied. De beeldwereld van religieuze vrouwen in de Zuidelijke Nederlanden, vanaf de 13de eeuw*, Brussels, 15–155.

Vanhoof, F., 1993, 'Prieuré de Vredenberg à Lierre', in *MB* VIII–2, 665–72.

Veelenturf, K. (ed.), 2000, *Geen povere schoonheid. Laat-middeleeuwse kunst in verband met de Moderne Devotie*, Nijmegen.

van der Veen, J., 1976, 'Het Diepenveense manuscript supplement 198 van de Athenaeumbibliotheek te Deventer', in *Verslagen en mededelingen van de vereeniging tot beoefening van Overijsselsch regt en geschiedenis* 91, 28–42.

van de Ven, J., 1990, *Handschriften en handschriftfragmenten in het bezit van de Theologische Faculteit Tilburg*, [Tilburg].

Verdeyen, P., 1981, 'De Middelnederlandse vertaling van Pomerius' werk "De origine monasterii Viridisvallis" ', *OGE* 55, 105–65.

—— 1994, *Ruusbroec and His Mysticism*, Collegeville, Minnesota, The Way of the Christian Mystics.

Verdeyen, R., and J. Endepols, 1914–17, *'Tondalus' visioen' en 'St. Patricius' vagevuur'*, 2 vols., Ghent, Koninklijke Vlaamsche Academie voor Taal- en Letterkunde (series 3–20).

Verheijen, L., 1967, *La Règle de Saint Augustin*, vol. 1, *Tradition manuscrite*, pt 2, *Recherches historiques*, Paris, Études augustiniennes (23–1 and 2).

Verschueren, L., 1949, 'Handschriften afkomstig uit het klooster Jerusalem te Venray', in *Miscellanea Mgr. Dr. P. J. M. van Gils* (= *Jaarboek van Limburgs Geschied- en Oudheidkundig Genootschap* 85), 693–730.

Völker, L., 1972, ' "Gelassenheit". Zur Entstehung des Wortes in der Sprache Meister Eckharts und seiner Überlieferung in der nacheckhartischen Mystik bis Jacob Böhme', in F. Hundsnurscher and U. Müller (eds.), *'Getempert und Gemischet'. Festschrift für Wolfgang Mohr*, Göppingen, Göppinger Arbeiten zur Germanistik 65, 281–312.

de Vooys, C. G. N., 1903, 'De Dietse tekst van Hendrik Mande's "Apocalipsis" ', *NAKG* 2, 78–97.

de Vreese, W., 1898, ' "Van swighen". Eene collatie van Johannes Brinckerinck', *Het Belfort* 13, 231–5.

Waaijman, K, 2000, 'Beeld en beeldloosheid; een uitdaging aan de devotie', in Veelenturf 2000, 43–66.

van der Wansem, C., 1958, *Het ontstaan en de geschiedenis der Broederschap van het Gemene Leven tot 1400*, Leuven, Universiteit te Leuven. Publicaties op het gebied der geschiedenis en der philologie IV–12.

Warnar, G., 1995, *Het "Ridderboec". Over Middelnederlandse literatuur en lekenvroomheid*, Amsterdam, NLCM 10.

—— *Ruusbroec.Literatuur en mystiek in de veertiende eeuw*, Amsterdam, 2003.

Wehrli-Johns, M., 1990, Review of U. Peters, *Religiöse Erfahrung als literarisches Faktum. Zur Vorgeschichte und Genese frauenmystischer Texte des 13. und 14. Jahrhunderts*, Tübingen, 1988, in *Beiträge zur Geschichte der deutschen Sprache und Literatur* 112, 326–32.

—— 1995, 'Das Selbstverständnis des Predigerordens im Graduale von Katharinenthal. Ein Beitrag zur Deutung der Christus-Johannes-Gruppe', in C. Brinker, U. Herzog, N. Largier et al. (eds.), *Contemplata aliis tradere. Studien zum Verhältnis von Literatur und Spiritualität*, Bern, 241–71.

Weiler, A. G. (trans.), 1984a, *'Getijden van de eeuwige wijsheid' naar de vertaling van Geert Grote*, Baarn.

—— 1984b, 'Recent Historiography on the Modern Devotion: Some Debated Questions', *AGKKN* 26, 161–79.

—— 1984c, 'Ervaring van onzekerheid in de late Middeleeuwen: twee wegen van Nederlandse spiritualiteit', *Speling* 36, 82–9.

—— 1985, 'De intrede van rijke weduwen en arme meisjes in leefgemeenschappen van de Moderne Devotie', *OGE* 59, 403–20. (Also in Andriessen, Bange and Weiler 1985, 293–308.)

—— 1992, 'De constructie van het zelf bij Geert Grote', in W. Verbeke (ed.), *Serta devota in memoriam Guillelmi Lourdaux*, vol. 1, *Devotio Windesemensis*, Leuven, Mediaevalia Lovaniensia I–20, 225–39.

—— 1995, 'Geert Grote en de begijnen in de begintijd van de Moderne Devotie', *OGE* 69, 114–32.

—— 1997, *Volgens de norm van de vroege kerk. De geschiedenis van de huizen van de broeders van het gemene leven in Nederland*, Nijmegen, MSt 13.

—— 2002, 'Het "Oetmoedighe fondament van Dyepenven" ', in W. Scheepsma (ed.), *Het ootmoedig fundament van Diepenveen. Zeshonderd jaar Maria en Sint-Agnesklooster 1400–2000*, [n.p], 113–28, 145–8 and 169–71.

Weinhold, K., 1880, *Lamprecht von Regensburg. 'Sanct Franciskus Leben' und 'Tochter Syon'*, Paderborn.

Weitlauff, M., 1981, 'Heinrich von Nördlingen', in *VL* 3, 845–52.

—— 1988, ' "Dein got redender munt machet mich redenlosz". Margaretha Ebner und Heinrich von Nördlingen', in P. Dinzelbacher and D. Bauer (eds.), *Religiöse Frauenbewegung im Mittelalter*, Cologne, 303–52.

Wierda, L., with I. Kok, 2000, *Middeleeuwse handschriften uit het klooster Diepenveen. Catalogus*, Deventer.
van de Wijnpersse, A. G. M., 1926, *De Dietse vertaling van Suso's 'Horologium aeternae sapientiae'*, Groningen.
Wilbrink, G. G., 1930, *Das geistliche Lied der Devotio Moderna. Ein Spiegel niederländisch-deutscher Beziehungen*, Nijmegen.
―― 1939, 'De schrijfster van het Diepenveense Hs. D', in *Album philologum voor Theodor Baader*, [Nijmegen], 157–71.
Willaert, F., M. M. Kors and H. Vekeman, 1992, 'De betekenis van de Nederlandse en vooral Brabantse mystiek voor de Europese spiritualiteit', *Trajecta* 1, 5–32.
Willems, J. F., 1842, 'Josina des Planques. Vlaemsche dichteresse', in: *Belgisch museum voor de Nederduitsche tael- en letterkunde en de geschiedenis des vaderlands* 9, 183–6.
Willeumier-Schalij, J. M., 1981, 'Ruusbroec's werk in het middeleeuwse tijdsbeeld', *OGE* 55, 298–393.
―― 1990, 'Middelnederlandse mystiek rond 1500: troost in gelatenheid', *OGE* 64, 227–53. (Also in Cockx-Indestege, Deschamps, Hendrickx *et al.* 1990, 527–53.)
Williams-Krapp, W., 1976, 'Studien zu "Der Heiligen Leben"', *Zeitschrift für deutsches Altertum und deutsche Literatur* 105, 274–303.
―― 1981, 'German and Dutch Legendaries of the Middle Ages: A Survey', in H. Bekker-Nielsen, P. Foote, J. H. Jørgensen *et al.*, *Hagiography and Medieval Literature. A Symposium*, Odense, 66–75.
―― 1986, *Die deutschen und niederländischen Legendare des Mittelalters. Studien zu ihrer Überlieferungs-, Text- und Wirkungsgeschichte*, Tübingen, Texte und Textgeschichte, Würzburger Forschungen 20.
―― 1986–7, 'Ordensreform und Literatur im 15. Jahrhundert', *Jahrbuch der Oskar von Wolkenstein Gesellschaft* 4, 41–51.
―― 1990, '"Dise ding sind noch nit ware zeichen". Zur Bewertung mystischer Erfahrungen in 15. Jahrhundert', *Zeitschrift für Literaturwissenschaft und Linguistik* 80, 61–71.
―― 1993, 'Frauenmystik und Ordensreform im 15. Jahrhundert', in J. Heinzle (ed.), *Literarische Interessenbildung im Mittelalter. DFG-Symposion 1991*, Stuttgart, 301–13.
―― 1995, 'Observanzbewegungen, monastische Spiritualität und geistliche Literatur im 15. Jahrhundert', *Internationales Archiv für Sozialgeschichte der deutschen Literatur* 20, 1–15.
van Woerkum, M., 1951, 'Het libellus "Omnes, inquit, artes" een *rapiarium* van Florentius Radewijns', *OGE* 25, 113–58 and 225–68.
―― 1955, 'Enige opmerkingen aangaande de methodische meditatie bij Moderne Devoten', *OGE* 29, 222–7.
Wolfs, S. P., 1985a, 'De Utrechtse wijbisschop Hubertus Schenck OP,

geestverwant van Geert Grote, en de eerste jaren van het dominicanessenklooster in Wijk bij Duurstede', *AGKKN* 27, 88–103.

—— 1985b, 'Moderne devoten en de dominicaanse observantiebeweging', *OGE* 59, 370–82. (Also in Andriessen, Bange and Weiler 1985, 259–70.)

Worstbrock, F. J., 1985, 'Konrad von Eberbach', in *VL* 5, 156–9.

van der Woude, S., 1947, *Johannes Busch. Windesheimer kloosterreformator en kroniekschrijver*, Edam.

—— 1949, 'Het calendarium van Windesheim', in *Huldeboek pater dr. Bonaventura Kruitwagen O.F.M. Aangeboden op Sint Bonaventura 14 juli 1949 ter gelegenheid van zijn gouden priesterfeest en zijn vijfenzeventigste verjaardag*, The Hague, 465–81.

—— 1953, *'Acta Capituli Windeshemense'. Acta van de kapittelvergaderingen der Congregatie van Windesheim*, The Hague, Kerkhistorische studiën 6.

Ypma, E., 1949, *Het Generaal Kapittel van Sion. Zijn oorsprong, ontwikkeling en inrichting*, Nijmegen.

Ziegler, J. E., 1992, *Sculpture of compassion: the Pietà and the Beguines in the Southern Low Countries c.1300–c.1600*, Brussels, Belgisch Historisch Instituut te Rome, Studies over Kunstgeschiedenis 6.

Zieleman, G. C., 1984, *De preek bij de moderne devoten*, Deventer.

Zumkeller, A., 1983, 'Jordan von Quedlinburg (Jordanus de Saxonia)', in *VL* 4, 853–61.

INDEX

Individuals are indexed by first (Christian) name, rather than surname.

Acco: 236
Acta Capituli Windeshemensis: 10 n. 37, 25 n. 93, 29 n. 104, 64 n. 50, 223
Adelhausen, *Schwesternbuch* of: 20 n. 74
Adriaen Mant: 68, 75 n. 107
Aechte Eernstes: 119, 120
Albert van den Beesten: 125 n. 66
Albertus Magnus: 151
Albrecht of Bavaria, count of Holland: 31
Aleid (sister of Brunnepe): 126, 127, 128
Alexander VI (pope): 101
Alijt Bake (see also: *Boeckxen vander passien / Een merkelike leeringhe*): 2, 17, 18 n. 66, 24, 25 , 26, 27, 28, 35, 86, 88, 90, 95, 98, 107, 194 n. 69, 197–226, 230, 240, 241, 242, 243
  Brief uit de ballingschap: 219, 220, 224
  Boeck der tribulatien, Dat: 216
  Lessen van Palmzondag, De: 211
  Louteringsnacht van de actie, De: 211, 212, 213
  Memorie der passien ons heren, Van die: 206, 208
  Mijn beghin ende voortganck: 25, 198, 199 n. 4, 200, 203, 205, 206, 208, 216, 217, 218, 219
  Ttrechter en de spin, De: 214, 223
  Vier kruiswegen, De: 201, 213, 226
  Weg der victorie, De: 211, 226
  Weg van de ezel, De: 211, 213
Alijt Bruuns: 79, 94, 103, 130
Alijt Comhaer: 138
Alijt Ooms: 156
Alijt Reijners: 140
Amsterdam: 7, 70
  convent of Mariënveld or Oude Nonnen: 12, 67 n. 63, 200 n. 8, 234
Angela van Zuylen: 171
Antwerp (see also: Facons): 47 n. 82, 171, 202, 210
Armgert van Lisse: 33 n. 10, 65, 76, 139, 149, 155 n. 74
Arnhem (see also: Marienborn): 10
  convent of Bethanië: 12, 69, 70, 166
  monastery of Monnikhuizen: 9, 157 n. 79
Arnold II, duke of Guelders: 32, 104
Augustina Baert: 216
Augustine: 72, 88, 179, 203, 233
  Epistola Augustini ad Cyrillum episcopum Hierosolymitanum de laude Jheronijmi: 88 n. 22
  Rule of, or *Praeceptum*: 8, 9, 10, 13, 14, 15, 30, 40, 50, 54, 63, 72, 93, 96, 111, 124, 182, 182, 224
Ave Maria: 81, 101, 104, 105, 109, 181, 183, 242
Ave Sonderlants: 15, 67, 119
Avignon: 4, 212

Barbara van Achterhout: 189
Barbara van den Dorpe: 169
Barbara van der Elst: 163
Barbare Speelberch: 48
Barberendaal, see: Tienen
Basel: 236
Bavaria: 235
Beatrijs van Nazareth: 20
Beatrix van der Beeck: 46, 66, 69 n. 79, 85, 105, 155, 156
Beernt Arborstier: 68, 75
Beerte Swijnkes: 237
Bede, Venerable: 72
Beguines: 3, 6, 7 n. 27, 12, 19, 80. 110 n. 99, 238
Belgium: 10, 12, 21
Belie van Düsseldorf: 120
Bernard (brother): 69
Bernard of Clairvaux: 20, 74 n. 103, 88, 118, 119, 150, 203, 233
Bernt van Dinslaken: 129
Berte van der List: 43
Bertha Jacobs: 26, 198
Berthold ten Hove: 9
Bertken, sister, see: Bertha Jacobs
Bethanië, see: Arnhem and Mechelen

INDEX

Boecken van den inwendighen gheestelike oefeninghe ende uutwendeghen lichameliken oefeninghen: 234, 235 n. 15

Boeckxen vander passien / Een merkelike leeringhe (see also: Alijt Bake): 213, 215, 218, 223 n. 86, 225, 226, 213 n. 54

Boeckxen van den inwendighen navolgen des levens ende des cruces ons heren: 226

Bonaventure: 20
 Meditationes vitae Christi: 101 n. 66
Bonn, convent of Engelendaal: 12
Book of Hours: 54, 94
Borken, convent of Mariënbrink: 114
Brabant: 23 n. 85, 34 n. 16, 151, 159, 173, 235, 236
Breviarium Windeshemense: 47 n. 82
Brielle, see: Rugge
Brothers of the Common Life: 7, 9, 46, 76, 80, 81 n. 131, 82
Brunnepe, convent of: 12, 37, 45, 107, 112, 125, 126, 127, 128
Brussels: 10, 107, 173
 convent of Jericho: 235
Burgundy: 163
Bursfeld, Congregation of: 11 n. 39

Caiaphas: 221
Catherine of Siena: 203, 212
Catharina Steeyncx : 64, 172
Cecilia van Marick: 79, 94, 130, 154, 156
Christianus Bloots, see: Kerstiaen van 's-Grevensande
Christina Mirabilis of St Truiden: 151
Christine Ebner: 236
Christine van Rijswijk: 33, 53, 167, 168
Christophorus Caers: 29, 171, 173, 174, 180 n. 29, 181 n. 33, 189, 234
 Naem- en doodtboeck: 29, 173, 190, 194 n. 67
 Register van het beginsel, voortganck ende gedenckweerdichste geschidenissen: 29, 172, 174, 202 n. 15
Clara 's Clercx: 161 n. 88
Clara Box: 173, 182
Clare of Assisi: 200, 203
Claus van Euskirchen: 129
Clemens van Sconenouwen: 120
Coesfeld, convent of Mariënbrink: 114
Coleta of Corbie: 200, 217
Cologne: 75 n. 105
 bishopric: 114

Chapter of: 13 n. 48
Constitutiones sanctimonialium ordinis Sanct Augustini Capituli Windeshemensis (CM): 28, 29 n. 108, 38, 47, 51, 62, 65, 73, 79, 84, 85, 86, 91, 96, 97, 111, 183, 202, 218, 233
Cornelius Beeke: 182 n. 35
Crayenstein: 143
Cusanus, see: Nicholas of Kues

David of Augsburg, *Profectus religiosorum*: 18, 21, 206, 234
Daya Dierkens: 34, 35 n. 17, 43 n. 63, 44, 145, 146
Deinze, convent of St Margaret: 224, 225
Delft, convent of St Barbara: 87, 89
Deliana Smolders: 162
Den Bosch: 7
 convent of Ten Orthen: 15
Deventer: 5, 6, 8, 125, 129, 130
 convent of Brandeshuis: 6
 convent of Buiskenshuis: 6, 129, 135 n. 2
 convent of Kerstekenshuis: 6
 convent of Lamme-van-Diezehuis: 6, 135 n. 2, 138
 convent of Meester-Geertshuis: 5, 6, 8, 80, 81 n. 132, 102, 113, 114, 117, 129, 130, 131, 135 n.2, 137, 139, 144, 146 n. 35, 152 n. 61, 153 n. 66, 170, 237
 Heer-Florenshuis: 6, 7, 22, 39 n. 40, 82 n. 137, 115, 125, 130, 131, 134, 137, 146 n. 33, 151 n. 57
Devote epistelen: 112, 120, 121, 122, 123, 125, 128, 239, 240
Diepenveen, convent of St Maria and St Agnes: *passim*
 sisterbook: 25, 26, 28, 29, 31, 35, 36, 39 n. 40, 40, 42 n. 57, 44, 50 n. 93, 51, 60, 66, 67, 71, 77, 87, 92, 94, 97, 102, 103, 104, 106, 110 n. 101, 113, 114, 124, 130, 132, 135, 136, 137 n. 5/n. 6, 139, 142, 145, 152, 153, 164, 165, 169, 222, 240, 241
Diessenhofen, convent of St Katharinental: 110 n. 99, 151 n. 56
Dikninge, convent of: 171, 182
Dionysius (the Areopagite): 203
Dirc van Delft, *Tafel van den kersten ghelove*: 103 n. 77
Dirc van Herxen, 'collatieboek' of: 82 n. 137

INDEX

Dirk Grave: 41, 126
Dit is van Magriete <b?>yen lee<r>inge: 188
Dominic Guzman: 2
Donaet (Donatus): 43
Dordrecht, convent of St Agnes: 12, 64, 69, 70
Dorstadt, convent of St Trinitatis: 12 n. 44
Dyliane Eernstes: 119
Dymme van Rijsen: 43 n. 58, 93 n. 42, 123 n. 58, 141

Eckhart, Meister: 19, 30, 89, 209 n. 40, 211, 212 n. 49, 236
Reden der Unterweisung: 89 n. 24
Eemstein, monastery of: 9, 10, 161, 162
Egbert van der Beeck: 39 n. 40
Egbert van Lingen: 144
Egypt: 117
Eldagsen, convent of: 140, 141
Elfsteyn, countess of: 161 n. 90
Elisabeth Kempfin: 137 n. 6
Elisabeth van Couwerven: 188, 189
Elisabeth van Daesdonck: 180 n. 29
Elisabeth van Naaldwijk: 33, 119, 170
Elsbeth Stagel: 89
Elsebe Hasenbroecks: 8, 32 n. 3, 36, 44, 45, 51, 54, 106, 138, 148, 149, 157, 158, 240 n. 25
Elseken van Steenren: 144
Elzegem, see: Ten Walle
Emmerich: 43 n. 58
  brotherhouse of St Gregory: 82 n. 137, 132 n. 87, 145
  convent of St Agnes: 135 n. 2, 152
Engelthal, convent of: 236
  Schwesternbuch of: 236
Epistola de vita et passione domini nostri Christi et aliis devotis exercitiis: 100, 101
Eugenius IV (pope): 11

Facons or Mariëndaal, convent of (Antwerp): 12, 24, 26, 28, 29, 45, 46, 54, 64, 68, 70, 75 n. 105, 107 n. 93, 108, 109, 110 n. 100, 171, 172, 174, 175, 177, 179, 181, 182, 183, 185, 187, 190, 191, 194, 196, 202, 219, 233, 237, 242, 243
Fenne Bickes: 44, 85
Fenne Godschalkes: 56

Fenne Stuermans: 60
Flanders, East: 224
Florens Radewijns: 6, 82 n. 137, 86, 90, 99 n. 60, 132 n. 87
Liber 'Omnes, inquit, artes': 117
Floris van Wevelinckhoven (bishop of Utrecht): 13
Francesco Petrarch: 17
De vita solitaria: 17 n. 64
Francis of Assisi: 2, 88, 151 n. 54, 203, 233
  Third Rule of: 12, 14
Frans Vervoort, *Bruygoms mantelken*: 226
Freckenhorst, convent of (near Münster): 43 n. 58, 167
Frederick (emperor): 161 n. 90
Frenswegen, convent of Mariënwolde: 114
  monastery of (Nordhorn): 114
Friesland: 65, 75
Fye van Galen: 43 n. 58
Fye van Marick: 154, 155 n. 74, 156

Gaesdonck, monastery of (Goch): 12, 237
Galilea, see: Ghent
Geert Grote: 5, 6, 9, 17, 18, 22, 34, 43, 54, 86, 113, 118, 122 n. 56, 131, 132 n. 87, 136, 146 n. 33, 228, 234
  Tractatus de quatuor generibus meditationum sive contemplationum: 110 n. 101
Geldern, convent of Nazareth: 74 n. 104
Gerard Leeu: 47 n. 82
Gerard of Frachet, *Vitae fratrum praedicatorum*: 151 n. 57
Gerard van Delft: 80
Gerard Zerbolt van Zutphen: 22, 23, 68, 81 n. 131, 85, 89, 99 n. 60, 122 n. 54, 147, 233
  Reformatione virium animae, De: 22 n. 84
  Spiritualibus ascensionibus, De: 22 n. 84
  (see also: *Super modo vivendi*)
Gerardus vanden Clooster: 48
Gerbergis Essink: 153 n. 69
Gerd Nyehof: 34
Gerlach Peters: 23, 68, 91, 231, 234
  Soliloquium: 83, 91
Gerlacus (cleric): 43
German: 11, 20 n. 72/n.73, 30, 32 n. 3, 43 n. 68, 75, 109, 140, 203
Germany: 5 n. 15, 7 n. 25, 10, 12, 13 n. 48, 21 n. 78, 30, 37 n. 36, 45 n. 73, 46 n.

273

INDEX

80, 105 n. 85, 114, 126, 134, 151, 167, 236, 237
Gert Velthuus: 34, 138 n. 7
Gertken Kocx van den Heveren: 69
Gertrud Boeckmans: 156
Gertrud Huginghes: 104, 105
Gertrud Monnickes: 53
Gertrud ten Voerde: 144
Gertrud ter Poorten: 67, 78 n. 118
Gertrud the Great: 20 n. 74, 195 n. 70
Gertrud van Rijsen: 141, 142, 190
Geseke (sister of Mariënberg, Helmstedt): 127
Gestant des heiligen landes, Vanden: 104
Ghent, convent of Bethlehem: 200
    convent of Galilea: 2, 12, 24, 25, 64, 75 n. 106, 88 n. 23, 197, 198, 199, 200, 201, 207, 208, 209, 210, 212, 214, 215, 217, 219, 222, 224, 225
    convent of St Agnes: 66 n. 57, 70 n, 85, 95, 235 n. 16
    convent of St Barbara: 224, 225
Gideon: 78, 81, 133
Gijsbert Dou: 12
Gijsel ter Aves: 156
Gisbertus Simoens: 182 n. 35
Gouda: 158
    convent of St Margaretha: 229 n. 3
Gregory the Great: 72
Griete Deghens: 103, 138 n. 8, 166
Griete des Vrien: 68 en n. 73, 69, 104 n. 82
Griete Essinchghes: 152, 153, 154, 155, 156, 158, 243
Griete Harbers: 78
Griete Koesters: 153, 158
Griete Koetgens: 104 n. 82, 110 n. 101
Griete Tasten: 103, 104
Griete ten Kolke: 103, 104, 140, 141 n. 18
Griete van Ahaus: 36 n. 26, 43 n. 58, 167, 168
Griete van Algeerden: 67, 68
Griete van Groenevelt: 120
Griete van Houdaen: 68
Griete van Naaldwijk: 31, 33, 41, 64, 65, 87, 97, 105, 106, 140 n. 17, 148
Griete Vromoeds: 69
Grobbendonk, see: Ten Troon
Groenendaal, monastery of: 10, 14, 22, 36, 89, 122 n. 56, 165, 199, 205, 219, 243
    Chapter of: 10
Groenlo: 113

Haarlem: 7
Hadewijch: 20, 27, 89, 203
Hail Mary, see: *Ave Maria*
Hattem, convent of Klaarwater: 200 n. 8
Heenvliet, Lady van: 31
Heiligen Leben, Der: 73
Heiningen, convent of St Petrus: 12 n. 44
Heinrich Seuse: 17 n. 63, 19, 30, 88, 89, 236
    Horologium aeternae sapientiae: 18, 54
Heinrich von Coesfeld: 134
Heinrich von Nördlingen: 236, 237
Helena (sister of Mariënberg, Helmstedt): 127
Helena van Bergen: 34 n. 11
Helfta, convent of: 20 n. 74
Helmstedt, convent of Mariënberg: 45, 112, 125, 126, 127, 128
Hendrik Mande: 8 n. 29, 23, 121, 122, 140 n. 17, 143, 231, 239
    Boecskijn van drien staten eens bekierden mensch, Een: 121, 122
    Spieghel der waerheit, Een: 122 n. 52
Hendrik Stappe: 5
Hendrik van Ahaus: 167 n. 103
Hendrik van Assel: 132
Hendrik van Bergen, bishop of Kamerijk / Cambrai: 34 n. 11, 171 n. 1
Hendrik van Loder: 114, 115, 239
Hendrik van Naaldwijk: 31, 143
Henricus Pomerius: 17 n. 63
    Origine monasterii Viridisvallis, De: 17 n. 63, 22 n. 83
Herent, monastery of: 11, 23 n. 85, 237
Herman Scoenbeke: 37 n. 34
Hermen Sticken: 113
Heylewich van Heenvliet: 119
Hic aliqua sequuntur ex vitisfratrum nostrorum: 82 n. 137, 133 n. 91
Hieronymus Bosch: 177
Hilbrandis Essink the older: 153 n. 69
Hilbrandis Essink the younger: 153 n. 69
Hildesheim: 125
Hille Sonderlants: 24, 25, 200, 202, 208 n. 36, 209, 215, 217, 225, 240
Hilwartshausen, convent of: 43 n. 68, 154 n. 72
Holland: 7 n. 25, 31, 42, 156 n. 77, 199
Holland, Chapter of: 13
Holy Land: 104
Hoog-Elten, convent of: 43 n. 58

Hoorn, see: Nieuwlicht
Hop (family): 69
Hours of the Virgin Mary: 53, 93, 168
Hubert van Lochem: 54
Hugo Goudsmit: 12

Ida (sister of Brunnepe): 126, 127, 128
Ijssel: 127
In quendam inordinate gradus ecclesiasticos et praedicationis officium affectantem: 81 n. 131
Innocent III: 2, 12
Innocent VIII: 171, 172

Jacob van Lichtenberg: 26
Jacob van Maerlant, *Wrake van Jerusalem*: 203
Jacoba of Bavaria: 199
Jacoba van Doenereyn: 80 n. 127, 169
Jacoba van Loon-van Heinsberg: 33, 95, 106, 107, 167, 168, 169
Jacobus de Voragine, *Legenda aurea*: 73, 74, 109 n. 98, 177, 234
  Sermoenen op die evangelien doer dat gehele jaer: 33 n. 9
Jacobus Isabeels: 216
Jacomijne Costers: 26–27, 28, 107 n. 93, 109, 110, 172, 173, 174, 175 n. 12, 178, 179, 180, 181, 182, 183, 184, 185, 187, 188, 208, 231, 238, 242
  Bereijdinghe tot het Heijlich Sacrament: 184
  Die op lanck leven stelt al sijn hopen: 187
  Drij beloften der religieusen, Vande: 185, 186
  O mijns herten lief eenich een: 186 n. 46
  Perfectie, Vande: 185, 186
  Previlesien van Sint Joannes Evangelist: 109, 110, 185, 186 n. 47, 204, 231
  Visioen en exempel: 172, 174, 175, 176, 177, 181, 182, 183, 184, 219 n. 73, 242
Jacques of Vitry: 236
Jan (Augustijns) van Peer: 163, 164 n. 95
Jan Bellens: 235
  Tractaet op den pater noster: 235
Jan Cele: 43
Jan Eggaert the older: 199
Jan Eggaert the younger: 199 n. 6, 201. 206, 224, 225, 241
Jan Gielis: 53
Jan Mombaer: 83 n. 2, 91, 107, 231

Rosetum exercitiorum spiritualium: 91, 108, 109
Jan Scutken: 23, 91, 101 n. 68
Jan van den Gronde: 5, 6
Jan van Leeuwen: 68, 89, 203, 205, 233
Jan van Luik (bishop): 167 n. 104
Jan van Naaldwijk: 241
Jan van Ruusbroec: 9, 10, 18, 22, 27, 89, 95, 106, 107, 203, 205, 206, 209, 219, 233, 239
  VII trappen, Van: 121 n. 50
  XII beghinen, Vanden: 107, 121 n. 50, 122
  Geestelike brulocht, Die: 121 n. 50, 124 n. 65, 209 n. 39
  Vier becoringhen, Vanden: 209 n. 39
Jan van Schoonhoven: 10, 89, 233, 234
  Letters to Eemstein: 68
  Ondersaten, Vanden: 116 n. 26
  Prelaten, Vanden: 116 n. 26
Janne van Diest: 165, 166
Janneke (sister of Facons): 54, 194, 196, 241
Jasper van Marburg: 129
Jean de Saint-Samson: 226
Jean Gerson: 10 n. 36
Jerome: 72, 203, 233
Jerusalem: 212
Jeruzalem, see: Utrecht
Joanna Dierix: 162
Joanna van Chaboth: 167, 168
Joanna vanden Hoede: 162
Johan de Waal: 113, 114
Johan van Delden: 157 n. 79
Johan Vos van Heusden: 23, 29, 100 n. 65, 114, 170 n. 118, 240
Johanna Eggaert: 199
Johanna Penninczac: 127
Johannes Brinckerinck: 1, 2, 6, 7, 8, 12, 24, 26, 31, 33, 34, 38, 39, 40, 46, 50 n. 93, 64, 77, 78, 79, 81, 82, 98, 112 n. 6, 113, 114, 118, 121, 122, 130, 132, 133, 134, 136, 137, 138, 146 n. 34, 147, 148, 152 n. 62, 153, 154, 181 n. 31, 231 n. 4, 232, 237, 239
  collations of: 82 n. 137, 97, 98 n. 54, 99, 112, 124, 129, 131, 133, 147 n. 39, 148 n. 48, 236, 237
Johannes Brugman: 96
  Speculum imperfectionis: 90, 91
Johannes Busch: 17 n. 63, 29, 37, 45, 52, 80, 83, 91, 100, 119, 120 n. 54, 125, 126, 128

Liber de origine Devotionis Modernae: 9 n. 34, 14 n. 42, 17 n. 63, 29 n. 106, 66 n. 61, 91
Liber de reformatione monasteriorum ordinum diversorum: 29, 125, 126 n. 69
Liber de viris illustribus: 29 n. 106
Johannes Mauburnus, see: Jan Mombaer
Johannes Meyer: 237
Johannes Ooms: 182
Johannes Tauler (see also: *Virginibus, De*): 19, 30, 75, 88, 89, 203, 206 n. 31, 209 n. 40, 211, 219, 226, 236
Johannes van Eyck: 182 n. 35, 233
Johannes van Warendorf: 75 n. 105
Johannes Veghe: 82 n. 138
John Cassian, *Collationes patrum*: 76
John Chrysostom: 72, 75 n. 105, 233
Joost Claesz: 31, 38, 39, 114
Jordan of Quedlinburg: 75 n. 106, 203, 211, 212, 213, 226
   Opus postillarum: 211
Jutte van Ahaus: 8, 9, 32 n. 3, 44 n. 64, 46, 47, 60, 64, 78, 81, 92, 94, 123 n. 58, 148, 167, 168, 169, 232
Jutte van Culemborg: 39 n. 40, 43 n. 58, 55, 56, 147, 153 n. 69, 156
Jutte van der Beeck: 60, 77

Kamerijk / Cambrai, bishopric of: 171 n. 1
Kampen (see also: Brunnepe): 126, 127
Katharina Holanders: 54 n. 15
Katharina Lippen: 67
Katharina Nots: 162
Katharina of Burgundy: 199
Katharina van Eppegheem: 162
Katharina van Gheldere: 220
Katharina van Giesen: 169 n. 113
Katharina van Naaldwijk: 31, 32, 33, 34, 35, 36, 39, 40, 41, 42, 43, 45, 55, 60, 64, 65, 85, 87, 88, 93, 94, 95, 97, 104, 119, 121, 124, 138, 139, 140 n. 17, 142, 143, 144, 147, 148, 158, 181 n. 31, 230, 231
Katharina van Rijsen: 101, 141, 231
Katharina von Unterlinden: 137 n. 6
Katherine Cauwericx: 95
Katrijne van Steenbergen: 144
Kerstiaen van 's-Grevensande or Christianus Bloots: 163, 164
Konrad von Eberbach, *Exordium magnum cisterciense*: 74 n. 103, 118, 150, 151 n. 54

Korsendonk, monastery (Oud-Turnhout): 14, 234, 237
Kortrijk, convent of Sion: 79 n. 124
Kroniek Bethanië, see: Mechelen
Kunegonda van Boxtel: 162 n. 92

Lambert (priest of Liège), *Life of St Agnes*: 19
Lamprecht of Regensburg: 237
   Tochter Syon: 235
Leiden, monastery of Hiëronymusdaal or Lopsen: 14, 21 n. 82
Leuven: 11
Libris teutonicalibus et de precibus vernaculis, De: 81 n. 131
Liège: 236
   bishop of: 54
   bishopric of: 15, 19
Liesbeth t'Overlaeck: 155 n. 74, 156
Liesbeth Tayen van Tiel: 160, 162, 165, 166, 167
Liesbeth van Arden: 53, 66, 156, 231 n. 4
Liesbeth van Bergen: 34 n. 11, 84 n. 6, 159, 160, 162, 171 n. 1
Liesbeth van Croenenborch: 162
Liesbeth van Delft or van Doesburg: 57 n. 27, 94, 120, 130, 133, 241
Liesbeth van Heenvliet: 44, 45, 64, 77, 78, 119, 138, 142, 143, 155 n. 74, 156
Liesbeth van Snellenberg: 144
Limborch, sisters of: 235
Lippstadt, sisters of: 114
Lopsen, see: Leiden
Lord's Prayer, see: Pater Noster
Low Countries (Northern): 5
Low Countries (Southern): 13 n. 48
Lubbe Snavels: 43, 44, 45, 67, 68, 85, 104 n. 80, 155
Lubbert Vyncke: 171, 172
Lübeck, convent of Sankt-Michaël: 14
Ludolf of Saxony, *Vita Jesu Christi*: 101 n. 66
Ludolf van Kampen: 140, 157
Lutgard van Buderick: 131
   vite of: 131, 153 n. 66
Lutgard van Tongeren: 151

Maaseik, convent of St Agnes: 74 n. 103, 87, 105
Maas-Rhine region: 3
Magdeburg, bishopric of: 37
Magnificat: 181

manuscripts:
  Anholt, Museum Wasserburg, Fürstlich Salm-Salm'sche Bibliothek, MS 45: 82 n. 137
  Arnhem, Openbare bibliotheek, 287: 69 n. 82
  Brussels, KB, 12.050–12.052 (1216): 75 n. 105
  Brussels, KB, 12.166 (3875): 74 n. 103, 151 n. 54
  Brussels, KB, 2283-4 (1167): 75 n. 105
  Brussels, KB, 643-4: 209 n. 40, 210, 211, 213, 214, 225, 226
  Brussels, KB, 8849–59 (manuscript B): 115, 133, 137, 158
  Brussels, KB, II 6644: 75 n. 106
  Brussels, KB, IV 50: 174 n. 6, 188
  Copenhagen, KB, Thott N 314^2 fol.: 234 n. 14
  Deventer, SAB, 113 B 8 KL: 108 n. 97
  Deventer, SAB, I, 12 (101 E 1): 101 n. 70, 153 n. 68
  Deventer, SAB, I, 13 (101 E 4): 101 n. 70
  Deventer, SAB, I, 23 (101 D 11): 144 n. 30
  Deventer, SAB, I, 33 (10 W 6): 74 n. 103
  Deventer, SAB, I, 35 (10 W 5): 75 n. 105, 88 n. 22
  Deventer, SAB, I, 43 (101 F 9): 74 n. 103
  Deventer, SAB, I, 46 (191 D 5): 74 n. 103
  Deventer, SAB, I, 49 (101 E 7): 68 n. 73
  Deventer, SAB, I, 50 (10 T 3): 68 n. 73
  Deventer, SAB, I, 55 (101 F 5): 68 n. 74
  Deventer, SAB, I, 57 (10 W 7): 88 n. 22
  Deventer, SAB, I, 61 (11 L 1): 82 n. 137
  Deventer, SAB, I, 71 (101 D 13): 75 n. 107
  Deventer, SAB, I, 72 (101 D 14): 75 n. 107
  Deventer, SAB, I, 73 (101 D 14): 75 n. 107
  Deventer, SAB, Suppl. 198 (101 E 26) (manuscript DV): 137, 138, 153, 154, 156, 157, 158, 170
  Deventer, SAB, Suppl. 208 (101 F 25) (manuscript G): 139, 144, 146 n. 35, 153 n. 66
  Düsseldorf, Heinrich Heine Archiv und UB, B 119: 132 n. 84
  Gaesdonck, Collegium Augustinianum, 15: 36 n. 27
  Ghent, UB, 3854: 216, 219
  Grubbenvorst, Ursulinen, archiefdepot Jerusalem (no shelfmark): 125 n. 66
  Grubbenvorst, Ursulinen, archiefdepot Jerusalem MS 11: 125 n. 66
  Hannover, Niedersächsischen Landesbibliothek, MS I 237: 141 n. 18
  London, Victoria and Albert Museum, George Reid MS 23: 67 n. 63
  Mechelen, Stadsarchief, EE XXIX/1: 159 n. 84
  Mechelen, Stadsarchief, S II,1: 36 n. 27
  Milan, Biblioteca Nazionale di Brera Gerli, MS 60: 69 n. 81
  Paris, Bibliothèque de l'Arsenal, 858: 101 n. 70
  The Hague, KB, 135 F 11: 234 n. 14
  Tilburg, Stichting Theologische Faculteit, Haaren 31: 67 n. 68
  Utrecht, UB, 8 L 16:
  Vienna, Österreichische Nationalbibliothek, s.n. 12.827: 174, 175, 184, 186, 188, 189, 190, 191, 196
  Zwolle, Rijksarchief Overijssel, coll. v. Rhemen (manuscript D): 137, 138, 150, 153, 157, 158
Margaret, Lame, of Magdeburg, see: Margaretha Contracta:
Margaretha Contracta of Magdeburg: 203, 212
Margaretha Ebner: 89, 236, 237
Margaretha van den Colke, see: Griete ten Kolke
Margarita van Achterhout: 45, 46
Margriet Block: 69
Margriete [Bijen]: 188
Margriete Hannemans: 162
Margriete Nots: 162
Margriete Oddyns: 48, 164, 169
Margriete van Geerdegeem: 162
Maria de Latere: 50 n. 93, 67 n. 62, 170
Maria van Boutershem: 167
Maria van Loon: 167 n. 104
Maria Weels: 68
Mariënberg, see: Helmstedt
Marienborn, monastery (Oosterbeek near Arnhem): 10, 14, 39 n. 40
Mariënburg, see: Nijmegen
Mariëndaal, see: Facons
Martin Luther: 16
Mary Magdalene: 198, 212, 213

Mary of Oignies: 89, 236
Mary: 98, 179, 180, 181, 184, 188, 202
Maximilian of Austria (Emperor): 161 n. 90
Mechelen, convent of Bethanië: 12, 24, 26, 33, 34 n. 11, 37, 53, 67 n. 62, 79 n. 103, 84 n. 6, 87, 95, 106, 107, 135, 136, 151 n. 54, 159, 163, 163, 165, 166, 167, 168, 170, 171 n. 1
   Kroniek Bethanië: 26, 28, 48, 80, 106, 159, 160, 161, 162, 163, 164, 165, 169, 234, 239
Mechthild of Hackeborn: 89, 195 n. 70
   Liber specialis gratiae: 194 n. 69
Mechthild of Magdeburg: 203, 212
   Fließende Licht der Gottheit, Das: 236
Mechtild van Rieviren: 26, 28, 54, 172, 174, 175, 184, 189, 190 n. 57, 191, 192, 193, 194, 195 n. 70, 196, 208, 242, 243
Medingen, convent of: 236
Mette van Linbeck: 154 n. 72, 156
Mettike Guestyn: 127
Muiden: 131 n. 83
Münster, Colloquium of: 13

Naaldwijk: 143
Naaldwijk, family: 39
Netherlands, the: 5 n. 15, 10, 12, 13 n. 48, 15 n. 54, 21 n. 78, 26, 30 n. 110, 42 n. 53, 80, 150
   Southern: 20, 110 n. 99, 177
Neurenberg, convent of St Katharina: 30, 73, 75, 79 n. 125
Neuss, Chapter of: 10
Nicolaas de Dinter: 71, 72, 234
Nicolaas van Duvendyc: 219, 224, 225, 241
Nicolaas van Oosterwijk or Sterts: 182 n. 35
Nicolas of Myra: 203
Nicholas of Kues: 15 n. 54, 80, 125, 241 n. 27
Nieuwlicht, monastery of (Hoorn): 10
Nijeklooster (Aula Dei), convent of (Scharnegoutum): 200 n. 8
Nijmegen, convent of Mariënburg: 12, 234
Nordhorn, see: Frenswegen

Odilia van Loon: 167 n. 104
Office of the Virgin Mary: 54
Oldenzaal: 8

Oostmalle, convent of Onze Lieve Vrouw Presentatie: 12 n. 44
Origen: 203
Otto of Passau, *Boeck des gulden throens of der XXIV ouden*: 33 n. 9
Otto Poten: 44, 45, 229
Oudenaarde, convent of Sion: 224, 225
Oudergem, see: Rooklooster
Oud-Turnhout, see: Korsendonk

Paris: 10 n. 36, 108
Parma, dukes of: 69
Pater noster: 101, 105, 109, 180, 183, 184, 242
Peter Hoorn: 136
   Vita Gerardi Magni: 22 n. 83
Peter van Os: 33 n. 9
Petrus Impens: 23 n. 85
   Compendium decursus temporum monasterii christifere bethleemitice puerpere: 23 n. 85
Petrus Trudonensis, *Catalogus scriptorum Windeshemensium*: 24
Philip (the Fair), duke of Burgundy: 163
Philip (the Good), duke of Burgundy: 199
Praeceptum, see: Augustine, Rule of
Princenhage (near Breda), convent of Vredenberg: 167 n. 104
Provence: 212
Purmerend, lord of: 199

Reinald IV, duke of Guelders: 32
Rembert van der List: 43 n. 59
Renkum, convent of Onze Lieve Vrouw: 12, 32, 114
Rhineland: 19, 21
Richard of St Victor: 88, 203, 233
Rijnsburg, convent of: 42
Rome: 4, 47, 53, 104, 105, 114
Rooklooster, monastery of (Oudergem): 37, 89, 161, 204 n. 21
Rudolf Dier van Muiden: 131, 136, 153 n. 66
   Scriptum: 34 n. 13, 131
Rugge, monastery of (Brielle): 31
Ruinen, Lord of: 8
Rulman Merswin: 203, 204 n. 20
   Neun Felsen Buch / Boek van de negen velden: 98, 203, 204, 205, 206

Salome Sticken: 24, 27, 35, 36, 42 n. 57, 50, 57, 59, 60, 61 n. 38, 66 n. 60, 77, 99,

113, 114, 115, 117, 121, 123, 124, 137, 138, 139, 144, 148, 231, 239, 240 n. 25, 241
   vite of: 58, 61
   Vivendi formula: 24, 28, 61 n. 38, 98, 99, 112, 114, 116, 117, 118, 123, 132, 151 n. 54, 239, 240
Salome van den Wiel the older: 39 n. 40, 112 n. 6
Salome van den Wiel the younger: 40, 41, 68, 155 n. 74, 156
Saxony: 45, 112, 125
Schoonhoven: 13
Schüttorf, convent of Mariëngarde: 114
Schwesternbücher: 20, 30, 89, 148 n. 46, 151, 152, 238 n. 23
Sibculo, Colligation of: 11 n. 39
Sint-Geertruidenberg, see: Eemstein
Sion, Chapter of: 13, 30, 54, 82 n. 139
Sisters of the Common Life: 6, 7, 14, 15, 17, 21, 30, 32, 80, 81, 82, 115, 129, 230, 240
Sneek: 65
Song of Songs: 235 n. 17
Sophia van Teilingen: 42
Souke van Dorsten: 65, 103 n. 75, 149, 156
Spaarnland, lord of: 199
St Agnes: 104
St Agnietenberg: 48, 91, 107
St Anne: 175, 188
St Barbara, life of: 74 n. 103
St Bridgitte of Sweden: 184
St Catherine: 141
St John the Baptist: 110 n. 99
St John the Evangelist: 109, 110, 179, 186, 231
St Lawrence: 220
St Patrick's Purgatory: 176
St Paul: 56, 75 n. 105, 95, 146
St Ursula and the Eleven Thousand Virgins: 105, 106
Stederborch: 127
Stine Groten: 149
Stine Tolners: 8 n. 29, 44, 104 n. 80, 140 n. 17, 142, 155, 156
Strasburg: 236
   convent of St Nikolaus in Undis: 30, 74 n. 104, 105
Sulta: 125
Super modo vivendi devotorum hominum simul commorantium (see also: Gerard Zerbolt): 80, 81 n. 131, 117 n. 30

Switzerland: 151

Tecla (sister of Brunnepe): 46, 126, 127, 128
Ten Troon, monastery of (Grobbendonk): 80, 161, 163, 234
Ten Walle, monastery of Onze Lieve Vrouw (Elzegem): 199, 224, 241
Teutonia: 30, 99
Thabor, monastery of (Tirns, near Sneek): 75
Theodericus Wiel: 132 n. 87
Theodoricus, see: Dirk van Grave
Thomas a Kempis: 89, 136
   Chronica Monte Sanctae Agnetis: 9 n. 34
   Dialogus noviciorum: 9 n. 34
   Imitatione Christi, De: 91, 230
Thomas Aquinas: 151
Thomas of Cantimpré: 151
   Bonum universale de apibus/ Liber apibus or *Bienboeck*: 14 n. 53, 21, 116 n. 26, 234
Thomas Vermoelen or Bel: 182 n. 35
Thonis van den Wiel: 39 n. 40
Thorn, imperial abbey: of 167, 168
Tielman Schuermans: 80, 164, 169
Tienen, convent of Barberendaal: 12, 37, 51 n. 5, 234, 235
Tractatus de vestibus pretiosis: 81 n. 131
Trude Schutten: 104, 105
Trude van Beveren: 55, 66, 81 n. 133, 102 103, 156
Trude van Compostel: 36 n.26
Truke Essinchghes: 56, 153 n. 69
Truke van der Beeck: 46, 71, 72, 76, 156
Tusculum: 236

Unterlinden, *Schwesternbuch* of: 20 n. 74, 137 n. 6
Utrecht: 7, 119, 198, 199
   bishop of: 8, 13
   Buurkerk: 26
   Chapter of: 12, 13, 14
   convent of In de Wijngaard: 15
   convent of Jeruzalem: 12, 26, 34 n. 16, 101 n. 70, 112, 119, 120, 121, 123, 124, 125, 128, 130, 200, 239
   convent of St Cecilia: 119
   hospital of St Barbara and St Lawrence: 199
   Schism of: 144

Venlo, Chapter of: 15, 30, 74 n. 103

INDEX

Venray, convent of Jeruzalem: 54, 96, 124, 125, 132
Vision of Tundale, The: 177
Vitae patrum: 150 n. 53, 234
Vreden, convent of: 8, 43 n. 58, 46, 64, 167
Vught: 15 n. 59

Walburg van Gelre: 32
Walburg van Meurs: 32
Wermbold Buscoop: 12
Westphalia: 8, 43 n. 58, 46, 114, 115, 239
Wilhelmina Eggaert: 199
Wilhelmus Zegers: 237
Willem Berwouts: 162, 165
Willem Clinckaert: 13
Willem Eggaert the older: 199
Willem Jordaens, *Mystieke mondkus, De*: 225, 226
Willem van Egmond and Bar: 32

Willem VI, count of Holland: 199
Windesheim, Chapter of: *passim*
  Liber ordinarius: 52 n. 5
  Manuale Windeshemense: 52 n. 5
  monastery of: 10
Wittenberg: 16
Wyse (sister of Diepenveen): 68

Zeeland: 156 n. 77
Zepperen, Chapter of: 13 n. 48
Zoniënwoud: 89
Zutphen: 6
Zweder van Rechteren, Lady of Ruinen: 8, 9, 32 n. 3, 36, 92, 93, 94, 141
Zwene ter Poorten: 67
Zwolle: 7, 9, 43
  Colloquium of: 13
  monastery of Bethlehem: 39 n. 40, 113